FOURTH EDITION

ESSAY ESSENTIALS

WITH READINGS

SARAH NORTON

BRIAN GREEN

D1309631

THOMSON
NELSON

Australia   Canada   Mexico   Singapore   Spain   United Kingdom   United States

THOMSON
™
NELSON

**Essay Essentials with Readings,
Fourth Edition**

Sarah Norton and
Brian Green

**Associate Vice President,
Editorial Director:**
Evelyn Veitch

Executive Editor:
Anne Williams

Marketing Manager:
Heather Leach

Managing Developmental Editor:
Lenore Spence

Permissions Coordinator
Karen Becker

Senior Production Editor:
Natalia Denesiuk

Copy Editor:
Sarah Robertson

Proofreader:
Karen Rolfe

Indexer:
Gillian Watts

Production Coordinator:
Ferial Suleman

Design Director:
Ken Phipps

Interior Design
Sonya V. Thursby, Opus House
Incorporated

Cover Design:
Rocket Design

Cover Image:
Rodolfo Arpia/ShutterStock

Compositor:
Carol Magee

Printer:
QuebecorWorld

**National Library of Canada
Cataloguing in Publication Data**

Norton, Sarah, date
    Essay essentials with readings /
Sarah Norton, Brian Green. — 4th
ed.

Includes bibliographical references
and index.
ISBN 0-17-640704-9

    1. Essay—Authorship.
2. Report writing. 3. English
language—Rhetoric. 4. College
readers. I. Green, Brian II. Title.

PE1471.N69 2005   808'.042
C2005-905302-X

This book is dedicated to the memory of Greg Darling, whose research provided much of the humorous trivia that we used as raw material for many of our exercises. A much-loved and respected film teacher at Niagara College for many years, Greg was famous for a sarcastic wit and gruff manner that served to disguise his kindness and generosity. His untimely death at the age of 50 meant the loss to us of an inspired researcher and close friend.

Preface: To the Instructor

Essay Essentials with Readings, Fourth Edition, is designed for Canadian university and college students who are learning to write for academic and professional purposes. The book has been revised to begin with a new chapter on style and usage; an expanded section on research and documentation, including APA style; a streamlined workbook, and 15 new essays, including 4 new pieces by student writers. Chosen for their value as good prose models as well as for their appeal to a broad spectrum of interests, the essays represent a variety of styles in the middle range of the language register. We have avoided the extremes of stiffly formal and slangy popular style and selected pieces that demonstrate the levels of language that are appropriate for most academic, technical, business, and public writing.

Essay Essentials is divided into six parts. The first three sections explain, exemplify, and provide practice in planning, drafting, revising, and editing.[1] Because most adults learn better and with more satisfaction together with other learners, many of the exercises are interactive. Some involve the whole class, but most are designed to be done in pairs or groups.[2] These exercises begin with a discussion to clarify the assignment and motivate students, proceed to a writing task, and conclude with a peer review to enhance and reinforce learning.

A primary goal of this book is to show students that effective writing necessarily involves revising and editing. To this end, we have incorporated these phases of the writing process throughout the book.

Part 4, Patterns of Essay Development, provides explanations and examples of the traditional rhetorical modes. The emphasis in this section is on exposition, the kind of writing students will be required to produce both in college and on the job. Part 4 begins with description and narration, strategies that are often required in expository writing, and concludes with argumentation, the most complex and difficult of the four modes. Each chapter contains a selection of readings to illustrate the pattern under discussion

---

[1]Note that answers to exercises marked with an asterisk are provided in Appendix C. Answers to other exercises are available in the Instructor's Manual and on our website.

[2]Of course, the instructor can choose to adapt these group exercises to individual assignments —and should do so if the latter model is appropriate to his or her course.

and concludes with a longer, more complex essay that employs a combination of writing strategies. In response to teacher requests, we have included three new documented essays in this section: one, "The Slender Trap," in MLA style; and two, "Labouring the Wal-Mart Way'" and "A City for Students," in APA style. The questions following each essay are designed to promote understanding of structure and development as well as to provoke thinking and discussion. Teachers will find suggested answers to these questions in the Instructor's Manual and on our website: http://www.essayessentials4e.nelson.com.

Part 5, The Research Paper, has been revised to include a fuller discussion of the responsible use of source materials and their documentation. In response to users' requests, we have included on our website a short but comprehensive overview of plagiarism. For essays on nonliterary topics, we encourage students to rely more on summary and paraphrase and less on direct quotation. Part 5 concludes with two model research papers, one on a topic of general interest and the other a critical analysis of a literary work. Purchasing *Essay Essentials* gives students access to InfoTrac®, a database that catalogues more than 600 periodicals and journals. Having an online library of easy-to-search reliable sources at their fingertips will facilitate students' learning in all of their courses as well as their mastery of the research and documentation skills covered in Part 5.

Part 6, the workbook section of the text, reviews the basics of syntax, grammar, punctuation, and spelling. We assume that many students will be working through this unit on their own, and answers to most of the exercises are provided in the back of the book; answers to the Mastery Tests are on the instructor's page of the website and in the Instuctor's Manual. The four sections of this unit can be covered in any order, but the chapters within each section are interdependent and should be studied sequentially since competency in later chapters often depends on mastery of previous ones.

Inside the front cover is a Quick Guide to Revision. We encourage students to use it as a checklist with which to revise and edit their work. Instructors can duplicate the guide, attach a copy to each student's paper, and mark ✔or ✘ beside each point to identify the paper's strengths and weaknesses. This strategy provides students with specific feedback in a consistent format. It also saves hours of marking time.

New to this edition is a website designed to support both teachers and learners (http://www.essayessentials4e.nelson.com). Students who need more practice than is included in the text will find additional exercises and self-scoring practice tests on the website. The site also provides information that could not conveniently be included in the text itself; for example, there is an overview of logical reasoning and common logical fallacies to supplement the introduction to argumentation in Chapter 17. In addition, the website provides students with definitions and examples of the parts of speech, sentence patterns, ESL tips, links to reference sites, a write-in "Ask the Authors" feature, and much more.

The instructors' page includes a teaching manual; interactive exercises to support many chapters of the text; suggested answers for most of the questions in Parts 1 to 5; answers to the chapter Mastery Tests in Part 6; PowerPoint slides and transparency masters; *The Essentials Test Manual* (a comprehensive bank of multiple-choice diagnostic and pre- and post-tests); reading and reference links; and a writers' forum—a direct link to the authors. We are eager to hear your comments, criticisms, questions, and dialogue on the text, on teaching, or on writing problems.

Acknowledgments

Much of the new material in this edition is attributable to the efforts of colleagues and friends from across Canada. We wish to record our special thanks to David Geiss, Laurie MacEachern, Michael Ruecker, and Trina Rys, whose work we are proud to introduce in this edition, and to Donna Fairholm (Humber College), Sharon Hamilton (Carleton University), Francie Greenslade (University of Regina), and Susan Johnston (University of Regina), who recommended these new student contributors. In addition to identifying errors and oversights, our reviewers offered helpful comments and suggestions: Phyllis Bishop, Conestoga College; Gail Clenman, Seneca College; Derek Hanebury, North Island College; Heather McAfee, George Brown College; Susan V. Piazza, St. Clair College; Cynthia Rowland, Algonquin College; Ritva Seppanen, Concordia University; and Anne Ward, Lambton College.

We are indebted to Sue Bartlett, research librarian at Niagara College, for her help in updating the book's information on research and documentation. We thank Centennial College for permission to reproduce portions of their *Revised Style Sheet* in Part 5 of the book and *Preventing Plagiarism Why? What? How?* on the website. And finally, we wish to acknowledge the support of two special people at Nelson: Sarah Robertson, editor *extraordinaire*; and Natalia Denesiuk, our Senior Production Editor, who cares as much about the details as we do.

Sarah Norton
Brian Green

Contents

Introduction: Why, What, and How to Learn to Write

Few people enjoy writing; after all, it's hard work. Writing is a complex process, a learned skill that requires patience, concentration, and persistence. Unlike most of the skills you acquire in a career program, however, writing is not job-specific. **The skills you learn from this book will be useful to you in all your college courses** and **in every job you hold throughout your working life.** If you have graduated from college or university, your prospective employer will assume that you are able to communicate in writing frequently, correctly, and in a manner that will do credit to the company. The higher you climb on the organizational ladder, the more you will write and the more complex your writing tasks will become. Furthermore, evaluations of your performance in any job will be based at least in part on your communication skills.

Essay Essentials will teach you to write essays of various kinds. The word "essay" comes from the French *essayer*, to try or attempt. **An essay is an attempt to communicate information, opinion, or emotion.** In the context of a college or university, an essay is an exercise that gives students an opportunity to explore and explain their own and others' thoughts about a subject. In the larger world, essays appear in newspapers and magazines as editorials, reviews, opinion pieces, and commentaries on news and public affairs.

If at times the essay form seems artificial or unrelated to the kinds of writing you expect to do in your profession, remember that thinking, organizing, and researching are basic to all practical writing tasks. **In this book, you will learn how to find and organize thoughts, to develop ideas in coherent paragraphs, and to express yourself clearly, correctly, and concisely.** Once you've mastered these basics, you can develop any job-specific writing styles that may be required of you. If you can write well-organized, convincing, and error-free essays of five or more paragraphs, you will have no difficulty adapting your skills to business or technical reports, instructions, proposals, memoranda, sales presentations, commercial scripts, or legal briefs.

The fact that literacy is in decline does not make the ability to write less important; rather, it means that those who can write competently are in high demand. **You can learn to write well if you are willing to work at it.** We have designed this text to enable you to master the theory of good writing and to practise it successfully. Because it is more fun and more efficient to learn with others than it is to struggle alone, we have included many group-based exercises. To make the process less onerous, we have also introduced a few humorous essays, and, in Part 6, as many entertaining exercises as we could think of. If you follow the guidelines in this book, you will produce effective essays in college and creditable communications in your career.

THE WEBSITE

In addition to the material in this book, you will find useful information and helpful exercises on our website. Go to http://www.essayessentials4e. nelson.com and click on "Student Resources" to find the menu of options available to you. Under "More Information" you will find helpful supplements to the book, and under "More Practice" you will find additional exercises for the chapters in Part 6. The answers to these exercises are marked automatically, so you will know instantly whether or not you have understood the material.

Also on the website are practice tests, reference links, and an "Ask the Authors" button that enables you to send us any questions you have about *Essay Essentials* or about your writing. We take your questions seriously and will answer as soon as we get your message. Purchase of this book also entitles you to free access to InfoTrac®, an easy-to-use online library of source materials you can use for your research in this and other courses. You will learn more about InfoTrac® and other databases in Chapter 18.

WHAT THE SYMBOLS MEAN

This symbol in the margin beside an exercise means the exercise is designed to be done by two or more students working together. Carefully read the directions that introduce the exercise to find out how many students should participate and what task is to be performed. Often you are instructed to begin work in a pair or group, then to work individually on a writing task, and finally to regroup and review your writing with your partner(s).

This symbol means "note this." We've used it to highlight writing tips, helpful hints, hard-to-remember points, and information that you should apply whenever you write, not just when you are dealing with the specific principle covered in the paragraph marked by the icon.

This icon attached to an exercise means that the exercise is a mastery test designed to check your understanding of the chapter you have just completed. The answers to these exercises are not in the back of the book; your instructor will provide them.

This symbol means that the *Essay Essentials* website has information or exercises to supplement the chapter you are working on. Log on to the website, click on the "More Practice" button, and then click on "Web Exercises." The information and exercises are arranged by chapter, so to get to the exercises for the apostrophe, for example, click on Chapter 38, and do the numbered exercises listed below the icon.

THE PROCESS OF WRITING

Writing is a three-step process consisting of
1. planning or prewriting
2. drafting
3. revising and editing

This book explains and illustrates two approaches to the process of writing: top-down and bottom-up. The **top-down approach** assumes that you know what you have to say before you begin to write. You identify your subject and main points, draft your thesis statement (the statement that orients your readers to the content of the paper), and plan your topic sentences (those sentences that identify the content of each paragraph). Research papers, business reports, and essay questions on exams are examples of writing that require a "top-down" approach.

The **bottom-up approach** is useful when you do not know ahead of time what you want to say. You discover your meaning through the act of writing. With this approach, you rely on prewriting strategies such as brainstorming and freewriting to get into the process of writing.

You will probably need to use both approaches. Sometimes you will discover your subject through writing; at other times, using "top-down" strategies will help you to express clearly what you already know. You should experiment with both approaches so that you can comfortably use whichever is more appropriate for a particular writing task.

WHAT YOUR READERS EXPECT

Whichever approach you use, your goal is to make your finished essay easy for your readers to read and understand. To achieve that goal, you must meet your readers' expectations.

Readers have five unconscious expectations when they begin to read a piece of extended prose. They expect to find

- paragraphs
- a sentence (usually the first) in each paragraph that identifies the topic
- unified paragraphs, each of which explores a single topic
- connections (transitions) within and between paragraphs
- a preview (in the introduction) of the content and organization of the paper

Keep in mind that readers want to obtain information quickly and easily, without backtracking. They rely on the writer—you—to make efficient reading possible.

Your readers will read more easily and remember more of what they read if you include a thesis statement to introduce them to the content and organization of the piece, and if you begin each paragraph with a topic sentence. If you do not organize and develop your paper and its paragraphs in a clearly identifiable way, readers will impose their own organization on the paper. The result will be longer reading time, or difficulty in understanding and remembering the content, or, worse, the assumption that a paragraph or even the whole paper has a meaning other than the one you intended. You can help your readers to read efficiently if you follow the old adage: "Tell them what you're going to tell them; tell them; then tell them what you've told them."

HOW TO BEGIN

Having a conversation with someone who never seems to get to the point is a tiresome and frustrating experience. Similarly, an essay—or any other form of written communication—that has no point and that rambles on will turn readers off.

How can you avoid boring, confusing, or annoying your readers? To begin with, you need to have something to say and a reason for saying it. Very few people can write an essay straight through from start to finish without spending a considerable amount of time thinking and planning. Some prewriting will help you to develop the structure more easily; freewriting and brainstorming (Chapter 3 will explain these) stimulate thinking.

Once you've determined what it is you want to say, you need to arrange your main points in the most effective order possible. If you organize your ideas carefully, you won't ramble. Writing an essay is like building a house. If you have a clear plan or blueprint, you can construct the house without the frustration of having to double back or even to start all over again from the beginning. A good plan saves time.

As a general rule, the more time you spend on prewriting and planning, the less time you'll need to spend on drafting and revising. Careful planning will enable you to produce papers that your readers will find clear and understandable.

THE PARTS OF AN ESSAY

An essay has a beginning, a middle, and an end. The most basic form is the five-paragraph essay, which teaches you everything you need to know about writing nonfiction prose. Think of this highly structured form of prose not as a straitjacket that stifles your creativity, but rather as a pattern to follow while you develop the skills and abilities you need to build other, more complex prose structures.

The beginning, or **introduction**, tells your reader the point, the purpose, and the scope of your essay. If your introduction is well crafted, its **thesis statement** will identify the main points you will discuss in the paragraphs that follow.

The middle, or **body**, of an essay consists of paragraphs that discuss in detail the points that have been identified in the introduction. In a short essay, each paragraph develops a separate main point. Each paragraph should contain three essential components:

- a **topic sentence**, which identifies the point of the paragraph
- development, or **support**, of the topic sentence. Supporting sentences provide the detailed information the reader needs in order to understand the point.
- a **concluding sentence** that either brings the discussion of the topic to a close or provides a transition to the next paragraph

The end, or **conclusion**, is a brief final paragraph. Unless your essay is very short, you summarize the main points to reinforce them for the reader, then say goodbye with a statement that will give your readers something to think about after they have finished reading your essay.

Bertrand Russell's "What I Have Lived For" is a good example of a well-structured essay. The introduction contains a clear thesis statement. Each paragraph of the body consists of a clearly identifiable topic sentence, development sufficient to explain it, and a concluding sentence. The conclusion is brief, pointed, and memorable.

WHAT I HAVE LIVED FOR

Bertrand Russell

INTRODUCTION

Thesis statement
Three passions, simple but overwhelmingly strong, have governed my life: the longing for love, the search for knowledge, and unbearable pity for the suffering of mankind. These passions, like great winds, have blown me hither and thither, in a wayward course, over a deep ocean of anguish, reaching to the very verge of despair.

BODY

Topic sentence

Support

Concluding sentence
I have sought love, first, because it brings ecstasy—ecstasy so great that I would often have sacrificed all the rest of life for a few hours of this joy. I have sought it, next, because it relieves loneliness—that terrible loneliness in which one shivering consciousness looks over the rim of the world into the cold unfathomable lifeless abyss. I have sought it, finally, because in the union of love I have seen, in a mystic miniature, the prefiguring vision of the heaven that saints and poets have imagined. This is what I sought, and though it might seem too good for human life, this is what—at last—I have found.

Topic sentence

Support

Concluding sentence
With equal passion I have sought knowledge. I have wished to understand the hearts of men. I have wished to know why the stars shine. And I have tried to apprehend the Pythagorean power by which number holds sway above the flux. A little of this, but not much, I have achieved.

Topic sentence

Support

Concluding sentence
Love and knowledge, so far as they were possible, led upward toward the heavens. But always pity brought me back to earth. Echoes of cries of pain reverberate in my heart. Children in famine, victims tortured by oppressors, helpless old people a hated burden to their sons, and the whole world of loneliness, poverty, and pain make a mockery of what human life should be. I long to alleviate the evil, but I cannot, and I too suffer.

CONCLUSION
This has been my life. I have found it worth living, and would gladly live it again if the chance were offered me.

Russell, Bertrand. "What I Have Lived For." Prologue. *The Autobiography of Bertrand Russell.* By Russell. Boston: Little, Brown, 1967. 3–4.

PART 1

Planning

1

Your Audience and You

Before you begin to write anything—an essay, a report, an e-mail message, or a set of instructions—you must have something to write about (your subject) and someone to write for (your audience). Writing is communication, and for communication to take place, you (the writer) must be able to make your ideas or message clear to your readers.

Addressing Your Readers

As you plan, draft, and revise your paper, ask yourself the following questions:

- How old are your readers?
- What is their level of education?
- What do they do for a living?
- What is their income?
- What is their cultural background?
- Are they male or female?

While you must be careful to avoid generalizing or stereotyping, the answers to these questions do influence most people's views, and you would be wise to consider them before you begin to write.

Before you begin to plan an essay, write at the top of the page the specific audience for whom your message is intended.

Naturally, your instructor will be reading your early (and your late) assignments, but, for your first draft, you should write at the top of the page the name of someone other than your instructor whom you might expect to be interested in your subject. Be creative: your high-school principal, a recent immigrant, a union official, a member of the Liberal Party, a religious leader, the CEO of a polluting company, someone receiving social assistance income. Keeping this reader in mind will help you to plan, develop, and write your assignment in a tone and style appropriate to your message.

Spend a little time thinking about your subject in relation to your audience. Consider carefully the following three questions when you are deciding what to include in your essay.

1. What does my reader know about my subject?
2. What is my reader's attitude toward my subject?
3. What are my reader's needs in regard to my subject?

READERS' KNOWLEDGE

The first question will help you choose the kind and amount of information that should be included. Are you writing for someone who knows little about your subject, or for someone with fairly detailed knowledge? Do you have to cover all the basics, or can you take it for granted your audience is familiar with them? You don't want to bore your readers by telling them things they already know. On the other hand, if you fail to provide information they need in order to understand your message, you'll turn them off or lose them entirely.

READERS' ATTITUDES

The second question helps you decide how to approach your subject. Will your readers be sympathetic to what you have to say? If so, you will aim to reinforce their agreement. You will probably state your opinion up front, to show you're on their side. If, however, you think they may be hostile to what you have to say, you might lessen their resistance by providing reasons and support for your ideas before revealing your point of view. Gentle persuasion is usually more effective than confrontation in writing, as it is in life.

READERS' NEEDS

The third question helps you to decide whether to persuade or instruct, to compare or classify, to describe or analyze. Which approach will give your readers the information they need about your subject? The answers to this question will determine whether your remarks should be fairly general or quite specific. Do you intend to add to or reinforce your audience's general knowledge, or do you want your readers to apply your information only in specific situations?

Reflecting Yourself

Once you are clear about who your readers are, what they know, and what they need to know, you should spend a little time considering your role in the communication process. Any time you speak or write, you present yourself in a particular way to your audience. We all play a variety of roles. We choose a role, often unconsciously, that we hope will suit the expectations of the people we are communicating with. These roles are not false or hypocritical; they are simply facets of our personality that we try to match to the needs of each situation. Choosing and maintaining an appropriate role is essential in successful communication.

Each day, for example, you meet a variety of people. Some of them you know well—parents, siblings, friends, classmates, teachers, coworkers, supervisors. Others you know only casually—the cashier in the restaurant, the police officer at the radar trap, the enumerator for the upcoming election, the checkout person in the grocery store. With each of these people, whether the contact is casual or intense, you consciously or unconsciously adjust your language in order to communicate. If you speak to your spouse as you might to your dog, you'll be sleeping on the couch. If you speak to a salesperson as you would to a love interest, you'll get arrested.

Consider the following three questions when you are deciding what role would be most appropriate in a particular communication situation.

1. What is my purpose in writing?
2. What is my attitude toward my subject?
3. What are my readers' expectations of me in this communication?

YOUR PURPOSE

The most common purposes of writing are to inform, to persuade, and to entertain. Your purpose will depend largely on the needs and expectations of your readers. It will influence your choice of supporting details to develop your points and will affect your tone. How you say something often has more impact on your audience than what you say.

YOUR ATTITUDE

The second question requires you to clarify your attitude to the subject of your paper. This involves more than simply asking, "Am I for or against it?" You should consider how strongly you feel about the subject because your attitude will influence your tone as well as the kinds of evidence you present. You should also think about how personal you want to be in presenting your ideas, or how balanced and objective you wish (or are able) to be. In answering these questions, consider how closely your attitude toward the subject aligns with your audience's attitude. If your views coincide, then a fairly informal approach may be appropriate; if they differ, then an impersonal, objective approach is preferable.

YOUR ROLE

The third question requires you to think about what role your audience is likely to expect of you. If you write as an authority, will you be credible? If you write as a peer or friend, will you be effective? What are your readers likely to expect from someone in your position writing to them on this subject? Taking the time to think about your readers' expectations will help you to make appropriate choices with respect to the point of view you take, the examples and support you provide for your ideas, and the level of language you use.

Levels of Standard English Writing

Good writing involves more than the meaning of words and sentences. It also requires the choice of appropriate language. No one would submit a book review that began, "This is an awesome book with, like, ideas that sort of make you think, you know?" You know instantly that the language is inappropriate. Similarly, if you were discussing the book with friends over coffee and announced, "This book contains provocative and stimulating ideas that engage and challenge the reader," your language would be equally inappropriate.

Written English (e-mail notwithstanding) is usually more formal than spoken English. Because writers have time to consider what they want to say and how best to say it, they can choose their words carefully, arrange them in meaningful sentences, and organize ideas into logical paragraphs. An appropriate level of language is an essential part of effective writing.

Choose a level that suits both your topic and your reader. There will be times when you need to compromise; for example, when you send one message to several people. In such cases, the safe bet is to aim at the highest level of receiver and trust that the others will understand.

Sometimes it isn't clear what level you should be using. At such times, your reader's preference should determine your choice. Many colleges and universities expect students to write academic papers in formal English, which requires, among other things, third-person pronouns (*he, she, one, they*). Informal writing, with its first- and second-person pronouns (*I, me, you*), may not be acceptable. (See page 496 for an explanation of pronoun "person.") Ask your instructor about your school's policy and follow it.

Similarly, because employers tend to favour formal letters of application over casual ones, if you want to get the job, you will write a formal letter. For a talk you give to your class, an informal, conversational style may be appropriate. Most of what you read and write falls somewhere in the middle. Business documents, for example, are usually written in general-level Standard English.

There are no fixed divisions of language use; the three levels we've identified often overlap. To help you choose the most appropriate level for your message and audience, the table below outlines the basic features of informal, general, and formal written English.

	Informal	General	Formal
Vocabulary and Style	Casual, everyday; usually concrete; some slang, colloquial expressions, contractions. Written in 1st and 2nd persons.	The language of educated persons; nonspecialized; balance of abstract and concrete; readily understood. Can use 1st, 2nd, and 3rd persons.	Often abstract, technical, or specialized; no contractions or colloquialisms. Written in 3rd person.
Sentence and Paragraph Structure	Sentences short, simple; some sentence fragments; paragraphs short.	Complete sentences of varying length; paragraphs vary, but are often fairly short.	Complete sentences, usually long, complex; paragraphs fully developed, often at length.
Tone	Conversational, casual; sounds like ordinary speech.	Varies to suit message and purpose of writer.	Impersonal, serious, often instructional.
Typical Uses	Personal letters, some fiction, some newspapers, much advertising.	Most of what we read: newspapers, magazines, novels, business correspondence.	Academic writing, some textbooks, scientific reports, journal articles, legal documents.

No one level is "better" than another. Each has its place and function. Your message, your audience, and your purpose in writing are what should determine the level you choose.

Read the following selections and consider each writer's purpose, the audience for whom the message is intended, and why the writer's level of language is appropriate to the readers, the subject, and the purpose.

INFORMAL

Love him or hate him, Michael Moore has turned the world of documentary film on its ear. Documentaries are stuffy and boring, aren't they? They certainly aren't supposed to be wildly popular or turn their directors into media stars. But starting with *Roger and Me* back in 1989, Moore has almost single-handedly made the documentary fun, personal, and popular. Like most film students, I began thinking I wanted someday to make blockbuster Hollywood hits like the movies Canadians Norman Jewison and James Cameron are famous for, but now I'm a convert to documentaries and that other Canadian production star: the NFB.

Who is the intended audience? This paragraph is intended for general readers, not people who are looking for a scholarly discussion of film. The writer assumes some interest in and knowledge of Michael Moore and his films.

What is the writer's role? The writer wants to inform readers in a personal way about his point of view. He plays the role not of expert or teacher, but rather of a friend or acquaintance supplying the information for discussion in a casual way.

Why is the level of language appropriate? The use of contractions and colloquialisms ("the world . . . on its ear," "stuffy and boring") and especially the use of first and second persons in direct address clearly mark this as an informal and friendly communication. Short sentences and a conversational style add to the informal tone.

GENERAL

What is a documentary film? The so-called father of documentary film, John Grierson, called it "the creative treatment of reality," but that definition is uncomfortably broad. For example, is *Alexander* a documentary? What about *Troy* or *Amadeus* or *Lawrence of Arabia*? All are about real people and contain a version of historical events, but few would classify them as documentaries. The purpose of these films is to entertain (if you discount their real purpose: to make money), and perhaps purpose lies at the heart of the definition. The primary purpose of a documentary film is to inform.

Who is the intended audience? Readers of this paragraph will be knowledgeable enough about films to have seen at least one of the three major releases mentioned, and interested enough in film to want to know more about the documentary genre.

What is the writer's role? The writer is providing information from an expert point of view, but in a friendly way rather than as a lecture or formal instruction. The use of humour and casual language makes the information easy to absorb, and the direct address and use of questions add a friendly tone to the paragraph.

Why is the level of language appropriate? The vocabulary and writing style are easily understood by general readers. The use of second person ("if you discount their real purpose") adds to the personal nature of the language, as do the questions directed to the reader. This message is designed to appeal to the widest audience possible.

FORMAL

John Grierson, best known as "the father of documentary film" and the founder of the National Film Board of Canada, called documentary "the creative treatment of reality." Since its inception in 1939, the NFB has been presenting reality to Canadians and the rest of the world in creative ways. While it has earned recognition in other cinematic fields (notably animation), the NFB has achieved most of its international acclaim from more than 60 years of producing first-class documentary films, many of them Academy Award winners.

Who is the intended audience? The readers of this passage are literate and well read. They are people whose education and experience have enabled them to appreciate that good films can be informative as well as entertaining.

What is the writer's role? The writer's purpose is to highlight the achievements of the NFB to an audience of educated peers who share his aesthetic interests. The writer presents himself not as an expert addressing nonexperts, but rather as an enthusiast who wants to share knowledge with a receptive audience.

Why is the level of language appropriate? The vocabulary is fairly sophisticated, and the sentences are fairly long and complex. There are no contractions or colloquialisms, no first- or second-person pronouns. The writer addresses his audience as peers—fellow film enthusiasts—but not as close friends. The objective tone would be suitable for an article in a professional magazine.

Exercise 1.1*

Read the excerpts below and discuss the intended audience, the author's role, and the appropriateness of the language. Answers for this chapter begin on page 512.

1. One of the most frequent complaints about Wal-Mart, which employs 1.4 million people worldwide, is its failure to pay workers a living wage. Store employees are paid 20–30 percent less than the industry average, making many of them eligible for social assistance. It is estimated that American taxpayers fork out $2.5 billion a year in welfare payments to Wal-Mart employees (Head, 2004). Because the retailer hires hard-to-place workers, like recent immigrants, seniors, and single mothers, its employees are often afraid they will not find work elsewhere. The kind of work Wal-Mart does offer is gruelling: stores are intentionally understaffed—the strategy behind the company's legendary productivity gains—so that existing employees will work harder (Head, 2004). It is alleged that systemic discrimination against women within the corporation has denied the majority of Wal-Mart workers the chance at promotion, a charge that is now the subject of the largest civil-rights suit in US history.

    Parmar, Deenu. "Labouring the Wal-Mart Way." 224.

Who is the intended audience? _____

_____

_____

_____

What is the writer's role? _____

_____

_____

_____

Why is the level of language appropriate? _____

_____

_____

_____

_____

2.   The "inletting" or "butt mortise" plane is designed to cut precise mortises for butt hinges, lock fronts, and strike plates, or to repair jambs, doors, furniture, and millwork, wherever the ability to do inletting is important. The plane has a completely open throat so that you can watch what you are doing. The 3/4" wide cutter is set at a 40 degree pitch for general work. This can be increased to 70 degrees (plus or minus) for difficult grain simply by inserting the blade bevel-up. For inletting, such as hinges, you set the blade extension at the hinge leaf thickness, score the outline and plane to depth, using overlapping strokes for a smooth bottom. The same technique would be used for a veneer repair on solid wood.

_____

Lee Valley Catalogue. Tenth Anniversary Issue, 1987–88. 23.

Who is the intended audience?   _____

_____

_____

_____

_____

What is the writer's role?   _____

_____

_____

_____

_____

Why is the level of language appropriate?   _____

_____

_____

_____

_____

3.   Doing business with the Chinese is an enterprise fraught with peril for the unwary Western business person. While in the West most business is ultimately conducted face to face between the principals, negotiations seldom if ever achieve this intimacy in the Orient. It is common for gatherings of ten or more to take part in the early stages of agenda-setting and prioritizing, and the hapless Westerner who has not engaged the services of a Chinese guide will have to sort out the Party overseers from the ineffectual hangers-on and try to hone in on the power brokers who often remain in the background to assess and evaluate before making themselves known. Often the early stages of business relationships are conducted in the very formal atmosphere of banquets, with hierarchical seating arrangements and ritual toasts. Coping with the exotic atmosphere, the oblique method of negotiation, the recondite formality, and the unidentifiable food is a formidable challenge: one that should be undertaken without assistance by only the most intrepid and experienced of Western entrepreneurs.

Czereczovich, Katlin. "Business Abroad." *Canadian Women Entrepreneurs* Spring 2002: 91.

Who is the intended audience? _____

_____

_____

_____

_____

What is the writer's role? _____

_____

_____

_____

_____

Why is the level of language appropriate? _____

_____

_____

_____

_____

4.   A parent quickly learns that no matter how much money you have, you will never be able to buy your kids everything they want. You can take a second mortgage on your house and buy what you think is the entire

Snoopy line: Snoopy pajamas, Snoopy underpants, Snoopy linen, Snoopy shoelaces, Snoopy cologne, and Snoopy soap, but you will never have it all. And if Snoopy doesn't send you to the poorhouse, Calvin Klein will direct the trip. Calvin is the slick operator who sells your kids things for eighty-five dollars that cost seven at Sears. He has created millions of tiny snobs, children who look disdainfully at you and say, "Nothing from Sears." However, Dad-Can-I fought back: I got some Calvin Klein labels and sewed them into Sears undershorts for my high fashion junkies.

Cosby, Bill. *Fatherhood*. New York: Doubleday, 1994. 41–42.

Who is the intended audience? _____

_____

_____

_____

_____

What is the writer's role? _____

_____

_____

_____

_____

Why is the level of language appropriate? _____

_____

_____

_____

_____

5.   The conclusion of *Jane Eyre* has Jane and Rochester married at last. Jane no longer needs to compromise herself in order to be with him, and his first wife is not the only obstacle that has been removed. The man who insisted that she abandon her conscience to live in sin has changed significantly. Rochester now complements Jane as never before. His mutilation has been referred to as a "symbolic castration" by Richard Chase (qtd. in Gilbert and Gubar 368), but it is his spirit rather than his masculinity that seems to have been honed. Rochester has been humbled, and the taste of humility has taught him wisdom. He is able to admit to Jane, "I did wrong: I would have sullied my innocent flower—breathed guilt on its purity"

(Brönte 495; ch. 37). During their first engagement, Jane was unsure and often uncomfortable about her place in Rochester's life. In her description of their marriage, however, she says that "we are precisely suited in character—perfect concord is the result" (Brönte 500; ch. 38). Such a perfect fit is only made possible by Rochester's movement away from his earlier extreme. He has become a close match for Jane on every level, and therefore becomes her ideal mate.

Friedland, Jess. "The Evolution of Moral Balance in Charlotte Brönte's *Jane Eyre*." 322–23.

Who is the intended audience? _____

_____

_____

_____

_____

What is the writer's role? _____

_____

_____

_____

_____

Why is the level of language appropriate? _____

_____

_____

_____

_____

Exercise 1.2

As a class, select one of the five paragraphs found on pages 16–20. First, be sure you all agree on the intended audience and purpose of the paragraph. Your objective is to "translate" the paragraph for a different audience. The purpose of your revision will be the same as that of the original, but the language and tone will be adapted to suit the audience for whom the new message is intended.

Next, in groups of three, choose an audience for your revision from the following list. (Each group must select a different audience.)

elementary-school children   very hip, very cool grade 12 students
your family   your English instructor
a close friend   *Globe and Mail* readers
an elderly relative   your college newspaper

Once all groups have completed their translations, compare the results by reading the newly translated paragraphs aloud. Try to guess who each other's intended audience is. How do you know? How does the language work to meet the needs of the new audience?

The following exercise will give you practice in communicating effectively by adjusting your level of language to suit your purpose, your message, and your audience.

Exercise 1.3

Imagine, in each of the following situations, that you must deal with three different audiences face to face. Before you begin, analyze each audience in terms of knowledge, attitudes, and needs; then clarify the purpose of your message, your attitude toward your subject, and your audience's expectations of you.

1. You prepared your company's sales presentation in PowerPoint and stored it on the hard drive of your notebook computer. On your way to a meeting with clients in Detroit, your notebook was handled roughly by customs inspectors at the airport. When you got to the sales meeting, your computer would not open PowerPoint.

   You made the sales presentation as well as you could, but the clients were not impressed, and your company did not get the contract. Explain these circumstances to

   • your supervisor in the sales department
   • the U.S. Customs complaint bureau
   • a representative of the computer company, which claims its notebook computers are practically indestructible

2. At 8:30 this morning, your friend Jaron phones you from a police station. He has been arrested because, according to the arresting officer, he has 37 unpaid parking tickets outstanding. He claims he's innocent; he's never had a parking ticket. He has called to ask you to come down and bail him out. If you do so, you will be very late for work. Jaron refuses to call his parents for help. Tell this story to

- your parents
- your boss
- Jaron's parents

3. You recently bought a pair of silk pants from Bottom Drawers Pants Company. They ripped in the crotch the first time you bent over. You were dancing enthusiastically with a very attractive partner and were deeply embarrassed. Before you could recover your composure, the owner of the club asked you to leave immediately. Tell your story to

- Bottom Drawers
- the owner of the club
- your dancing partner

4. After only three weeks at your new job, you felt you had to tell someone that your fellow employees were routinely stealing office supplies, sales samples, and even tools and equipment. After speaking to your union steward and your manager, you were laid off without any explanation or warning, and as a probational employee you have no protection. Explain your situation to

- the president of your union
- a longtime employee of the company who doesn't know why you were let go
- an employment counsellor

5. You are short of money—so short you can't even buy gas for your car. If you can't get gas money, you will be late for work, and your boss is annoyed because you've been late twice this week already. Ask for money from

- your parents
- a friend
- someone who owes you money

6. Turn one of the 15 role-playing situations above into a written assignment.

Exercise 1.4

This exercise is designed to reinforce your understanding of the importance of knowing your reader. An effective communicator figures out ahead of time not only what his or her readers need to know, but also what they do not need to know. Some information is necessary and some is superfluous, with the mix varying widely from audience to audience. With this in mind, describe one of the following topics to three different audiences: choose one from each of the three groups listed below.

Topics: a favourite musician or group, a favourite standup comic or other performer

Group A: a grandparent, a teacher, an employer

Group B: a coworker, a classmate, an old friend you haven't seen in years

Group C: The president of your college or university or the Student Council Social Committee, whom you are trying to persuade to support a fundraising event featuring your topic.

2

Choosing the Right Words

In this chapter, we provide a brief introduction to language that is accurate and appropriate for your message and your audience. Our assumption is that you are writing for readers in academic and professional environments. Our goals are to help you convey your message clearly and in a way that will leave your readers with a positive impression of you and your ideas.

Before you get started, you need to equip yourself with a few essential resources and some basic knowledge of what kinds of language are inappropriate when you write.

The Writer's Toolkit

In addition to basic skills, all workers need tools. As a general rule, the better their tools, the better their work. Every writer comes equipped with a set of language skills acquired from birth. In most cases, however, these skills are not sufficiently developed to handle the complex task of producing clear, error-free prose in a professional style. Fortunately, tools are available to assist writers in bringing their language skills up to the standards required by professional environments. Collectively, we call these indispensable aids the Writer's Toolkit.

No one expects a writer to write without assistance. In fact, our first recommendation to beginning writers is to GET HELP! Every writer needs three basic tools and to know how to use them.

1. Buy and use a good dictionary.

A dictionary is a writer's best friend. You will need to use it every time you write, so if you don't already own a good dictionary, you need to buy one. For Canadian writers, a good dictionary is one that is Canadian, current, comprehensive (contains at least 75,000 entries), and reliable (published by an established, well-known firm).

A convenient reference is the *Gage Canadian Dictionary*, available in an inexpensive paperback edition. It is the dictionary on which we have based the examples and exercises in this chapter. Also recommended are the *ITP Nelson Canadian Dictionary of the English Language*, the *Canadian Oxford Dictionary* (2nd ed., 2004), and, for those whose native language is not English, the *Oxford Advanced Learner's Dictionary*. Unfortunately, no comprehensive Canadian dictionary is available on the Internet.

Begin by reading the "Guide to the Dictionary" in the front matter. The information in the Guide may not be very entertaining, but it is essential if you want to understand how to read your dictionary accurately. No two dictionaries are alike. In order to use your dictionary efficiently, you need to be familiar with its symbols, abbreviations, and the format of its entries.

Knowing what is in the dictionary guide will also save you time. For example, you may not need to memorize long lists of irregular plurals. Good dictionaries include irregular plurals in their entries. They also include irregular forms of verbs, adjectives, and adverbs. And if you've forgotten how regular plurals, verbs, adjectives, and adverbs are formed, you'll find that information in the guide as well.

2. Use spelling and grammar checkers responsibly.

Good spell-check programs can find typing errors and common spelling mistakes that distract your readers and make you look careless. They do have limitations, however. As we'll see, they can't tell if you meant to write "your" or "you're" and will not flag either word, even if it's used incorrectly. (You'll learn more about such words in Chapter 37, "Hazardous Homonyms.")

Also, since we use Canadian English, our spelling is frequently different from American spelling, which is the standard on which most word-processing programs are based. Set your program to Canadian spelling if the option exists. If it does not, be aware that words such as *colour, honour*, and *metre*—all correct Canadian spellings—will be flagged as errors.

Another useful tool is a hand-held spell checker. Conveniently pocket-sized and not expensive, these devices contain a large bank of words and can provide the correct spelling if the "guess" you type in is not too far off. Some checkers even pronounce the word for you. Ask your instructor if you can use this device (sound turned off, please) when you are writing in class and during exams.

The best advice we can give you about grammar checkers (they announce their presence by producing wavy green lines under words or sentences as you write on your word processor) is to use them with caution. So far, no grammar checker has been able to account for even most, let alone all, of the subtleties of English grammar. A grammar program is as likely to flag a perfectly good sentence, even to suggest a "fix" that is incorrect, as it is to ignore a sentence full of errors. "I done real good on my grammar test," for example, escapes the dreaded wavy green line.

3. Buy and use a good thesaurus.

If you repeat yourself, using the same words again and again, you won't communicate your thoughts interestingly, let alone memorably. Worse, you will bore your reader. A thesaurus is a dictionary of synonyms—words with similar meanings. For any word you need to use repeatedly in a document, a good thesaurus will provide a list of alternatives.

Synonyms are *not* identical in meaning. Your dictionary will help you decide which of the words listed in your thesaurus are suitable for your message and which are not. We do not recommend that you rely on the thesaurus in your word-processing program. For any given word, a word-processing thesaurus provides a list, in alphabetical order, of more-or-less synonyms, with no usage labels or examples. "More-or-less" is not good enough. At the very least, you need to know whether the synonyms offered are nouns or verbs and whether they are in general use or are informal, technical, derogatory, or even obsolete. For this information, buy a good book-form thesaurus and use it in conjunction with your dictionary. Two thesauruses are available in inexpensive paperback editions: the *Oxford Thesaurus of Current English* (2003) and *Roget's 21st Century Thesaurus in Dictionary Form* (3rd ed., 2005).

Use the information you find in a thesaurus with caution. Inexperienced writers sometimes assume that long, obscure words will impress their readers. In fact, most readers are irritated by unnecessarily "fancy" language. For more information on this topic, see the "Pretentious Language" section on pages 31–32.

NEVER use a word whose meaning you do not know. When you find a potential but unfamiliar synonym, look it up in your dictionary to be sure it's the word you need.

So far, we've introduced you to the tools you'll need as a writer and to the levels of language you can choose from when writing a message for a particular audience. Let's turn now to the writing errors you must not commit, no matter what message you're sending or the audience to which you're sending it: wordiness, slang and jargon, pretentious language, clichés, sexist language, offensive language, and "abusages."

The Seven Deadly Sins of Writing

1. WORDINESS

Wordiness—words and phrases that are not essential to the communication of your message—is annoying to readers, no matter what topic you are writing about. Good writing communicates a message as concisely as possible. Wordy messages take up your readers' time and try their patience. If you want to please your audience, be brief.

Sometimes wordiness results from a failure to revise carefully. In the editing stage of writing, you should be looking for the best words to express your meaning. Wordy expressions and awkward phrasing often pop into your mind when you are struggling to express an idea, and they often make their way into a first draft. There is no excuse for them to survive a careful edit and make their way into the second draft, however.

Here's an example of what can happen when a writer fails to prune his or her prose:

> In my personal opinion, the government of this country of ours needs an additional amount of meaningful input from the people of Canada right now.

This wordy sentence could be nicely condensed into "In my opinion, our government needs to hear more from the people." The writer has chosen impressive-sounding phrases (*meaningful input, this country of ours*) and has slipped in unnecessary and meaningless words that should have been caught during editing (*personal opinion, an additional amount*). The result is a sentence that is so hard to read that it isn't worth the effort to decipher.

As you can see from the above example, one of the symptoms of wordiness is redundancy, or saying the same thing twice. Another is using several words where one or two would do.

The following list contains some of the worst offenders we've collected from student writing, corporate memoranda, form letters, and advertisements.

Wordy	Concise
a large number of	many
absolutely nothing/everything/ complete/perfect	nothing/everything/ complete/perfect
actual (*or* true) fact	fact
almost always	usually
at that point in time	then
at the present time	now
consensus of opinion	consensus
continue on	continue
could possibly (*or* may possibly, might possibly)	could (*or* may, might)
crisis (*or* emergency) situation	crisis (*or* emergency)
due to the fact that	because
end result	result
equally as good	as good
few and far between	rare
final conclusion	conclusion
for the reason that	because
free gift	gift
I myself (*or* you yourself, *etc.*)	I (*or* you, *etc.*)
I personally think/feel	I think/feel
in actual fact	in fact
in every instance	always
in my opinion, I think	I think
in the near future	soon
in today's society/in this day and age	now (*or* today)
is able to	can
many different kinds	many kinds
mutual agreement/cooperation	agreement/cooperation
my personal opinion	my opinion
no other alternative	no alternative
personal friend	friend
real, genuine leather (*or* real antique, *etc.*)	leather (*or* antique, *etc.*)
red in colour (*or* large in size, *etc.*)	red (*or* large, *etc.*)
repeat again	repeat
return back	return (*or* go back)
really, very	*These words add nothing to your meaning. Leave them out.*
8:00 a.m. in the morning	8:00 a.m.
such as, for example	such as

Wordy	Concise
take active steps	take steps
totally destroyed	destroyed
truly remarkable	remarkable
very (most, quite, almost, rather) unique	unique

Exercise 2.1*

Working with a partner, revise these sentences to make them as concise and clear as possible. Then compare your answers with our suggestions on page 513.

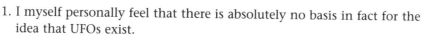

1. I myself personally feel that there is absolutely no basis in fact for the idea that UFOs exist.
2. Basically, I myself prefer modern contemporary furniture to old antiques.
3. I personally think Alison is faking her illness and pretending to be sick so she can stay at home and not have to go to work.
4. It has come to my attention that our competitor's products, though not equally as good as ours are, are nevertheless, at this point in time, selling better than those which we produce.
5. In my opinion, I believe that my essay is equally as good as Jill's and deserves equally as good a mark, which it would have got if it weren't for the fact that the professor hates me.
6. In my opinion, I doubt that this particular new innovation will succeed in winning much in the way of market share.
7. In my view, I feel that an English course that teaches the basic fundamentals is an essential prerequisite before a person can succeed in college, the business world, and the community at large.
8. "As a new beginning teacher," we told our English instructor, "you should try to understand the utter impossibility of gaining and holding the respect of us students so long as you are so completely and totally devoted to insisting that we follow grammar rules and regulations that totally inhibit the creativity in our writing."
9. I myself believe that, in all probability, this trend can be turned right around if we return back to basic fundamentals in our design process and introduce a few new innovations in our manufacturing process.
10. Due to the fact that the law, not to mention our company's policy, rules, and regulations, absolutely prohibits any mention of race, age, sex, religion, or marital status in official documents such as personnel documents, we have made sure that all such descriptors are entirely eliminated from our files, resulting in the fact that all our personnel documents are now almost virtually identical.

2. SLANG AND JARGON

Slang is "street talk": nonstandard words and phrases used by members of a group—people who share a culture, interest, or lifestyle. The group may be as large as a generation or as small as a high-school clique. Do you know what "amped," "badload," "busting," and "hodger" mean? Probably not. The whole point of slang is its exclusivity. It's a private language and thus not appropriate for a message aimed at a general reader.

Another characteristic of slang is that it changes quickly. Terms that were "in" last month are "out" today. Except for a few expressions that manage to sneak across the line that separates private language from mainstream English, most slang expressions are quickly outdated and sound silly. And finally, slang is an oral language. It is colloquial—that is, characteristic of casual speech—and not appropriate for use in professional or academic writing.

When you aren't sure if a word is appropriate for a written message, consult your print dictionary. The notation *sl.* or *slang* appears after words that are slang or have a slang meaning. (Some words, such as *house, cool,* and *bombed,* have both a general and a slang meaning.) If the word you're looking for isn't listed, chances are it's a recent slang term, and you should avoid using it in writing. Taking the time to choose words that are appropriate to written English increases your chances both of communicating clearly and of winning your readers' respect.

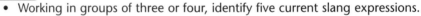

Exercise 2.2

- Working in groups of three or four, identify five current slang expressions.
- Now list five slang expressions that are no longer in use among your peers.
- Finally, define each current slang term in language appropriate to a general reader. (If you don't have a clear picture of a "general reader," write each definition in words your parents and teachers would understand.)

Jargon is similar to slang because it, too, is the private language of a subgroup; however, whereas the subgroups for slang are formed by culture or lifestyle, the subgroups who speak jargon are formed by profession or trade. The jargon of some professions is so highly technical and specialized it amounts almost to a private language.

Although jargon is useful, even necessary, in the context of some jobs, it is inappropriate in most writing because it does not communicate to a general reader. Our vocabulary and even the content of our writing are influenced by the contexts within which we work and live. In the following paragraph, D. E. Miller explains the extent to which our individual perceptions are influenced by our life experience.

A group of people witness a car accident. What each person sees, and how he or she describes it, is determined to a large extent by the language each one normally uses. A doctor or nurse would see and describe contusions, lacerations, and hemorrhages. A lawyer would think in terms of civil liabilities and criminal negligence. A mechanic would see crushed fenders, bent axles, and damaged chassis. A psychologist would be concerned about stress reactions, trauma, and guilt. You or I might see and describe the pain and injury caused by a driver's error in judgement or lapse of skill.

Miller, D. E. *The Book of Jargon.* New York: Collier, 1981. 26.

Jargon restricts your audience to those who share your specialized vocabulary and limits or destroys your ability to reach a wider audience. The cure for jargon is simple: unless your readers share your technical background, use nonspecialized language.

Exercise 2.3

Working in small groups, list as many examples of technical jargon as you can for each of the following occupations.

1. police officer (e.g., perpetrator, murder two)
2. nurse (e.g., bug, elopement risk)
3. car enthusiast (e.g., shift throw, stance)
4. financial analyst (e.g., beauty contest, fallen angel)
5. filmmaker (e.g., sync sound, M.O.S.)

Choose five technical terms from your own career field and write a general-level equivalent for each one.

---

3. PRETENTIOUS LANGUAGE

One of the challenges writers face when trying to adapt their style from the familiar to the formal level is a tendency to overcompensate. Many beginning writers try so hard to impress their readers that they forget that the purpose of writing is to communicate. Writing filled with abstract nouns, multi-syllable words, and long, complicated sentences is **pretentious**. All readers hate pretentious writing because they have to take the time to "translate" it into language they can understand. (Most teachers and supervisors won't bother. They'll just return the piece to the student or employee for revision.)

Sometimes called "gobbledygook," pretentious language has sound but no meaning:

> Our aspirational consumer strategy must position the brand's appeal to women shoppers who are seeking emblematic brands that are positively identified with health-oriented and fitness-centred lifestyles, so they can align their personal images with those lifestyle indicators.

This sentence, part of a marketing presentation to senior management, was written by a middle manager for a major yogurt company. What the poor writer is trying to say is that the company's customers want to be seen as people interested in fitness and health, so the company should advertise its yogurt accordingly.[1]

One symptom of pretentious writing is "buzzwords." These are words and phrases that become popular because they reflect the latest academic or psychological fad. They are often nouns with *-ize* added to them to make them into verbs: *utilize, verbalize, conceptualize*. What's wrong with *use, say*, and *think*? Every teacher knows this annoying trick; so do most managers. Instead of impressing readers, pretentious writing makes readers impatient and causes them to lose respect for the writer. If you really want to get your message across, write plainly and clearly in language your readers can understand.

Exercise 2.4*

Rewrite the following sentences, expressing the ideas in a way that allows the reader to grasp your meaning clearly, easily, and quickly. Then compare your answers to our suggestions on page 513.

1. We were forced to utilize the moisture-removing apparatus in our motorized personal conveyance when precipitate liquid impacted our windshield.
2. The chronologically less advanced generation sometimes achieves a communication deficit with authority figures and parental units.
3. The witness was ethically disoriented truthwise when she claimed that her interface with the accused resulted in his verbalization of an admission of guilt.
4. The parameters of our study vis-à-vis the totality of research in the field demonstrate that surveywise our validity is on a par with that of other instruments.

---

[1] This anecdote is paraphrased from Doug Saunders, "Aspiration Nation: Life Is but a Brand-name Dream," *Globe and Mail* 3 Jul. 2004: F3.

5. The cancellation of IMF funds to the Pacific Rim countries could lead to negative distortion of mutual interrelationships between developed and developing nations.

4. CLICHÉS

Unless you're a career civil servant or a longtime bureaucrat, writing pretentious language is a time-consuming and tiring task. You have to look up practically every word in a thesaurus to find a polysyllabic equivalent. Clichés, on the other hand, are easy to produce: they represent language without thought.

A **cliché** is a phrase that has been used so often it has lost its ability to communicate a meaningful idea to a reader.

In this day and age, it seems that anything goes in our private lives. But in our professional lives, the name of the game is what it has always been: the bottom line.

In this day and age, anything goes, the name of the game, and *the bottom line* are clichés. Readers know what these phrases are supposed to mean, but they have been used so often they no longer communicate effectively. Cliché-filled writing will not only bore readers, but also affect their reaction to your message: "There's nothing new here. It's all been said before."

Spoken English is full of clichés. In the rush to express an idea, we often take the easy way and use ready-made expressions to put our thoughts into words. There is less excuse to use clichés in writing. Writers have time to think through what they want to say. They also have the opportunity to revise and edit. Writers are expected to communicate with more care, more precision, and more originality than speakers.

Clichés are easy to recognize if you are a native speaker. When you can read the first few words of an expression and automatically fill in the rest, the phrase is a cliché: free as a _____; a pain in the _____; last but not_____; it goes without _____. It is difficult to get rid of *all* clichés in your writing, but you can be aware of them and use them as seldom as possible.

The solution to a cliché problem involves time and thought. Think carefully about what you want to say; then say it in your own words, not everyone else's.

As you read through Exercise 2.5, notice how hard it is to form a mental picture of what the sentences mean and how hard it is to remember what you've read—even when you've just read it!

Exercise 2.5

Working with a partner, rewrite these sentences, expressing the ideas in your own words. When you're finished, exchange papers with another team and compare your results.

1. The boardroom was so quiet you could hear a pin drop.
2. It was raining cats and dogs, but we slept like logs through the storm.
3. When you are playing poker, you should keep your cool; otherwise, you could lose your shirt.
4. The CEO could not find a way to stay afloat, so she threw in the towel.
5. I burned the midnight oil and managed to finish the assignment at the crack of dawn.
6. Is this concept a flash in the pan or an idea whose time has come?
7. If we can nip this problem in the bud, there will be light at the end of the tunnel!
8. She stopped dead in her tracks. Lying on the floor was her son, crying his eyes out.
9. Your proposal is as good as they come; however, until the deal is signed, sealed, and delivered, we had better not count our chickens.
10. Even though I sweated it out night after night and kept my nose to the grindstone, I didn't meet my sales quota. As a result, I am sadder but wiser.

5. SEXIST LANGUAGE

Any writing that distracts your readers from your meaning is weak writing. Whether the distraction is caused by grammatical errors, spelling mistakes, slang, or the use of sexist language, your readers' concentration on your message is broken, and communication fails. **Sexist** (or gender-biased) **language** includes the use of words that signify gender (e.g., *waitress, sculptress, actress*) and the use of the pronouns *he, his, him* to refer to singular antecedents such as *everybody, anyone, no one*. Some readers object to terms that draw attention to gender differences, such as *man and wife* or *host and hostess*, preferring instead gender-neutral, inclusive terms such as *married couple* and *hosts*.

It is easy to dismiss nonsexist writing as "politically correct," but the language we use is a powerful force that influences the way we think. If we consistently refer to a *chairman* or *businessman*, we are perpetuating the idea that only men qualify for these positions. Far from being a politically correct fad, the use of inclusive or neutral words is both accurate and evenhanded.

Here are three tips to help you steer clear of sexist writing.

- Avoid using the word *woman* as an adjective. There is an implied condescension to phrases such as *woman athlete* and *woman writer* and *woman engineer*.

- Be conscious of the dangers of stereotyping. Physical descriptions of women are appropriate only where you would offer a similar description if the subject were a man. Just as some men can be excellent cooks, some women can be ruthless, power-hungry executives. It is possible for men to be scatterbrained and gossipy, while women can be decisive, tough, even violent.

- When making pronouns agree with singular antecedents, be careful that your pronouns do not imply bias. For example, "A teacher who discovers plagiarism must report it to *his* supervisor." Either use masculine and feminine pronouns interchangeably, or switch to a plural noun and avoid the problem: "Teachers who discover plagiarism must report it to their supervisors."

Exercise 2.6*

Correct the use of sexist or gender-biased language in the following sentences. Exchange papers with a partner and compare revisions. Then turn to pages 513–14 and compare your answers with our suggestions.

1. The well-known female producer Elaine May often regrets that she cannot go out in public without attracting the attention of fans and photographers.
2. Amy King, an attractive, blonde mother of two, first joined the company as a saleswoman; 10 years later, she was promoted to president.
3. A businessman sitting in the first-class cabin rang for the stewardess, a friendly gal who quickly arrived to assist him.
4. The list of ingredients on food packages contains information that may be important to the housewife, especially if she is the mother of young children.
5. The typical working man with a wife and two children is often hard-pressed to find time for recreation with his bride and the kids.

---

6. OFFENSIVE LANGUAGE

The last thing you want to do when you write is to offend your reader, even if you are writing a complaint. As we've seen above, some words occasionally used in speech are always inappropriate in writing. Swear words, for example, are unacceptable in a written message. So are obscene words, even "mild" ones. Offensive language appears much stronger in print than in speech and can provoke, shock, or even outrage a reader. Racist language and blasphemy (the use of names or objects that are sacred to any religion) are deeply offensive and always unacceptable.

Many writers have experienced the acute embarrassment of having a message read by people for whom it was not intended. What might have seemed at the time of composition to be an innocent joke may prove hateful to the unintended audience and mortifying to the writer.

It is wise to avoid all questionable, let alone unacceptable, expressions in your writing. Language has power: as many linguists have observed, our language actually shapes as well as reflects our attitudes and values. Those who use racist, blasphemous, sexist, or profane terms not only reinforce the attitudes contained in those terms, but also project a profoundly negative image of themselves to their readers.

7. ABUSAGES

Some words and phrases, even ones we hear in everyday speech, are *always* incorrect in written English. Technically, they are also incorrect in speech, but most people tolerate them in informal conversation. If these expressions appear in your writing, your reader will assume you are uneducated, ignorant, or worse. Even in some conversations, particularly in academic and professional environments, these expressions make a poor impression on your listeners.

Carefully read through the following list and highlight any words or phrases that sound all right to you. These are the ones you need to find and fix when you revise.

allready	A common misspelling of *already.*
alot	There is no such word. Use *much* or *many.* (*A lot* is acceptable in informal usage.)
anyways (anywheres)	There is no *s* in these words.
between you and I	The correct expression is *between you and me.*
can't hardly couldn't hardly	Use *can hardly* or *could hardly.*
could of (would of, should of)	The helping verb needed is *have,* not *of.* Write *could have, would have, should have.*

didn't do nothing	All double negatives ("couldn't see nothing," "couldn't get nowhere," "wouldn't talk to nobody") are wrong. Write *didn't do anything, couldn't see anything, couldn't get anywhere, wouldn't talk to anyone.*
for free	Use *free* or *at no cost.* (Also "free gift." Is there any other kind of gift?)
in regards to	Use *in* (or *with*) regard to.
irregardless	There is no such word. Use *regardless.*
media used as singular	The word *media* is plural. The singular is *medium.* Newspapers and television are mass *media.* Radio is an electronic *medium.*
most all	Use *most* or *almost all.*
off of	Use *off* alone: "I fell *off* the wagon."
prejudice used as an adjective	It is wrong to write "She is *prejudice* against blondes." Use *prejudiced.*
prejudism	There is no such word. Use *prejudice.* "A judge should show no *prejudice* to either side."
real used as an adverb	"Real good," "real bad," and "real nice" are wrong. You could use *really* or *very,* but such filler words add nothing to your meaning.
reason is because	Use *the reason is that*: "The reason is that my printer blew up."
suppose to	This expression, like *use to,* is nonstandard. Use *supposed to* and *used to.*
themself	Also "theirself," "ourselfs," "yourselfs," and "themselfs." These are all nonstandard words. The plural of *self* is *selves: themselves, ourselves,* and so on. Don't use "theirselves"; it's another nonstandard word.
try and	Use *try to.*
youse	There is no such word. *You* is the singular and plural form of the pronoun.

Exercise 2.7*

Correct the following sentences where necessary. Suggested answers are on page 514.

1. Irregardless of what you think, the problem between her and I has nothing to do with you.
2. If you want to be in the office pool, I need $5.00 off of you today because there will be no spots left by tomorrow.
3. Because they didn't finish the job theirself the way they should of, we will have to work real late to get it done.
4. I didn't feel like seeing nobody, so I went home, turned on the TV, and didn't do nothing for the rest of the night.
5. This use to be a real good place to work, but now we are suppose to work a full shift every day, or a penalty is deducted off of our pay.
6. Alot of young people today fight against prejudism not only in society but also within themselfs.
7. I'm suppose to ask youse if the reason for the delay is because there has been another bomb threat.
8. It's unresponsible of us to blame television or any other media for causing violence.
9. Television is partly responsible, however, for the fact that alot of ungrammatical expressions sound alright to us.
10. Between you and I, the reason I didn't speak to no one about Elmo's cheating is because he would of broke my arm.

3

Selecting a Subject

Approximately one-third of the time you devote to an essay should be spent on the planning stage (and the remainder to drafting and revising.) If you take the time to analyze your audience, find a good subject, and identify interesting main points to make about that subject, you will find that the mechanics of writing will fall into place much more easily than if you try to sweat your way through the paper the night before it's due. After you have considered your readers' background, needs, and expectations, the next step is to choose a satisfactory subject to write about.

Even when you are assigned a topic for an essay, you need to examine it, focus it, and consider different ways of approaching it. Depending on your knowledge of the topic and the readers you are writing for, the range of specific subjects for any broad topic is almost endless. For example, given the broad topic "Research sources," here are some of the approaches from which you might choose.

Can you trust Internet sources?
Interviewing to develop original source material
Books: still the best "random access device"
Journal indexes: an underused source of mountains of material
How to do an effective Internet search

Your first task, then, is to choose a satisfactory subject, one that satisfies the basic principles of the **4-S test**:

A satisfactory subject is significant, single, specific, and supportable.

If it passes the 4-S test, your subject is the basis of a good essay.

MAKE YOUR SUBJECT SIGNIFICANT

Your subject must be worthy of the time and attention you expect your readers to give to your paper. Can you imagine an essay on "How to buy movie tickets" or "Why I hate pants with button flies," for example, as being meaningful to your readers?

Exercise 3.1*

From the list below, choose those subjects that would be significant to a typical reader. Revise the others to make them significant, if possible. If not, suggest another, related subject that is significant. When you have finished this exercise, compare your answers with those provided on page 514.

1. Tips for travelling with small children
2. Using the reference library
3. Page-turning techniques
4. The perfect vacation spot
5. How to use the number pad on a calculator
6. Television is a threat to Canadian independence
7. Why you should write on one side of the page only

MAKE YOUR SUBJECT SINGLE

Don't try to crowd too much into one paper. Be careful that your subject is not actually two or three related subjects masquerading as one. If you attempt to write about a multiple subject, your readers will get a superficial and possibly confusing overview instead of the interesting and satisfying detail they expect to find in a well-planned paper. A subject such as "The problem of league expansion in basketball and other sports" is too broad to be dealt with satisfactorily in one essay. More manageable alternatives are "The problems of league expansion in the NBA" or "Why Montreal can't get an NBA franchise."

Exercise 3.2*

From the following list, choose the subjects that are single and could be satisfactorily explored in a short essay. Revise the others to make them single.

1. Causes of unemployment among college students and new graduates
2. Pub night at different colleges
3. How to change a tire and adjust the timing
4. The importance of accuracy in newspaper and television reporting
5. Methods of preventing the spread of STDs

6. Causes of injury in industry and professional sports
7. Nursing and engineering: rewarding careers

MAKE YOUR SUBJECT SPECIFIC

Given a choice between a broad, general topic and a narrow, specific one, always choose the specific one. Most readers find concrete, specific details more interesting than broad generalizations. It would be difficult to say anything very detailed about a huge subject such as "The roles of women in history," for example. But with some research, you could write an interesting paper on "The roles of 19th-century prairie women" or "Famous female pilots."

You can narrow a broad subject and make it more specific by applying one or more *limiting factors* to it. Try thinking of your subject in terms of a specific *kind, time, place, number,* or *person* associated with it. By applying this technique to the last potential subject above, you might come up with "Amelia Earhart's last flight."

Exercise 3.3*

In the list below, identify the subjects that are specific and could be explained satisfactorily in a short essay. Revise the others to make them specific by applying one or more of the limiting factors to each one.

1. Summer employment opportunities in my home town
2. Modern heroes
3. How to enjoy winter weather
4. The effects of government cutbacks on low-income families
5. The problems of urban living
6. How to repair your home appliances
7. Binge drinking among college women

MAKE YOUR SUBJECT SUPPORTABLE

You must know something about your subject (preferably more than your readers know), or you must be able to find out about it. Remember, your readers want information that is new, interesting, and thought provoking—not obvious observations familiar to everyone. You must be able to include *specific examples, facts, figures, quotations, anecdotes,* or other *supporting details.* Supporting information can be gathered from your own experience, from the experience of other people, or from both. If you don't know enough about your topic to write anything but the obvious, be prepared to do some research.

Exercise 3.4*

From the subjects given below, choose those that are clearly supportable in a short essay. Revise the others to make them supportable.

1. My career as a student
2. Movie review: *Star Wars: Episode III—Revenge of the Sith*
3. Crisis in the Canadian airline industry
4. The Chinese secret service
5. Space travel in the year 2100
6. Art through the ages
7. The hazards of working in a fast-food outlet

Exercise 3.5*

Together with a partner, discuss the acceptability of the potential subjects listed below. Indicate with check marks (✔) whether each subject below passes the 4-S test by being significant, single, specific, and supportable. Revise each unsatisfactory subject (fewer than four check marks) to make it a satisfactory subject for a short essay.

The 4-S Test

Subject	significant	single	specific	supportable	Revision
1. Computers	☐	☐	☐	☐	_____
2. Insomnia and other stress-related disorders	☐	☐	☐	☐	_____
3. The Arctic 200 years from now	☐	☐	☐	☐	_____
4. Dressing for an interview	☐	☐	☐	☐	_____
5. Architecture	☐	☐	☐	☐	_____

GO TO WEB

EXERCISE 3.1

Exercise 3.6

Write down three subjects that you think pass the 4-S test. When you've finished, exchange papers with another student and carefully check each other's
work.

Once you have selected an appropriate subject, it's time to move on to
the next stage: identifying solid main points to support that subject.

4

Managing the
Main Points

While you were selecting subjects and testing them against the four principles presented in Chapter 3, you were thinking, consciously or unconsciously, about what you could say about them. **Main points** are the two or three or four most important things you have to say about your subject. Selecting them carefully is a vitally important part of the writing process.

Generating Main Points:
The Bottom-Up Approach

If you are feeling intimidated by your task and unsure about how to present your subject, some prewriting activities can be helpful. Writers use several methods to stimulate thinking and prepare for a productive first draft. Two techniques are especially effective: freewriting and brainstorming. Either will get your creative juices flowing; we recommend that you try both to see which works best for you in particular situations.

Understand that you employ these techniques when you already have the necessary material in your head. Either you are writing from personal experience or you've done some research. (You'll learn about research in Part 5.) Freewriting and brainstorming are designed to get your ideas on the page in any order, shape, or form. Don't worry about making a mess. You can clean it up later.

FREEWRITING

Freewriting does what its name implies. It sets you free to write without worrying about any of the possible writing errors you might make that block the flow of your ideas. Forget about grammar, spelling, word choice, and so on, for a while, until you get some ideas down on the page. Here's how to go about freewriting:

1. Put your watch and a pad of paper on your desk. If you can type faster than you can write, open a new document on your computer. (Some writers find it helpful to turn the monitor off.) Write your subject at the top of the page or tape it to the top of your computer monitor. Ideally, your subject will have passed the 4-S test, but if you're really stuck, you can begin with just a word or a phrase.

2. Make a note of the time and start writing. Don't stop until you have written for three, five, or even ten minutes straight. Write anything that comes to mind, even if it seems boring or silly. If you get stuck for words, write your subject or even the last phrase you've written over and over until something new comes to mind. (Don't worry, it will!)

3. Write as quickly as you can. Don't pause to analyze or evaluate your ideas, and don't scratch out or delete anything. This technique is designed to get thoughts into words as quickly as possible without self-consciousness.

4. When the time is up, stop and stretch. Then read over what you've written. Underline anything that is related to your subject. Much of your freewriting will be irrelevant nonsense that you can delete. But what you have underlined will be useful in the next step: identifying the main points you will focus on to explain your subject.

5. Turn the phrases, fragments, and sentences you have underlined into clear, understandable points. If you don't end up with at least 10 points, continue freewriting for another few minutes and see what new ideas you can discover.

6. On a separate piece of paper, list the points you have identified. Study the possible relationships among these points and cluster them under two or three headings. These are your main points. Now you can move on to the next step: testing each main point to be sure it is satisfactory for your essay.

Here is an example of the freewriting technique. The assigned topic, for a course in law enforcement fundamentals, was "Crime and Punishment." Victor Chen was interested in the difference between crime as it is portrayed in the media and the reality of Canada's justice system. After doing some research and finding statistics that he thought might be useful, he drafted the following on his computer in 15 minutes.

What's really happening in our system in terms of crime and punishment is really different from what we see in the media. Look at TV crime shows. It used to be that all the courtroom shows were about defence lawyers trying to prove their clients' innocence. The prosecutors were the bad guys doing everything they could to put the defence attorney's client in jail or worse. There has been a big shift in the last five years or so and now we seem to have developed a taste for law and order. Now it's the prosecutors who are the good guys and the defence attorneys are trying to prevent their sleazy clients from escaping justice. The sad thing is that we form opinions about what goes on in real courtrooms based on stories like these. Almost all of the courtroom dramas on TV are American, and what goes on in American courtrooms is different from Canada's court procedures, so we are definitely not very aware of how our justice system really works.

To prove this, look at the study that was done by Roberts and Doob. They took a group of people and gave them the newspaper articles about a trial. When they had read the stories, they were asked about the trial. Most of them thought the criminal had gotten a sentence that was too light and only 15 percent thought the sentence was too tough. Then they took another group and gave them the court documents and transcripts of what actually went on in the trial. This group was reversed, more than half of them thought the sentence was too tough. Less than 20 percent agreed with the majority in the other group that the criminal should have got a longer sentence. This shows that we are getting a distorted impression of reality when we read about violent crime in the papers or on TV. It's like we're living in two worlds, the imaginary media one and the real one we don't know about. Also the news distorts violence. Reading the papers or watching TV, you'd think there was an epidemic of crime and that our streets are unsafe and murder was a common occurrence. This is so they can sell more papers and attract more viewers. In fact crime rates are falling. About half the crime reported in the news is violent while violent crime is actually less than 12 percent of cases that are reported. Murders are less than 1 percent of violent crimes but they are 25 percent of crime stories. If all you did was read the papers and watch TV you'd think that violence and murder were very common but actually they are quite rare. It's easy to see how we get the idea that violence in our society is a real problem. So it's really important that the people who make the laws don't rely on the media, because it is very distorted information.

After completing this freewriting exercise, Victor underlined all the points that he considered significant, supportable, and related to the subject. He quickly realized that the paper would be too long, and that one of his points was based on personal observation rather than provable facts. He crossed out everything related to television shows and then rearranged the other information into a rough outline of an essay with two main points.

Intro: the reality of the justice system and the media accounts of it are two different things. Take two examples: violence and court proceedings.

1. Crime
   - murders in reality vs. murders in the media
   - violent crime in reality vs. violent crime in the media
2. Courts—the Roberts and Doob study
   - opinions of group that read newspaper accounts of a trial
   - opinions of group that read court documents of a trial

Conclusion: lawmakers need to base decisions on reality and not on the media or public opinion.

Working from this rough outline, Victor developed a first draft. In reading it over, he noted where he needed to add more support to make the contrast clearer and more emphatic. After two more revisions and a careful edit, he submitted "Justice and Journalism," which you will find on pages 209–10.

Exercise 4.1

Choose a subject, or work with an assigned subject. Follow the six steps outlined on page 45 to see what main points you can come up with. Don't worry if your work is messy. Freewriting is a record of your thoughts, and thinking is messy.

BRAINSTORMING

In **brainstorming**, you write down a list of every idea you can think of about a specific subject. You can brainstorm alone, with a partner, or—best of all—in a group. If you run out of ideas too quickly, then try the age-old journalist's technique: ask the questions *who, what, why, when, where,* and *how* about your subject. Here's how to proceed. (The first three steps below assume you are working with a partner or in a small group. You can also do them by yourself, but you'll have less fun.)

1. Write your topic at the top of the page. Again, you will save time if you've checked your subject against the 4-S test. Decide how much time you will spend on this exercise: three, five, or more minutes. As in freewriting, working against the clock can bring surprising results.
2. Write down in short form—words or phrases—every idea you can think of that is even vaguely related to your subject. Choose the fastest writer in your group to be the recorder. Work quickly. Don't slow yourselves down by worrying about grammar or repetition.

3. When the time is up, relax for a minute, then go over the list carefully. Underline the points that seem most clearly related to your subject and scratch out any duplicates or any ideas that are vague, trivial, or irrelevant. If you don't end up with at least three or four points that are meaningful to you, brainstorm again for a few minutes, using the six journalist's questions to generate more ideas.

4. Working alone now, take your three or four most significant points and rephrase them in clear sentences on a new sheet of paper. Now you're ready to move on to the next step: testing your main points to ensure that they are suitable for use in your essay.

The following example demonstrates how brainstorming can be used to overcome the most frustrating inertia. The subject was "Your college English course." As you might expect, the class groaned when the subject was assigned, but one group's quick brainstorming produced some unique and interesting approaches to the topic. The time limit given for this exercise was four minutes. After brainstorming, at least one student was convinced that her career opportunities would improve if she learned how to communicate better.

Your College English Course

- have to take it
- should like it but I don't
- writing is important
- speaking's easier than writing
- bosses will hire you if you can write
- you can get a job
- letter of application
- have to write on the job
- have to write to the boss, other departments
- have to write to customers
- embarrassed about my writing
- people don't respect a poor writer
- writing helps you think
- writing helps you read better
- have to write reports
- need to know how to write a good report
- have to prepare slides for presentations
- need to write to get promoted

This list contains several significant points along with some irrelevant and trivial ones, which the group deleted. Then they talked about possible relationships among the remaining items on the list.

At this point, each student began working alone. After one student had underlined the points she felt were most important, she noticed that these points could be divided into two related ideas: what college English teaches and why it is useful. She then combined these two ideas into a thesis (a point of view about a subject). Here is her list of revised points.

College English is useful because
- it improves writing and thinking skills
- you will communicate better on the job
- you will get promoted

Exercise 4.2

In groups of four or five, brainstorm as many topics as you can in five minutes. Do not censor or cut any ideas. You should end up with at least 20 topics. Then exchange papers with another group, and edit that group's topics, crossing out any that are too broad or too narrow. Switch papers again, with a different group, and choose four topics that pass the 4-S test. Finally, select the best of the four topics and present it to the rest of the class, explaining why it's a good choice for an essay.

Exercise 4.3

Choose one of the two prewriting techniques presented in this chapter: freewriting or brainstorming. Generate as much information as you can in five minutes about one of the topics presented to the class in Exercise 4.2. Then narrow your information down to three main points, decide how to present them, and write a brief outline (no longer than the example given at the top of this page) for a short essay.

Generating Main Points:
The Top-Down Approach

Another way to find out what you have to say about a subject is to ask specific questions of it. Questioning lets you "walk around" your subject, looking at it from different angles, taking it apart and putting it back together again. Each question is a probe that enables you to dig below the surface and find out what you know. The top-down approach is more structured than the strategies we have discussed so far, but it has the advantage of producing clear main points with few or no off-topic responses. It also identifies for you the kinds of development you can use in your essay.

Questioning your subject works best if you know it well or have done some research but are not sure how to approach it. Any subject can be approached in a number of ways. The needs of your audience and your purpose in writing should determine the approach you choose.

Here's how to use the questioning technique to generate ideas:

1. Begin by writing your proposed subject at the top of the page, or tape it to your monitor.
2. Now apply the 12 questions listed below, one at a time, to your subject to see which ones "fit" best. That is, find the questions that call up in your mind answers that could be used as points to develop your subject. As you go down the list, you will probably find more than one question for which you can think up answers. Do not stop with the first question that produces answers. The purpose of this idea-generating technique is to discover the *best* approach for your target audience and writing purpose.
3. Go through the entire list and record your answers to any questions that apply to your subject. Ignore the questions that make no sense in relation to the subject.
4. Finally, study the questions that produced answers and choose the one that generated the ideas that are closest to what your reader needs to know and what you want to say.

The questions listed in the left-hand column lead to the kinds of essay development listed in the column on the right. Don't worry about these now. We'll discuss them in detail in Part 4.

The Answers to This Question	Produce This Kind of Paper
1. What does your subject *look, feel, sound, smell*, and/or *taste* like?	*Description*
2. How did your subject *happen*?	*Narration*
3. How is your subject *made* or *done*? 4. How does your subject work?	*Process*
5. What are the main *kinds* of your subject? 6. What are the component *parts* of your subject? 7. What are the significant *features, characteristics,* or *functions* of your subject?	*Classification/ Division*
8. What are the *causes* of your subject? 9. What are the *effects* or *consequences* of your subject?	*Cause/Effect*
10. What are the *similarities* and/or *differences* between your subject and *X*?	*Comparison/ Contrast*
11. What are the main *advantages/disadvantages* of your subject? 12. What are the reasons *in favour of/against* your subject?	*Argument/ Persuasion*

Here is an example of how the process works. Alice Tam, a recent college graduate, has decided to write about her first job as a management trainee. Her target audience is general readers, not experts in her field. The subject passes the 4-S test: it is significant, single, specific, and supportable.

1. **What does my job feel like?**
   At first glance, this question doesn't make much sense. A *job* can't feel; the *employee* does. However, by interpreting the question loosely, Alice could describe her nervousness, her desire to do well, the pressures she felt, and the rewards of the job.

2. **How did my job happen?**
   This question doesn't sound promising. How Alice landed her job would be of interest to her family and friends, but probably would not appeal to a broader audience unless her experience was highly unusual or could be instructive to others.

3. **How is my job done?**
   The answer to this question is basically a job description, which would be of little interest to anyone other than Alice's close friends, her supervisor, or the person hired to replace her. Let's move on.

4. **How does my first job work?**
   All jobs are different; this question doesn't take us anywhere.

5. **What are the main kinds of first jobs?**
   This question might lead to an acceptable topic for a research paper on the kinds of entry-level jobs graduates from specific programs can expect to get, but the answers won't produce the sort of personal experience essay Alice wants to write.

6. **What are the component parts (i.e., main requirements) of my job?**
   Our writer might use this question as a starting point for a discussion of her main job functions, but this information would be of interest only to those in her career field, not to a broad, general audience.

7. **What are the significant features of my job?**
   This question has possibilities. Alice could tell her readers about those aspects of her job that apply to all first-time employees, perhaps limiting her focus to the aspects of the working world that she hadn't expected, that in fact surprised her.

8. **What were the causes of my first job?**
   This question doesn't produce useful answers. Most people work because they have to support themselves. The answer is self-evident.

9. **What are the effects of my first job?**
   This question raises some interesting answers. What effect has full-time employment had on Alice's life? She might discuss the self-esteem that

replaced her earlier insecurity and fear of the job search; she might discuss her new independence, both financial and social.

10. What are the similarities (or differences) between my first job and . . . what? A second or third job?
    Our writer is still on her first job and so can't really comment on this question.

11. What are the main advantages (or disadvantages) of my first job?
    This question produces answers that are easy to explain—and that's the problem with it. Unless Alice has a very unusual first job, the answers to this question are predictable and therefore of little interest to a broad audience.

12. What are the reasons in favour of (or against) my first job?
    This question leads to answers that overlap with those produced by question 11. It would lead to an average essay, but not to anything outstanding or memorable.

After patiently going through the list, our writer found two questions, 7 and 9, that produced answers she felt she could work with. She especially liked the possibilities suggested by question 7. As Alice focused her thoughts, she realized that what she wanted to write about was the unexpected challenges she confronted when she joined the world of work. So she refined the question to capture what she wanted to write about ("What are the most significant challenges I faced in my first job?") and came up with three solid answers: the expectations of my boss, my coworkers, and myself. The essay that resulted from this process, "On-the-Job Training," appears on pages 188–89.

Generating main points is a time-consuming but worthwhile process. The more time you spend at this stage, the less time it will take you to draft your essay. To sharpen your skills, study the examples given below. Each consists of a 4-S test–approved subject, a question about that subject, and some answers the question produces that would form solid main points to support, explain, or prove the subject of the essay.

Subject	Selected Question	Main Points
Hockey violence	What are the reasons in favour of violence in hockey?	• releases aggression • keeps players alert • attracts fans
Law enforcement officers	What are the main functions of law enforcement officers?	• preventing crime • apprehending criminals • enforcing the law • acting as role models

Subject	Selected Question	Main Points
Job interviews	How do you make a negative impression in a job interview?	• be late • be inappropriately dressed • be ignorant about the company • complain about former employers
Essay topics	What are the characteristics of a satisfactory essay topic?	• single • significant • specific • supportable

Exercise 4.4

Working in pairs, apply the questions on pages 51–52 to each of the subjects listed below. Select the question that produces the answers you both like best, and list three or four of these answers as main points.

Subject	Selected Question	Main Points
1. Procrastination		• • • •
2. E-mail		• • • •
3. SUVs		• • • •

4. Business dress
   codes

-
-
-
-

5. Ice cream

-
-
-
-

Exercise 4.5

In pairs, choose two subjects that you think would be suitable for short essays. Be sure all are significant, single, specific, and supportable. For each subject, list at least three strong main points. Use the questions on pages 51–52 to help you identify main points. When you've finished, exchange your ideas with another team, critique each other's main points, and make suggestions.

Subject _____

Selected Question _____

Main Points
-
-
-

Subject _____

Selected Question _____

Main Points
-
-
-

Testing Your Main Points

Now that you've practised identifying main points using freewriting, brainstorming, and the questioning approach, the next step is to examine the points you've come up with to make sure each is going to work as a major component in your essay. Some may be too minor to bother with; some may overlap in meaning; some may even be unrelated to your subject. Here's how to test your main points to be sure they are satisfactory. Whether you've arrived at your main points through freewriting, brainstorming, or questioning, the test is the same.

Main points must be significant, distinct, and relevant.

ARE YOUR MAIN POINTS SIGNIFICANT?

Each main point should be worth writing and reading about. If you can't write at least one interesting and informative paragraph about a point, it is probably not significant enough to bother with. Don't waste your readers' time with trivial matters. In the following example, one of the main points does not have the same importance as the others; it should be eliminated or replaced. Which one would you discard?

Reasons for attending college
- to learn career skills
- to improve one's general knowledge of the world
- to enjoy the social life
- to participate in student government

ARE YOUR MAIN POINTS DISTINCT?

Each of the main points you choose must be different from all the others; there must be no overlap in meaning. Check to be sure you haven't given two different labels to what is really only one aspect of your subject. Eliminate or replace any main points that duplicate other points or that can easily be covered under another point. Here's an example of a list that contains a redundant main point. Which point would you eliminate?

Advantages of cycling

- improves fitness
- stimulates enjoyment of surroundings
- keeps one in shape
- doesn't damage the environment

ARE YOUR MAIN POINTS RELEVANT?

The main points you choose must be clearly and directly related to your subject. They all must be aspects of that subject and must add to the development of your readers' information on the subject. In this example, the third main point listed should be eliminated because it does not relate to the stated topic.

The miseries of winter

- numbing cold
- layers of uncomfortable clothes
- Christmas presents
- dangerous driving conditions

Exercise 4.6*

At least one main point in each item below is unsatisfactory. Identify each faulty point and explain why it should be deleted. When you have finished, compare your answers with those on page 515.

1. Business communication devices
   - telephone
   - e-mail
   - fax
   - mail
   - cell

2. Advantages of locating a business outside the city
   - cheaper cost of living
   - calmer pace
   - distance from suppliers and markets
   - government subsidies and tax benefits

3. Kinds of television commercials
   - boring
   - clever
   - misleading
   - puzzling
   - repetitive

4. Causes of college failure	• lack of preparation in high school • procrastination • poor study habits • irregular attendance
5. How to choose a place to live	• determine your needs • determine your budget • find a reliable real-estate agent • seek expert advice
6. Reasons for high staff turnover	• salary lower than industry standard • no chance for advancement • uncomfortable work environment • competitors offer better pay

Organizing Your Main Points

After you've identified the main points for your essay and checked to make sure they are satisfactory, your final task in the planning process is to list them in order. (This list of points is sometimes called a plan of development or a path statement.) Main points are like menu items on a website: the more logically they are arranged, the easier it is to navigate your way through them.

> There are four ways to order your main points: chronological, climactic, logical, and random.

CHRONOLOGICAL ORDER

When you present your points in order of time from first to last, you are using **chronological order**. You will find it most appropriate in process essays, but it can be used in other essays as well. Here are two examples.

Subject	Main Points
The process of writing a paper	• select an appropriate subject • list and edit the main points • write a thesis statement • write an outline for the paper • write a first draft • revise, edit, and proofread
The evolution of a relationship	• meeting • attraction • discovery • intimacy • disillusionment

CLIMACTIC ORDER

Persuasion most often uses a climactic arrangement, but climactic order is also common in papers based on examples, comparison or contrast, and classification or division. In **climactic order**, you save your strongest or most convincing point for last (the climax of your argument). You lead off your essay with your second-strongest point, and arrange your other points in between, as in this example.

Subject	Main Points
Advantages of a college education	• development of skills and knowledge • friendships and contacts with compatible people • potential for higher income • discovery of one's own potential

LOGICAL ORDER

Cause-and-effect essays, or any writing in which one point must be explained before the next point can be understood, are based on **logical order**. Your main points have a logical relationship, and you cannot take them out of order without confusing your readers. Consider the following sequence.

Subject	Main Points
Main causes of youth crime	• lack of opportunity or motivation for work • lack of recreational facilities • boredom • quest for "kicks"

The logical links here are clear: because of unemployment, recreational facilities are needed. Because of both unemployment and inadequate recreational facilities, boredom and the quest for "kicks" become problems. Readers must grasp each point before the next can be explained and understood.

RANDOM ORDER

On the rare occasions when your points can be explained in any order without affecting your readers' understanding, you can use **random order**. A random arrangement is possible only if all your main points are of equal significance and if they are not linked together logically or chronologically. In this example, all three points have equal weight.

Subject	Main Points
The garbage disposal crisis	• disposal sites are hard to find • cartage costs are high • new technologies are not yet fully developed

---

Exercise 4.7

Choose the type of order—chronological, climactic, logical, or random—you think is most appropriate for each of the following subjects. Arrange the main points in that order by numbering them in the spaces provided.

Subject	Order	Main Points
1. How to impress a client	_____	_____ firm handshake _____ friendly closing _____ well-prepared sales presentation _____ knowledge of client's needs _____ appropriate business attire
2. How to handle tax preparation	_____	_____ do your own _____ don't bother to file a return _____ go to a franchise tax-preparation company _____ hire an accountant

3. Reasons for   _____   _____ it offers informative
   listening to   programs
   the CBC   _____ your taxes are paying for it
                                                                                      _____ it provides a sense of
                                                                                         Canadian unity

4. Methods of   _____   _____ nicotine patch
   quitting smoking   _____ cold turkey
                                                                          _____ gradual withdrawal

5. Causes of   _____   _____ incompetent or unfriendly
   dissatisfaction   supervisor
   with employment   _____ incompatible coworkers
                                                                 _____ inappropriate pay for skills
                                                                                   and effort
                                                                     _____ unfulfilling work
                                                                     assignments

GO TO WEB

EXERCISE 4.1

Exercise 4.8

Now go back to the subjects and main points that you developed in Exercise 4.5. First, reconsider your main points: are they all significant, distinct, and related to the subject? Next, put the main points in the order that is most appropriate for the subject to which they belong.

When you've finished this task, exchange papers with another student and check each other's work. Can your partner identify the order of points you have chosen? Does he or she agree with your choice?

In this chapter, you've learned how to identify main points, how to test them for suitability, and how to arrange them in the most appropriate order. You're ready now to go on to the next step: writing the thesis statement—probably the most important sentence in your paper.

5

Writing the Thesis Statement

The key to clear organization in any paper is a thesis statement near the beginning that announces the paper's subject and scope. The thesis statement not only helps a reader to see how you are going to approach the subject, but also serves to keep you, the writer, on track.

A **thesis statement** is one or more sentences that clearly and concisely indicate the subject of your paper, the main points you will discuss, and the order in which you will discuss them.

In business communication, technical writing, and some academic writing (e.g., research papers and dissertations) it is important to indicate the subject and scope of your paper at the outset. Readers expect this sort of preview.[1]

The number of sentences in a thesis statement depends on what the subject is, how best to phrase it, how many points there are, and how complex they are. A thesis statement in a short paper is usually a single sentence at the end of the first paragraph, but in a lengthy paper on complicated issues, it might be several sentences or even a paragraph long. Occasionally (in a technical description, for example), a writer will choose a short thesis and omit the main points from the thesis statement.

To write a thesis statement, you combine your subject and your main points. Here is a simple formula for constructing a thesis statement:

---

[1]In less formal writing, such as newspaper or magazine articles and informal essays—including some of the essays in this book—a thesis statement is unnecessary.

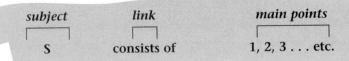

subject	*link*	*main points*
S	consists of	1, 2, 3 . . . etc.

These three elements can be combined in various ways. For example:

The most prolific producers of unnecessary jargon are politicians, sports writers, advertising copy writers, and educators. (Subject and main points are linked by *are*.)

Because the United States influences Canada's foreign policy, dominates its culture, and controls its economy, Canada is little more than an American satellite. (Main points precede subject and are linked to the subject by *because*.)

Fad diets are not the quick fix to weight problems that they may appear to be. On the contrary, they are often costly, ineffective, and even dangerous. (Subject is one sentence. Main points are in second sentence, linked to the first by *On the contrary*.)

Two cheers for democracy: one because it admits variety, and two because it permits criticism. (E. M. Forster) (Subject and main points are linked by a colon.)

Once you have mastered the basic formula, you can experiment with creative ways of expressing a thesis statement. Just be sure that it is appropriate in form, language, and tone to the kind of paper you are writing. The thesis statements in the exercise below range from short to long, formal to informal, and serious to flippant.

Exercise 5.1*

In each of the following thesis statements, underline the subject with a double line and the main points with a single line. When you have finished all seven, compare your answers with those on page 516.

1. Students who try to combine a full-time job with a full-time program face problems at school, at work, and at home.
2. To be successful in a broadcasting career, you must be talented, motivated, and hardworking.
3. The ideal notebook computer for business applications is reliable, lightweight, powerful, and flexible.
4. Establishing a local area network would increase efficiency and flexibility in the office.

5. The chairperson's job calls for a responsible and sensitive person, someone who is knowledgeable about company policy, sensitive to personnel issues, and a creative problem solver. It wouldn't hurt if he or she could also walk on water.

6. The business traveller can learn much from the turtle. Carry everything you need with you. Move slowly but with purpose and consistency. Keep your head down until you are sure you know what's going on.

7. Large energy producers and some provincial governments say we cannot afford to live up to the terms of the Kyoto Accord, which seeks to reduce the production of greenhouse gases. But can we afford not to comply with this international agreement? Can we afford to compromise the health of Canadians by continuing to pollute? Can we afford to risk the effects of global warming on our environment? Can we afford to fall behind the rest of the world in research and development leading to a solution to the problem of greenhouse gases?

Exercise 5.2

Each of the five introductions below contains a thesis statement. Working with a partner or in groups of three or four, identify the thesis statement in each paragraph.

1. What does an interviewer look for in a new job applicant? Good credentials, good preparation, good grooming, and good communication skills are essential features for anyone who wants a job. No interviewer would seriously consider an applicant who comes to an interview without the required educational background and work experience, without information about the job and the company, without appropriate clothing, and without the ability to present ideas clearly in the interview.

2. In the traditional manufacturing sectors, sales growth has stagnated in Canada over the past five years. Our products and services have secured as large a market share as we can expect, and we can anticipate further decline over the next 10 years as a result of increased competition. For these reasons, we have undertaken a study to determine where our best expansion opportunities lie. The following report outlines growth opportunities in the emerging markets of China and India.

3. Suddenly a man steps into the road in front of me. He's wearing a uniform and he's waving his hand for me to pull over to the side. My heart pounds and my pores prickle with anxiety. I feel guilty, but I don't know what I've done wrong—maybe speeding 10 kilometres over the limit, but no more. Anyone who has been caught in a radar trap knows this momentary feeling of panic, guilt, and resentment. We fear that the police officer will be brusque and blaming, but we are often surprised. There are as many kinds of police officers as there are people. Four kinds, however, dominate the profession: the confident veteran, the arrogant authoritarian, the cocky

novice, and the friendly professional. As I roll down my window, I wonder which kind of police officer has stopped me.

4.   After a hard day's work, do you relax with two or three stiff drinks? Do you enjoy a few beers while watching a game on TV? Do you believe mixed drinks make a party more fun? Do you cool off with gin fizzes on a hot afternoon? If you answered "yes" to most of these questions, you are probably abusing alcohol. The line between excessive social drinking and a serious addictive habit is a blurry one. Most alcoholics don't know they are hooked until they try to stop drinking. What are the signs that a drinker is no longer drinking for pleasure only? If a person "needs" a drink, or drinks alone, or can fall asleep only after a few drinks, or can find enjoyment only when drinking, that person is probably in trouble.

5.   Ours is a transient society. Most of us travel more kilometres in a year than our grandparents travelled in a lifetime. We move from one city to another, one province to another, and one country to another. In the course of moving, we inhabit many homes. The family home of the past might have been inhabited by several generations, consecutively or concurrently. Today's average Canadians will probably have 10 or more addresses during their adult lives. Our restlessness is particularly hard on the children in our migrating families: they have to leave familiar surroundings and friends, and they must adjust to a new environment, new habits, and sometimes a new language. These children pay a heavy price for the mobility of modern impermanence.

Phrasing Your Statement of Subject

The first part of a thesis statement is the statement of subject. It identifies *your idea about* or *your approach to* your subject. It states a viewpoint that must be explained or proved. (The main points provide the explanation or proof.)

Your statement of subject should be as clear and concise as you can make it. It must not be boring, however.

Beginning writers often fall into the trap of stating the obvious: "In this paper, I am going to discuss . . ." or "The subject of this memo is . . ." Your readers *know* it's your paper; you needn't hit them over the head by pointing out the fact that the paper contains your ideas. Here are three examples of faulty subject statements and their revisions.

Poor	Better
In this essay, I am going to discuss violence in hockey. (What about it?)	Violence in hockey is misunderstood by the nonplaying public.

This paper is about Canada's multiculturalism policy. (What about it?)

Canada's multiculturalism policy is neither practical nor desirable.

I am going to examine the influence of Wal-Mart in Canada. (What about it?)

With over 200 stores in Canada and plans for expansion, Wal-Mart's effects on labour are worth considering.

As soon as you write, "In this essay . . ." or "I am going to discuss (write about, explore) . . . ," you trap yourself into simply announcing your subject, not stating your idea or opinion about it. Avoid these traps. Always let your reader know *what it is about your subject* that your paper will explain or prove.

Phrasing the Main Points

When you combine your statement of subject with your main points to form your thesis statement, be sure that all your main points are phrased in the same way, in grammatically parallel form. If point 1 is a single word, then points 2, 3, and so on must also be single words. If point 1 is a phrase, then all the points following it must be phrases. If point 1 is a clause or a sentence, then the succeeding points must also be in clause or sentence form.

The following sentence contains a main point that is not parallel with the others.

Of the many qualities that combine to make a good nurse the three most important are strength, intelligence, and she must be compassionate.

Here is the sentence rewritten to be grammatically parallel:

Of the many qualities that combine to make a good nurse the three most important are strength, intelligence, and compassion.

Or, the sentence could be rewritten this way:

Of the many qualities that combine to make a good nurse the three most important are that she or he be strong, intelligent, and compassionate.

If you have trouble with grammatical parallelism, turn to Chapter 26 before you try the exercise below.

Exercise 5.3

In each of the following lists, one point is not parallel with the others. Rephrase the incorrect item so that all are in grammatically parallel form.

1. Our employees are
   a. motivated
   b. good training
   c. knowledgeable
2. Our doctor is
   a. full of compassion
   b. competent
   c. hard-working
3. I've noticed that my friends are increasingly
   a. concerned about smoking
   b. interested in fitness
   c. environmental awareness
4. To upgrade our educational system, we need
   a. more effective teacher training
   b. better liaison between levels of education
   c. students must be motivated to learn
5. An investment strategy must be
   a. based on current information
   b. appropriately diversified
   c. the client has to be tolerant of the degree of risk

Exercise 5.4

Work in pairs to develop two thesis statements for potential essays. Phrase the two thesis statements so that one has a poor statement of subject and the other lacks parallelism. Switch your creations with another team and identify each other's problems. Then correct the sentences. Exchange papers again. Did the other team identify and correct the problems you thought you'd created? If not, revise your own team's faulty sentences.

Exercise 5.5

Working with a partner, combine each of the following subjects with its main points to form a clear thesis statement that is expressed in grammatically parallel form.

1. Causes of stress
   - change of employment
   - financial problems
   - death of family member

Thesis statement: _____

_____

_____

_____

_____

2. Steps in finding a job
   - conduct an Internet job search
   - prepare a letter of application
   - perform well in the interview

Thesis statement: _____

_____

_____

_____

_____

3. How to save money
   - automatic payroll deductions
   - keep a record of expenditures
   - reduce impulse buying
   - establish and maintain a budget

Thesis statement: _____

_____

_____

_____

_____

4. Evolution of a recession
   - unemployment causes general economic slowdown
   - consumer buying decreases, resulting in inflation
   - inflation causes fear and further decrease in consumer demand

68 · PART 1: PLANNING

Thesis statement: _____

_____

_____

_____

_____

Exercise 5.6*

Working independently, combine each of the following subjects with its main points to form a grammatically parallel thesis statement. Then compare your answers to our suggestions on page 516.

1. Comparison between McDonald's and Wendy's (or any other two fast-food restaurants)
   - food
   - atmosphere
   - service
   - price

   Thesis statement: _____

   _____

   _____

   _____

   _____

2. Effects of urban overcrowding
   - traffic jams
   - too much air pollution
   - high rate of homelessness
   - violence on the streets

   Thesis statement: _____

   _____

   _____

   _____

   _____

3. Characteristics of a successful small business
   - adequate capital
   - marketable product
   - personnel that are dedicated
   - workable business plan

NEL

Thesis statement: _____

_____

_____

_____

_____

_____

Exercise 5.7

In groups of three or four, share the thesis statements you developed for Exercise 5.6 and discuss your decisions. As a group, revise each statement until you are all satisfied they meet the criteria for satisfactory thesis statements.

You have now covered all the steps leading to the construction of a good thesis statement. The exercises above have given you practice in the skills you need to phrase subjects and main points correctly and effectively.

Exercise 5.8 will walk you through the process of developing a thesis statement for a subject of your own choice. As you fill in the blanks in this exercise, you will be reviewing the first five chapters of this book and also testing your mastery of the writing skills they presented.

Exercise 5.8

1. Select a subject.

_____

_____

2. Test whether your subject is significant, single, specific, and supportable.

3. Using either a bottom-up or a top-down approach to generate ideas, identify three to five main points in support of your subject.

_____

_____

_____

_____

_____

4. Test whether your main points are all significant, distinct, and clearly related to your subject.

5. Arrange your main points in the order that is most likely to guarantee your readers' understanding of your subject: chronological, climactic, logical, or random.

_____

_____

_____

_____

_____

6. Rewrite your main points so that they are grammatically parallel: all single words, all phrases, or all clauses.

_____

_____

_____

_____

_____

7. Combine your statement of subject with your main points to produce your thesis statement.

_____

_____

_____

_____

_____

The seven points listed in Exercise 5.8 summarize the steps to follow in planning an essay. Keep this outline handy and refer to it when you start your next paper or research report.

6

Preparing an Outline

Writing a paper is like building a house: you save much time and frustration if you start with a plan. For anything longer than about 250 words, writers need a plan or outline to guide them as they begin to build words into sentences, sentences into paragraphs, and paragraphs into the final product, whether it's a term paper, a research report, a business plan, or a market analysis.

Wise writers treat an outline as tentative, not something chiselled in stone. As you draft your paper, you may discover new ideas or a new structure that better suits your purpose. If so, change your thesis statement and outline to accommodate it. (It's a good idea to make these changes in pencil or in a new file because you may decide at the end of the draft that these new ideas weren't so great after all.)

If you have access to a word-processing program with an outline feature, try it out. These programs can be a great help to an inexperienced writer with little knowledge of how to plan a writing assignment.

As we have seen, all written messages consist of an introduction, a body, and a conclusion, but each of these may vary from one to several paragraphs in length, and from simple to sophisticated in style. The model format on the next page is a basic outline for a five-paragraph essay. Once you've mastered this basic structure, you can modify, expand, and develop it to suit any of the kinds of writing you'll be called upon to do.

Outline Format

Title _____

INTRODUCTION _____

Attention-getter* _____

_____

_____

Thesis statement <u>Subject consists of 1, 2, and 3.</u>

BODY <u>Topic sentence introducing main point 1 goes here.</u>

Support for first main point
- _____
- _____
- _____
- _____

<u>Concluding (or transition) sentence goes here.</u>
<u>(Transition or) Topic sentence introducing main point 2 goes here.</u>

Support for second main point
- _____
- _____
- _____
- _____

<u>Concluding (or transition) sentence goes here.</u>
<u>(Transition or) Topic sentence introducing main point 3 goes here.</u>

Support for third main point
- _____
- _____
- _____
- _____

<u>Concluding (or transition) sentence goes here.</u>

CONCLUSION _____

Summary
- _____
- _____

Memorable statement*
- _____.

Note: Occasionally, a writer will begin a body paragraph with a transitional phrase or sentence. Variety adds interest to writing style. You will see examples of this technique in Part 4.

———————

*Terms marked with an asterisk are explained and illustrated in Chapter 8.

The outline below follows the format on page 72. The final version of "Ready, Willing . . . and Employable" appears after the outline.

Ready, Willing . . . and Employable	*Essay title*
What are employers looking for today?	*Attention-getter*
Employers are looking for a new breed of employee: one who has knowledge, flexibility, and the right attitude.	*Thesis statement*
Knowledge is still first on the list.	*1. Topic sentence*

- colleges offer a broad range of programs to meet employers' needs
- graduates must know current trends as well as theory
- some employers test for knowledge
- some rely on college's reputation plus recommendations of professors and recruiters

Support for first main point

Adaptability is essential for a prospective employee.

2. Topic sentence

- today's jobs require multitasking
- flexible workers are more cost-effective and better problem solvers
- flexible workers can adapt to change
- students need to broaden their education and learn a variety of skills

Support for second main point

Employers complain about graduates' poor attitude.

3. Topic sentence

- graduates lack the ability to take direction, use team skills, communicate well, and motivate themselves
- similar problems show up in class
  —chronic lateness
  —lack of cooperation
  —laziness
- students need to correct these attitude problems on their own

Support for third main point

Students must be ready, able, and willing to work.

Summary of main points

With these skills, a good résumé, and professional contacts, graduates can enter the workforce with confidence.

Memorable statement

READY, WILLING . . . AND EMPLOYABLE

Attention-getter

What are employers looking for in today's job market? Several recent surveys point to a subtle shift in the requirements of businesses looking to hire college and university graduates. Only a few years ago, knowledge was the prerequisite to employment in most industries. Employers needed workers with the highly specialized skills of an emerging high-tech workplace. Now many of

Thesis statement

those skills are taken for granted, and other characteristics have become increasingly important. Employers are seeking a new breed of employee: one who has the knowledge required to do the job, the flexibility to adapt, and—most important—the attitude to succeed.

Topic sentence

Knowledge of how to do the job is, understandably, still first on the shopping list that employers bring to job fairs. Colleges across the country have responded to marketplace requirements with an array of programs designed to prepare students to meet the needs of industries from broadcasting to photonics, from microelectronics to winemaking. Graduates are expected to have

Support for first main point

up-to-the-minute information on current trends in their fields, as well as solid grounding in the theory and practice of their specialty. Some employers test applicants for this knowledge; others rely on the reputation of the institution, the recommendation of professors with whom they have professional connections, and the insights of recruiters. As valuable as knowledge is to the employer,

Concluding statement (transition)

however, an employee's flexibility is quickly becoming just as important.

Topic sentence

"Multitasking" is a buzz word often used to describe the ability to move quickly and easily between projects and work environments, bringing a wide range of skills to bear on a variety of situations. Adaptability is an essential characteristic of any prospective employee. Workers who can use their expertise simultaneously on several different tasks within a project are valuable not only because they are more cost-effective than several single-task specialists, but also because they tend to see projects holistically and are better problem solvers as

Support for second main point

a result. In addition, flexible workers are those who most quickly and easily adapt to changes in technology or work practice, and such changes are a way of life in today's work environment. Students must prepare themselves to be flexible workers by broadening their education and by learning as many skills as possible. Unlike their parents, workers in the current generation have little hope of finding a job that will require only one skill set over the course of a career. Adaptability is a critical skill, but even when combined with knowledge,

Concluding statement

it is not enough to ensure employability. Increasingly, attitude is the determining factor in who gets hired (and promoted!).

Transition

Employers continually complain to colleges and universities that students on placement and graduates in their first position fail to impress, not from lack of knowledge, skill, or preparation, but from a broad range of inadequacies best summed up as "poor attitude." Among the faults cited under this broad heading are inability to take direction, failure to work well with colleagues, inability to communicate effectively, and lack of enthusiasm and initiative. How can such problems be corrected before graduates reach the workplace? Colleges do not offer courses in attitude adjustment, but perhaps they should. Most of these problems have surfaced in classes long before graduation. Students who are chronically late, frequently uncooperative, constantly complaining, or visibly lazy are those who, with all the skills and ability in the world, will not succeed in any job worth having. Even highly motivated and ambitious graduates have sometimes had difficulty adjusting to entry-level positions when they find themselves working under the supervision of people they consider less talented or skilled. It is up to students themselves to correct their attitudinal deficiencies. They need to pay attention to the criticisms of teachers, classmates, even family members, and make an honest evaluation of consistently noticed faults. Only when such attitude faults have been identified and acknowledged can they be corrected, and only when they have been corrected will the student be an asset to an employer.

Topic sentence

Support for third main point

Concluding statement

As graduation draws near, most students view their coming transformation into workers with eagerness liberally mixed with anxiety. Statistics tell us that most college and university graduates find employment in their fields within a year of graduation. Armed with this encouraging information, together with a good résumé, professional contacts, and the knowledge, flexibility, and attitude to succeed, graduates can face employers and the workplace with confidence.

Summary and Memorable statement

Exercise 6.1

Read "Of Men and Machines in the 21st Century" (pages 189–91) and "Lightweight Lit." (pages 218–19). Identify in each essay the sentences that correspond to the major structural items in the outline formats that follow. If you're working through this textbook in order, you may not have studied some of the terms mentioned, but you should be able to make a good guess at identifying the attention-getter and the memorable statement. To make your task easier, the sentences in each essay have been numbered.

OF MEN AND MACHINES IN THE 21ST CENTURY

INTRODUCTION

Attention-getter   Sentence(s) _____

Thesis statement   Sentence(s) _____

BODY PARAGRAPH #1

Topic sentence   Sentence(s) _____

Support for first main point   Sentence(s) _____

Conclusion/Transition   Sentence(s) _____

BODY PARAGRAPH #2

Topic sentence   Sentence(s) _____

Support for second main point Sentence(s) _____

Conclusion/Transition   Sentence(s) _____

BODY PARAGRAPH #3

Topic sentence   Sentence(s) _____

Support for third main point   Sentence(s) _____

Conclusion/Transition   Sentence(s) _____

CONCLUSION

Summary/Reinforcement   Sentence(s) _____

Memorable statement   Sentence(s) _____

LIGHTWEIGHT LIT.

INTRODUCTION

Attention-getter   Sentence(s)   _____

Thesis statement   Sentence(s)   _____

BODY PARAGRAPH #1

Topic sentence   Sentence(s)   _____

Support for first main point   Sentence(s)   _____

Conclusion/Transition   Sentence(s)   _____

BODY PARAGRAPH #2

Topic sentence   Sentence(s)   _____

Support for second main point   Sentence(s)   _____

Conclusion/Transition   Sentence(s)   _____

BODY PARAGRAPH #3

Topic sentence   Sentence(s)   _____

Support for third main point   Sentence(s)   _____

Conclusion/Transition   Sentence(s)   _____

CONCLUSION

Summary/Reinforcement   Sentence(s)   _____

Memorable statement   Sentence(s)   _____

Exercise 6.2

1. With a partner, choose either "The Train Ride" (pages 160–61), "A Slender Trap" (pages 221–23), or "A City for Students" (pages 242–43). Read the essay carefully and create an outline for it, following the format on page 72.
2. Compare outlines with another team that selected the same reading. Are there significant differences between the two outlines? If so, which outline best reflects the components of the introduction, body, and conclusion of the essay?

PART 2

Drafting

7

Understanding Paragraph Form and Function

What Does a Paragraph Look Like?

Essays are divided into paragraphs. **Paragraphs** are sentence groups that are separated from each other in their physical presentation and in their content. They usually have an indentation at the beginning (on a typed page, the first word begins five spaces in from the left margin) and some white space at the end (the last line is left blank following the paragraph's last word). Between the indentation and the final period comes the paragraph—a group of sentences that explains a single idea or topic.

If you were to draw a blueprint for a single paragraph, it would look like this:

A sentence that introduces the **topic** (or main idea) of the paragraph goes here.

Three or more sentences that specifically support or explain the topic go in here.

A sentence that concludes your explanation of the topic (or provides a transition to the next paragraph) goes here.

How Does a Paragraph Function?

Readers expect a paragraph to present a unit of thought or a single, developed idea. The white space at the beginning and end of each paragraph defines your thought units and also serves two other functions.

1. Paragraphs provide visual cues that make your writing "reader friendly." Imagine how intimidating the page you are now reading would be if were one continuous block of print: no headings, no indentations, no paragraphs.
2. Paragraphs divide your writing into linked but separate sections. Without paragraphs, ideas would blur and blend one into another. Readers would find it difficult to identify them, let alone follow the organization and development of the writer's thoughts.

In a typical essay, an introductory paragraph is followed by paragraphs that add details and depth to the ideas set out in the introduction. A concluding paragraph brings all the ideas together again and leaves the reader with a complete understanding of the writer's thinking.

Readers can tell a great deal about your thinking just by glancing at a page of your paper. A number of short paragraphs indicates a series of ideas, briefly (and perhaps superficially) explained. Long paragraphs—half a page or longer—suggest complex ideas that require explanation and details. They signal serious thought but are more difficult to read because they require close attention.

As a general rule, you explore one major idea or main point in each paragraph. When you have finished exploring one topic and wish to move on to another, you signal this shift to your readers by beginning a new paragraph.

How Long Should a Paragraph Be?

The answer to this question depends on the topic, your readers' familiarity with it, and your purpose in writing. If your topic is complex, your readers' knowledge is limited, and your purpose is to persuade readers who do not share your point of view, then you'll probably need a fairly long paragraph to accomplish your goal. On the other hand, if you're writing about a topic your readers are likely familiar with, and your purpose is simply to share with them your understanding of that topic, you may be able to accomplish your task in a few sentences.

Work in groups of five or six. Each group will take one of the paragraphs below to read and analyze by answering the following questions. Share your analysis with the class.

- What is the topic of the paragraph, stated in a few words?
- How much knowledge of the topic does the writer assume the readers have?
- What is the writer's purpose in this paragraph?

1. Violence as a way of achieving racial justice is both impractical and immoral. It is impractical because it is a descending spiral ending in destruction for all. The old law of an eye for an eye leaves everybody blind. It is immoral because it seeks to humiliate the opponent rather than win his understanding; it seeks to annihilate rather than to convert. Violence is immoral because it thrives on hatred rather than love. It destroys community and makes brotherhood impossible. It leaves society in monologue rather than dialogue. Violence ends by defeating itself. It creates bitterness in the survivors and brutality in the destroyers. A voice echoes through time saying to every potential Peter, "Put up your sword." History is cluttered with the wreckage of nations that failed to follow this command.

King, Martin Luther, Jr. "Three Types of Resistance to Oppression." *Stride Toward Freedom*. New York: Harper & Row, 1958. 215.

2. Take William Lyon Mackenzie King, our prime minister through the war and, so it seemed, for all time until Pierre Trudeau came along and seemed to be prime minister for all time. King held power longer than any other Western politician in this century. How did such a pudgy, mundane little man do it? The truth is, he did it deliberately. He was shrewd and self-effacing, and he told his friends that he made every speech as boring as possible because then no one would ever remember what he said and hold it against him. Twenty-two years in power, droning on and on over the airwaves, and meanwhile, he was as crazy as a loon.

Callaghan, Barry. "Canadian Wry." *Canadian Content*. Ed. Sarah Norton and Nell Waldman. 2nd ed. Toronto: Harcourt, 1992. 92.

3. *Vinaya* means humility; it is the complete surrendering of the self on the part of the *shishya* [the disciple] to the *guru*. The ideal disciple feels love, adoration, reverence, and even fear toward his *guru*, and he accepts equally praise or scoldings. Talent, sincerity, and the willingness to practise faithfully are essential qualities of the serious student. The *guru*, as the giver in this relationship, seems to be all-powerful. Often, he may be unreasonable, harsh, or haughty, though the ideal *guru* is none of these. Ideally, he should

respond to the efforts of the disciple and love him almost as his own child. In India, a Hindu child, from his earliest years, is taught to feel humble toward anyone older than he or superior in any way. From the simplest gesture of the *namaskar*, or greeting (putting the hands palm to palm in front of the forehead and bowing), or the *pranam* (a respectful greeting consisting of touching the greeted person's feet, then one's own eyes and forehead with the hands held palm to palm) to the practice of *vinaya* or humility tempered with a feeling of love and worship, the Hindu devotee's vanity and pretension are worn away.

Shankar, Ravi. "Studying Music in India." *My Music, My Life.* Delhi: Vikas Publications, 1968. 11–12.

4.   When I found [the snakeskin], it was whole and tied in a knot. Now there have been stories told, even by reputable scientists, of snakes that have deliberately tied themselves in a knot to prevent larger snakes from trying to swallow them—but I couldn't imagine any way that throwing itself into a half hitch would help a snake trying to escape its skin. Still, ever cautious, I figured that one of the neighborhood boys could possibly have tied it in a knot in the fall, for some whimsical boyish reason, and left it there, where it dried and gathered dust. So I carried the skin along thoughtlessly as I walked, snagging it sure enough on a low branch and ripping it in two. . . . I saw that thick ice still lay on the quarry pond and that the skunk cabbage was already out in the clearings, and then I came home and looked at the skin and its knot.

Dillard, Annie. *Pilgrim at Tinker Creek.* New York: Harper's Magazine Press, 1974. 73.

5.   [T]here needs to be a thorough revision of the maximum-penalty structure to remove the incongruities that riddle the current Criminal Code. Should forgery or certain kinds of fraud really have the same maximum penalty as sexual assault with a weapon? The maximum penalties are also much too high; most were created many decades ago, when our perceptions of the seriousness of various crimes differed from those today. The maximum penalty for breaking and entering is life imprisonment, for example, but in practice the average sentence is well under one year. This is called "bite and bark" sentencing; the system barks more loudly than it bites, and creates false expectations among the public.

Roberts, Julian V. "Three Steps to Make the Punishment Fit the Crime." *Globe and Mail* 7 Dec. 1993: A25.

Exercise 7.2

Write a short paragraph (five to seven sentences) that demonstrates your understanding of paragraph form and function. Choose any topic you like. When you have finished, exchange papers with another student and check each other's paragraph for

- Form: Is there a clear introduction to and conclusion of the topic?
- Function: Is the paragraph sufficiently developed for the reader to understand the topic clearly? The reader should have no questions left unanswered.

Crafting the Topic Sentence

The **topic sentence** in each paragraph is the sentence that clearly identifies what the paragraph is about—its main idea. The topic sentence focuses the paragraph, helps to unify it, and keeps you and your readers on track. In professional writing, the topic sentence is not always the first sentence of the paragraph. Sometimes it is more effective to announce the topic in the second, third, or even the last sentence. But professional writers, through years of practice, have earned the right to break the rules. Beginning writers should remember this: *most readers assume that the first sentence of a paragraph identifies the topic of that paragraph.* If your first sentence doesn't do this, then your readers may go through your paragraph assuming the topic is something other than what you intended. Miscommunication frustrates readers and wastes their time. To be absolutely clear, identify your topic up front.

A good topic sentence does three things:

1. It introduces the topic of the paragraph.
2. It makes a point about the topic.
3. It makes a statement that is neither too broad nor too narrow.

Readers appreciate writers who get to the point quickly, make the point clearly, and support or explain it adequately. They also appreciate writers who can make their points in an interesting way. Take the time to write topic sentences that are something more than straightforward, flat announcements of your main idea. Compare the following pairs of topic sentences.

Weak	Strong
I am going to explain why I love "trash."	I'm ashamed to confess my secret vice, but because we're friends, I can tell you: I love "trash."
This paragraph is about violence.	Violence as a way of achieving social justice is both impractical and immoral (Martin Luther King, Jr.).

A good way to introduce the topic so that it is both interesting and effective is to make a point about it. You save your readers' time and eliminate the risk of confusion if you make clear at the outset your idea about or your attitude toward your topic. Consider these examples.

Weak	Strong
Many people around the world enjoy music.	Nothing bridges gaps between cultures like music.
Canadians are different from Americans.	Canadians should be thankful for their differences from Americans.

Finally, the topic you choose must be "the right size"—neither so broad that you cannot support it adequately in a single paragraph, nor so narrow that it doesn't require support. The 4-S test that you used to determine whether a subject was suitable for a paper can also be applied to potential paragraph topics. If your topic is single, significant, specific, and supportable, it should form the basis for a solid paragraph. Take a look at these topic sentences.

Weak	Strong
The legal system in Canada discriminates against men. (too broad)	Single fathers who seek custody of their children are often treated unfairly in family court.
My children won't eat peas, broccoli, or spinach. (too narrow)	Getting young children to eat a balanced diet is not an easy task.
Cars should be banned from city streets. (too broad)	Cars should be banned from the downtown core from 7:00 a.m. to 7:00 p.m.

Exercise 7.3*

Read through each of the following paragraphs, then underline the topic sentence.

1.   The third consideration is perhaps the most important. Canada makes no economic sense. There may be excellent reasons for Canada's existence historically, socially, culturally, and even geographically, but the lines of trade and commerce flow north–south. If a government's chief concern is the economy, that government will naturally draw the country closer and closer to the United States, cinching in those belts of commerce that bind Canada to her southern partner. Only governments whose major goals are cultural or social will loosen the longitudinal ties and seek east–west bonds.

2.   Winston Churchill said, "Golf is a game whose aim it is to hit a very
small ball into an even smaller hole with weapons singularly ill-designed
for the purpose." It has been said that baseball is an activity where 14 men
stand idly by while two play catch. In fact, all sports can be made ridiculous because the essence of sport is rules. If you really want to put a ball
into a hole in the ground, it's very easy to do: pick it up, carry it to the
hole, and drop it in. The fun in golf, as in all sports, is that the task is
made challenging by very rigid and complex regulations. Reduced to its
essential, sport is the attempt by one person or group to win dominance
over another while encumbered by complicated rules. The rules in a game
like hockey or baseball are enormously complex, while those in soccer or
bowling are less so; however, the objective of all games is the same as the
objective of war. Luckily, civilized humans have a love of rules and laws,
and can take out their aggressions within the very rigid confines of the
rule book.

3.   Seen by scanning electron microscope, our taste buds look as huge as
volcanoes on Mars, while those of a shark are beautiful mounds of pastel-
colored tissue paper—until we remember what they're used for. In reality,
taste buds are exceedingly small. Adults have about 10,000, grouped by
theme (salt, sour, sweet, bitter), at various sites in the mouth. Inside each
one, about fifty taste cells busily relay information to a neuron, which will
alert the brain. Not much tasting happens in the center of the tongue, but
there are also incidental taste buds on the palate, pharynx, and tonsils,
which cling like bats to the damp, slimy walls of a cave. Rabbits have
17,000 taste buds, parrots only about 400, and cows 25,000. What are they
tasting? Maybe a cow needs that many to enjoy a relentless diet of grass.

Ackerman, Diane. *A Natural History of the Senses*. New York: Vintage-Random House, 1991.
138.

4.   Scholarly explanations of humor fall into three major categories.
According to superiority theories, we laugh at the henpecked husband
and the woman hit with a banana cream pie because the misfortunes of
others make us feel better about our own lot. The 17th century philoso-
pher Thomas Hobbes, for example, described laughter as a result of the
"sudden glory" of increased self-esteem at the expense of others.
Incongruity theories . . . stress the cognitive jolt of bringing together
unrelated ideas. Thus the infant who chuckles when Mommy eats the
baby food is savoring the incongruity of a grown woman making a fool
of herself. Finally, tension-relief theories attribute our laughter to a
sudden release from strain. Freud argued that our jokes, like our dreams,
allow pent-up sexual and aggressive images to suddenly leap into consciousness, albeit in a disguised form.

"What's So Funny?" *Psychology Today* June 1978: 101.

5.　　"Why do you want it?" This should be the first question a good computer salesperson asks a prospective customer. With the huge variety of computers now on the market, the determining factor in a purchase should be the job the machine will be expected to do. While a network card, premium audio system, and 21-inch VDT are great for watching movies, a user who wants a basic word processor would be throwing away money to buy them. Home users and small businesses often get carried away with the desire for gigantic memory capacity, lightning speed, and high resolution capability, but these are advertising gimmicks rather than useful purchases for most small users. On the other hand, it can be a costly error for a buyer to underestimate long-term computer needs and buy a machine that must be upgraded or replaced in a year.

Now compare your answers with ours on page 516.

GO TO WEB

EXERCISE 7.1

Exercise 7.4

Each of the following thesis statements contains a subject and main points. Working with a partner or in a small group, develop the main points of each thesis statement into effective topic sentences.

1. Volunteering is a valuable addition to a college education because it provides work experience, develops professional contacts, and enhances self-esteem.
2. Unemployment, poverty, and loneliness are factors that may lead to depression.
3. Canadians emigrate to other countries for three main reasons: a warmer climate, better job opportunities, and new cultural experiences.

Exercise 7.5

For each of the thesis statements below, develop the main points into effective topic sentences. Make sure each topic sentence you write introduces the topic clearly, makes a point about the topic, and is neither too broad nor too narrow.

1. The driver who caused your accident last weekend was probably one of four types: a road hog, a tailgater, a speed demon, or a Sunday driver.

2. There are three types of supervisor in this world: the good, the bad, and mine.
3. The thought of moving to the country is attractive to many city dwellers because of the slower pace, the healthier environment, and the closer-knit communities.

Developing the Topic

Once you've written your topic sentence, the next step is to develop it. An adequately developed paragraph gives enough supporting information to make the topic completely clear to the readers. Unless you are writing from a detailed outline listing all the supporting material you need, it's time to focus once again on your intended audience. Put yourself in your readers' place.

- How much information do your readers already have about your topic?
- Are they inclined to agree or disagree with you?
- What do your readers need to know to understand your point clearly?

There are seven ways to develop a topic. Not all will be appropriate in every case, and some will be more effective than others. Let your topic and your audience guide you in choosing the most appropriate kind(s) of development.

1. Tell a story. Everyone loves to read a story if it's relevant and well told. An anecdote can be an effective way to help your readers not only understand your idea but also remember it. Below are two examples that illustrate the use of narration to develop a topic.

I first experienced culture shock when I travelled to Egypt. I was walking down the main street on the day of my arrival when it suddenly struck me that the crowds on the street were stepping aside to make way for me. It was 1980, and my height, blond hair, and blue eyes were so unusual to the Egyptians that I was an object of intense curiosity. The staring and pointing followed me everywhere. Finally, unable to cope any longer with being constantly on display, I took refuge in the Canadian Embassy and spent a couple of hours quietly leafing through back issues of *Maclean's* magazine.

Imagine that two accountants do similar jobs for similar companies. One day they make the same discovery: with almost no chance of getting caught, they can embezzle a large sum from their employers. They can both use the money to pay off debts or buy a new car. The first accountant right away says to himself, "It's wrong to steal," and never considers the matter again. But the second accountant is torn. She, too, knows that stealing is wrong, but she's tempted and at first decides to go ahead. Then she decides she won't, and then that she will. Finally, after weeks of agonizing, she decides not to embezzle. Who is the morally better person?

Hurka, Thomas. "Should Morality Be a Struggle? Ancient vs. Modern Ideas about Ethics." *Principles: Short Essays about Ethics*. Toronto: Harcourt Brace, 1994. 83.

Exercise 7.6

Using a story to develop your topic, write a paragraph on one of following, or choose a topic of your own.

1. A road-rage experience
2. The day I became an adult
3. The customer is not always right
4. How not to treat employees
5. Defusing a tense situation

2. **Define your topic.** A definition paragraph explains and clarifies the meaning of a word or idea. Use the definition paragraph to explain a term that may be unfamiliar to your readers. (Write your own definition, please. Quoting from a dictionary is an overused and boring way to start a paragraph.) Below are definitions of two terms that the authors wanted to be sure their readers would understand from the *writers'* point of view.

Culture shock is the inability to understand or cope with experiences one has never encountered before. It commonly affects travellers who journey to lands whose climate, food, language, and customs are alien to the traveller. In addition to confusion and anxiety, culture shock may even produce physical symptoms: chills, fever, trembling, and faintness.

A hybrid is a cross between two established varieties of plant, animal, . . . or technology. The hybrid bicycle, for example, combines the features of a road bike with those of an off-road bike to produce a comfortable and efficient bicycle for short distance cycling. For most people, however, the word "hybrid" signifies a fuel-efficient, low-emission automobile. Hybrid car technology combines a gasoline or diesel internal combustion engine with a battery-powered electric motor. Its objective is to maximize the best properties of both the gas engine and the electric motor.

Howerth, Sara R. "The Gas-Electric Hybrid Demystified." 207.

You should include a definition, too, if you're using a familiar term in an unusual way. Here Martin Luther King defines what he means by "the length of life":

Now let us notice first the length of life. I have said this is the dimension of life in which the individual is concerned with developing his inner powers. It is that dimension of life in which the individual pursues personal ends and ambitions. This is perhaps the selfish dimension of life, and there is such a thing as moral and rational self-interest. If one is not concerned about himself he cannot be totally concerned about other selves.

King, Martin Luther, Jr. "The Dimensions of a Complete Life." *The Measure of a Man.* 1959. Philadelphia: Pilgrim Press, 1969.

Exercise 7.7

Choose one of the following topics (or select one of your own) and write a paragraph in which you develop the topic by defining it.

1. Burnout
2. A good boss (employee, customer, colleague)
3. An extrovert (introvert)
4. A great artist (musician, actor, writer, etc.)
5. A bad habit

---

3. **Use examples.** Giving examples is probably the most common method of developing an idea and supporting a statement. Readers can become confused or suspicious when they read unsupported statements of "fact," opinion, or ideas. One of the best ways to support your topic is by providing clear, relevant examples.

Sometimes, as in the paragraph below, one extended example is enough to allow your readers to see clearly what you mean.

Culture shock can affect anyone, even a person who never leaves home. My grandfather was perfectly content to be an accountant until he retired, and was confident that his company would need his services for the foreseeable future. Computers were "silly toys" and modern business practices just "jargon" and "a new fad." When he was laid off four years before his retirement, he went into shock. It wasn't just the layoff; it was the speed of change— the idea that he was stranded in a new and unfamiliar culture for which he was unprepared, and in which he had no useful role.

Sometimes a number of examples may be necessary to develop a point, as in this paragraph.

All sports may be reduced to a few basic skills, which, if learned properly at the outset and drilled until they are instinctive, lead to success. Tennis is no exception; however, few people seem willing to spend the time needed to master the basics. Having been shown the proper grip and swing for a forehand, backhand, and serve, my students seem to feel they can qualify for Wimbledon. The basics are not learned that easily. Many tennis schools are now using a system first developed in Spain that is very successful in establishing the correct stroke in new players: for the first month of lessons, they aren't allowed to use a tennis ball. For that first month, correct positioning, proper swing, footwork, and technique are drilled without any of the distractions of keeping score, winning or losing, or chasing errant balls. That's how important the basics are to winning tennis.

Green, Brian. "How to Play Winning Tennis." 173.

Exercise 7.8

Using examples to develop your topic, write a paragraph on one of following, or choose a topic of your own.

1. Parents and privacy
2. Computers: the biggest time-wasters of modern life
3. Childless by choice
4. Adjusting to life away from home
5. The incompetence (incomprehensibility) of men (women)

4. **Use a quotation or paraphrase.** Occasionally you will find that someone else—an expert in a particular field, a well-known author, or a respected public figure—has said what you want to say better than you could ever hope to say it. Relevant and authoritative quotations, as long as they are kept short and are not used too frequently, are useful in developing your topic. Two sources of quotations on practically any subject are *John Robert Colombo's Famous Lasting Words: Great Canadian Quotations* (Vancouver: Douglas & McIntyre, 2000) and *Bartlett's Familiar Quotations* (http://www.bartleby.com/101/). **Never forget to acknowledge the source of your quotation!** In the paragraph below, the writer introduces his topic with a thought-provoking quotation.

"Although one can experience real pain from culture shock, it is also an opportunity for redefining one's life objectives. Culture shock can make one develop a better understanding of oneself and stimulate personal creativity." As with any experience that forces us out of our comfort zone and shatters our complacency, culture shock can be an opportunity for growth and development, as this quotation from the College of Education at San Diego State University makes clear. The trick is to recognize this unpleasant experience as a starting point for personal change. Here's an opportunity to re-examine our preconceptions about our place in society, about our interactions with others, even about the path we have chosen to take in life: has it become a rut?

A **paraphrase** is a summary in your own words of someone else's idea. Remember to indicate whose idea you are paraphrasing, the way the author of "The Myth of Canadian Diversity" does in the following paragraph.

. . . [O]ur much-discussed ethnic differences are overstated. Although Canada is an immigrant nation and Canadians spring from a variety of backgrounds, a recent study from the C.D. Howe Institute says that the idea of a "Canadian mosaic"—as distinct from the American "melting pot"—is a fallacy. In *The Illusion of Difference*, University of Toronto sociologists Jeffrey Reitz and Raymond Breton show that immigrants to Canada assimilate as quickly into the mainstream society as immigrants to the United States do. In fact, Canadians are less likely than Americans to favour holding on to cultural differences based on ethnic background. If you don't believe Mr. Reitz and Mr. Breton, visit any big-city high school, where the speech and behaviour of immigrant students just a few years in Canada is indistinguishable from that of any fifth-generation classmate. (321–22)

Exercise 7.9

Choose one of the following topics (or select one of your own) and write a paragraph in which you develop the topic by using quotations and/or paraphrase.

1. The most inspiring (uninspiring) teacher you have known
2. Everything I know I learned from my mother (father, brother, etc.)
3. A favourite book (movie, website)
4. The wisdom of children
5. Father knows (does not know) best

5. Use a comparison. A comparison shows similarities between things; it shows how two different things are alike in a particular way or ways. If you have a difficult or abstract topic to explain, try comparing it to something that is familiar to your readers, as this writer does.

Being left on your own in a foreign land is a bit like being forced to play a card game when you're the only one who doesn't know the rules. As the stakes get higher and the other players' excitement and enjoyment increase, you get correspondingly more frustrated and miserable. Finally, in desperation, you want to throw your cards on the table, absorb your losses, and go home.

In this next paragraph, the writer uses an **analogy**—an extended comparison—between a date and a car to make the point both clear and interesting.

The economy-model date features cramped conditions and a lack of power. The econo-date thinks that his personality can make up for the fact that you never go anywhere except for walks and never do anything that costs money. He tends to be shy, quiet, and about as much fun as an oil leak. It's not that he doesn't have money to spend; it's that he doesn't use any imagination or creativity to compensate for his lack of cash.

Exercise 7.10

Choose one of the following topics (or select one of your own) and write a paragraph in which you develop the topic by using comparison.

1. The modern workplace
2. E-mail
3. Two consumer products
4. Type A (Type B) personalities
5. Engineering (or computer science, arts, or nursing) students

6. **Explain steps or stages in a process.** Sometimes the most effective way to develop the main idea of your paragraph is by explaining how something occurs or is done—that is, by relating the series of steps involved. Make sure you break the process down into its component parts and detail the steps logically and precisely.

The first sign of culture shock is usually anxiety. The traveller feels uncomfortable and ill at ease; nothing looks, smells, sounds, or tastes familiar. Next, he may become resentful, even angry, and withdraw from his new surroundings, seeking isolation in safe, familiar territory—his room. Unfortunately, solitude reinforces anxiety and makes the situation worse. Over time, the victim of culture shock may begin to perceive the environment not as "strange but neutral" but as "strange and hostile." Friendly interaction with others and positive experiences in the new culture are the cure, but one is not likely to encounter either while cocooned in a small boarding house or hotel room. Fortunately, most travellers find that culture shock diminishes with rest. As anxiety lessens, curiosity grows, and they begin to venture out to participate in the life of the new country. In extreme cases, however, travellers suffering from culture shock can develop flu-like symptoms: fever, chills, sleeplessness, and a debilitating loss of energy. When these symptoms strike, it's time to call home for moral support and encouragement to get out and enjoy the sights and scenes one has travelled so far to experience.

In writing a process paragraph, you need to pay particular attention to transitions, which are discussed in the next chapter, or you'll leave your readers gasping in the dust as you gallop through your explanation. The paragraph below illustrates a simple yet effective use of transitions.

In 1983, a Harvard Medical School team led by Dr. Howard Green found a revolutionary way to repair burned skin. Here is how it is done. Doctors cut up a small patch of skin donated by a patient, treat it with enzymes, then spread it thinly onto a culture medium. After only ten days, colonies of skin cells begin linking up into sheets, which can then be chopped up and used to make further sheets. In twenty-four days, enough skin will be produced to cover an entire human body. About ten days later, the gauze is removed, and the skin soon grows into a surface much smoother and more natural-looking than the rough one a normal skin-graft usually leaves.

Ackerman, Diane. *A Natural History of the Senses.* New York: Vintage-Random House, 1990. 69–70.

Exercise 7.11

Choose one of the following topics (or select one of your own) and write a paragraph in which you develop the topic by describing the series of steps or stages involved in the process.

1. Career planning
2. Buying a used car
3. Understanding women (men)
4. Writing a business report
5. Getting out of debt

---

7. **Provide specific details.** Concrete, specific, descriptive details can be an effective way to develop your main idea. In the paragraph below, the writer uses specific detail to describe treatment for culture shock.

Culture shock can be alleviated by taking action to reduce the impact of the cause, and then treating each of the symptoms separately. Prevention is the best cure: introduce yourself gradually to a new environment. Explore in small stages, while keeping contact with safe and familiar surroundings. Don't plunge into the bazaar within an hour of your arrival in Marrakesh, but begin your exploration in the Western quarter and gradually expose yourself to the sights, sounds, and smells of areas that seem threateningly foreign. If you should come down with symptoms of shock, go to bed, stay warm, drink lots of bottled water, and sleep as much as you can. When you begin to feel better, take things slowly and avoid stressful situations where you have to make decisions or confront the unexpected. A guided bus tour of the city is a good way to begin familiarizing yourself with a new physical and cultural environment, and discovering what's available that you want to explore.

In some paragraphs, numerical facts or statistics can be used to support your point effectively. However, in keeping with Benjamin Disraeli's immortal comment ("There are three kinds of lies: lies, damned lies, and statistics"), critical readers tend to be suspicious of statistics. Be very sure that your facts are correct and that your statistics are current.

Canadians are great travellers. We not only travel around our own country, exploring every nook and cranny from Beaver Creek in the Yukon Territory to Bay Bulls in Newfoundland, but we also can be found touring around every other country on Earth. Statistics Canada reports that we take about 150 million overnight trips a year within our own borders. Abroad, we favour our next door neighbour by a wide margin above other destinations, averaging around 15 million overnight trips a year to the United States. The United Kingdom is our second favourite destination, with over 800,000 visits, followed by Mexico (over 600,000) and France (over 400,000). Of the Caribbean islands, Cuba is our favourite winter escape. Cuba ranks fifth overall, with 350,000 annual visits by Canadians. Of the Asian nations, Hong Kong, in tenth place, tops the list with 115,000 visits. Australia, in fourteenth place with about 90,000 visits, ranks just ahead of Japan. Rounding Canada's population off to about 30 million, we can use these figures to deduce that, on average, a Canadian travels within Canada five times every year and takes a trip abroad twice in three years.

Exercise 7.12

Using specific details to develop your topic, write a paragraph on one of following, or choose a topic of your own.

1. A web page
2. A migraine headache

3. The myth of the shorter work week
4. The best team in basketball (baseball, football, soccer, lacrosse)
5. Money can't buy happiness

In writing your own paragraphs, you will often need to use more than one method of development to explain your point. The seven methods described in this chapter can be used in any combination you choose.

How Do You End a Paragraph?

A good paragraph doesn't just end; like a door, it should close firmly, with a "click." Finish your paragraph with a statement that serves either as a **clincher**—an unmistakable and appropriate conclusion—or a **transition** to the new idea that will be developed in the next paragraph.

Exercise 7.13

Turn back to the paragraphs in Exercise 7.1 (pages 83–84). Reread each one and decide whether it ends with a clincher or a transition sentence.

Exercise 7.14

To stretch your imagination and improve your mastery of the kinds of support you can choose from to develop a topic, write a paragraph on one of the following topics, using two or more methods of development. Your target audience is your instructor and your classmates.

1. Getting along with coworkers
2. Performance appraisal
3. Training a new employee
4. Life is like a game of _____
5. Canadians don't appreciate how lucky they are

8

Keeping Your Readers with You

As you write, remember that it is your responsibility to make it as easy as possible for your readers to follow you through your essay. Unity, coherence, and tone can make the difference between a paper that confuses or annoys your readers and one that enlightens and pleases them.

Unity

Unity means "oneness." The contents of a paragraph must relate to a single main idea. All supporting sentences in the paragraph must clearly and directly relate to the topic sentence of that paragraph.

Achieving unity requires care. Your job is to develop the points that you have set out to make, not other points that may occur to you as you write. (The time to set down whatever happens to come to mind is in the prewriting stage, not the paragraph development stage.) Any material that does not clearly support the topic sentence should be deleted or moved to another paragraph in the essay—assuming, of course, that it is directly relevant there.

Take a look at the following paragraph. It contains several sentences that spoil the unity of the paragraph because they do not clearly relate to the topic.

(1) I knew I wanted to return to school, but did I want to be a full-time or a part-time student? (2) The major consideration was, not surprisingly, money. (3) If I chose to go to college full-time, then I would have to give up my full-time job. (4) The resulting loss of income would reduce my buying power to zero. (5) Even the tuition fees would be beyond my reach. (6) Also, my choice of program would be a difficult decision, because I still wasn't sure which career path to follow. (7) My other option was part-time education. (8) If I kept my full-time job,

I could at least pay for food, rent, and a modest amount of clothing. (9) Also, I could afford the tuition fees. (10) Going to school part-time costs less per year because the expenditure is spread over a longer period of time than it is in the full-time program. (11) Therefore, I chose to educate myself part-time, through continuing education courses. (12) While working, I could learn new skills in my spare time. (13) My career choice would still be in doubt, but I would have a longer time in which to make up my mind. (14) Money is scarce for a full-time, self-supporting student, but as a part-time student I could have the best of both worlds: a steady income and a college education.

Draw a line through the sentences that do not logically and directly support the topic of the paragraph: the writer's decision whether to be a full-time or part-time student.[1]

Exercise 8.1[*]

The paragraphs below contain some irrelevant sentences that disrupt unity. Read each paragraph and then, with a partner, find and cross out the sentences that don't belong. Answers for exercises in this chapter begin on page 517.

1. (1) A good pizza consists of a combination of succulent ingredients. (2) First, you prepare the foundation, the crust, which may be thick or thin, depending on your preference. (3) I like my crusts thick and chewy. (4) The crust is spread with a layer of basil- and oregano-flavoured tomato sauce. (5) Next, a rich smorgasbord of toppings—pepperoni, mushrooms, green peppers, bacon, anchovies—should be scattered over the tomato sauce. (6) *Smorgasbord* is a Swedish word meaning a buffet meal; *pizza* is Italian in origin. (7) Last of all, a double-thick blanket of grated mozzarella cheese should be spread over all. (8) Pizza is simple to make—all you need is dough, tomato sauce, vegetables, sausage, herbs, and cheese—but the combination has an unbeatable taste.

2. (1) Keeping a job is not easy in a tight market in which well-educated job-seekers are plentiful. (2) Here are a couple of hints you will find helpful in maintaining your "employed" status. (3) First, you should not only apply your specialized knowledge on the job every day, but also continually update it by taking seminars and evening courses to enhance your skills. (4) Doing your job effectively is difficult without becoming burned out. (5) Second, good communication—with the public, your fellow workers, and your supervisor—is perhaps the most important factor in keeping you on the payroll. (6) Upgrading your education and improving your communication skills are your best defences against the pink slip.

---

[1]The sentences that you should have crossed out because they do not belong in this paragraph and detract from its unity are 6, 12, and 13.

3.   (1) Comedies are my favourite way to relax. (2) Horror films terrify me, and adventures become tedious after the tenth chase, but comedies entertain and refresh me after a long shift at work. (3) Woody Allen pictures, especially the early farces, help me to take my mind off the stress of the day. (4) For example, *Bananas*, a satire about American politics in the 1960s, is more relaxing for me than a double martini. (5) It's also less fattening, and I've been trying to give up drinking. (6) *Sleeper*, a futuristic spoof, has me laughing, on average, twice a minute. (7) Perhaps my favourite, however, is *Annie Hall*. (8) After viewing it, I am so weak with laughter that I can go to sleep within minutes. (9) Now that all of Allen's comedies are available on DVD, I never need to feel tense and worn out for longer than it takes to insert a disc.

4.   (1) My department's job is to produce reports. (2) We research and prepare year-end reports, stockholders' reports, reports on the competition, on the customers, on the suppliers, and on just about everything else. (3) We think of ourselves as creative rather than technical writers because there is no future in our company for anyone who is critical or who dares to tell the truth if truth isn't what the senior managers want to hear. (4) Instead of fixing the problem, they punish the person who tells them what's wrong; that is, they "shoot the messenger." (5) I believe this saying originated in ancient days, long before there were guns, so presumably the original idea was "knife the messenger" or "behead the messenger." (6) If employees understand this management practice, however, they can protect themselves. (7) For example, our department has developed three rules to help us produce reports that are guaranteed a favourable reception. (8) First, teamwork is essential; without it, you have no one else to blame. (9) Second, when you don't know what you're doing, do it neatly. (10) Third, if at first you don't succeed, destroy all evidence that you ever tried. (11) With these rules to guide us, our department has survived three new managers in the past two and a half years.

5.   (1) The office manager who demands that all employees not only arrive on time but actually get in early to demonstrate their enthusiasm and drive is actually damaging productivity. (2) Such a manager is, of course, always in the office at least an hour early herself, and because she attributes her success to this habit, she demands it of others. (3) Not everyone is suited to an early start. (4) Individual biorhythms vary widely, and some employees may be better suited to demonstrating their keenness by staying late at night. (5) The old adage "The early bird gets the worm" is based on some truth, but there are many exceptions. (6) Besides, what office worker wants a worm, anyway? (7) For that matter, there are lots of other sayings and aphorisms that can apply just as readily to the situation. (8) If your manager cites this tired old phrase as her justification for demanding unreasonably early hours, you may want to point out that another saying is equally true: "The second mouse gets the cheese."

Coherence

Coherence means "sticking together." The sentences within each paragraph need to cohere, as do the paragraphs within an essay. If your sentences and paragraphs are not coherent, your reader will have great difficulty trying to fit together your bits of information to make sense of the whole. Sorting out sentences as if they were pieces of a puzzle is not the reader's job. It is the writer's responsibility to put the pieces together to form a complete and clear picture.

Coherence is achieved in two ways.

1. First, you need to arrange the sentences in each paragraph according to an organizational principle. Remember the options you chose from to arrange ideas in Chapter 4, "Managing the Main Points"? You should arrange your development within paragraphs in the same ways: chronological, climactic, logical, or, infrequently, random order. (Turn to pages 57–59 to review these.)
2. Second, you achieve coherence by providing **transitions**. Transitions are connections between one idea and the next within a paragraph, and between one paragraph and the next within an essay. Why are transitions needed? Read the paragraph below and you'll see clearly that something is missing. The paragraph has adequate development, but no transitions.

We were bored one day. We didn't know what to do. It was Friday. We thought about going to the library. No one really wanted to do schoolwork. We went to the mall. For a short time we window-shopped. We discussed what to do. It was agreed that we would drive to the American side of the border. We would do our shopping. It was a short drive. We went to a discount mall. The bargains were great. We spent much more money than we intended to. We went home. We discovered that with the American exchange, prices were better at home. We should have gone to the library.

Not very easy to read, is it? Readers are jerked abruptly from point to point until, battered and bruised, they finally reach the end. This kind of writing is unfair to readers. It makes them do too much of the work. The ideas may all be there, but the readers have to figure out for themselves how the ideas fit together. After a couple of paragraphs like the one above, even the most patient readers can become annoyed.

Now read the same paragraph, rewritten with transitions.

Last Friday we were so bored we didn't know what to do. We thought about going to the library, but no one really wanted to study, so we went to the mall and window-shopped for a while. After a long discussion about what to do next, we agreed to drive to the American side of the border for some serious shopping. A short drive later, we arrived at a discount mall, where the bargains were so great that we spent much more money than we had intended. Finally, we returned home, where we discovered that, with the American exchange, prices were better at home after all. We should have gone to the library.

In this paragraph, readers are gently guided from one point to the next. By the time they reach the conclusion, they know not only what ideas the writer had in mind, but also how the ideas fit together to form a unit. The transitions make the reader's job easy and rewarding.

You can choose from an array of strategies to improve the coherence of your writing. There are five techniques to master. Be sure to use a variety of these techniques every time you write. Nothing improves the polish of your prose more than the use of coherence strategies.

1. **Repetition.** Repetition focuses the reader's attention on an idea and creates a thread of meaning that runs through a paragraph or a paper, tying the whole thing together. Don't overdo it, though.

2. **Synonyms.** Frequent repetition of a key word can become monotonous after a while. You can keep the reader focused on the idea by using synonyms—different words that convey the same meaning.

3. **Pronoun references.** Another way of maintaining the focus but varying the wording is to use appropriate pronouns to refer to a key noun. (This technique involves pronoun–antecedent agreement, a topic covered in Chapter 32.)

4. **Parallel structure.** Phrasing your sentences in parallel form helps to maintain focus, reinforces the unity of your thoughts, and adds emphasis. Parallelism adds "punch" to your writing. (More punch is served in Chapter 26.)

5. **Transitional words and phrases.** Transitional words and phrases show the relationships between points in a paragraph as well as between paragraphs in an essay. They act like tape, sticking together the elements of a paragraph or a paper so your reader does not fall between the cracks. Use them the way you use turn signals on a car: to tell the person following you where you're going.

Here are some transitional phrases that will help make your writing read smoothly.

Transitional Function	Words/Phrases Used
1. To show a time relationship between points	• first, second, third • now, simultaneously, concurrently, at this point, while • before, to begin, previously • after, following this, then, later, next • finally, last, subsequently • during, meanwhile, presently, from time to time, sometimes
2. To add an idea or example to the previous point	• and, in addition, also, furthermore, besides, moreover, for the same reason • another, similarly, equally important, likewise • for example, for instance, in fact
3. To show contrast between points	• although, nevertheless, on the other hand, whereas, while • but, however, instead, nonetheless • in contrast, on the contrary, in spite of, despite
4. To show a cause-and-effect relationship between points	• since, because, thus, therefore, hence • as a result, consequently, accordingly
5. To emphasize or repeat a significant point	• in fact, indeed, certainly, undoubtedly • in other words, as I have said, that is to say
6. To summarize or conclude	• in brief, on the whole, in summary, in short • therefore, as a result, last, finally

The paragraph below illustrates the use of all five coherence strategies to achieve unity. As you read, pay particular attention to the writer's use of repetition and parallelism.

While the Internet can be a useful tool for some businesses, studies have shown that in most workplaces it is a time-wasting drain on resources. As a result of one such study, Deloitte and Touche have issued a report pointing out the "five G's": risks of allowing employees unsupervised Internet activity during business hours. A company risks Giving, handing trade or business secrets over to the competition or the general public. A company risks Gawking, time-wasting employee fascination with particular sites, including pornography. A company risks Gambling, an increasingly common and potentially addictive lure for surfers. A company risks Goofing off, the pointless surfing of sites that are unrelated to the task at hand. A company risks Grabbing, the downloading of virus-infected material and copyrighted software. To counter the five G's, Deloitte and Touche recommend that companies establish clear policy on Internet use.

Owner Manager Advisor newsletter. *Globe and Mail* 25 Jan. 1998: B15.

Exercise 8.2*

Working with a partner, identify the transitional words and phrases that create coherence in each of the sentence groups below.

1. The spruce budworm threatens B.C.'s forests, killing trees that have resisted all other predators. Therefore, governments at both the local and provincial levels have begun a controlled burn program.
2. The two women spent the whole day tramping from car dealer to car dealer. Finally, they found a used Toyota they could live with, but the price was higher than they had hoped to pay.
3. There are many jokes about cats. Unfortunately, however, in most of them the cat is either very unhappy or dead.
4. There are those who think Quebec would thrive as a separate state. On the other hand, some feel that its economic viability depends on a close relationship with the rest of Canada.
5. Although we fear the size and power of our big banks, we must admit that they serve us well when compared with the banking institutions of other countries. For example, Canadian banks are second only to Japanese banks, and ahead of those in the United States and Germany, in the number of ATMs per person they provide. In addition, they lead all three of these countries in the number of full-service branches per capita.

Exercise 8.3

In each of the following sentences, supply transitional words or phrases that help the meaning become clearer and make the sentence more coherent. When you've finished, exchange exercises with another student and check each other's answers. If you disagree with any of your partner's choices, explain why.

1. My first impression of my supervisor was that he was aloof and arrogant; _____, I discovered I was wrong. He was painfully shy.

2. Many bestsellers have become pathetic movies, now long forgotten. _____ many poor novels have been turned into movie classics, such as *Gone with the Wind*, that last forever.

3. Many sports were discovered by accident. _____, one day at Rugby school in the 1830s, an English schoolboy, during a game of rugby, threw the ball overhand down the field. Football (as we call it in North America) was born.

4. Architecture in the 20th century has become more streamlined, geometrical, and uniform. _____, it has become monotonous.

5. The Bush administration believes that an expensive and unproven missile defence system is needed to protect North American from a non-existent threat. _____, Canadians disagree.

Exercise 8.4*

Read the paragraphs below and identify the transitional strategies that contribute to coherence. Both paragraphs contain examples of all five techniques listed on page 102.

1.   Finally, developing the proper attitude is the true key to winning tennis. I define winning tennis as playing the game to the best of your ability, hitting the ball as well as you know you can, and enjoying the feeling of practised expertise. Winning tennis has nothing to do with beating an opponent. Naturally, if you play winning tennis by learning the basics, practising sufficiently, and concentrating, you'll win many matches, but that is the reward of playing well, not the reason for playing well. People who swear and throw their racquets when they lose are very useful; they are the most satisfying players to trounce. But I don't understand why they play a game that causes them such pain. Tennis players who enjoy the feel of a well hit ball and the satisfaction of a long, skilfully played rally are winners, regardless of the score.

2.   Travel abroad offers you the best education you can get. For one thing, travel is a course in communication skills. In order to function in a foreign language, you must practise every aspect of the communication process from body language to pronunciation. In fact, just making yourself understood is

a lesson in creativity, a seminar in sign language, and a lab in communication theory. Another educational aspect of travel is the history, geography, and culture that you learn about almost unconsciously. Everywhere you go, you encounter memorable evidence of historical events you may dimly recall from school, and you are continually confronted by the practical realities of geography as you try to find your way around. As for culture, no book or course of study could provide you with the understanding and appreciation of another society that living in it can. A third way in which travel educates is through teaching you about yourself. Your ability—or inability—to cope with unfamiliar customs, with language difficulties, and with the inevitable problems of finding transportation and accommodation will tell you more than you might want to know about yourself. Without the safety net of family and friends, perhaps without even the security of knowing where you'll spend the night, you develop self-reliance or you go home. Either way, you learn valuable lessons. While you may not get a diploma from Travel U., you'll learn more about the world, about people, and about yourself than you will in any classroom.

Now compare your answers to ours on pages 517–18.

Exercise 8.5

Now consider the ways coherence strategies can be used to promote the smooth flow of ideas throughout an essay. Identify the transitional techniques used in Bertrand Russell's "What I Have Lived For," on page 6.

Tone

As you write the paragraphs of your paper, be conscious of your **tone**. Your audience, purpose, and subject will all influence the tone you choose, which must be appropriate to all three. The words you use, the examples, quotations, and other supporting materials you choose to help explain your main points—all these contribute to your tone.

When you are trying to explain something to someone, particularly if it's something you feel strongly about, you may be tempted to be highly emotional in your discussion. If you allow yourself to get emotional, chances are you won't be convincing. What will be communicated is the strength of your feelings, not the depth of your understanding or the validity of your opinion. To be clear and credible, you need to restrain your enthusiasm or anger and present your points in a calm, reasonable way.

Here are a few suggestions to help you find and maintain the right tone:

- Be tactful. Avoid phrases such as "Any idiot can see," "No sane person could believe," and "It is obvious that. . . . " What is obvious to you isn't necessarily obvious to someone who has a limited understanding of your subject or who disagrees with your opinion.

- Don't talk down to your readers as though they were children or hopelessly ignorant. Never use sarcasm, profanity, or slang.

- Don't apologize for your interpretation of your subject. Have confidence in yourself. You've thought long and hard about your subject, you've found good supporting material to help explain it, and you believe in its significance. Present your subject in a positive manner. If you hang back, using phrases such as "I may be wrong, but . . . " or "I tend to feel that . . . ", your reader won't be inclined to give your points the consideration they deserve. Keep your reader in mind as you write, and your writing will be both clear and convincing.

The following paragraph is an example of inappropriate tone. The writer is enthusiastic about the topic, but the tone is arrogant, bossy, and tactless rather than persuasive.

It is time that governments at all levels did something completely out of character: take action. We need laws requiring the addition of 10 percent ethanol to gasoline. Ethanol burns cleaner than gas and also boosts octane, so it's completely obvious that the oil companies don't have to put so many poisonous additives in the gas to make our already too powerful cars go even faster. For another thing, anybody who has done any reading knows that ethanol is made out of corn, which is grown on farms and is a renewable resource. Growing it will make farmers happy, and drivers should also be cheerful because it can be produced for less than the outrageous prices we pay for straight gasoline. Adding 10 percent of the cheaper fuel should bring pump prices down, although I'm sure the oil companies will find a way to gouge the consumer. Obviously, the government is going to have to pass laws forcing the oil companies to add ethanol because there's no way these corporate creeps are going to do what is good for the environment and the economy at the expense of lining their own pockets. However, relying on government to do the right thing is just as precarious a proposition; I wouldn't hold my breath.

Now read the paragraph below, which argues the same point but in a courteous, tactful way.

Legislation requiring the addition of ethanol to gasoline is both sensible and overdue. The addition of 10 percent ethanol to the gasoline that is sold at the pump is sensible for two reasons. First, it makes the fuel that is burned in our cars and trucks cleaner. Ethanol burns hotter than gasoline and burns up more of the pollutants, rather than sending them out of the tailpipe. Because it provides a higher octane fuel, ethanol also eliminates the need for some of the toxic additives currently used to boost octane. Second, ethanol is a renewable source of energy that will provide jobs in rural Canada because it is made from corn. At current oil prices, ethanol is cheaper than gasoline, so its addition to our fuel will help to reduce costs for consumers. Why should governments have to legislate such a sensible course of action? The petroleum industry, from exploration to retail, is not about to voluntarily dilute its product—or, more important, its profits—by any amount, let alone 10 percent!

Exercise 8.6*

The following paragraph is a draft written for a general reader. The writer's purpose is to persuade her audience that city dwellers should be more aware of the labour that lies behind every packaged product we eat. Revise the paragraph to make it appropriate to its audience and purpose by deleting or rewording any lapses in tone. Then compare your answer with ours on page 518.

I'm from the city, so I may not know much about the subject, but it seems to me that we urbanites have lost touch with the food we eat. By this I mean, obviously, that we no longer appreciate the farmers and farm workers who supply the food that we enjoy every day. Anyone with half a brain should realize that most of the food we buy is prepackaged in Styrofoam, wrapped in plastic, or precooked and frozen by huge corporations whose goal is to make humongous profits by selling us the packaging, not the contents. Do any urban consumers understand that their ketchup is made from farm-grown tomatoes? Do any advertising-driven supermarket shoppers really think about the fact that those overpackaged frozen pork chops, so irresistible with their sprig of parsley, were once a pig, raised by a farmer? Not only are we ignorant, but also we could care less about the journey our food makes from farm to fridge. My guess is that if you asked most city kids where their food comes from, they'd say, "the food factory."

Exercise 8.7

Revise the following paragraph, adding transitions and moderating its tone.

The armed forces of most nations are trained to be psychopaths. Canada's military personnel face a greater challenge: they need to be schizo-phrenics. The boot-camp training that recruits undergo, together with instruction in combat and weaponry, produces efficient and remorseless killers—psychopaths. The role of Canada's armed forces over the past 50 years has been to keep the peace. When the Nobel Peace Prize was awarded to the United Nations peacekeeping forces, Canada, as the only nation to have participated in every mission, considered the prize largely hers. Canada's elite forces played a traditional military role as hunters and killers in Afghanistan. Is Canada's military adequately trained for these two con-tradictory roles? Our country needs highly trained units of efficient psy-chopaths. The majority of armed forces personnel need training in mediation, conflict resolution, cultural sensitivity, basic medical treatment, and infrastructure repair. This is a hard concept for fans of the military to get through their thick skulls: soldiers trained to prevent violence. Peacekeeping is still the Canadian military's primary function. Canada's armed forces have two roles. Both must be prepared for.

9

Writing Introductions and Conclusions

All of the concepts you have studied so far can be applied to any paragraph. Two paragraphs, however—the first and the last—serve special purposes and need extra care. All too often, the introduction and the conclusion of a paper are dull or clumsy and detract from its effectiveness. But they needn't be dull or clumsy. Here's how to write good ones.

The Introductory Paragraph

The introduction is worth special attention because that's where your readers either sit up and take notice of your paper or sigh and pitch it into the wastebasket.

There are two parts to an introductory paragraph:
1. an attention-getter
2. a thesis statement

Getting and Holding Your Readers' Attention

Your readers must be attracted to your writing or there's no point in putting pen to paper or fingers to keyboard. The attention-getter must be appropriate to the content of your essay and to your intended readers. If your audience is known for a solemn approach to life and your topic is serious (environmental ethics, for instance, or equal opportunity policies in the workplace), then there is no point in leading off with a pun or joke, no matter how witty. Such an opening would be inappropriate and probably offensive to your readers.

Your attention-getter does not have to be a single sentence; in fact, good ones are often several sentences long. Your readers will be committing varying amounts of personal time to reading your writing. You owe it to them to make your opening sentences clear, interesting, and creative.

An effective attention-getter should be followed by an equally effective thesis statement, one that slides smoothly and easily into place. Your readers should be aware only of a unified paragraph, not of two separate parts in your introduction.

Below are eight different kinds of openings you can choose from to get your readers' attention and lead up to your thesis statement. In each of the example paragraphs, note how the attention-getter and the thesis statement are solidly linked to form a unified whole. To demonstrate that you can take many different approaches to a subject, depending on your purpose and your audience, we have used the same subject—physical fitness—in all of the introductions.

1. Spell out the significance of your subject. If your subject's significance can catch your readers' interest, they will want to know more about it, especially if it is a subject that affects them directly.

More and more young people are dying of heart disease. Despite the statistics that say most people in our society are living longer thanks to advances in medicine and surgery, the figures can be misleading. It is a fact that people in their thirties and forties are dying from coronary problems that once threatened people in their fifties and sixties. What has caused this change? Certainly, the increase in stress, the fatigue of overwork, the rise in obesity, and the decline in physical activity are all contributing factors. To combat the risk of cardiovascular disease, we need physical activity. Regular exercise can forestall the ravages of heart disease and promote longevity.

2. Begin with a well-phrased quotation. You might choose a famous statement, a popular slogan, or a common saying. Use a quotation when it sums up your point of view more succinctly and effectively than your own words could. As a rule, you should identify the source of the quotation.

"Who can be bothered?" "I'm much too busy." "I get all the exercise I need at the office." We've all heard excuses like these, excuses for avoiding regular exercise. Modern life, with its distractions and conveniences, tends to make people sedentary and lazy, but the human organism cannot tolerate inactivity and stress indefinitely. Eventually, it begins to break down. Those who want to keep in shape for the challenges of modern life should consider the benefits of working out a few times a week. Regular exercise can rejuvenate the body, refresh the mind, and improve self-confidence.

3. **Use a startling statement.** Sometimes a surprising remark (not an insult or a false exaggeration) is effective in getting readers' attention. A little-known or striking fact will have the same effect.

After the age of 30, the average North American puts on 10 to 20 kilograms of fat. Presumably, the cause for this startling increase in avoirdupois is a combination of metabolic changes, decreased physical activity, and hundreds of kilos of junk food ingested since childhood. It's difficult to stop the spread of middle-aged corpulence, but experts tell us we *can* resist the rise in flab by reducing our caloric intake and increasing our physical activity. Regular exercise can rejuvenate the body, refresh the mind, and improve self-confidence.

4. **Ask a question or two.** Questions are often an effective way to encourage interest because your readers will find themselves thinking of answers. Some questions are rhetorical; that is, they will not have specific answers. Others might be answered in your essay.

Have you been feeling sluggish and exhausted lately? Has your blood pressure increased along with your waistline in the past few years? Are you stalled in front of the television set every night with potato chips and a beer? If so, you are probably suffering from a common middle-aged ailment called *flabitis*. This malady strikes most people over 30: they put on weight, have trouble concentrating, tire easily, and prefer watching sports to participating in them. Fortunately, there is a cure for flabitis: a three-times-weekly dose of exercise. With regular exercise, you can rejuvenate your body, refresh your mind, and improve your self-confidence.

5. **Begin with a generalization related to your subject.** Generalizations can be useful for suggesting the context and scope of your subject. They must, however, be narrowed down carefully to a focused thesis statement.

Until the 20th century, physical exercise was part of the normal workday. Our ancestors were farmers, pioneers, sailors, and so on. Few of our parents, however, made their living by ploughing the land or chopping down trees. Since the early 1900s, the trend in work has been away from physical exertion and toward automation. Today's generation uses technology to reduce physical activity even further: they pick up the phone, ride the elevator, and take the car to the corner store. Modern inactivity has negative consequences that only physical exercise can counter. To sustain good health, sharpen your mental edge, and have fun, you should take up aerobics or sports and use your body in the way it was intended—actively.

6. Challenge a common opinion. Perhaps your readers have also doubted a popular belief. Your thesis statement can assert that an opinion is false, and the body of your paper can contain evidence to support your opposing view.

Physical activity is for kids. Adults don't have time to hit a baseball or run around a field chasing after one, or to do aerobics and lift weights in a gym. They have to earn a living, raise families, and save money for retirement. They can leave exercise to their children. I firmly believed this until one morning when, late for work, I ran after a bus. My heart pounded; my lungs gasped; my head swam. It had been some years since my last stint of exercise, and I realized I wouldn't be around to do my job, support my family, or enjoy retirement unless I got into the habit of doing something physical to maintain my health. Regular exercise can rejuvenate the body, refresh the mind, and broaden one's interests.

7. Begin with a definition. A definition is a good way to begin if you are introducing a key term that you suspect may be unfamiliar to your readers. If the subject of your essay depends on a personal meaning of a term that most people understand in a different way, a definition is essential.

Myocardial infarction: the very term is frightening. It occurs when a person's muscles slacken from disuse, the veins clog up with sticky fats, and the heart has to work too hard to sustain even minor exertion such as raking leaves or shovelling snow. The muscles of the heart become strained to exhaustion or balloon outward because the veins cannot pass blood quickly enough. In plain English, a myocardial infarction is a heart attack. If the victim is lucky enough to survive, physicians prescribe a regimen of less stress, low fat intake, and regular exercise.

8. Describe an interesting incident or tell an anecdote related to your subject. Readers like stories. Keep yours short and to the point by narrating only the highlights. The incident or anecdote you select might be a story from the media, an event involving family or friends, or a personal experience.

Last year, I got a free invitation in the mail to a fitness club. I responded, out of curiosity, but I needed to be convinced. After all, I was 35, had grown a little paunch, and was a bit short of breath on the stairs; 10 years had passed since I had last played sports. My first workout was a nightmare. My joints ached, my muscles throbbed, and my head spun. I was in worse shape than I thought. After a few weeks, those symptoms disappeared, and I began to enjoy myself. My paunch vanished and my muscles toned up. My capacity for concentration increased. Also, I met some new people who have become friends. Obviously, 10 years is too long between workouts, given that exercise not only rejuvenates the body and refreshes the mind but also improves one's social life.

Exercise 9.1

In small groups (four or five people), consider five movies you have all seen within the past year. How did each of these movies begin so that the audience was "locked in"? How do these movie "grabbers" relate to the kinds of attention-getters you have just read?

Exercise 9.2

Each of the following paragraphs is the introductory paragraph of an essay. Work in pairs and, using the strategy given in parentheses, write an appropriate attention-getter for each paragraph.

1. (significance of subject) _____

_____

TV commercials that portray unrealistic and unattainable lifestyles should be banned. Although I do not support censorship, I believe there is sufficient evidence of the damage done by these advertisements to justify eliminating them in the name of public interest. The objectionable commercials promote sexual stereotyping, set up unrealistic and dangerous expectations, and encourage irresponsible consumerism.

2. (quotation) _____

_____

Every sport has its strange expressions, just as every sport has its devoted fans, its famous teams, and its legendary heroes. A sport that gets very little attention in Canada but is very popular in many parts of the world, especially Commonwealth countries, is cricket. Like the sports that millions of Canadians follow enthusiastically, cricket is an exciting and fascinating game once you become familiar with its rules and style. In fact, it compares very favourably with baseball in skill, pace, and strategy.

3. (startling statement) _____

_____

Canadian roads are overrun by drivers who are a danger to themselves, their passengers, and others on the road. Inept drivers demonstrate their inadequacies in so many ways that it would be impossible to list them all in one short paper. Nevertheless, bad drivers can be broadly categorized as traumatized turtles, careening cowboys, and daydreaming dodos.

4. (question) _____

_____

Arranged marriages are a very important part of my culture. When my family moved to Canada, we left behind many of the traditions and customs that were as natural to us as breathing. However, my parents retained their right to choose a wife for me, even though they are aware that this custom is at odds with the Canadian way of life. Although their decision was at first difficult to accept, I believe there are good reasons that an arranged marriage may be best for me. The decision will be made by mature people in a thoughtful manner, uninfluenced by the enthusiasms of youth; the decision will be made by people who have at heart the best interests of our family, the bride's family, and me; and the decision will be made in accordance with a centuries-old tradition that has proven its success generation after generation.

5. (generalization) _____

_____

My first project manager was the sort of person that nightmares are made of. It's been a year since she was finally transferred to another department, but I still shudder when I recall our six months together. Denise was rude, bossy, and, worst of all, thoughtless.

6. (opinion you challenge) _____

_____

The evidence strongly suggests that overexposure to the sun can cause several forms of cancer at worst and premature aging at best. We can't completely avoid the sun's rays, but there are several measures we can take to prevent the damage that normal outdoor activity might cause. To enjoy the summer without fear, use an effective sun block, cover sensitive skin completely, and limit your time in the sun.

7. (definition) _____

_____

The choice of corrective lenses is an individual matter, but many people go through a tough decision-making process when confronting the issue. In deciding whether contact lenses or eyeglasses are more suitable, one should examine factors such as comfort, convenience, and appearance.

8. (anecdote or incident) _____

_____

Black flies are just one of the pests that make life less than comfortable in Canada during the spring, but they tend to be the most irritating. No method of combatting the pests is foolproof, but there are several methods that can be employed, either singly or together, to repel most of them. The campaign against the black fly begins with protective clothing, follows up with an effective repellent, and goes over the top with the secret weapon: garlic.

Exercise 9.3

With the class divided into four or five teams, consider the following essay topics. Each team will take one of the topics and develop the first sentence of an introductory paragraph for it. The sentence will then be passed in sequence to the next group, who will add a sentence to the paragraph. Continue this exercise until each paragraph contains both an attention-getter and a thesis statement. When each team gets back the paragraph it initiated, it will revise and polish the paragraph, identify the kind of attention-getter that has been developed, and underline the thesis statement. Share the results with the rest of the class. (Keep these paragraphs; you will need them later.)

1. Why I want to be a _____ (fill in your career choice)
2. Why I chose _____ (fill in your school)
3. How not to treat a coworker
4. My favourite TV show
5. The trouble with customers (parents, teachers, etc.)

The Concluding Paragraph

Like the introduction, the conclusion of your paper has a special form. Think of your favourite television sitcom. The last section of the show wraps up the plot, explains any details that might still be unresolved, and leaves you with a satisfying sense that all is well, at least until next week. A concluding paragraph works in a similar way.

The last paragraph of your paper has two functions.
1. It summarizes or reinforces the main points of your paper.
2. It ends with an appropriate memorable statement.

Your **summary statement** should be as concise as you can make it, and must be phrased in such a way that it does not repeat word for word the portion of your thesis statement that identifies the main points. (Note that a summary is not needed in a very short essay.)

A **memorable statement** is a sentence designed to leave your readers feeling satisfied with your essay and perhaps taking away with them something for further thought. Never end without a clincher. Don't just quit writing when your main points are covered, or you'll leave your readers hanging, wondering what to make of it all.

Six strategies you can choose from when you write a concluding paragraph are listed below. Each strategy is illustrated by an example paragraph. Identify the summary and the memorable statement in each conclusion.

1. End with a relevant or thought-provoking quotation. You can use this type of ending in two ways: repeat an earlier quotation but give it a new meaning, or place your subject in a larger context by supplying a new quotation from a recognized authority in the field.

Since I began lifting weights every second day, I have lowered my blood pressure, improved my productivity at work, and made some new friends at the fitness club. I will never be Arnold Schwarzenegger, but that isn't my goal. My muscles are pleasantly sore after a good workout, but as Arnold says, "No pain, no gain." As long as the pain is so little and the gain is so great, I will continue to enjoy my regular workouts.

2. Offer a solution to a problem discussed in your paper. You can plan an organization for your paper that will allow you to resolve a problem or neutralize negative consequences in your conclusion.

I've got the best intentions in the world. I know that exercise benefits me physically, mentally, and emotionally—but I still don't have the time. I didn't, that is, until last month, when I was home from work for a week because I sprained my ankle while walking the dog. That never would have happened if I had been in shape. Since then, I have forced myself to manage my time to allow for a fitness program. Four hours of exercise a week is not a very big investment of time compared with four days of lying on the couch with a painfully swollen foot.

3. End with one or more relevant or thought-provoking questions. The advantage of clinching with a question is that readers tend automatically to pause and consider it: questions stimulate thought. Before they know it, readers will begin to formulate answers to your question—and that activity will make them remember your points. Be sure your question relates directly to your subject.

> My life has improved considerably since I took up jogging three times a week: I enjoy better health, less brain-fog, and more confidence. And I'm inspired to continue jogging by the fact that coronary disease runs in my family. My father and grandfather both suffered heart attacks in their fifties. If they had done regular exercise, could they have reduced their chances of coronaries? Would they still be alive today?

4. Point out the value or significance of your subject to your readers. If you emphasize your subject matter at the end of your paper, you can stamp its importance on your readers' memory.

> Regular exercise is the best way to stay in shape, be sharp, and feel strong; it is the best way to reduce the risk of arthritis, arterial decay, and heart dysfunction. In a country where the most common cause of mortality is coronary collapse, everyone needs to consider the value of consistent exercise. It is a small daily inconvenience that pays large and long-term rewards.

5. Make a connection to a statement made in your introduction. This strategy provides your readers with a sense of closure. They will recall your earlier statement and feel satisfied that the loose ends have been tied up.

> Having exercised now for six months, I can run for the bus without losing my breath, sweating profusely, or feeling dizzy. My body is in better trim; my endurance and confidence on the job have grown. After a lapse of 20 years, I have even taken up bicycling again: I go riding along local bike trails with friends. And now, when my children are playing baseball in the yard, I don't think, "Baseball is for kids." I'm first at the plate. Batter up!

6. End with a suggestion for change or a prediction about the future. Your suggestion for change will influence your readers if they have been persuaded by your arguments. Your predictions of events that might occur should not be misleading or exaggerated, or your readers will be skeptical. Make predictions that are possible and plausible.

If those of us who still prefer junk food, overwork, and television don't shape up, then the incidence of coronary disease will continue to rise. Moderate exercise will benefit body, mind, and spirit. If we follow common sense and change our habits of self-pollution and self-destruction, all of us can lead long, active, and healthy lives.

Exercise 9.4

Each of the following is the concluding paragraph of an essay. Working in pairs, underline the summary statement and write a memorable conclusion. See if you can use a different kind in each paragraph.

1. Both games are enjoyable for spectators and create real enthusiasm among fans. High schools that have chosen soccer have seen no reduction in school spirit or fan support. For educational institutions to make the switch from football is really a "no-lose" proposition because soccer provides dramatic advantages in reducing player injury, increasing player fitness, and shaving thousands of dollars from school expenses.

   _____

   _____

   _____

   _____

2. In retrospect, the NHL lockout was completely avoidable. It had been predicted and discussed for two years prior to the date of the lockout, yet neither side made a meaningful move to prevent it. Only when the 2004–05 season was on the edge of cancellation did the players and owners begin to make concessions that moved them closer to a settlement. Had these moves been made a year or even half a year earlier, the lockout need never have happened. But both sides engaged in brinksmanship in the hope that the other would cave in, and we are all living with the results.

   _____

   _____

   _____

   _____

3. Although the causes of dropout among first-year students are as individual as the students themselves, the effects are easier to categorize. Conflict with parents and others whose expectations have not been met

comes first, followed by a loss of self-esteem. The determination to succeed despite this unfair setback is common, but statistics show that low-paying, dead-end jobs are the norm for the college dropout. The situation is much worse, of course, for those who don't complete high school.

---

4.   Employers who need to replace retiring workers with skilled young people must take into account the major differences between the generation of retiring boomers and the generation that is replacing them. Unlike their parents, who were raised to respect age and authority, members of Generation Y (broadly defined as anyone born after 1980), are used to calling their teachers and their parents' friends by their first names; they think of themselves as less experienced equals. They believe that their opinions count, that their feelings matter, and that they should be heard. While they lack the relentless career ambition and drive of their parents, they seek career satisfaction in enjoyable work, opportunities for growth, and more leisure time. They see "the good life" not as their parents did, as a matter of accumulating wealth, but as a satisfying balance between their professional and personal lives.

---

5.   Drinking and driving must be stopped. To stop it will require substantial commitment from all levels of government, both in terms of money and in terms of political will. The penalties for driving while under the influence of alcohol must be increased, and more money must be spent for education and publicity. But, more than these measures, it will take the individual will of every Canadian to make the promise not to drive after drinking. Nothing will bring my sister back, but there are lots of other sisters out there—and brothers and mothers and fathers—who can be saved.

Exercise 9.5

With the class divided into the same teams as in Exercise 9.3, write concluding paragraphs to complement the introductions you developed. Here's how to proceed:

- Review the paragraph you developed for Exercise 9.3.
- Write the first sentence of a concluding paragraph for this same topic.
- Pass your sentence, together with your introductory paragraph, along to the next team, who will write a second sentence for the conclusion.
- Continue this process until the conclusion contains both a summary or reinforcement and a memorable statement.
- Return the paragraph to the team that initiated it for revising and polishing.
- Share the results with the rest of the class.

PART 3

Revising

10

The Three Steps to Revision

No one can write in a single draft an essay that is perfectly organized and developed, let alone one that is free of errors. The purpose of the first draft is to get down on paper something you can work with until it meets your reader's needs and expectations. Planning and drafting should take about half the time you devote to writing a paper. The rest should be devoted to revision.

Revision is the process of refining your message until

- it says what you want it to say,
- your reader(s) will understand it, and
- your reader(s) will receive it favourably.

These three goals are the essentials of good communication. You can achieve them only if you keep your readers in mind as you revise. Because a first draft reflects the contents of the writer's mind, it often seems all right to the writer. But in order to transfer an idea as clearly as possible from the mind of the writer to the mind of the reader, revision is necessary. The idea needs to be honed and refined until it is as clear to your reader as it is to you. By revising from your reader's point of view, you can avoid misunderstandings before they happen.

What Is Revision?

Revision means "re-seeing." It does *not* mean recopying.

The aim of revision is to improve your writing's organization, accuracy, and style. Revising is a three-stage process. Each step requires that you read through your entire essay. The goal of your first reading is to ensure that your reader's information needs are met. In your second reading, you focus on paragraph and sentence structure. Your third reading concentrates on correctness. Here are the steps to follow in revising a paper:

1. Improve the whole paper by revising its content and organization.
2. Refine paragraph and sentence structure, and correct any errors in grammar.
3. Edit and proofread to catch errors in word choice, spelling, and punctuation.

Inexperienced writers often skip the first two stages and concentrate on the third, thinking they will save time. In fact, they waste time—both theirs and their readers'—because the result is writing that doesn't communicate clearly and won't make a positive impression.

The best way to begin revising is to let as much time as possible pass between completing your first draft and rereading it. Ten minutes, or even half a day, is not enough. The danger in rereading too soon is that you're likely to "read" what you think you've written—what exists only in your head, not on the paper.

If you haven't allowed enough time for this cooling-off period, there are two other things you can do to help you get some distance from your draft. If your first draft is handwritten, type it out. Reading your essay in a different form helps you to "re-see" its content. Alternatively, read your paper aloud and try to hear it from the point of view of your reader. Listen to how your explanation unfolds, and mark every place you find something unclear, irrelevant, inadequately developed, or out of order.

Step 1
Revise Content and Organization

As you reread your paper, keep in mind the three kinds of changes you can (and probably should) make at this stage:

1. You can rearrange information. This is the kind of revision that is most often needed but least often done. Consider the order in which

you've arranged your paragraphs. From your reader's point of view, is this the most effective order in which to present your ideas?

2. You can add information. Adding new main ideas or more development is often necessary to make your message interesting and convincing as well as clear. It's a good idea to ask a friend to read your draft and identify what needs to be expanded or clarified. (Be sure to return the favour; you can learn a great deal by critiquing other people's writing.)

3. You can delete information. Now is the time to cut out anything that is repetitious, insignificant, or irrelevant to your subject and reader.

Your outline is the best place to begin checking the adequacy and organization of your information. Keep it beside you and change it as your revise your essay. In most cases, your paper will be improved by rearranging, adding, and subtracting ideas.

The thesis statement is your contract with your reader, so it should be the guiding principle of your paper. It should contain nothing that is not developed in the body of the essay, and there should be nothing in the essay that is not directly related to your thesis statement. When you find a mismatch between the thesis statement and the paper, change one or the other or both until the two agree. Using a word processor to move blocks of text around is as easy as shuffling a deck of cards.

If you are not already using a word-processing program, now is the time to begin. Before you start to revise, change the computer's settings to meet the format requirements of your paper: set the spacing, margins, font style and size, etc. (See Chapter 21 for instructions and examples.) Most people find it easier to revise from a paper copy, so print out your draft double- or triple-spaced. Read it through carefully, making notes for changes in the margins or in the spaces between the lines; then go back to the computer to make the changes.

Remember to save your work frequently. It takes only a split second to click on the Save icon, but that split second could save you hours—even days—in the event of a computer disaster. Learn to save your work in a systematic and easy-to-find filing system. Calling a paper "draft" or "essay" will cause frustration later when you want to reopen the file to revise it but can't remember the name of the file you were working on. Give each file a distinctive name (or name and number), and save each draft separately just in case you want to go back and use material from a previous version of your document.

Use the checklist that follows to guide you as you review your paper's form and content.

CONTENT AND ORGANIZATION CHECKLIST

ACCURACY

- Is your information consistent with your own experience and observations or with what you have discovered through research?
- Are all your facts and evidence up to date?

COMPLETENESS

Have you included enough main ideas and development to explain your subject and convince your reader? Remember that "enough" means from the reader's point of view, not the writer's.

SUBJECT

Is your subject

- significant? Does it avoid the trivial or the obvious?
- single? Does it avoid double or combined subjects?
- specific? Is it focused and precise?
- supportable? Have you provided enough evidence to make your meaning clear?

MAIN POINTS

Are your main points

- significant? Have you deleted any unimportant ones?
- distinct? Are they all different from one another, or is there an overlap in content?
- relevant? Do all points relate directly to your subject?
- arranged in the most appropriate order? Again, "appropriate" means from the reader's perspective. Choose chronological, climactic, logical, or random order, depending on which is most likely to help the reader make sense of your information.

INTRODUCTION

Does your introduction

- catch the reader's attention and make him or her want to read on?
- contain a clearly identifiable thesis statement?
- identify the main points that your paper will explain?

CONCLUSION

Does your conclusion

- contain a summary or reinforcement of your main points, rephrased to avoid word-for-word repetition?
- contain a statement that effectively clinches your argument and leaves the reader with something to think about?

Exercise 10.1*

Read the following draft outline for a short essay on how to write effective e-mail in a business environment. Working with a partner, rearrange the main points in chronological order, delete any unnecessary supporting points, and write a thesis statement to produce a working outline for the essay. Then compare your answer with our suggestion. Answers for exercises in this chapter begin on page 519.

E-Mail Excellence

Attention-getter: As the recipient of approximately 1,000 business-related e-mail messages every month, I am something of an expert on what is effective and what is not in e-mail correspondence.

Thesis statement: _____

_____

_____

_____

Main points:

  I. Subject line

      A. always include one

      B. make sure it states clearly what the message is about

      C. never use vague subject lines such as "hello," or "message," or "are you there?"

      D. never leave the subject line blank

 II. Attachments

      A. use sparingly

      B. may carry viruses

      C. take time to transfer and to open

      D. attach text-only files unless a graphic is absolutely necessary

      E. use only if necessary

III. Message

    A. Content

        1. be concise and to the point

        2. tell the reader what action is needed, by whom, and when

        3. don't be a novelist or a "Chatty Cathy"

        4. use plain English, not "cyberspeak"

        5. use an appropriate level of language in your message as well as in your salutation and signature

    B. Format

        1. use bullets to identify points you want to emphasize

        2. leave white space between points

        3. avoid sending your message in uppercase letters (shouting)

        4. avoid smilies and other "cute" computer shorthand symbols

Summary: If you follow my recommendations on these three points whenever you write an e-mail, you will make the recipient of your message very happy.

Memorable statement: Especially if you're writing to me.

Step 2
Revise Paragraphs and Sentences

Here, too, you should allow time—at least a couple of days—between your first revision and your second. Read your draft aloud, and use this list of questions to help you improve it.

PARAGRAPH AND SENTENCE CHECKLIST
PARAGRAPHS
Does each paragraph
- begin with a clear, identifiable topic sentence?
- develop one—and only one—main idea?
- employ one or more kinds of development appropriate to the main idea?
- contain clear and effective transitions to signal the relationship between sentences? Between paragraphs?

SENTENCES

Sentence Structure
1. Is each sentence clear and complete?
   - Are there any fragments or run-ons?
   - Are there any misplaced or dangling modifiers?
   - Are all lists (whether words, phrases, or clauses) expressed in parallel form?
2. Are your sentences varied in length? Could some be combined to improve the clarity and impact of your message?

Grammar
1. Have you used verbs correctly?
   - Are all verbs in the correct form?
   - Do all verbs agree with their subjects?
   - Are all verbs in the correct tense?
   - Are there any confusing shifts in verb tense within a paragraph?
2. Have you used pronouns correctly?
   - Are all pronouns in the correct form?
   - Do all pronouns agree with their antecedents?
   - Have any vague pronoun references been eliminated?

When you're sure you've answered these questions satisfactorily, go to the third and last stage of the revision process.

Exercise 10.2*

Here is the first draft of the essay on e-mail. Revise it to correct errors in paragraph structure, sentence structure, and grammar. Then compare your answer with our suggestion on pages 519–20.

1   As the recipient of approximately 1,000 business-related e-mail messages every month, I am something of an expert on what is effective and what is not in e-mail correspondence. The three areas that need attention in most e-mail messages are the subject line, the content, and format of the message and the use of attachments.

2   Some people leave the subject line blank, this is a mistake. I want to know what the message is about before I open it so I can decide if it needs my immediate attention. Or can wait until later. A message with no subject line or with a line that didn't tell me nothing about the content of the e-mail get sent to the bottom of my "to-do" list. There are lots of readers like me busy people who receive tons of e-mail, much of it unsolicited advertising that clutter up their in-boxes. For this reason the subject line should always clearly state the subject of the message and should never be vague or cute like "hello" or "message" or "are you there?"

3   As for the message itself, it's function should be to tell the reader what action one wants, you need to be clear about this and be as brief as possible. What is it that you want the recipient to do. Who else needs to be involved. By when does the action need to take place. Communicate your message in plain English, not in "cyberspeak" Not everyone knows Net lingo, and even some who are famliar with it find it irritating not charming. Use an appropriate level of language (general level Standard English will always be appropriate) to convey you're message. Use the same level of language in you're salutation and closing or "signature." One should definitely not sign off a message to you're client or you're boss with "love and kisses." Format you're message so that the recipient will be able to read it quickly and understanding it easily. Use bullets to identify points you want to emphasize, separate the bullets with white space so they can be read at a glance and

reviewed individually if necessary. There are some important points of e-mail etiquette that you should observe. Don't type you're message in upper case letters, that's considered "shouting." Do avoid "smilies" and other "cute" computer shorthand symbols. Some of you're readers won't understand them others will have seen them so often they will be turned off.

4 Attachments should be included only if they are really necessary, for one thing, they may carry virruses and some people won't open them. Another disadvantage is that they take time to send download and open. Unless I am sure that an attachment is both urgent and vitally important—the agenda of tomorrow's meeting, for example—I don't bother to open it, for all I know, it might contain not only a virus but also footage of the sender's toddler doing her latest photogenic trick. As a general rule attach only what you must and attach text-only files. Try to include everything you need to say in the message itself and use attachments only as a last resort. Think of them as equivalent to footnotes supplementary to the message not an essential part of it.

5 If you follow my recommendations on these three points whenever you write an e-mail, you will make the recipient of your message very happy, especially if you're writing to me.

Step 3
Edit and Proofread

By now you're probably so tired of refining your paper that you may be tempted to skip **editing**—correcting errors in word choice, spelling, and punctuation—and **proofreading**—correcting errors in typing or writing that appear in the final draft. But these final tasks are essential if you want your paper to make a positive impression.

Misspellings, faulty punctuation, and messiness don't always create misunderstandings, but they do cause the reader to form a lower opinion of you and your work. Careful editing and proofreading are necessary if you want your writing to be favourably received.

Most word-processing programs include a grammar checker and a spell checker. The newer programs have some useful features. For example, they will question (but not correct) your use of apostrophes; they will sometimes catch errors in subject–verb agreement; and they will catch obvious misspellings and typos. But don't make the mistake of assuming these programs will do all your editing for you. Many errors slip past them. Only you or a knowledgeable and patient friend can find and correct all errors.

If spelling is a particular problem for you, you should first run your paper through a spell checker. After that, you're on your own. Read your paper backward word by word, from the end to the beginning. Reading backward forces you to look at each word by itself and helps you to spot those that look suspicious. Whenever you're in doubt about the spelling of a word, look it up! If you find this task too tedious to bear, ask a good speller to read through your paper for you and identify any errors.

Here are the questions to ask yourself when you are editing.

EDITING CHECKLIST
WORDS

Usage
Have you used words to "mean" rather than to "impress"?
- Have you eliminated any slang, pretentious language, or offensive language?
- Have you cut out any unnecessary words?
- Have you corrected any "abusages"?

Tone
- Is your tone consistent, reasonable, courteous, and confident throughout your essay?

Spelling
Are all words spelled correctly?
- Have you double-checked any homonyms?
- Have you used capital letters where they are needed?
- Have you used apostrophes correctly for possessives and omitted them from plurals?

PUNCTUATION

Within Sentences

- Have you eliminated any unnecessary commas and included commas where needed? (Refer to the comma rules on pages 417–22 as you consider this question.)
- Have you used colons and semicolons where appropriate?
- Are all quotations appropriately marked?

Beginnings and Endings

- Does each sentence begin with a capital letter?
- Do all questions—and only questions—end with a question mark?
- Are all quotation marks correctly placed?

Exercise 10.3*

Read the following sentences carefully and edit them to correct any errors in usage, spelling, and punctuation. Then compare your answers to our suggestions on pages 520–21. (Our thanks to *Fortune* magazine for collecting these howlers from real résumés and cover letters.)

1. I demand a salary commiserate with my qualifications and extensive experience.

2. I have lurnt Microsoft Word and Excel computor and spreasheet progroms.

3. I received a plague for being salesperson of the year.

4. Reason for leaving last job; maturity leave.

5. You will want me to be Head Honcho in no time.

6. I am a perfectionist and rarely if if ever forget details.

7. Marital status: single. Unmarried. Unengaged. Uninvolved. No commitments.

8. In my previous job I became completely paranoid, trusting completely no one and absolutely nothing.

9. As indicted, I have over five years of analyzing investments.

10. I was responsible for ruining the entire operation for a Western chain store.

TIPS FOR EFFECTIVE PROOFREADING

By the time you have finished editing, you will have gone over your paper so many times you may have practically memorized it. When you are very familiar with a piece of writing, it's hard to spot the small mistakes that may have crept in as you produced your final copy. Here are some tips to help you find those tiny, elusive errors:

1. Read through your essay line by line, using a ruler to guide you.
2. If you've been keeping a list of your most frequent errors in this course, scan your essay for the mistakes you are most likely to make.
3. Use the "Quick Revision Guide" on the inside front cover of this book to make a final check of all aspects of your paper.
4. Use the list of correction marks on the inside back cover to check for errors your instructor has identified in your writing.

Your "last" draft may need further revision after your proofreading review. If so, take the time to rewrite the paper so that the version you hand in is clean and easy to read. If a word processor is available to you, use it. Computers make editing and proofreading almost painless, since errors are so easy to correct.

At long last, you're ready to submit your paper. If you've followed the three steps to revision conscientiously, you can hand it in with confidence that it says what you want it to say. One last word of advice:

DON'T FORGET TO KEEP A COPY FOR YOUR FILES!

Exercise 10.4*

Now go through the revised first draft of the e-mail essay that you produced in Exercise 10.2. This is your last chance to make this essay error-free. Use the Editing Checklist and the Tips for Effective Proofreading to guide you as you make your final pass through this document. Then compare your answer with our suggestion on pages 521–22.

GO TO WEB

EXERCISE 10.1

Is the following essay ready for submission? Go over it carefully, correcting any errors. Then get together with another student and compare your proofreading skills. (There are 20 errors in this exercise.)

According to a recent survey in Maclean's magazine, only 43 percent of Canadians are satisfied with their jobs. What can you do to ensure that you will not be one of the 57 percent who are unhappy with the work they do. There are three questions to consider when seeking employment that will provide satisfaction as well as a paycheque.

First are you suited to the kind of work you are applying for. If you enjoy the outdoors, for example, and like to be active, your not going to be happy with a nine to five office job, no matter how much it pays.

Second is the job based in a location compatible with your prefered lifestyle. No matter how much you like your work, if you go home every night to an enviorment you are miserable in, it will not be long before you start transfering your disatisfaction to your job. If you like the amenities and conviences of the city, you probably will not enjoy working in a small town. If, on the other hand, you prefer the quiet and security of small town life, you may find the city a stressful place in which to live.

Finally, is it one that you want to work for. Do you need the security of generous benifits, a good pension plan, and incentives to stay and grow with one company? Or are you an ambitous person who is looking for variety, quick advancement, and a high salary. If so, you may have to forego security in favour of commissions or cash incentives and be willing to move as quickly and as often as opportunities occur. Some carful self-analysis now, before you start out on your career path, will help you chose a direction that will put you in the 43 percent minority of satisfied Canadian workers.

Exercise 10.6

This exercise will serve as a review of the three stages of the revision process. Below is a first draft of an essay. Applying all the principles you have learned in Chapter 10, revise this essay to make it a model of good communication: complete, correct, concise, and courteous. When you have finished, exchange papers with another student and compare your results. What errors did you miss? If this assignment were worth 20 percent of your final grade, would you hand it in now, or would you revise it again?

We are having a garbage crisis. There is so much waste being produced in North America, we no longer have any idea of were to put it. Toronto's garbage problem is so great that they are trucking thousands of tonnes of it to Michigan every year. But how long will that last? We must act now, and we must act as individuals. We cannot wait for the Government to save us from this crisis. We produce the garbage; we must solve the problem. In very practical, down to earth, concrete terms, here are some things we can do to reduce, recycle, and reuse.

First we must reduce the amount of garbage we produce. We can do this be refusing to buy products that are over packaged, like fast food that comes in styrafoam containers and chocolates that have a paper wrapping, a box, lining paper, a plastic tray for the candies, and foil wrap around each chocolate. By not purchasing such wasteful items, we say to the manufacturer, Either reduce the packaging in your product or lose business to your competition. We can also be less wastful in our own habits by carpooling, for example, or by using cloth diapers or biodegradable disposables.

We must recycle everything we can instead of sending it to the dump. Old cloths can be sent to the Salvation Army, the Scott mission, or other charitable organizations. As can furniture, appliances, books, and most other household items. There are dozens of ways to make useful items from packaging that would otherwise be thrown away, such as bird feeders from plastic jugs, braided rugs from old rags, and fire logs from newspapers. We don't need to consume as much as we do, and it won't hurt us to use things longer instead of buying new items before the old ones are completely worn out. Many companies now manufacture products from recycled goods, and we should be on the lookout for their products to support their efforts and to reduce the waste that is dumped into landfills.

Third, we can reuse most things. Composting vegetable garbage is a good way to put waste to valuable use. Or we can offer the things we no longer want to others through lawn sales and flea markets.

This is an absolute necessity. If we do not stop producing so much waste, we will inevitibly destroy our own enviornment. Unlike most efforts to improve things, the move to recycle, reuse, and reduce has one other advantage: it doesn't cost any money. In fact, it can save every household that practices it hundreds of dollars a year.

PART 4

Patterns of Essay Development

Introduction

College papers, like most professional writing, fall into three broad categories:

1. descriptive and narrative writing
2. expository writing
3. persuasive writing

These categories are not separate and distinct. In general-interest, business, and technical prose, they often overlap. (In fact, one could argue that *all* writing is persuasive, because all writing attempts to convince readers that the information presented is reasonable and true.) It is useful, however, to consider the three categories one at a time and to learn the techniques involved in each separately before you attempt to combine them in an essay or report.

All effective writing depends to some extent on *description* and *narration*, the subjects of the next two chapters. Whether you are describing the exact layout of a retail space you're designing or narrating your experiences at a professional conference, you'll find these techniques useful again and again.

Expository writing includes *process analysis, classification and division, cause and effect*, and *comparison and contrast*. These patterns of development are often required in on-the-job writing: Why is a component manufactured by one supplier better than the one made by another? Explain to a new employee how to perform a complex procedure. Why did sales decline in the last quarter? We look at the techniques involved in effective exposition in Chapters 11 to 16.

Chapter 17 focuses on *persuasive* writing, which has a wide variety of applications—from a letter of application to a marketing proposal; from sales letters to budget requests.

Each chapter begins with a definition of a particular prose pattern, together with an outline of its practical applications. Next, we offer tips on how to write that kind of paper and present four or five short examples, followed by questions designed to help you understand their structure and technique. The last selection in each chapter is a longer piece that illustrates the pattern used in combination with other writing strategies.

11

Description

Description covers many writing applications in academic and professional contexts. Architecture, interior design, biology, botany, anthropology, archaeology, engineering, criminology, and the health sciences are just some of the fields in which practitioners must be skilled in writing precise, concrete descriptions. A description is a verbal picture of an object, a scene, a person, or an event. In all descriptive writing, the objective is to provide readers with a picture of what it was like to be there.

By learning to write good description, you will become better at all kinds of writing. Enabling your readers see what you have seen, even in your imagination, is the essence of communication.

Tips on Writing Description

1. Engage all the senses, if possible: sight, sound, smell, touch, and taste.
2. Describe precisely, using words that create specific images. Don't say that something is "beautiful" or "impressive" or "wonderful" without telling your readers specifically how the object or event exhibits those qualities.
3. Select words with care. Never use a general word where a more specific, descriptive one could be used.

Example: The man walked toward the figure standing in the shadows.

Examples with specific words replacing general ones:
   The *detective crept* toward the *suspect lurking* in the shadows.
   The *old man hobbled* toward the *puppy cowering* in the shadows.
   Dirty Harry bounded toward the *villain crouching* in the shadows.

4. Choose a viewpoint for your description. As the describer, take a position and describe what you see from that spot. Tell what is visible from left to right or from far to near, or "walk" your readers around an object or along a defined pathway, but don't confuse them by changing your view point unnecessarily.

Read the following descriptive papers and answer the questions that follow each essay.

DIAMONDS ARE FOREVER

Brian Green

1   Toronto's Dome, Houston's Astrodome, and Florida's Tropicana Field are wonderful places for loyal subjects to pay homage to baseball's royalty. We can watch the game in air-conditioned comfort, fearing neither rain nor cold, just as though we were at home viewing the proceedings on TV. Whereas modern stadiums are fittingly lavish for highly paid major-leaguers to perform their feats, baseball for most Canadians has a much different atmosphere. Many of us have in common the sights, sounds, smells, and "feel" of the dirt diamonds, grass outfields, wooden bleachers, and hometown crowds of small-time baseball.

2   Where I grew up, baseball meant the hometown Star Cleaners in their white uniforms with red trim. The infield of our diamond was hard red clay, raked over and loosened prior to game time so that by the middle innings the players were covered in fine rust; latecomers could tell what inning it was by the degree of colour in the uniforms. A fastball would explode in the catcher's mitt in a satisfying cloud of dust, and a slide at second would sometimes be obscured from the bleacher crowd. In the early part of the season, the outfield grass was always bright green and as lush as a cemetery lawn. As the dry weather of August approached, however, brown patches would appear, until, by playoff time, the outfield was straw brown relieved by the odd green patch.

3   The newly mown outfield grass and, especially, the perfume of fried onions from the Lions Club snack bar behind the stands remain the most vivid scents of summer, and the thwack! of ball hitting leather the most exciting sound. The yelling of the hometown fans stirred excitement, and the hilarious jibes of the local wit in the back row of the bleachers brought comic relief, but the sounds on the field were what we were all there for. The smack of the bat on a well-hit ball, the umpire's guttural exclamations, the grunt of a player's effort, cries of encouragement from the players' benches: all these blended together in a happy symphony. But the slap of the ball into the leather of the first-baseman's glove, that breathless moment when so much is at stake—that's the sound that I crouched in the front row of the bleachers to hear.

4   Individual great plays still raise the hair on the back of my head when I recall them: "Moose" Christie catching a line drive in his bare, pitching hand; the reserve player/coach (his name now forgotten) who came off the bench in the sixteenth inning to hit a game-winning triple; my fifth-grade teacher, "Squirt" Dunsmore, striking out the side in the ninth inning; the entire, delirious game on a sunny Sunday when the Star Cleaners won the provincial championship. I love the Astros and Devil Rays and adore the Blue Jays, and I live and die with them all season long. But somehow, their game is plastic, artificial, and remote beside the baseball being played on dirt diamonds by men and women who play for the love of it.

Questions for Discussion

1. Sight, sound, smell, and touch are the senses engaged in this essay. Identify specific words the author has used to appeal to each of these senses.

    Sight: _____

    _____

    Sound: _____

    _____

    Smell: _____

    _____

    Touch: _____

    _____

2. From what viewpoint does the author describe his subject?
3. This essay has elements of comparison/contrast. How do they add to the description?
4. In the introduction, the author begins with a brief description of other places before shifting to the real theme of the essay. Is this an effective way to start? Why?
5. Draft an outline for the essay, listing the main and supporting points.

CAITHREAM[1]

Laurie MacEachern

1   As I let my eyes wander over this modern-day battlefield, I can feel a nervous flutter bubbling within me. The task at hand is rumoured to be the fruit of King Malcolm Canmore's defeat of MacBeth. Such was Canmore's joy

---

[1] Caithream, *n.* battle cry (Scots Gaelic)

that he laid his sword upon the earth, crossed his opponent's on top of it, and danced over them in victory. Soldiers later adopted the king's impromptu display of wartime success as their own pre-battle tradition and would foresee the results of upcoming battles in how well the sword dance was performed. Brushing a sword with your foot meant injury in combat, while kicking one meant certain death. Today, a misstep leads to a disqualification: an untimely end to the dancer's hopes and dreams stemming from years of diligent training. As such, the dance is an overwhelming and intimidating art, and many weary dancers have stood nervously, as I do now, readying themselves for the challenge ahead.

2   Suddenly, with the pipes droning in their broken breaths, I begin. I bow to the audience, thankful for their presence. Then, with choreographed precision, I step to my right and then to my left, addressing the swords as I move around them: a turn followed by another, an extension of the legs, and a leap all in succession. Despite my concentration, I hear a voice calling to me, although I cannot tell from where. "Put up your arms!" it says. I put them up, hold them above my head, and keep them firm with all the strength I can gather while I jump.

3   I lower my arms and repeat the sequence again before stepping forward and arching my foot, my internal voice instructing me to touch down with my toes and to place them—really place them, not hover them—in their rightful spots. I mustn't appear weak; I must assert myself, for I have no words: my voice is in my dance. But I'm tired now, and my legs can hardly bear my weight. I'm less than halfway through, and it's much too soon to be feeling the strain. Where's my energy? Where's my strength? No longer dancing outside the swords, but rather within them, I must double my efforts to make each movement sharp and strong. Too much is at stake now to risk a false step. I must go on, and I must do it well.

4   I struggle to take a deep, calming breath, clap, and begin a third sequence: the fast-paced anticlimactic ending to my minute-and-forty-second-long battle. With eyes downcast, I jump over the swords from quarter to quarter and across the centre, repeating the pattern until I find my way back to where I had started. I long for the voice to guide me through this moment, but it seems I am visibly alone as I think ahead to the final movement. I count the last four bars, taking solace in the music's familiar indication that the end is drawing near. Why should I play the Roman fool and die on my own sword? Having made it this far, I will not wave my white flag. I move away and into the final steps, lowering my arms and resting them on my hips as I do so.

5   One two three four and step, close, and bow.

Questions for Discussion

1. This essay describes a personal "battle" the author engaged in at some point in the past, yet she writes her account in the present tense. Why do you think she made this choice? (Hint: Rewrite the fourth paragraph in the past tense and contrast the effect with that of the original.)

2. The author begins with an analogy: she compares the modern art of sword dancing to its origins in the ancient art of warfare. While she does not use this analogy directly again, she continually draws us back to the idea of the dance as a battle. Identify at least three words, phrases, and images that metaphorically link "dance" and "battle."

3. In your own words, identify the thesis of this essay.

4. Punctuated according to traditional rules of grammar, the concluding sentence would read as follows: "One, two, three, four, and step, close, and bow." Why do you think the writer chose to punctuate the sentence the way she did? Is it an effective ending to this piece? Why? (In your answer, consider the style as well as the meaning of the sentence.)

5. Consult the InfoTrac database to find out more about the history and cultural lore of sword dancing. Note that keying "sword dance" in the title search line produces limited results. What keywords were effective in your own search? Which article did you find provided the most relevant information?

THE WHITE DARKNESS

Wade Davis

1   The challenge of travel is to find a way to isolate and understand the germ of a people, to measure and absorb the spirit of place. In Haiti one begins in Port-au-Prince. The capital lies prostrate across a low, hot, tropical plain at the head of a bay flanked on both sides by soaring mountains. Behind these mountains rise others, creating an illusion of space that absorbs Haiti's multitudes and softens the country's harshest statistic: a land mass of only ten thousand square miles inhabited by 6 million people. Port-au-Prince is a sprawling muddle of a city, on first encounter a carnival of civic chaos. A waterfront shantytown damp with laundry. Half-finished public monuments. Streets lined with *flamboyant* and the stench of fish and sweat, excrement and ash. Dazzling government buildings and a presidential palace so white that it

doesn't seem real. There are the cries and moans of the marketplace, the din of untuned engines, the reek of diesel fumes. It presents all the squalor and all the grace of any Caribbean capital.

2   Yet as you drive through the city for the first time, down by the docks perhaps, where the shanties face the gleaming cruise ships and men with legs like anvils haul carts loaded with bloody hides, notice something else. The people on the street don't walk, they flow, exuding pride. Physically, they are beautiful. They seem gay, jaunty, carefree. Washed clean by the afternoon rain, the entire city has a rakish charm. But there is more. In a land of material scarcity, the people adorn their lives with their imagination—discarded Coke cans become suitcases or trumpets, rubber tires are turned into shoes, buses transformed into kaleidoscopic *tap-taps*, moving exhibits of vibrant, naive art. And it isn't just how things appear, it is something in the air, something electric— a raw elemental energy not to be found elsewhere in the Americas. What you have found is the lens of Africa focused upon the New World.

Davis, Wade. "The White Darkness." *Shadows in the Sun: Essays on the Spirit of Place.* Edmonton: Lone Pine, 1992. 50–51.

Questions for Discussion

1. The author begins this piece by announcing its purpose in a subtle thesis statement. In the paragraphs that follow, find specific descriptive details that develop the "measure" and the "spirit" of Haiti.

2. What overall impression of Haiti does Davis convey? List at least five negative details and five positive details that contribute to this impression. What single sentence best sums up the paradoxical nature of this island?

3. Which of the physical senses does Davis appeal to in this verbal picture of Haiti? Give examples for each.

4. The first paragraph contains a number of sentence fragments. How do these fragments help contribute to the dominant impression the writer wishes to communicate?

5. What does the last sentence mean? Why is it an effective conclusion?

A NATIONAL BILLBOARD

Witold Rybczynski

1   An embassy is unique among building types. It is culturally and legally foreign, even though it may be a familiar part of the city. It is usually forbidding—not altogether private, nor yet really public; indeed, most people never

go inside an embassy, and when they do, it is likely to be that of another country, not their own. The first Canadian embassy that I visited was in New Delhi. I was not sure what to expect. Once through the front door, I felt immediately at home. Not only the familiar accents of the embassy staff but the furnishings—the desks and chairs, the pictures on the wall, even the staplers—were recognizably Canadian. The building itself made little impression; it was merely one more official edifice along embassy row, distinguished only by its maple-leaf flag and its Canadian diffidence.

2   On the other hand, visitors to the Canadian embassy in Washington, DC, cannot help noticing the architecture. Officially opened in 1989, this is an unusual design, an unusual embassy, . . . and, not the least, unusual for a building representing Canada.

3   The . . . embassy is, indeed, a very beautiful building. The walls, of cream-and-grey-streaked stone, are lovely; so are the hanging roses, azaleas, and hawthorn blossoms that cover the stepped-back façade inside the courtyard. The materials are assembled with great attention to detail. There are satisfactions for the ear as well as for the eye: a sheet of water spills over to sheathe the base of the rotunda and gurgles mysteriously into a gap beside the sidewalk. There is also the pleasure of movement—up a wide stair, between columns, and under the building—and of shifting views.

4   The twelve pillars of the rotunda are intended to symbolize the ten provinces and the two territories of Canada. As if anticipating Canadian expansion or subdivision, the circle is not quite closed—space is left for one or two more pillars. Oddly, the provincial pillars don't stand on solid ground but emerge from water, like islands. Is this a sly comment on the state of Canadian federalism? The rotunda is dwarfed by a row of six mammoth fluted columns inside the court. Here the symbolism is less clear. Do these represent the federal government? If so, why are these columns headless? And why do they support nothing more substantial than a giant planter?

5   The difficulty with the game that [architect] Erickson is playing is that it raises precisely such questions. The results demonstrate not so much the limits of his talent as the limits of the modernist approach, at which he is usually so adept. As a beautiful abstract sculpture, the building is a success; as a post-modern symbolic architectural statement, it sends ambiguous messages.

6   The interiors, by contrast, are strictly in the modernist idiom, which is to say cool, metallic, and, to my mind, uncongenial. There is a handsome semi-circular staircase, but the lobby is rather too splendid. It makes the casually attired staff and Bermuda-shorted visitors look out of place. The offices—and an embassy is really an office building—are unremarkable, except for the ambassador's suite, which is a concoction of puffy decor and cream-coloured leather furniture. I cannot image that it will be too long before they are replaced by dark wood panelling and sensible Georgian wing chairs.

7   As one approaches from the streets and climbs the stair leading to the court and the main entrance, which is marked by an unprepossessing, pyramid-roofed pavilion, the sequence is so smooth, so skilfully orchestrated, that one never notices the absence of a fence or gate, or of a barrier of any kind. When I visited, people were strolling around the court, children were throwing coins into the fountain, and two tourists were testing the acoustics of the rotunda dome. There were no members of the Protective Service (a uniformed division of the U.S. Secret Service) accosting loitering photographers, no security guards on view. As everyone knows, the land on which an embassy is built is extraterritorial, in this case a piece of Canada; here is a piece of Canada that is open even to the most casual passerby.

8   This unrestricted access is partially continued inside; there are a public art gallery and a library, also open to the public. The decision to make a large part of the embassy in effect a public place is a truly unusual one and required a range of security devices: strategically located checkpoints, zoned access, much bulletproof glass, and, I assume, a battery of hidden electronics. Whatever the cost of such gadgetry—and a spokesman for the Department of External Affairs would provide no figures, although he assured me that it was "not inexpensive"—it was well worth it. Such openness makes this embassy, as far as I know, unique, and both the client and the architect deserve much credit for the achievement.

Rybczynski, Witold. "A National Billboard." *Looking Around: A Journey through Architecture.* New York: HarperCollins, 1992. 167–72.

Questions for Discussion

1. The first two paragraphs constitute the introduction of this essay. The attention-getter contains a generalization about embassies and a short example of "usual" embassies. Sketch an outline of the rest of the piece, beginning with its thesis statement in paragraph 2. Which paragraphs develop the first main point? The second? Why is the third main point not developed separately from the others?

2. For what audience is this piece intended? Does the use of architectural jargon make the essay difficult for a layperson (a general reader) to understand? If you think it does, identify two or three examples of jargon that you, as a layperson, were not familiar with.

3. After reading this essay, do you have a clear picture of the Canadian embassy in Washington? Assuming the author's purpose was to enable you to picture the building's public space, could the description have been made more effective? What additional details would you need before you could draw a rough sketch of the exterior and the interior of the building?

4. Rybczynski mentions symbolism as part of his description. What architectural and design features in the Canadian embassy might be considered symbolic, and what do you think these features might symbolize?

Exercise 11.1*

In pairs, brainstorm at least 10 characteristics for any one of the persons listed below. Then, individually, write a paragraph about this person that incorporates at least seven of the characteristics you've identified by brainstorming. Share the results with your partner.

a petty criminal
a fitness instructor
your girlfriend/boyfriend, past or present
a small child
an accident victim

a grandparent
your favourite comedian
your present boss
a homeless person
a cafeteria or restaurant
   employee

Exercise 11.2

1. In pairs, identify a famous person, hero, or historical figure whom you and your partner know something about and are interested in.
2. Imagine that this famous person has recently been invited to write a description of a special place he or she recently visited. This piece will be posted on the person's website to be read by fans.
3. After you have finished your description, share it with another pair. Discuss how the writing is affected by the author's role, the intended audience, the subject, and the purpose of the piece.

Exercise 11.3

In pairs, select a site or a building that pertains to your career. Then, working alone, write a paragraph describing the physical appearance of the site or building. When you have finished, exchange papers with your partner and critique each other's descriptions. What similarities do you find in your two paragraphs? What differences? What accounts for these similarities and differences?

Exercise 11.4

To the paragraph you wrote in 11.3, add a paragraph describing the sounds, smells, and feelings (if any) you might experience if you were at the site or in the building you are describing. Again, share the results with your partner and discuss the similarities and differences between the details each of you chose to include.

Exercise 11.5

1. Write a paragraph describing a well-known contemporary man or woman. Do not name the person in your paragraph. The purpose of your description is to make him or her come alive for your reader. Specific details (including mannerisms, appearances, unique characteristics, activities) will bring the subject to life more than abstract descriptions of his or her personality, and a detailed physical description will help to convey a clear picture.

2. When you have completed your description, exchange papers with another student and see if you can identify each other's subjects. If you cannot, what additional details do you need to know?

12

Narration

Narration is the kind of writing you do when you want to tell your readers how something happened. The ability to write good narration is required in any career that draws on personal interviews in its practice or research. Social work, education, health sciences, and criminology are just a few examples.

Your purpose in telling a story may be to illustrate a point or to persuade, but all good narrative papers follow a basic pattern:

- The introduction presents a thesis or an overall theme for the story.
- The story unfolds, usually in chronological order, with sufficient detail and description that your readers can experience the events along with you.
- The conclusion brings the story to a satisfying end and reinforces its point.

Like description, narration is seldom found in its pure form in academic or professional writing. It is usually used in combination with other kinds of development. For example, explaining a process (how something works or is done) is a special kind of narration; explaining a cause–effect relationship frequently involves narration, as does arguing a position.

Almost everything you write will include at least some description and narration; that is why we are dealing with these two forms first. Because they depend on specific details for their effect, narration and description add interest to whatever kind of writing you do. They enable readers to *see* and *feel* what you are saying, and they make your ideas easier to understand and remember.

Tips on Writing Narration

1. The story you tell must have a clear purpose; it must have a point. Good narration tells who did what to whom, where, when, and how. It also states or clearly implies why the event or incident is significant. Remember: the subject of your essay is the point you are making, not the story you are telling.

2. Draft an outline of your story and then fill in descriptive details. Outlining will help you to arrange your events in chronological order and to group the events appropriately. Begin a new paragraph after a natural break in the narrative. Be sure to use transitions to ensure the coherence of your narrative. (See pages 102–04.)

3. Make sure that your opening paragraph introduces the scene and major characters fully enough that your readers are not confused. In your closing paragraph, draw the events of the story together to leave your readers with a feeling of satisfactory closure.

4. Dialogue is a common device in narration, but use it sparingly. Traditionally, each piece of dialogue is given a separate paragraph, so it takes up a lot of space. Paraphrase and summary are more efficient but less vivid.

5. Don't use so much description that events are drawn out beyond their natural length; you may make your readers impatient.

6. Don't try to include too many events in a short narrative.

Read the four narrations that follow and answer the questions after each one.

FROZEN TEARS

Michael Ruecker

1   I bolted into the house, slammed the door behind me, and started bawling. My teacher had let our class out five minutes late, and as I was walking alone across the vast, deserted fields between the school and my house, a monstrous sixth grader started chasing me. Somehow, I made it home safely, but I was still terrified. My dad appeared in the entranceway to the kitchen. "What's wrong?" he asked bluntly. I tried to answer, but, in my hysteria, I could barely string two words together. Dad interrupted immediately. "I can't understand you when you're crying like that. Now stop crying and tell me what's wrong." I tried to stop crying. I tried desperately. "Well, I'm not going to talk to you until you stop crying," Dad declared as he turned around and went back to the kitchen. I wiped my eyes and looked for my mom. She was still at the grocery store.

2   I was seven years old then, and still afraid of Dad. My three brothers and I learned at a very young age that if we needed comfort or assurance, Dad was not the person to look for. Consolation was Mom's responsibility: Dad was all business. If we had a question that required a simple answer, we could ask Dad, but when we had a more complex problem, we always sought out Mom. We were always wary about what we said to Dad since we never quite knew what would set him off. We wouldn't dare to argue with Dad; when something upset him, he would often become volatile. Luckily, he didn't get angry that day when I came home from school in tears, but even so, I was still fearful of him all the time. It wasn't the same gripping fear I had of the sixth grader; it was a more deep-seated, nagging fear that lingered in the back of my mind. Mom was the parent we trusted. Dad was the one we obeyed.

3   Mealtime was when the difference in our relationships with Mom and Dad was most apparent. For most of my life, Dad worked nights, so during the week we would always have supper without him. These meals were always unpredictable. Sometimes we would laugh so much we could barely find time to take a bite. Some nights Mom would ask us a question, and we would have a calm discussion as we ate. Some nights we ended up screaming at each other over incredibly inconsequential matters, such as what kind of cheese was on the pasta. Those meals were always more enjoyable than the ones with Dad. When Dad was there, we had to eat quietly and quickly. If we were laughing instead of eating, Dad would order us to stop. If we laughed again, he would start to yell. Sometimes one of us would start to cry, which only heightened Dad's anger. Meals were an agonizing chore for Dad; he wanted them over with as soon as possible, regardless of whether or not we had anything to do afterwards.

4   As I got older, I started to figure Dad out. I started to predict how he would react in certain situations, and I started to become less afraid of him. I still obeyed him, but more grudgingly and with more protest. If I felt sad, I turned my wretchedness into resentment. I taught myself to keep from crying. Though I didn't realize it, I was becoming like Dad. It was the only way to overcome my fear of him. I could tell that my brothers were awed by my behaviour, and it was probably that awe that gave me the courage to get into my first argument with Dad when I was eleven. Not surprisingly, it happened during a meal. I began to talk to my brothers about a particular episode of *The Simpsons,* and we started to laugh. Not only did Dad disapprove of the laughter, but he also had a vendetta against *The Simpsons* at the time, so this situation upset him more than usual. He firmly told us to be quiet and eat. My brothers were about to continue with their meal, but I said, "No." Dad became enraged. We started shouting at each other. He was adamant that because he was the father, I must never question his word; I tried to tell him that there was no reason for us not to have conversations during meals. I ended up being sent to my room. From there, I could hear a new argument beginning between Mom and Dad. Mom had taken my side.

5   Arguments like this one continued to happen periodically over the next few years. When I started high school, they got worse. Any time I couldn't see the reasoning behind one of Dad's commands, I would refuse to obey. Our arguments never led anywhere, of course, because I would demand to know the reasoning behind his orders while he would insist that I obey without a reason. By this point, my brothers were following my lead and also questioning Dad's authority. In addition, Mom would often take our side in these disagreements. Dad began to see us all, to some degree, as adversaries, and he fought to maintain the level of control he had once had over us. He would often step in to try to settle any minor dispute between me and my brothers, simply to assert his own authority. We all had problems with Dad during those years; however, I am certain that I was his biggest enemy. I had the most self-confidence and the least respect for his authority. I was no longer afraid of him; he was now afraid of me. While tensions would rise and fall between him and other members of the family, Dad and I were at odds throughout my high-school years, right up to the day I graduated.

6   Graduation day was a big deal for my family. The ceremony was on a sunny Saturday morning in June, and all sorts of relatives and friends came to my high-school gymnasium to witness the event. It was a pleasant ceremony, perhaps a bit long, but still enjoyable. When it was over, everyone went outside to mingle on the front lawn. I had won a few scholarships and awards, so everywhere I went, people were congratulating me. Grandparents, aunts, uncles, cousins, classmates, teachers, principles, pastors, parents of friends—it was all pretty overwhelming. People I didn't even recognize came running up to give me hugs. And through all this pandemonium, Dad was silent. He talked to a few other people, but he didn't say a word to me. Afterwards, we went to Pizza Hut for lunch with my grandparents. Dad and I sat at opposite ends of the table; still he said nothing. I noticed his silence, but it didn't really bother me. I figured that even if he did say something, his words would be impersonal and meaningless.

7   We went home in the afternoon; our class had our supper that evening, followed by our dance and after-grad, and I wanted to get some rest. I changed clothes and lay down on the couch in front of the TV. I was half asleep when Dad walked into the room. "Hi," he said. "I just wanted to say that I'm proud of you." I sat up and looked at him. His eyes were shifting around the room, and he was blinking rapidly. He swallowed hard and focused his eyes on me. "When your Dad feels like he's about to cry, you know it's a special occasion," he chuckled, and left the room. I was stunned. I had never imagined that anything could move my dad to tears. Not only that, he was crying because he was proud of me. My family left me alone for the rest of the afternoon, but I didn't get any sleep.

8   Since that day, my relationship with my father has been drastically different. We still don't talk about personal, emotional issues with each other, but we aren't at each other's throats all the time anymore. Dad was raised to

believe that the father is the head of the household, that the father's word is law, and it is obviously excruciatingly difficult for him to let go of those beliefs. I have realized that Dad is not cold and emotionless as I had once thought, but he feels that his role is to be a strong provider for our family. I decided a long time ago that when I have children, I will be a very different father than Dad was. I have also learned that by being the son he wants me to be, I can help my dad regain some of his pride in his manhood and fatherhood.

Questions for Discussion

1. In a sentence or two, summarize the point of this story. What is the author trying to convey to his audience? Do you think he has successfully communicated his thesis?
2. Only the father is directly quoted in this story. Why? How would the impact of the story change if the author had included direct quotations from his mother and/or one or more of his brothers?
3. The incidents that make up this narrative are presented in chronological order: we are told the author's experiences as (1) a little boy, (2) a preadolescent, and (3) a high-school graduate. Draft a rough outline that presents these incidents in a different time line: 3, 1, 2, or 2, 1, 3. How does the effect of the narrative change? What is gained or lost in the reordering of the author's experiences?
4. How does the behaviour of the parents in this essay compare to that of your own parents (or parent, if you grew up in a single-parent family)? Were they authoritarian, as the writer's father was, or permissive, like the writer's mother? Or did your parents adopt a collaborative approach to rearing you, involving you in decisions that affected the family? Write a short narrative essay that illustrates how your mother and/or father's parenting style shaped and influenced you.
5. Search the journals in InfoTrac to find out more about father–son relationships. Some of the articles you will find are sympathetic to the authoritarian father role. With this information in mind, reread "Frozen Tears" and write the story from the father's point of view.

BABA AND ME

Shandi Mitchell

1   In 1922, my father, at the age of two, came to Canada with his parents and five brothers and sisters from the Ukraine. They landed at Pier 21 in Halifax and headed west to homestead in northern Alberta. They lived in a sod and log house and suffered the prejudice of the times and the poverty of a barren

existence. Forty years later, I was born into a lower-middle-class Canadian existence.

2   In that short span, the Ukrainian culture had been lost to me. My Baba (grandmother) never learned to speak English and I knew no Ukrainian. She was as much a stranger to me as were her customs, foods, thoughts, and life. As a child, I was frightened of her.

3   I knew nothing of her past and none of her secrets. No one spoke of my grandfather. I remember the family visiting a weed-infested lot set aside from the main cemetery. It wasn't until many years later that I was told he had killed himself.

4   It was then 1938: the prairies were choking on dust and Baba was newly widowed, with six children to support. In the next town over, Old Man Kurik's wife had died in childbirth. And so began Baba's next marriage. The old man used the kids as field hands and boxing bags, excepting his own son, whom he schooled to become a "gentleman." Then World War II exploded. One by one all of Baba's children left for the cities. They ran from the wheat fields and their rich, decaying earth.

5   They ran to the plastic, shiny chrome worlds filled with starched sailors and armed forces personnel. They ran to heroes' deaths and cowards' retreats. They fell in love and became "Canadians" or "Americans." They changed their names and became Marshalls, Smiths, and Longs. They traveled the world and sent postcards back home to Baba. She saved the exotic images in a cookie tin under her bed. Eventually, even Baba and Old Man Kurik moved to town. Baba became a grandmother and was asked not to speak Ukrainian around her grandchildren.

6   Baba wrote letters in Ukrainian to the old country, but they remained unanswered. Undaunted by political barriers, she continued to save her pennies, quarters, and nickels for her visit home. She didn't believe that she wouldn't be let in. Her children shushed her when she spoke of her Communist brother. It was as if the world grew up around Baba. Then one day, she found herself a widow again. That morning, she opened every window and door in the house and breathed deeply. It was January.

7   My Baba got old in the seventies. Sometimes, she babysat my brother and me. My parents would drop us off for the weekend. I hated going there. She didn't speak any English, and I blocked out her Ukrainian. She dressed funny, she cooked funny, and she smelled of garlic. She tried to teach me about Ukrainian things. I didn't want to know. My friends were outside playing, the first McDonald's in town was opening down the street, and the Bay City Rollers had a new record. . . . I had better things to do than hang around with Baba. Back then, I didn't know the word "ashamed."

8   Baba didn't need English in the town where she lived. There were Ukrainian newspapers, TV and radio stations, stores, neighbours, churches

and all the essentials in this weed of a town poking up out of nowhere in northern Alberta. The town of 1600 was divided neatly into French in the north, Ukrainians in the south, Assiniboine in the east, English in the centre, and everyone else crammed into the west. It was in Baba's town that I first learned about poverty, alcoholism, domestic abuse, and racism.

9   When the old man next door died, his house was boarded up, and it became a popular place to sniff glue and drink aftershave. The neighbours pretended not to see. In the safety of daylight, we kids would venture in and gather up the few bottles amongst the cans and then cash them in at the confectionery for nickel candy. Once, we thought we'd found a dead body, but he had only passed out. Baba tended her garden, seemingly oblivious to the world next door, and kept on planning her trip home to the old country.

10   When the neighbourhood began to gentrify with condos and supermarkets and it was decided that Baba's best friend, Mrs. Westavich, couldn't keep her chickens anymore, Baba rallied to help her and used her precious savings in the process. When the two old women lost their battle, they took the chickens out to the front yard. Baba swung the axe while Mrs. Westavich held the birds down. They chopped their heads off one by one and let the birds' bodies flail and flop over the manicured lawns.

11   When the family decided it was best for Baba to go into a Home, there was no one left to fight for her. The first place was called Sunnyvale. The kids pulled her out from there when they found that she hadn't been bathed in a month and was covered in bed sores; also, her bank account was unaccountably low. Baba liked the new place better. She had a window box there, and grew tomatoes. I went to visit her, once. I called out, "Hi Baba!" and twenty wizened babas turned expectantly to me.

12   I hear Baba's house rents cheap now. The garden is filled with three cars up on blocks. I don't know what happened to her belongings. Her body is buried in Edmonton. I think the family felt it was a greater tribute to be buried in a city lot.

13   So here I sit in front of my computer with cell phone in hand and a coffeemaker brewing, and wonder about my grandmother. I have only one black and white photograph of her. She is squat and round, with huge breasts. She wears a cotton shift dress. Her nylon stockings are bunched at her ankles. A babushka covers her head. She stands shyly beside a shiny late-model 1950s car. Next to her is my mother, with dark glasses, over-sized sun hat, and wasp waist, posed very much like Greta Garbo. I stand at the edge of the frame, a skinny kid looking as if I'm about to run.

Mitchell, Shandi. "Baba and Me." *Confluence*. Edmonton: Grant MacEwan College, 2001. 53–55.

Questions for Discussion

1. What is the author's purpose in this essay, other than chronicling the life of her grandmother? State in one sentence what you think the purpose or "lesson" of the story is. How did the story affect you?
2. Identify the separate events of this story. In what order are they arranged? In point form, write an outline of the narrative.
3. What transitional techniques does the author use to link paragraphs 1 and 2? 4 and 5? 7 and 8?
4. The concluding paragraph is a description of a photograph. What do the specific details tell you about the people in the photograph: the grandmother, the mother, and the author as a child? What does the author imply about the relationship between these people?

THE TRAIN RIDE

Therese Y. Siemers

1   Willow River, B.C., a hamlet so small it isn't even on most road maps, is located about 20 miles from Prince George in the heart of huge, wild forests. Twenty years ago, life was simpler and slower-paced, and a car was almost a luxury. . . . Consequently, trains were still a central part of life in Willow River, and a train ride was an exciting treat for a five-year-old boy. People still took pride in their work, [found] time for the little things in life, and [showed] an interest in others' feelings.

2   . . . I can still picture the day I set out for the doctor's appointment, hurrying my two freshly scrubbed small sons, Benny and Dougie, over the path, through the stiff wire fence, to the tiny CNR way station. Catching the train was a risky adventure, and it was important to arrive before the only passenger-freight train whistled by at noon.

3   Nattily attired in their cowboy boots and matching shirts, heads topped with cowboy hats, shoulders squared, the boys led the way. As a special treat, they were allowed to bring their own considerable earnings which they had amassed selling pop bottles. Each had the huge sum of *one whole dollar*. Dougie entrusted his savings to my care, but Benny proudly patted the back pocket that contained his fortune in a brand-new plastic wallet.

4   The boys soon got restless waiting for the train and began exploring their surroundings. Through the deserted station's rooms, over the path, under the pilings, and over the railings they climbed to pass the time. Finally, the train arrived. [Nothing can compare to the excitement of a small boy rushing] to the edge of the elevated platform, holding a red flag to signal that huge, smoking monster diesel to a screeching, chugging, whistling stop. Holding

onto the railing, the boys were assisted up the steel steps by the conductor. We made our way up the long, narrow aisle to a seat. Slowly, the train started chugging on its way, and soon the conductor ambled down the aisle to collect [the fares]. As I dug into my purse for my wallet, Benny, not realizing that children under six travelled free, reached for his back pocket, proudly telling the conductor, "I have a dollar. I can pay for my own ticket!" To his dismay, he couldn't find the wallet. It was gone!

5   Slowly it sank in: the realization that he had no more wallet, no more money. He was going into town, and he couldn't get a treat. Bravely, Benny tried to make the best of it. He sighed, "Oh well, we can find it when we get back." Unhappily, I had to remind him that many other children played around the train station and that his wallet was unidentified. By the time we returned on the midnight train, there would be little hope of retrieving his wallet. I was trying to console my little boy when suddenly, . . . the train whistled, screeched, lurched and came to a grinding halt.

6   Everybody looked around, wondering why we had stopped. Then the train started to back up. Benny looked around with mounting interest. Realization dawned. Could it be possible? Was this mile-long freight train returning to the station? Dared he hope? Would the train back up as far as Willow River station? Was this just for him? The suspense was unbearable as the trees sped by. After what seemed an interminable time, the train slowed its backward journey and crept to a halt. The door of the very car we were in stopped directly in front of the station.

7   Wordlessly, the same conductor who had collected the fares strolled unhurriedly down the aisle. He reached the door, turned, and slowly descended the steps, still without saying a word. Excitedly, Benny crept up to the door. He watched, beaming. Sure enough, the conductor was looking around the station. And there it was, the little white wallet with the Indian chief on the front, just a few steps from where Benny had boarded the train. Slowly, deliberately, and with no hint of emotion, the conductor bent down . . . and picked up the wallet. He climbed back on board and silently returned the [prize] to Benny. Still no emotion crossed his face as he received a big hug from the ecstatic little boy.

8   Silently, this anonymous stranger, a conductor who had a job to do, who was responsible for keeping this passenger-freight train on schedule, made his way down the aisle: back to work, no more time for delays. But yes, something was there as he made his way down the aisle: just a hint, a ghost of a grin; the satisfaction of a job well done . . . and the immeasurable reward of a little boy's gratitude.

Siemers, Therese Y. "The Train Ride." *Contest: Essays by Canadian Students.* Ed. Murray McArthur. 3rd ed. Toronto: Harcourt, 1998. 54–56.

Questions for Discussion

1. Most narratives do not contain a fully developed thesis statement. (To be successful, a narration must involve suspense. If the reader knows at the outset what the ending will be, why would he or she bother reading on?) What about this piece? Identify the thesis statement and explain why the piece would (or would not) be less effective without it.
2. Siemers' essay is a story about a single incident. Is the effect of the piece limited to the reader's response to that single incident, or does the essay have a wider application? What point is Siemers making in this story?
3. Good films are based on strong narratives. Do the visual images in this story allow you to picture the scene and the action? Identify as many images as you can that would translate effectively to a film treatment of this story.
4. The story of the train ride ends in paragraph 7. What is the function of the last paragraph? Would the essay be equally effective if the author had not included paragraph 8? Why?

GROWING UP NATIVE
Carol Geddes

1   I remember it was cold. We were walking through a swamp near our home in the Yukon bush. Maybe it was fall and moose-hunting season. I don't know. I think I was about four years old at the time. The muskeg was too springy to walk on, so people were taking turns carrying me—passing me from one set of arms to another. The details about where we were are vague, but the memory of those arms and the feeling of acceptance I had is one of the most vivid memories of my childhood. It didn't matter who was carrying me—there was security in every pair of arms. That response to children is typical of the native community. It's the first thing I think of when I cast my mind back to the Yukon bush, where I was born and lived with my family.

2   I was six years old when we moved out of the bush, first to Teslin, where I had a hint of the problems native people face, then to Whitehorse, where there was unimaginable racism. Eventually I moved to Ottawa and Montreal, where I further discovered that to grow up native in Canada is to feel the sting of humiliation and the boot of discrimination. But it is also to experience the enviable security of an extended family and to learn to appreciate the richness of the heritage and traditions of a culture most North Americans have never been lucky enough to know. As a film-maker, I have tried to explore these contradictions, and our triumph over them, for the half-million aboriginals who are part of the tide of swelling independence of the First Nations today.

3   But I'm getting ahead of myself. If I'm to tell the story of what it's like to grow up native in northern Canada, I have to go back to the bush where I was born, because there's more to my story than the hurtful stereotyping that depicts Indian people as drunken welfare cases. Our area was known as 12-mile (it was 12 miles from another tiny village). There were about 40 people living there—including 25 kids, eight of them my brothers and sisters—in a sort of family compound. Each family had its own timber plank house for sleeping, and there was one large common kitchen area with gravel on the ground and a tent frame over it. Everybody would go there and cook meals together. In summer, my grandmother always had a smudge fire going to smoke fish and tan moose hides. I can remember the cosy warmth of the fire, the smell of good food, and always having someone to talk to. We kids had built-in playmates and would spend hours running in the bush, picking berries, building rafts on the lake and playing in abandoned mink cages.

4   One of the people in my village tells a story about the day the old lifestyle began to change. He had been away hunting in the bush for about a month. On his way back, he heard a strange sound coming from far away. He ran up the crest of a hill, looked over the top of it and saw a bulldozer. He had never seen or heard of such a thing before and he couldn't imagine what it was. We didn't have magazines or newspapers in our village, and the people didn't know that the Alaska Highway was being built as a defence against a presumed Japanese invasion during the Second World War. That was the beginning of the end of the Teslin Tlingit people's way of life. From that moment on, nothing turned back to the way it was. Although there were employment opportunities for my father and uncles, who were young men at the time, the speed and force with which the Alaska Highway rammed through the wilderness caused tremendous upheaval for Yukon native people.

5   It wasn't as though we'd never experienced change before. The Tlingit Nation, which I belong to, arrived in the Yukon from the Alaskan coast around the turn of the century. They were the middlemen and women between the Russian traders and the Yukon inland Indians. The Tlingit gained power and prestige by trading European products such as metal goods and cloth for the rich and varied furs so much in fashion in Europe. The Tlingit controlled Yukon trading because they controlled the trading routes through the high mountain passes. When trading ceased to be an effective means of survival, my grandparents began raising wild mink in cages. Mink prices were really high before and during the war, but afterwards the prices went plunging down. So, although the mink pens were still there when I was a little girl, my father mainly worked on highway construction and hunted in the bush. The Yukon was then, and still is in some ways, in a transitional period—from living off the land to getting into a European wage-based economy.

6   As a young child, I didn't see the full extent of the upheaval. I remember a lot of togetherness, a lot of happiness while we lived in the bush. There's a very strong sense of family in the native community, and a fondness for children, especially young children. Even today, it's like a special form of entertainment if someone brings a baby to visit. That sense of family is the one thing that has survived all the incredible difficulties native people have had. Throughout a time of tremendous problems, the extended family system has somehow lasted, providing a strong circle for people to survive in. When parents were struggling with alcoholism or had to go away to find work, when one of the many epidemics swept through the community, or when a marriage broke up and one parent left, aunts, uncles, and grandparents would try to fill those roles. It's been very important to me in terms of emotional support to be able to rely on my extended family. There are still times when such support keeps me going.

7   Life was much simpler when we lived in the bush. Although we were poor and wore the same clothes all year, we were warm enough and had plenty to eat. But even as a youngster, I began to be aware of some of the problems we would face later on. Travelling missionaries would come and impose themselves on us, for example. They'd sit at our campfire and read the Bible to us and lecture us about how we had to live a Christian life. I remember being very frightened by stories we heard about parents sending their kids away to live with white people who didn't have any children. We thought those people were mean and that if we were bad, we'd be sent away too. Of course, that was when social workers were scooping up native children and adopting them out to white families in the south. The consequences were usually disastrous for the children who were taken away—alienation, alcoholism, and suicide, among other things. I knew some of those kids. The survivors are still struggling to recover.

8   The residential schools were another source of misery for the kids. Although I didn't have to go, my brothers and sisters were there. They told stories about having their hair cut off in case they were carrying head lice, and of being forced to do hard chores without enough food to eat. They were told that the Indian culture was evil, that Indian people were bad, that their only hope was to be Christian. They had to stand up and say things like "I've found the Lord," when a teacher told them to speak. Sexual abuse was rampant in the residential school system.

9   By the time we moved to Whitehorse, I was excited about the idea of living in what I thought of as a big town. I'd had a taste of the outside world from books at school in Teslin (a town of 250 people), and I was tremendously curious about what life was like. I was hungry for experiences such as going to the circus. In fact, for a while, I was obsessed with stories and pic-

tures about the circus, but then when I was 12 and saw my first one, I was put off by the condition and treatment of the animals.

10   Going to school in Whitehorse was a shock. The clash of native and white values was confusing and frightening. Let me tell you a story. The older boys in our community were already accomplished hunters and fishermen, but since they had to trap beaver in the spring and hunt moose in the fall, and go out trapping in the winter as well, they missed a lot of school. We were all in one classroom and some of my very large teenage cousins had to sit squeezed into little desks. These guys couldn't read very well. We girls had been in school all along, so, of course, we were better readers. One day the teacher was trying to get one of the older boys to read. She was typical of the teachers at that time, insensitive and ignorant of cultural complexities. In an increasingly loud voice, she kept commanding him to "Read it, read it." He couldn't. He sat there completely still, but I could see that he was breaking into a sweat. The teacher then said, "Look, she can read it," and she pointed to me, indicating that I should stand up and read. For a young child to try to show up an older boy is wrong and totally contrary to native cultural values, so I refused. She told me to stand up and I did. My hands were trembling as I held my reader. She yelled at me to read and when I didn't she smashed her pointing stick on the desk to frighten me. In terror, I wet my pants. As I stood there fighting my tears of shame, she said I was disgusting and sent me home. I remember feeling this tremendous confusion, on top of my humiliation. We were always told the white teachers knew best, and so we had to do whatever they said at school. And yet I had a really strong sense of receiving mixed messages about what I was supposed to do in the community and what I was supposed to do at school.

11   Pretty soon I hated school. Moving to a predominantly white high school was even worse. We weren't allowed to join anything the white kids started. We were the butt of jokes because of our secondhand clothes and moose meat sandwiches. We were constantly being rejected. The prevailing attitude was that Indians were stupid. When it was time to make course choices in class—between typing and science, for example—they didn't even ask the native kids, they just put us all in typing. You get a really bad image of yourself in a situation like that. I bought into it. I thought we were awful. The whole experience was terribly undermining. Once, my grandmother gave me a pretty little pencil box. I walked into the classroom one day to find the word "squaw" carved on it. That night I burned it in the wood stove. I joined the tough crowd and by the time I was 15 years old, I was more likely to be leaning against the school smoking a cigarette than trying to join in. I was burned out from trying to join the system. The principal told my father there was no point in sending me back to school so, with a Grade 9 education, I started to work at a series of menial jobs.

12 Seven years later something happened to me that would change my life forever. I had moved to Ottawa with a man and was working as a waitress in a restaurant. One day, a friend invited me to her place for coffee. While I was there, she told me she was going to university in the fall and showed me her reading list. I'll never forget the minutes that followed. I was feeling vaguely envious of her and once again, inferior. I remember taking the paper in my hand, seeing the books on it and realizing, Oh, my God, I've read these books! It hit me like a thunderclap. I was stunned that books I had read were being read in university. University was for white kids, not native kids. We were too stupid, we didn't have the kind of mind it took to do those things. My eyes moved down the list, and my heart started beating faster and faster as I suddenly realized I could go to university, too!

13 My partner at the time was a loving supportive man who helped me in every way. I applied to the university immediately as a mature student but when I had to write Grade 9 on the application, I was sure they'd turn me down. They didn't. I graduated five years later, earning a Bachelor of Arts in English and philosophy (with distinction). . . .

14 Today, there's a glimmer of hope that more of us native people will overcome the obstacles that have tripped us up ever since we began sharing this land. Some say our cultures are going through a renaissance. Maybe that's true. Certainly there's a renewed interest in native dancing, acting, and singing, and in other cultural traditions. Even indigenous forms of government are becoming strong again. But we can't forget that the majority of native people live in urban areas and continue to suffer from alcohol and drug abuse and the plagues of a people who have lost their culture and have become lost themselves. And the welfare system is the insidious glue that holds together the machine of oppression of native people.

15 Too many non-native people have refused to try to understand the issues behind our land claims. They make complacent pronouncements such as "Go back to your bows and arrows and fish with spears if you want aboriginal rights. If not, give it up and assimilate into white Canadian culture." I don't agree with that. We need our culture, but there's no reason why we can't preserve it and have an automatic washing machine and a holiday in Mexico, as well.

16 The time has come for native people to make our own decisions. We need to have self-government. I have no illusions that it will be smooth sailing—there will be trial and error and further struggle. And if that means crawling before we can stand up and walk, so be it. We'll have to learn through experience.

17 While we're learning, we have a lot to teach and give to the world—a holistic philosophy, a way of living with the earth, not disposing of it. It is critical that we all learn from the elders that an individual is not more important than a forest; we know that we're here to live on and with the earth, not to subdue it.

18   The wheels are in motion for a revival, for change in the way native people are taking their place in Canada. I can see that we're equipped, we have the tools to do the work. We have an enormous number of smart, talented, moral Indian people. It's thrilling to be a part of this movement.

19   Someday, when I'm an elder, I'll tell the children the stories: about the bush, about the hard times, about the renaissance, and especially about the importance of knowing your place in your nation.

Geddes, Carol. "Growing Up Native." *Canadian Content.* Ed. Sarah Norton and Nell Waldman. 4th ed. Toronto: Harcourt, 2000. 41–46.

Questions for Discussion

1. What is the author's purpose in this essay? Which paragraphs most clearly state that purpose?
2. This narrative is filled with specific detail. Choose one paragraph and identify the details the author has included to help the reader form a vivid mental picture.
3. Look at paragraph 10. What does the anecdote in that paragraph tell you about the author? About her teacher? Find another anecdote in the essay that also illustrates the clash between two cultures.
4. A good narrative introduces the scene and major character(s) in the opening paragraph. Consider Geddes' first paragraph. Do you think it is effective? Why?
5. How does the concluding paragraph contribute to the unity of the piece?

Exercise 12.1

You hear narration every day when your friends, family, classmates, and teachers tell you about incidents that happened to them. Most of these are insignificant incidents that seemed important at the time but are soon forgotten. What makes a narrative memorable? What kinds of stories stick in your mind long after you have heard them? Why?

Exercise 12.2

Narration relies on the same principle as description in that it is a detailed account that appeals to the senses. However, effective narration goes a step further than description: it answers the question "What was it like to be there when this event happened?" Imagine yourself as a central figure in a career-related event. Write a paragraph that conveys to your readers some of the important details of the event and your thoughts as a participant. For example, you might choose to write about presenting a sales pitch to prospective clients; dealing with an angry, dissatisfied customer; or trying to help a member of your work team solve a problem he or she has with another member of the team.

Exercise 12.3

Using the same incident that you created in Exercise 12.2, write a third-person account of the event as a witness might have experienced it, perhaps as one of the clients in the first example, as another customer overhearing the discussion in the second example, or as another employee listening in on your conversation with your colleague.

Exercise 12.4

In good narration, the story told is often used as an example to illustrate a general theme. Briefly outline a story you might tell from personal experience to demonstrate one of the following themes, but do not name the theme.

frustration	the reward (or futility) of hard work
leadership	loss
fear	jealousy
peer pressure	injustice

Exercise 12.5

Using the outline you produced in Exercise 12.4, write a narrative paper. Remember that good stories are carefully planned and structured; poor ones are often the products of writers who begin at the top of the page and stumble downward until the story comes to an end. When you have completed your work, exchange papers with another student. Can you identify the point of each other's narratives—what theme the story is intended to illustrate? Discuss how each piece could be made more effective.

Exercise 12.6

Embarrassing incidents often make good narratives, both because most are entertaining and because listeners and readers can often learn a lesson from the embarrassing mistakes of others. Briefly outline, in point form, a narrative of the most embarrassing experience you have ever had. Use third-person pronouns (he/she); that is, outline the story as if it had happened to someone else. This may make a good paper when you are assigned a narrative to write. It might also be good therapy!

With a partner, identify a movie you have both seen and remember clearly. It's not important that you both like it; in fact, you may get better results if you disagree on the movie's merits. Working independently, narrate the plot of that movie, giving important details, not just the simple facts of the story. Try to make your paper as specific and vivid as the movie itself. Then exchange papers and critique each other's work. How similar are your plot outlines? What do you think might account for any differences?

Your life is full of experiences that you share with others: your first day at school, your first day at work, your wedding day, a memorable vacation, and so on. However, no two of these experiences are the same; each person's is unique. Below is a list of "first" or "last" or "only" experiences. Only you can narrate how yours happened. Plan and develop one of these events into a paper of approximately 300 to 500 words. Remember to focus on a limited time frame and to give most attention to highlights.

a speeding ticket	my first speech
my first car purchase	my first time skiing (or another sport)
an equipment failure	moving day
the last day on a job	the day my childhood ended
my first day in college	my first business venture

13

Process

Like narration, **process** writing explains events that follow one another in time. There are two kinds of process analysis: one instructs or directs the reader how to perform a task, the other informs the reader how something is done, is made, or works.

1. **Instructional/directional process:** When you explain how to get from the registrar's office to the resource centre, how to start a wet motor, how to make perfect pastry, or any other how-to topic, your purpose is to enable your readers to perform the process themselves. Giving instructions or directions is often done in point form: think of a recipe, for example, or the instructions that come with a child's toy, a barbecue, or a piece of furniture from Ikea. Instructions are usually written in the second person (*you*) and include commands (e.g., "Allow to dry for 10 minutes," "Leave yourself time to revise").

2. **Informational process:** This type of process analysis describes how something is done, or is made, or works. In explaining how hamburger gets from the farm to the table, how snowflakes form, or how the stock market operates, you do not expect your readers to be able to reproduce the process. Your purpose is simply to inform them about it.

Process analysis is usually written in the third person (e.g., "Wise writers leave plenty of time for revision") and often includes the passive voice ("When the paper has been edited, it is ready for submission"). The tone of your essay, and the amount and kind of detail you include, will vary depending on your audience and purpose.

Whether you are writing instructions or analysis, keep your language simple and clear. Remember that your readers probably do not share your expertise on the subject (if they did, they wouldn't be reading your explanation). If you use highly technical language or skip over steps that are obvious only to an expert, you will confuse or mislead your readers.

Consider the following instructions, written for inexperienced anglers who want to learn how to cast a fly:

> To execute the cast, play out about 10 metres of fly line in front of you. Ensure that there is no slack in the line, and begin your back cast. As the rod tip reaches about one o'clock, stop the backward motion and begin a crisp forward motion, loading the rod. On the back cast, the line must straighten behind you, parallel to the ground, before the forward motion begins.
>
> The quick forward thrust, stopping abruptly at about ten o'clock, will result in an aerodynamic loop that will travel the length of the fly line, straightening the line in front of you, and resulting in the perfect cast.

These directions break the process of fly casting down into chronologically arranged steps, but the writer has forgotten the most basic rule of good writing: remember the reader. Only someone who already knows what the writer is talking about would be able to follow these instructions.

An effective process paper, whether instruction or analysis, takes into account the readers' familiarity—or lack of it—with the process, their experience, and their level of vocabulary. Finally, it communicates the steps of the process in a way that holds the readers' interest.

One of the most challenging aspects of process analysis is making sure that you have included all the necessary steps. Only an expert, someone who knows what the result should look like, can leave out a step or two, or combine steps, or take shortcuts. As you write, try to imagine yourself in the reader's position: someone with little or no experience who is reading the instructions or description for the first time.

Tips on Writing Process Papers

1. Plan carefully. Prepare an outline listing all the steps of the process. Include everything that your readers need to know, and use language they can understand. Now put the steps in chronological or logical order. (See pages 57–59 for definitions and examples.) Be prepared to revise your list several times before your steps are arranged correctly. Too much detail can be as confusing as too little, so if there are many small steps, group them into a number of more easily manageable stages.
2. Write the introduction. State your purpose, and include any background information or theory (for example, identify any necessary equipment).
3. Write a thesis statement that makes it clear what your readers are about to learn. If it is appropriate, include a preview of the major steps you will describe. Consider the following examples.

The steps involved in becoming a winning tennis player can be summed up in four words: basics, practice, concentration, and attitude.

Getting married is a process that involves fulfilling arcane legal requirements, enduring an official ceremony, and surviving the abuse of one's in-laws.

For the executive chef, creating a signature dish is a process that involves selecting fresh, local ingredients, preparing them to bring out the best of their flavours in combination, and presenting the finished product with imagination and flair. (Niagara Culinary Institute)

4. Develop each step in a paragraph. Be sure to use transitions both within paragraphs and between paragraphs. Transitions help your reader follow the sequence of the process; they also make your writing easier to read. Review the list of transition techniques on pages 102–04 before you begin your essay.

5. Avoid shifts in person. Inexperienced writers often start with the third person and then switch to *you* and give commands. If you focus on your purpose—either to instruct or to inform—as you write, you will be less likely to use pronouns inconsistently.

6. Write the conclusion. Sometimes a brief summary is useful, especially if the process is a complex one. Alternatively, you could end your paper with an evaluation of the results, or remind your readers of the importance or usefulness of the process.

7. When revising, put yourself in the position of someone who knows nothing about the process and see if you can follow the instructions or description with ease. Have you included all the steps or stages? Have you defined any technical terms? Better yet, ask someone who really is a novice to read your paper and try to follow your directions or understand your description.

In the five essays that follow, you will find examples of both kinds of process analysis. Read each selection and answer the questions that follow.

HOW TO PLAY WINNING TENNIS

Brian Green

1   As a tennis instructor for the past three summers, I have watched many people waste their money on hi-tech racquets, designer outfits, and professional lessons, and then complain loudly that in spite of all the expense they still can't play the game. Unfortunately for them, a decent backhand is one thing that money can't buy. No matter what level of player you are, though,

or what level you wish to be, there are four steps to accomplishing the goal of winning tennis. They can be summed up in four words: basics, practice, concentration, and attitude.

2   All sports may be reduced to a few basic skills, which, if learned properly at the outset and drilled until they are instinctive, lead to success. Tennis is no exception; however, few people seem willing to spend the time needed to master the basics. Having been shown the proper grip and swing for a fore-hand, backhand, and serve, my students seem to feel they can qualify for Wimbledon. The basics are not learned that easily. Many tennis schools are now using a system developed in Spain that helps new players establish the correct stroke. For the first month of lessons, they aren't allowed to use a tennis ball. For that first month, correct positioning, proper swing, footwork, and technique are drilled without any of the distractions of keeping score, winning or losing, or chasing errant balls. That's how important the basics are to winning tennis.

3   Having acquired the basics, a beginning player must now practise and practise and practise to remember and refine those important skills. It isn't very much fun sometimes to play against a ball machine that never swears or sweats and doesn't care whether you hit a winning return. Drills and exercises won't do much for your social life while your friends are on the next court playing "pat-a-ball" with a couple of good-looking novices. Those basic strokes that you must keep hitting correctly hundreds of times a day aren't as impressive as the sexy spins and tricky between-the-legs shots the club players are perfecting . . . but if you're going to play winning tennis, practice is vital. Your feet must move instinctively to get you to the ball properly positioned for an effective stroke; a smooth backhand must become automatic from everywhere on the court; a crisp forehand, hit with accuracy, must be as nat-ural as breathing.

4   When you're finally ready for competition, everything seems calculated to make you forget all you've learned. It requires enormous concentration to shut out distractions and continue to practise the basics that are essential to your game: watch the ball, keep your head down, turn 90 degrees from the path of the ball, keep your feet moving, and so on and so on. With an opponent opposite you, people watching, and your own self-esteem on the line, it's difficult to keep your mind from wandering. Tennis is about 50 per-cent mental effort. Successful players are those who are able to block out dis-tractions and concentrate on making the racquet meet the ball with precision.

5   Finally, developing the proper attitude is the key to winning tennis. I define winning tennis as playing the game to the best of your ability, hitting the ball as well as you know you can, and enjoying the feeling of practised expertise. Winning tennis has little to do with beating an opponent. Naturally, if you play winning tennis by learning the basics, practising sufficiently, and con-centrating, you'll win many matches, but that is the reward of playing well,

not the reason for playing well. People who swear and throw their racquets when they lose are very useful; they are the most satisfying players to trounce. I don't understand why they play a game that gives them such pain. Tennis players who enjoy the feel of a well-hit ball and the satisfaction of a long, skillfully played rally are winners, regardless of the score.

Questions for Discussion

1. Describe the audience the author may have been thinking of. Consider their interests and goals.
2. What is the role of the author?
3. What are the main points the author covers in explaining the steps of improving performance in the game? Roughly outline the main and supporting points of this essay.
4. What functions does the introductory paragraph serve in this essay?
5. Discuss the final paragraph as an effective conclusion to the essay.

FORGING: THE BLACK ART
Paul Allen

1   The art of shaping metal by forging is as old as civilization itself. Its significance to human progress is evident in the names we give to historical periods: the Bronze Age, the Iron Age. Forging is the working of metals by heating them until they are pliable, and then hammering or pressing them into shapes. The process can be used to produce objects ranging from giant propellers to tiny manicure scissors. Whether the end product weighs tonnes or grams, the procedure is the same: the metal to be forged must be prepared, processed, and finished.

2   The first step in the process is to identify precisely the material to be forged and to determine its weight and grade. The carbon content and the presence of any alloying elements, such as nickel or molybdenum, will determine the temperature and duration of the heating process. Once the calculations are complete, the metal can be heated. While it heats to forging temperature (1200°C), any tools that are required for shaping should be prepared. Punches are needed if rings are being forged; blocks of varying thicknesses are required if bars or shafts are being formed.

3   Forging begins when all the preparations have been completed and the material has reached forging temperature. The part is removed from the furnace and taken to the forging hammer or press. Hammer forging involves shaping the metal by a series of swift blows; press forging squeezes the metal

into shape. Press forging is slower than hammer forging, but it can produce closer tolerances in shape and size.

4   Finishing is the final stage of the process. When a part has been forged, it must be inspected to ensure that it is precisely the right size and configuration. Inspection is crucial because if required tolerances are not met, the part may need to be forged again or scrapped. Manufacturers have good reasons for wanting to get the piece right the first time: the materials range from a few cents to $150 a kilogram, and labour costs are as high as $15 a minute. Once the forging has passed inspection, each piece is stamped with an identification mark such as the customer's name and order number. The part can now be allowed to cool before any finishing or fine shaping. Materials that may crack if they lose heat too quickly require slow cooling in a specially prepared furnace.

5   Forging is not just "metal beating," as some have described it; it is a complex operation requiring highly skilled workers. Metalworking is sometimes called "the black art," and the descriptor is apt. There is something magical about the transformation of a cold lump of steel into parts for a jet engine, a submarine, or a nuclear generator. To produce a high-quality forged part requires considerable skill and careful judgment. Neglect or carelessness in preparing, processing, or finishing means the loss of time, effort, and money.

Reprinted by permission of the author.

Questions for Discussion

1. What is the purpose of this essay? Is it intended to teach readers how to perform the process themselves? How do you know?
2. For what audience is this essay intended? How would the piece be different if the target readers were six to eight years old? Retired steelworkers?
3. What is the author's attitude toward forging? What clues provide an indication of this attitude?
4. Study the introductory and concluding paragraphs. Identify the attention-getter, the thesis statement, the summary, and the memorable statement. Are these clear? Effective? Why?

    How does the concluding paragraph contribute to the unity of the essay?
5. Not many readers are likely to be familiar with the process described in this essay. How has the author made his subject accessible to general readers?
6. An essay like this is often accompanied by photographs. Which points in the process would you like to see illustrated?

HOME OFFICE ERGONOMICS FROM A TO Z
Tina Verna

1   As a writer for a decorating magazine, I have the privilege of working at home. Aside from having to endure my own bad coffee, I find the solitude and flexibility suit me well. Recently I was asked to write an article on the concept of ergonomics for the home office. Ergonomics involves designing a tool, a piece of equipment, or a space so that it is both safe and efficient. As my research progressed, I became aware that some of the aches and pains I was experiencing might be resolved by making some ergonomic adjustments to my own work environment. So I put my research to practical use and set about designing a better organized, more efficient, and healthier workspace. If you are a student or a professional working from home, and you experience headaches, a sore neck, or pain in your wrists and forearms, you might consider doing the same. Re-evaluating your office furnishings, lighting, and the placement of key pieces of equipment can do much to alleviate work-related discomfort.

2   Your first consideration should be office furniture. It's easy to drag one of your kitchen chairs into your workspace, but it isn't a good idea. One of the most important items in an ergonomic office is a good chair. It should be stable and solid, with five floor rollers. All parts should be adjustable so that you can fine-tune the chair's height, tilt, angle, and armrests. Adjust the seat height so that your thighs are parallel to the floor when you are sitting at your desk. The chair should be firmly cushioned and its back should be wide enough to support your shoulders. If you can afford it, a chair with a high back or headrest is well worth the investment—your neck and shoulders will thank you! After you have selected an appropriate chair, the next thing to look for is a suitable office desk. It must be large enough to allow you to organize your workspace to minimize physical strain. Heavy objects and items that you use regularly should be placed within easy reach so that you can avoid unnecessary twisting and stretching. Rather than buying a desk from an office outlet, you might consider building in a custom-fit MDF board, cut to fill the available space and installed at just the right height for you and your computer. This option is surprisingly inexpensive, and if you design it yourself, you can ensure that the desk surface is deep enough to accommodate your most-used reference books behind and on either side of your computer. You can tuck filing cabinets, a wastebasket, and even the family dog underneath. A multi-purpose office desk, combined with a high-quality chair, can be costly, but so can regular visits to a chiropractor!

3   After you have selected appropriate furniture, the next item on your list of ergonomic "musts" is adequate lighting. Eyestrain is one of the most common hazards of working in a poorly designed environment. Bright natural

light glancing off your computer screen is very hard on the eyes. Install drapes or blinds to reduce the glare on your monitor. Thoughtfully designed artificial lighting is essential. Recessed lamps brighten a room without being hard on the eyes. Small, adjustable pot lights are good for illuminating specific work areas such as the computer monitor, keyboard, drafting table, and notepad. The new low-watt, long-life halogen bulbs provide full-spectrum, natural-looking light. Be sure to adjust these fixtures so that the light is directed at your work surfaces, not your eyes. Good lighting is essential to a comfortable work environment, eye health, and freedom from vision-related headaches.

4   Once you have designed your lighting strategy, give some thought to the placement of equipment. Where you sit in relation to the monitor and keyboard is critical. Be sure that the computer screen is slightly below eye level when you look straight ahead. You should sit approximately 50 to 60 cm away from the monitor, with your forearms parallel to the floor and your elbows bent at a 90-degree angle. Keyboard and mouse-related injuries are common problems that an ergonomic design can alleviate. Your wrists are the joints that are most susceptible to injury, so an adjustable, pullout tray that holds your keyboard and mouse is a good investment. With or without a tray, the ideal position for your keyboard is below your work surface and slightly tilted, so that when your fingers are on the keyboard, your wrists are in line with your forearms. Avoid bending, twisting, or straining your wrists while you work. If you spend most of your time at the keyboard, take regular breaks, relax your hands, flex your fingers, and go into the kitchen to make a cup of tea or get a beverage from the fridge. On a related note, the one piece of equipment that has benefited me more than any other is a headset that attaches to my phone. The headset leaves my hands free so that when I have to type and talk on the phone simultaneously, I no longer have to bend my neck at a painful angle to hold the phone between my ear and my shoulder.

5   A well-designed home office can help to diminish fatigue, physical stress, and the hazards of RSI (repetitive strain injury). But even the best office furniture, lighting, and equipment layout will not protect you from injury if you neglect your body. Wear comfortable clothing. Consciously sit upright, with your spine straight, and take periodic breaks to give your eyes a rest. Do a few spine, leg, and arm stretches every hour or so. Who cares if you're in your pyjamas? You're at home! Physical comfort, occasional exercise breaks, and a thoughtfully designed workspace will result in a healthier, happier, and more productive you.

Questions for Discussion

1. Why does this essay begin with personal information about the author? How is the reader affected by knowing that she writes for a decorating magazine and has experienced workspace-related "aches and pains"?

2. A good instructional process paper must provide enough information to enable the reader to follow the instructions without being overwhelmed by too much detail. Does this essay achieve that balance? Is any critical information missing? Are any details superfluous or distracting? Give examples to support your opinion.

3. When giving instructions, you need to motivate your readers to want to accomplish the goal of the process. How has this author attempted to motivate her audience to follow her directions? Find two or three examples. Are these motivational efforts successful? Why?

4. What sorts of transitional devices does the author use to maintain coherence within and between paragraphs? Identify at least five examples.

5. If you key the word "ergonomics" in the InfoTrac title search, you'll get more than 4,000 hits (and over 20,000 hits if you use the contents search). Clearly, ergonomics is an important issue in today's office and industrial environments. Find an article that deals specifically with the ergonomics of the home office and compare its advice with that given in this essay.

FIGHTING FIRE WITH FIRE

Zoe Zacharatos

1   Forest fires are generally considered destructive forces that should be prevented at all costs. Yet, fire can be a friend as well as a foe. Across Canada, forestry managers rely on prescribed burns in locations where fire does not occur naturally but can be useful in restoring the ecosystem. The term "prescribed burn" applies to fires that are set intentionally in a controlled environment in order to achieve a specific goal. The procedure can be remarkably successful when it is well planned, carefully prepared, and skillfully executed.

2   The planning stage is probably the most intensive and time-consuming part of a prescribed burn. The first step is to establish goals for the burn. What is the desired outcome? Reducing the potential hazard of wildfires by clearing underbrush and dead wood? Restoring a particular plant species? Preventing the spread of an infestation or disease? To ensure a safe and effective burn, fire experts carefully study the specifics of the target region and identify clear goals for its biosphere. They also examine the region's weather patterns and develop contingency plans in the event that the weather shifts unpredictably. The planning stage also involves gathering and testing equipment, educating staff, and obtaining necessary permits.

3   Once the goals and logistics of the burn have been determined, preparation of the land begins in earnest. A "fireguard"—the predetermined boundary that will contain the prescribed burn—must be meticulously prepared in advance. The fireguard might be a pre-existing boundary (such as a stream or road) or something that fire crews create by wetting the vegetation

that forms the perimeter of the burn area. Heavy fuels such as logs and dense brush are moved away from the fireguard to prevent the fire or sparks from jumping outside the boundaries. The preparation process also involves alerting local authorities (fire departments, police, etc.), community members, and businesses. In addition, fire specialists study weather-related data pertaining to both the day before the burn and the day of the burn; temperature, wind, and humidity all influence the success of a burn, so weather conditions must be exactly right.

4   Now comes the easy part: the burn itself. Typically, a "backfire" is started at one end of the prescribed area; where it is set depends on the direction of the wind and how many people are available to control the burn. Crew members are then dispatched to various points around the perimeter to light what are known as "flank fires." When the fire supervisor considers these to be burning safely, a "head fire" is lit to burn up the remaining fuel on the forest floor. (Each type of fire serves a specific purpose; hence each has a different name.) Fire crews watch the perimeter of the burn to ensure that it is well contained and actively monitor the burn area for several days after the fire to confirm that all flames, hot coals, and smoldering ashes have been extinguished.

5   There is no doubt that any type of fire poses risks. But ironically, our long-standing practice of suppressing and extinguishing wildfires has produced conditions that leave forests vulnerable to even more intense and dangerous blazes. Prescribed burning can reduce the hazard created by wood and brush build-ups by clearing fire-prone areas—a preventive measure that is particularly important near populated areas. Controlled fires can also be used to promote a healthy forest landscape in which threatened plant species (e.g., Ponderosa pine, white and black spruce) can regenerate, and to transform forest environments that were too dense with brush and fallen timber to support animal life into ecosystems in which animals can thrive. For hundreds of thousands of years, wildfires achieved these objectives, but not without cost: loss of human, animal, and plant life, as well as valuable timber. A successful burn helps sustain and improve our forest ecosystems without loss of life or property.

Questions for Discussion

1. This essay contains a great deal of information, most of it unfamiliar to the general public. What strategies does the author employ to make her information accessible to her readers? (Hint: Before looking at the paragraphs individually, write an outline of the information contained in the essay.)
2. What is the function of the first sentence in paragraph 3?
3. Identify three kinds of paragraph development that the author uses to support her main ideas.

4. Consider the last two sentences of paragraph 1. What is the function of each sentence?

5. Use InfoTrac to find four articles supporting the author's thesis that fires, contrary to their popular image as a destructive force, can help to regenerate forests.

A TREE-PLANTING PRIMER

Danny Irvine

Tape # 1: Introduction

1 "Welcome to the wonderful world of tree-planting. You are about to embark on an adventure of awesome proportions, fending for yourself in the coniferous Klondike—the very heartland of Canada. Are you intimidated? Don't be. You can rest assured that any stories you may have heard about the grueling savagery of the tree-planting experience, about inhospitable land-scapes, maimed bodies, and inhuman exhaustion are wild exaggerations, nothing more than hallucinations of former planters who are suffering the residual effects of some obscure psychological trauma.

2 "The wilderness is a nurturing, healing place, and it is well known that physical labour can be a contemplative, therapeutic activity. You can see its effects in the euphoria of the planters at the end of the season. Nevertheless, you may still be a little apprehensive about the planting contract and may feel somewhat alien in your new environment, so far away from the familiar com-fort of the city, with its paved roads and snowless summers, its docile elements and herbivorous wildlife. We encourage you to think of the North as your 'home away from home': the trees and rocks your walls and floors, the darkening clouds your vaulted ceiling, the bears and wolves your friendly neighbours. What's more, you have this primer, which is designed to help you to survive and to profit from your silvicultural experience."

Tape # 2: Equipment

3 "By this time, you will have been given your tree-planting equipment. Your planting bags—three pouches of high-tensile nylon, suspended from a padded, ergonomic belt and adjustable shoulder straps—are the first order of business. You will wear this set of bags all day, every day, for the duration of the contract. They will be your uniform, the armor of the noble tree planter; they will adorn and distinguish you; they will soak up your sweat and bear your scent. Think of them as indispensable articles of clothing, a sort of 'second underwear,' which you put on as soon as you awake and without which you never leave home. Do not get caught without your planting bags. Since this second underwear will be weighted with more than 20 kg of trees,

you will want to adjust the belt and shoulder straps to the position most closely approximating comfort. Ignore any uncomfortable chafing you may experience; this abrasion will soon become too familiar to be troublesome.

4   "The second piece of equipment: your shovel. Hold it in your hand. Grip it. Swing it. Can you feel the earth part before you? No? Swing it again. Hit something with it. This is no ordinary shovel; this is your livelihood. This is your weapon. This steel-spaded, wood-shafted, D-handled shovel is the instrument with which you will split the earth and subdue the forests. It will be your trusty machete when you encounter obstructive branches and brush. It will be your means of carving yourself bathroom facilities when you are miles from civilization. It will be your sure defense in the event of an encounter with squirrels, raccoons, or small, sickly black bears. For these rea- sons, it is important that you respect your shovel. Never let it out of your sight. Take care of it. Name it. Talk to it. It will be your best and only friend in the long days of solitude out on the clear-cut. At first, your shovel may feel awkward and heavy, but after several weeks of continuously gripping it, you will feel as if it were a fifth limb. You and your shovel will form such a bond that you will find it almost unbearably painful to unclench your grip at night."

Tape # 3: Getting Started

5   "Once you have familiarized yourself with your equipment, you are ready to plant. To begin, put your planting bags around your waist. If the belt slips, readjust it. If it continues to slip, duct-tape the straps together. If even duct tape fails to maintain a fit, the problem is probably faulty belt buckles. Find a fellow planter with undamaged bags and inconspicuously swap your bag for hers. Write your name on your new bag with a waterproof magic-marker and avoid that planter for a few days.

6   "Next, decide how many trees you are willing to carry in one trip, and load up your bags. This is not a casual decision. On the one hand, since you are being paid per tree, there is financial reward in carrying as many trees as you can squeeze into your bags. On the other hand, a heavy load will weigh and slow you down. You will tire quickly, and you will not be able to stop for a rest until your bags are fully unloaded. What's that? You don't plan on taking any breaks? That's the attitude! Heavy or light: you must find a middle road. Forestry is, after all, fundamentally a matter of balance: harvesting lumber without decimating the sustainable forests, planting new growth without destabilizing the ecosystem, working harder than a machine without destroying your body, keeping the bugs away without developing cancer from insect repellent.

7   "Once you have packed up your trees, scan the area and pick up any trees you may have inadvertently dropped. The forestry company has paid a good deal of money for these trees, and you will find that they get quite upset if they discover any lying on the ground. Throw any fallen trees into your bag, or, alternatively, onto the ground where another planter has been working.

8   "Packing up your trees, or 'bagging up,' as you will become conditioned to call it, can, admittedly, be a time-consuming procedure. Having to sit in one place to perform it can be particularly irritating if it happens to be raining or snowing; if it happens to be in the frigid early months or the scorching later months of the season; or if the blackflies, mosquitoes, horseflies, or deerflies happen to be out. But never mind. Having packed up your bags, knowing precisely how many trees you are carrying, you are ready to go. What? You didn't keep track of how many you put in? Well, you'd better take them all out and count again.

9   "Once you have confirmed your count, take your shovel in your right or left hand, whichever is the stronger. This will be your 'shovel hand'; your weaker hand will be your 'bag hand.' Your bag hand is the hand that will pick up and plant each tree; that is why you have put the trees into the pouch on that same side. What? You didn't know this, and put the trees into the pouch on the side of your stronger hand? Well, you'd better take them all out and start again.

10   "Your bags strapped and loaded, your shovel firmly gripped, you are at long last ready to plant your first tree. Make your way to the piece of land, 'the block,' that has been allotted to you. The block may be a short, convenient distance from your tree depot. More often, however, you will have a long hike to get to the entrance to your land. You may be compensated if this travel time is unusually lengthy or particularly grueling. But don't count on it. Your employer is more likely to consider this trek an opportunity for you to explore the untamed wilderness and reflect on your contribution to the development of our country's sustainable resources."

Tape # 4: Planting a Tree

11   "Planting a tree is an art that requires control and precision and, for many individuals, takes years to learn. In Japan, for instance, bonsai-tree planters are chosen while they are still infants and taken to mountain pagodas, where they spend their youth in rigorous training under the tutelage of revered masters. Each day they spend hours in the forest, learning respect for the trees; they participate in disciplined physical exercises, developing scrupulous control of their bodies; and only after seven years of bare-handed labour in the stony Japanese soil are they permitted to handle a shovel.

12   "You, on the other hand, have the good fortune to live in a much less demanding culture. With this guide to help you, you can easily learn to plant a tree without years of arduous training. To be a successful tree planter, you need to learn two things. First, you must understand and accept the essential, organic, and spiritual union of body and land—a dynamic, beautiful marriage of arms, legs, back, and shovel with tree and soil. Second, you must learn to harness and relentlessly exploit this union for your own purposes.

13   "Begin by retrieving a tree from your bag with (you guessed it) your bag hand. At the same time, step forward with the corresponding leg, pinpoint the spot where you wish to plant a tree, and, with your shovel hand, raise your shovel.

14   "This is probably a good point at which to discuss generating and maintaining motivation and morale while out on the clear-cut. As everyone knows, a certain degree of mental fortitude is helpful when you are repeatedly performing even the simplest of tasks. The oppressive, dark, and forbidding clouds that perpetually crowd the skies this far north may already have suggested to you that not every planting day will be a sunny outing in the woods. Some planters have even experienced moments of mild discouragement at their work.

15   "If ever you should feel a twinge of despair over your ability to fulfil the planting contract, to meet the quota of trees that you have set as a standard for yourself; if ever you are worried that you will not earn enough money to pay off your student debts and will have to sell the family heirlooms to pay your tuition; if you have been planting in a swamp for three weeks and have not spoken to another soul for days; if you notice the extremities of your body turning numb from the cold, from insect bites, or from the pesticides on the trees; if the zipper on your tent has torn and your boots have holes in them and your leg is broken and infected and your girlfriend or boyfriend has stopped writing letters and your mother has forgotten about you and rented out your room to a new son or daughter and you are on the verge of impaling yourself on your own planting shovel, do not be dismayed. Stop. Look about you at the miles of muddied and overturned land, at the endless expanse of barren clear-cut, at the infinitely distant and uncompromising sky, and reflect on your relative insignificance. Remember that compared to the immensity and mysterious purposefulness of the universe, your life and worries are inconsequential. Then, your mind cleared and reinvigorated, take a deep breath, and get back to work.

16   "So, with your shovel aloft in your shovel hand, and with a tree in your tree hand, take a second step forward—this time with your other leg, the one that corresponds to your shovel hand. Bring down your shovel with a swift, heavy stroke, stabbing the blade into the earth as deeply as possible. If your shovel doesn't penetrate the surface, it is likely that you have struck a rock or some sort of impervious sun-fired clay. Nevertheless, you must plant a tree as close to this spot as you can. Move to the next nearest planting spot. If the soil in this location visibly leeches water when you step on it, it is too wet and will drown your tree. Move to the next closest location. If this one is within two metres of a tree that has somehow miraculously survived the clear-cutting, bulldozing, and chemical spraying that has otherwise sterilized the land, keep moving. Eventually, you will find a patch of acceptable soil, a sufficiently rotten stump, or a sizable pile of bear droppings in which to plant your tree.

17   "With your shovel plunged in the earth, take the third and final step, again with the leg that corresponds to your bag hand. Twist the D-handle of your shovel away from you in a wide outward arc, laying open a hole in the ground, and, with the tree still in your bag hand, bend down over your

shovel. Poke the roots of the tree into the freshly dug hole and hold the seedling in place while pulling your shovel from the soil. As you straighten your back, slide your fingers up the length of the tree until they gently grip the tip. Remember, the needles of the trees are laced with pesticides, so avoid pricking your fingers. Once you are upright, close the hole by lightly stomping on the ground immediately beside the tree. Finally, give the seedling a small tug to ensure that it is snug in the soil.

18   "Congratulations! You have planted your first tree. Know that you are following in a great human tradition, one that began when agricultural man first informed the flora and fauna of the world that he knew better than they did how and where they should grow. Since then, humankind has been proudly asserting its place in the natural world and now you, too, are a part of this noble history. Your father and mother are every farmer who ever pressed a seed into the soil, every gardener who ever ripped a weed from its bed, every farm hand who ever forced a bit into a horse's mouth.

19   "All that stands between you and fortune are three easy steps, a swift bend, and a few fluid motions with your shovel—repeated three or four thousand times a day. You have planted your standard. Eventually, one tree at a time, you will own the North.

20   "Unless, of course, your tree is not within the two- or three-millimetre margin of depth; unless it is leaning; unless it is crooked, or its roots are not straight; unless it is less or more than the permitted distance from any other tree, natural or planted; unless the tree is unhealthy, diseased, smothered by loose dirt or missing its tip; or if, as you filled the hole, it got stepped on, or . . ."

Reprinted by permission of the author.

Questions for Discussion

1. What is a "primer"? Is this essay is a good example of a primer? Why? Find at least five examples of words you are unfamiliar with and look up their definitions.

2. The author assumes the role of an expert providing instructions and advice to the reader, but is this in fact an instructional process? Does the author really intend to teach readers how to succeed as tree planters? If not, what is his true purpose?

3. In an essay not intended to be taken seriously, the author uses sophisticated vocabulary and many long, convoluted, sentences. Why? What is the effect of the contrast between the stated subject—a simple process—and the formal, complex style in which the subject is explained?

4. List, in order, the steps in planting a tree. Why does the author provide so much descriptive detail about each step? Does it overwhelm the reader? What purpose does it serve, if not to explain how to plant a tree?

5. After 13 paragraphs of instruction that bring us to the point of actually planting a tree, the author suddenly breaks off and begins discussing how to maintain "motivation and morale while out on the clear-cut." Why? What are the effects of this digression?

6. Paragraph 15 opens with a 12-line run-on sentence. The author stops punctuating the clauses about two-thirds of the way through the sentence. Why? How does the structure of the sentence reinforce its content?

7. Consider the author's concluding paragraphs. Identify the summary. There is no real conclusion to this essay; the last sentence is deliberately incomplete. Why? Given the author's purpose, is this ending effective?

Exercise 13.1

It is five years in the future, and you are an internationally recognized leader in your chosen field. A national news magazine wants a short biography highlighting how you got to where you are. Write an informational analysis of your rise to fame.

Exercise 13.2

You have some expertise that is not shared by others. Your skill may be making friends, serving customers, eating spaghetti, or designing web pages. Choose an activity at which you excel and write a short instructional process essay that describes how to do what you do so well.

Exercise 13.3

Write a process essay on one of the following topics or on any topic of your choice, so long as it requires an explanation of *how* to do something or *how* something works. Review the tips on pages 171–72 before you begin.

How my family came to Canada
How to cope with stress
How to perform well in a job interview
How to get fired
How to get along in a language you don't speak
How to cure a hangover
How not to treat a babysitter
How to get a bargain
How a biological process works (e.g., how skin heals, how the lungs function)
How a fuel cell works (or any other mechanical, chemical, or electronic device)

14

Classification and Division

Classification and **division** are based on our instinct to arrange and analyze things. We group like things into categories or classes, and we separate the component parts of something in order to understand them better. For example:

- College students could be grouped into undergraduates and graduates (classification).
- An undergraduate class might be divided by programs or majors such as engineering, nursing, arts and science, and so on (division).
- Food on a restaurant menu is listed in categories such as appetizers, entrées, desserts, and beverages (classification).
- A meal is divided into courses: soup, salad, entrée, dessert (division).

The process of **definition** involves both classification and division. We define a concept (e.g., a good student) by identifying the features or characteristics that are shared by all members of the class to which it belongs: a good student is one who is motivated, hard-working, and creative. Writing a classification paper requires grouping similar things together to identify them as belonging to one of several categories. Writing a division paper requires examining one entity and breaking it down into constituent parts or features or characteristics. Here are some examples of classification and division topics:

Classification

Saturday a.m. TV
- cartoons
- sports shows
- interview programs

Division

Saturday a.m. TV
- infantile
- infuriating
- informative

Classification		Division	
Patients doctors hate to treat	• clingers • deniers • demanders	The ideal patient	• cooperative • knowledgeable • self-disciplined
Types of bad parents	• overprotective • uninterested • disengaged	A good parent	• kind • firm • consistent

Tips on Writing Classification and Division Essays

1. The key to a good paper is choosing your main points carefully. Make sure that all points are of approximately equal significance and that the points do not overlap.
2. If you have deliberately left out some aspects of the subject, briefly let your readers know this and why you have limited your discussion. Some topics are too complex to discuss exhaustively in a short paper. You are better off discussing a few representative points in detail than skimming over all the categories or components.
3. Your thesis statement should set out your subject and its main points, as in the following examples.

Inanimate objects can be classified into three major categories—those that don't work, those that break down, and those that get lost.

An appropriate wardrobe for work consists of outfits that are comfortable, easy to maintain, and, within limits, distinctive.

Our softball team is made up of has-beens, might-have-beens, and never-weres.

The following five essays illustrate classification and division. In the first essay, the writer explains her subject by dividing it into its main features. The two pieces that follow show how subjects (here, men and methods of conflict resolution) can be classified into categories. Next comes an essay on the characteristics of good news blogs. The last essay analyzes the ingredients of a consumer product. Read the essays and then answer the questions that follow.

ON-THE-JOB TRAINING
Alice Tam

1   What can you expect from your first job after you leave college? As a recent graduate from a technical program, I entered the workforce fully prepared to do the job I was hired to perform. What I was *not* prepared for were some of the expectations and challenges posed by my employer, my coworkers, and—surprisingly—myself.

2   During the hiring process, the employer makes sure that you have the knowledge and skills that the position calls for. However, once you are on the job, you will discover that he or she has many other expectations of you as well. Basic job requirements such as being on time should come as no surprise, but volunteering for tasks outside working hours, cheerfully taking on additional responsibilities, and demonstrating work habits that go beyond the basic requirements of the job are all unspoken expectations that employers have of new employees. In my first month on the job, I attended a managers' weekend retreat; joined the company's health and safety committee and United Way campaign; and, on the advice of my supervisor, accepted an offer to serve on my college program's advisory board. My social life suffered, but I felt that I was becoming a valued member of the company's management team.

3   Coworkers present a different challenge. Those who did not attend college may question the value of your diploma or degree; they learned the business the hard way, on the job, and they want you to know that your "book learning" will carry you only so far. You will cope with this hostility more easily if you understand that it is caused by insecurity. Many employees feel intimidated by colleagues who have qualifications they lack; their aggressive stance is their defence. Even those whose college or university days are long behind them may display this attitude. If you show them that you are willing to learn from their experience, you will prove to them that you have the skills and attitude the job requires. One of the unwritten responsibilities of any job is earning the respect of your colleagues. This is not an easy task. It requires time and humility, but, in the long run, it is critical to be an accepted part of the team. Outsiders don't get past the first or second rung on the long ladder to career success.

4   Finally, your expectations of yourself may surprise you. In your first job out of college, the stakes are higher than any you have ever experienced. The pressure to succeed can create real stress and even hamper your performance. One of the grads who was hired the same month that I was became so nervous about doing well that he couldn't make decisions in case he was wrong, wouldn't take on extra jobs in case he couldn't handle them, and drove himself (and those around him) crazy by compulsively checking and

rechecking everything he did to be sure he hadn't made a mistake. As a new employee, you should expect some performance anxiety. The best way to deal with it is to channel it productively by working extra hours or volunteering for charity work until you develop the confidence to be satisfied with just doing your best at your job.

5   I celebrated my first year as a full-time employee just a month ago, and when I look back on the past year, I can't believe how fast it has gone or how much I have learned. Because of my college training, I certainly had the ability to do the job, but it has taken me almost the full year to become comfortable with the culture and attitudes of the workplace and to get my own expectations under control. I wish I'd been given this essay to read while I was in school, and I hope it will be helpful to you!

Questions for Discussion

1. This essay is clearly and precisely organized. Draft a point-form outline for it (follow the format in Chapter 6, page 72).

2. Drawing on your own work experience, do you agree that a critical part of on-the-job training is learning how to fit in with your colleagues, even if it means extra time (e.g., volunteering for community or charity work) and extraordinary patience (e.g., holding your tongue when coworkers belittle your education)?

3. The author uses all three pronoun "persons" in this essay. She writes about her own experience in the first person ("I"); addresses the reader in the second person ("you"); and describes the behaviour of a colleague in the third person ("he"). Why do you think Tam has chosen to vary her point of view in this way? Would her essay be more effective if she had told her story as a first-person narrative, or as a second-person instructional process, or as a third-person division analysis? Support your opinion with evidence from the essay.

4. Use InfoTrac to find at least one article that supports the author's view of her first year on the job and at least one article that contradicts this view. Briefly summarize the main points of each article.

OF MEN AND MACHINES IN THE 21ST CENTURY

Francine LaPlante

1   [1]There has got to be a better way! [2]The North American system of mate selection, dating, is so inefficient and fraught with embarrassing perils that I wonder why it works even as often as it does. [3]If we were forced to select cars

using the same methods we employ to choose a mate, few of us would bother driving. [4]Imagine buying a vehicle you were allowed to test drive only under certain restrictions: no manual, no performance reviews, no information on reliability, maintenance costs, major repairs, or previous owners—what you see is what you get. [5]Dates and cars have a few basic things in common: a body, an image, some kind of motive power, and, if you're lucky, insurance. [6]Reflecting on these similarities got me thinking about further parallels, and I've concluded that cars and dates can be classified into three general types: the econo-box, the SUV, and the exotic sports model.

2   [7]The econo-box is the least a car can be. [8]It features a no-frills interior, bland exterior design, and lack of power. [9]Similarly, the econo-date lacks charm or personality, is undistinguished in appearance, and lacks anything resembling authority or charisma. [10]The problem is not that he doesn't have a lot of money to spend; it's that he doesn't use any imagination or creativity to compensate for his lack of cash. [11]Heck, the old Beetle, the Citroen CV, even the original Mini were cheap, but they had imagination, personality, pizzazz! [12]The econo-date's interests are comic books, computers, and Star Wars movies; he is quiet, unassertive, and about as much fun as an oil leak. [13]Ironically, his ambition is often as lofty as it is futile: when he grows up, he'd like to be an SUV.

3   [14]The SUV is more than a car ought to be, at least on the outside. [15]Its muscular skin, monstrous size, and ridiculously large engine suggest the rugged outdoors, but in reality it's a commuter vehicle for insecure drivers who are afraid of bumping into something and getting hurt. [16]So it is with the SUV date. [17]He's big, ruggedly handsome, loud, and aggressive, but he has the sensitivity of a bumper and the brains of a hubcap. [18]He'll buy you an expensive but ordinary meal, then tip lavishly for poor service, all the while confident that he's impressing you. [19]He is showy, aggressive, and sure he's the best thing that could happen to you. [20]Unfortunately, he can't talk about anything except himself and (occasionally) sports. [21]He aspires to a career in real estate so he can spend most of his time playing golf. [22]The SUV date dwells on top of his world and feels inferior to nothing and no one—except an exotic sports type.

4   [23]The exotic sports car is expensive, sophisticated, smooth, gorgeous, fast, and temperamental. [24]While there is an undeniable initial thrill to driving one, that thrill quickly wears off with the outrageous loan payments, the breathtakingly expensive (and frequent) repairs, and winter driving conditions. [25]These are seasonal cars: good for six months of the year at most. [26]The exotic date is also a showpiece. [27]You'll be the envy of all your friends for a while. [28]But you will soon learn that your function in the relationship is to be impressed, to stroke his vanity, to adore. [29]He is so aware of his superiority that he treats most creatures who cross his path as dust beneath his wheels. [30]He's also unreliable. [31]As often as not, he has another commitment—per-

haps to his club, his friends, or his travels abroad. [32]There's nothing wrong with Jaguars, Porsches, or Lamborghinis, but you'd better have deep pockets, unlimited patience, and consummate driving skills to handle one. [33]My mother used to say, "Handsome is as handsome does," and the exotic sports model date is a prime example of what she meant.

5   [34]If these comments sound pessimistic, I guess perhaps they are. [35]If only dates came with professional performance reviews, websites that outlined their merits and faults, and the observations of previous owners about their idiosyncrasies and upkeep! [36]If only we could research a potential mate as thoroughly and carefully as we select a car! [37]Given the randomness of our dating system, my fear is that I'll end up with something with the power of an econo-box, the maneuverability of an SUV, and the maintenance costs of a sports car.

Questions for Discussion

1. What audience did the writer have in mind for this essay? Identify four or five characteristics that the intended readers would be likely to have in common.

2. This essay is based on analogy. It comments on different kinds of men by describing them in terms of cars. Keeping in mind that the author intends to be humorous, do you find the analogies accurate? Are they effective for the target audience? Would they be likely to offend some readers? Why?

3. The conclusion makes a serious point. What is it? In your opinion, does it qualify as a "memorable" statement?

4. Use InfoTrac to find articles that review two or three new cars in different categories (e.g., a luxury sedan, a hybrid car, or a Smart car). Using the author's technique as a model, develop analogies of your own between the characteristics of the automobiles you've chosen and the personalities of dates you've known or friends you've had.

METHODS OF CONFLICT RESOLUTION
Eva Tihanyi

1   Imagine you are the supervisor of a call centre that employs a full-time staff of 40 telephone sales representatives. During the past few months, there has been an increase in employee requests for schedule changes in order to accommodate personal needs. These employees, of course, would prefer not to lose pay, so they want to make sure they work their regular number of

weekly hours. Unfortunately, the growing number of schedule changes is having an adverse effect, creating confusion and inconvenience for you, the payroll department, and the employees in general. You, as the person in charge, recognize that you must deal with this situation quickly and fairly—before it escalates. There are four methods of conflict resolution to consider: deference, competition, compromise, or co-operation.

2   If the scheduling issue is not a major one, you might opt to defer; in other words, "let the other side win." Employees could continue to ask for schedule changes as they saw fit, and you would do your best to accommodate them and ignore the inconvenience. Maintaining employee morale would be more important than enforcing a smooth scheduling process.

3   If, on the other hand, you view the scheduling issue as so important that it must be resolved to the company's advantage, you will want to exercise your authority and insist on a no-change policy. Employees would be assigned to particular shifts, and if they wanted time off, they would have to take it without pay. There would be no re-scheduling. This is a competitive approach, one which ensures that you "win" while the other side "loses"—and one which also ensures that your relationship with the "losers" will be tarnished.

4   A more empathetic way of managing the situation would be to compromise. You could circulate a memo in which you laid out parameters, specific guidelines for how and when schedule changes could occur. This would allow some flexibility, but would at the same time limit the frequency and nature of schedule change requests. In this way, both you (i.e., the company) and the employees would "win"—partially. Both sides would get a part of what they wanted, but both would also lose a part. And so long as both sides were satisfied, this could be an effective solution.

5   Finally, if you're a supervisor who believes in the concept of mutual benefit, in the notion that it's possible for both sides to "win," you will choose the method of co-operation. You and the employees might brainstorm the scheduling issue together and in the process discover new ways in which it might be settled to the satisfaction of both sides—not compromise, but resolution. Because co-operation produces no "loser," it fosters an atmosphere of trust and respect; and, although certainly more time-consuming than the other three methods, it is generally the best way to encourage goodwill in the workplace.

6   Deference, competition, compromise, and co-operation are all viable ways of handling conflict. The one you choose will most likely depend on how significant the issue is, how much time you have to deal with it, to what extent you value employee morale, and what the word "winning" means to you.

Tihanyi, Eva. "Methods of Conflict Resolution." 1999.

Questions for Discussion

1. What introductory strategy does the author use to set up her thesis? (See pages 111–14 for a review of eight different ways to introduce an essay.) A good introduction intrigues readers, involves them in the subject, and makes them want to read on. How does Tihanyi's introductory paragraph accomplish these goals?

2. Describe the audience this writer had in mind: approximate age, level of education, special interests, and any other details you can.

3. One of the reasons this essay is so easy to read is that the author has structured it very carefully. She outlines the problem in paragraph 1, then offers four different solutions to the problem, using a single pattern of development, in paragraphs 2 to 5. For each possible solution, she offers a definition, remarks on the practical effects of its implementation, and comments on how the implementation would affect company morale. Identify these three components in paragraphs 2, 3, 4, and 5.

4. Another reason this essay is easy to read is that the author has made skillful use of transitional devices. Turn to pages 102–04 to review the five transitional techniques that an author can employ. Which ones does Tihanyi employ in this essay? Identify one example of each technique.

5. In Chapter 9, you learned that a good conclusion should (a) summarize or reinforce the main points of the paper and (b) end with a memorable statement. Does Tihanyi's conclusion satisfy these criteria?

THE BEAUTY OF BLOGS

Jody Moritsugu

1   "Blog": such an ugly word to describe a beautiful and powerful phenomenon. A blog—short for "weblog"—is a personal, professional, or political journal that is posted on the Internet. The activity of maintaining a blog is known as "blogging"; "bloggers" are people who write online dissections of subjects ranging from Alberta and Alzheimer's to Zaire and Zambonis; and the "blogosphere" is the community of all blogs on the World Wide Web. What explains the growing international audience for blogs? The news blogs that I participate in provide some clues: they present a forum for stimulating, immediate, and democratic communication that is increasingly missing from conventional media.

2   You might think that reading other people's opinions is boring, but if a blog is well researched and well written, the ideas it presents can be illuminating. A good blogger pays close attention to the news of the day—a time-consuming

task in our information-saturated world—and then publishes an alternative analysis: interpreting, making connections, and drawing conclusions not found in mainstream sources. The blogs I read often contain information not covered by traditional news media, partly because of time and space limitations imposed on network news outlets and partly because of political restrictions. The Internet has no such limits or restrictions.

3   One of the most appealing features of blogs is their immediacy. Blogs are dynamic, real-time sources of information. Bloggers can respond virtually instantly to any event; some routinely post their opinions several times a day. The liveliest blogs give readers the opportunity to post their own messages—messages that, unlike the letters to the editor found in traditional print media, are not edited for content or length. The opportunity for online dialogue engages readers more deeply than the one-way communication offered by mass media.

4   Beyond the immediacy and ever-changing forum of ideas and information they offer, blogs have the potential to be vehicles for genuine democracy. Blogging is revolutionizing the way people worldwide get and distribute information. In stark contrast to the authoritarian, "voice of God" stance adopted by most mass media, blogs encourage a wide range of voices to speak up and be heard. Bloggers can post anything they wish (so long as they observe the laws governing hate messages or child pornography, for example). In the blogosphere, there are no gatekeepers to distort or limit information, no editors to chop your prose to pieces, no owners whose political biases must be catered to. Such unfettered freedom of speech is not without risk, but once you learn how to separate the well-informed, trustworthy blogs from the uninformed rubbish—and there is lots of it—you gain access to dynamic, thought-provoking media sources that can be just as (if not more) reliable than the increasingly scandal-plagued traditional print and electronic media.

5   Good blogs are intellectually challenging, dynamic, and current. They provide forums for debate and discussion, a precondition for democracy. Blogs give ordinary people like you and me the power of information and the opportunity to share our opinions with the rest of the world.

Questions for Discussion

1. Who are the author's intended readers? What is her purpose in writing this essay?
2. Summarize this essay in a one-sentence thesis statement that includes both the author's thesis and her main points.
3. The term "blog" is a fairly new addition to the English language: it was first used in 1999 and did not appear in a major dictionary until 2004. How does the author ensure that her readers understand the meaning of blog and its related terms?

4. Are you a blog enthusiast? If so, what kinds of blogs do you monitor and/or contribute to? How reliable is the information presented on these blogs? What are your criteria for evaluating their reliability?

5. Use InfoTrac to find five or six articles that express opinions about blogs. Are the majority of the articles you found pro-blog or anti-blog? How do the opinions they express about blogs differ from Moritsugu's views?

PUCKER UP

David Bodanis

1   Until quite recently, respectable women did not wear make-up. Colour on the face suggested passion, and passion was what they were supposed to avoid. Shortly after the First World War, lipstick was referred to as only being appropriate "to repair the ravages of time and disease on the complexion of coquettes." They were probably the only ones to put up with it, too, as it was then little more than a greasy rouge, containing crushed and dried insect corpses for colouring, beeswax for stiffness, and olive oil to help it flow—this latter having the unfortunate tendency to go rancid several hours after use. The New York Board of Health considered banning lipstick in 1924, not because of what it might do to the women who wore it, but because of worry that it might poison the men who kissed the women who wore it.

2   For the liberated woman of today, the product has been transformed, re-thought, entirely remade. Insect corpses have been expunged as a barbarity; beeswax and olive oil have been rejected too. What goes in tubes of lipstick today is only what the best of late 20th century cosmetic science can devise.

3   At the centre of the modern lipstick is acid. Nothing else will burn a colouring sufficiently deeply into the lips for it to stay. The acid starts out orange, then sizzles into the living skin cells and transforms into a deep red where it sticks to them. Everything else in lipstick is there just to get the acid into place.

4   First, it has to be spread. Perhaps at some time you've noticed children playing with softened food shortening, smearing it over their faces. Such shortening (hydrogenated vegetable oil, as in Crisco) spreads very well, and accordingly is one of the substances found mixed in with almost all lipsticks on the market. Soap smears well too, and so some of that is added as well.

5   Unfortunately, neither soap nor shortening are good at actually taking up the all-crucial acid that's needed to do the dyeing. Only one smearable substance will do this to any extent: castor oil. Good, cheap castor oil, used in varnishes and laxatives, is one of the largest ingredients by bulk in every lipstick, from the finest French marks on down. The acid soaks into the castor oil,

the castor oil spreads on the lips with the soap and shortening, and so, through this intermediary, the acid is carried where it needs to go.

6   If lipstick could be sold in modified shortening jars or castor oil bottles, there would be no need for the next major ingredient. But the whims of the lip-conscious consumer do not allow for such ease of packaging; the mix has to be sold in another form. It must be transformed into a rigid, streamlined stick, and to do that nothing is better than heavy petroleum-based wax. Such wax can soak up the shortening, soap, and acid-impregnated castor oil, and it will still have enough stability in its micro-crystalline structure to stand up firm. It's what provides the "stick" in lipstick.

7   Of course, certain precautions have to be taken in combining all these substances. If the user ever got a sniff of what was in there (all that castor oil) there might be some problems in continuing consumer acceptance. So a perfume is poured in at the manufacturing stage before all the oils have cooled—when the future cosmetic is still what the engineers call a "molten lipstick mass." At the same time, food preservatives are poured in the mass, because apart from smelling rather strongly, the oil in there would go rancid . . . without some protection.

8   All that's lacking now is the glisten. Women who smear on lipstick expect to get some glisten for their troubles, and their wishes do not go unheeded. When the preservatives and perfume are pouring, something shiny, colourful, almost iridescent—and, happily enough, not even too expensive—is added. That something is fish scales. [They are] easily available from the leftovers of commercial fish packing stations. The scales are soaked in ammonia then bunged in with everything else.

9   Is that it then? Shortening, soap, castor oil, petroleum wax, perfume, food preservatives, and fish scales? Not entirely. There is still one thing missing: the colour. The orange acid that burns into the lips only turns red on contact. That means another dye has to be added to the lipstick, a soothing and suggestive red one this time, so that what you see in the tube looks at least vaguely lip colour and not a horrifying orange-juice orange. Which means, if you think about it, that the red dye you see in the tube has only a little to do with the colour that's going to end up on your lips.

Bodanis, David. *The Secret House: 24 Hours in the Strange and Unexpected World in Which We Spend Our Days and Nights.* New York: Simon & Schuster, 1986. 45–47.

Questions for Discussion

1. This essay analyzes lipstick by dividing it into its component parts. Identify each ingredient and the paragraph(s) in which it is described.

2. Why did the author not reveal in the thesis statement the aspects of the topic that are described in the body paragraphs of the essay? What would the effect on the reader have been if the author had named all the ingredients up front?

3. Identify six or seven examples of the author's use of vivid descriptive details to help communicate key points. Bodanis uses words that are very different from those we are familiar with in advertisements that describe the same product. What effect does the author's diction have on the reader?

4. Identify two or three specific examples of the author's ironic humour. How would you describe the tone of this piece? Do you find the tone appealing or alienating? Why?

5. What was the author's purpose in writing this piece? Is there a serious intent behind the obvious fun he had in shocking his readers?

Exercise 14.1

This exercise is designed to improve your skill in identifying *unity* within classification or division. In each of the following thesis statements, cross out any irrelevant, insignificant, or overlapping points.

1. A good teacher doesn't bark at the students, give last-minute assignments, study for a test the night before, or grade unfairly.

2. Computer applications commonly used in business environments include word processors, spreadsheets, CD-ROMs, and database managers.

3. A journalist has four major tasks: to report news accurately, to entertain with social information, to collect a big salary, and to resist government control of information.

4. Finding the right career depends on careful planning: getting all the education you can, continually monitoring your enthusiasms and interests, being flexible enough to shift focus as circumstances change, and having luck on your side.

5. The music I enjoy can be divided into five distinct categories: blues, jazz, light rock, vocal, hip hop, and rap.

6. Newspapers are my main source of information. At least twice a week I read the *Halifax Gazette*, *Le Devoir*, *The Globe and Mail*, and *People* magazine.

7. It's not easy to work for a perfectionist. She wants perfect results, twice the work in half the time, unpaid overtime, and memos for everything.

Exercise 14.2

Humans have a strong instinct to classify everything including themselves. List at least seven classifications (groups or categories) to which you belong.

Exercise 14.3

To help explain what things are, we usually divide them into their constituent parts. For each of the following terms, list four or five characteristics that would help to define it. After discussion, agree on the best three.

- a good manager/team leader/coach
- a good résumé
- an ideal vacation
- a worthwhile college course
- a good talk show (TV or radio)

Exercise 14.4

Select one of the terms you used in Exercise 14.3 and expand your list of characteristics into an essay.

Exercise 14.5

Think of an example of a test question on a recent exam that required you to classify or divide in order to explain, or make up a possible test question that would require a classification or division essay in response.

Exercise 14.6

Sports analogies are very common ("He can't get to first base," or "Just when she was making the right moves, she dropped the ball"). For each of the following subjects, give an analogy and an example that would enhance your readers' understanding in a classification or division essay.

Subject	Analogy	Example
Overwork	electronics	When the brain's circuits are overloaded, a fuse can blow, resulting in nervous breakdown.

Physical fitness   auto mechanics   _____

_____

_____

Marriage   a journey   _____

_____

_____

The aging process   _____   _____

_____

_____

Exercise 14.7

Focus each of the following general topics into a specific subject suited to a classification or division paper. For each, identify three types or categories; or three parts, characteristics, functions, or features.

Restaurants   Subject _____
- _____
- _____
- _____

Managers   Subject _____
- _____
- _____
- _____

Television   Subject _____
commercials
- _____
- _____
- _____

Drivers   Subject _____
- _____
- _____
- _____

Computer   Subject _____
experts
- _____
- _____
- _____

Exercise 14.8

Here is an outline for an essay on the characteristics necessary for career success. The thesis statement and main points are provided. Working in pairs, fill in appropriate topic sentences and support. When you are both satisfied, turn your outlines into full essays and compare your results.

Career Success

Attention-getter _____

_____

_____

Thesis statement To be successful in your career, you must prepare adequately in college, work hard on the job, and communicate well with employers, colleagues, and the public.

1. Topic sentence: _____
(Preparation)

_____

_____

Support _____

_____

_____

2. Topic sentence: _____
(Hard work)

_____

_____

Support _____

_____

_____

3. Topic sentence: _____
(Communication)

_____

Support _____

_____

_____

_____

_____

_____

_____   *Summary*

_____

_____   *Memorable
statement*

_____

_____ **Exercise 14.9**

Write an essay on one of the following subjects.

The main kinds, types, or categories of	• employees • believers • sports fans • small businesses • movies • alternative medicine practitioners • body piercing
The characteristics of	• an ideal job • an ideal marriage • a bad movie • a successful interview • a good employer • a good web page • an average Canadian
The component parts of	• an oral presentation • a citizenship hearing • a love affair • a winning hockey team • a golf swing (or slap shot, or save, etc.) • a business plan • a religious service or ceremony

15

Comparison and Contrast

If you are focusing on the similarities between two things (or ideas or concepts or points of view), you are writing a **comparison**. If you are focusing on the differences, you are writing a **contrast**. Most people, however, use the term "comparison" to cover both (as in "comparison shopping"), and similarities *and* differences are often discussed together in a paper.

You can choose from two approaches when you are organizing a comparison. In the first option, you discuss one item fully and then turn to the other item. This approach is called the **block method** of organizing. The alternative option is to compare your two items **point by point**. For example, suppose you decided to compare Russell Crowe and Brad Pitt. You might identify the following three points:

- physical appearance
- acting technique
- on-camera heroics

Using the block method, you would first consider Crowe in terms of these three points; then you would do the same for Pitt. You would need to outline only four paragraphs for your essay:

1. Introduction
2. Crowe's physical appearance, acting technique, and on-camera heroics
3. Pitt's physical appearance, acting technique, and on-camera heroics
4. Conclusion

The block method works best in short papers, where the points of comparison are easy to understand and remember. As comparisons get more complex, your readers will be able to understand your points better if you present them point by point. You would then need to write an outline of five paragraphs for your essay:

1. Introduction
2. Physical appearance of Crowe and Pitt
3. Acting technique of Crowe and Pitt
4. On-camera heroics of Crowe and Pitt
5. Conclusion

The introductory paragraph in the comparison essay usually tells readers what two things are to be assessed and what criteria will be used to assess them. The concluding paragraph may (or may not) reveal a preference for one over the other.

Tips on Writing a Comparison or Contrast

1. Make sure that the two items you have chosen are appropriately paired; to make a satisfactory comparison, they must have something in common. Both might be baseball teams or world leaders; but to compare the Toronto Blue Jays and the Calgary Stampeders or to contrast Queen Elizabeth and your Aunt Agatha would be futile and meaningless.
2. Your main points must apply equally to both items. Reject main points that apply to one and have only limited application to the other. For example, in a comparison of digital and analog instruments, a category for dial configuration would be pointless.
3. Your thesis statement should clearly present the two items to be compared and the basis for their comparison. Consider these examples.

   E-mail and interoffice memos differ not only in format but also in style and purpose.

   The major points of comparison in automobiles are performance, comfort, and economy, so I applied these factors to the two cars in the running for my dollars: the Saturn and the Mazda 3.

4. Use transitional words and phrases within and between paragraphs to provide coherence. (See pages 102–04.)

The following four examples demonstrate different approaches to writing comparisons and contrasts. After reading each essay, answer the questions that follow it.

THE CANADIAN CLIMATE
D'Arcy McHale

1   The student who comes to Canada from a tropical country is usually prepared for cold Canadian winters, a sharp contrast to our hot northern summers. What the student may not be prepared for is the fact that Canadian
personalities reflect the country's temperature range but are less extreme.
Canadian personalities fall into two categories: warm and cool. The two
groups share the Canadian traits of restraint and willingness to compromise,
but they are dissimilar in their attitudes both to their own country and to the
foreign student's country of origin.

2   Warm Canadians are, first of all, warm about Canada and will, at the first
sound of a foreign accent, describe with rapture the magnificence of the
country from the Maritimes to the West Coast, praising the beauty of the
Prairies, the Rockies, and even the "unique climate of the Far North."
Canadian leisure activities are enthusiastically described with a special place
reserved for hockey. "So you've never skated? You'll learn. Come with us;
you'll have a great time." The Warm Canadian wants the newcomer to share
in the pleasures of life in Canada. When she turns her attention to the foreign
student's homeland, she seeks enlightenment, asking questions about its
geography, social and economic conditions, and other concerns not usually
addressed in travel and tourism brochures. The Warm Canadian understands
that the residents of tropical countries are not exotic flower children who sing
and dance with natural rhythm but are individuals who, like Canadians, face
the problems of earning a living and raising a family.

3   Compared to the Warm Canadian, who exudes a springlike optimism, the
Cool Canadian is like November. Conditions may not be unbearable for the
moment, but they are bound to get much colder before there is any sign of
a thaw. The Cool Canadian's first words on hearing that the foreign student is
from a warm country are, "How could you leave such a lovely climate to come
to a place like this?" Not from him will one hear of Banff, or Niagara Falls, or
anything except how cold and dark and dreary it gets in the winter. It sometimes seems that the Cool Canadian's description of his own country is
designed to encourage foreign students to pack their bags and return home
at once. As for the foreign student's country of origin, the Cool Canadian is
not really interested, although he may declare, "I hear it's beautiful. I'd love
to go there." Beyond that, however, he has no interest in information that
may shake the foundations of his collection of myths, half-truths, and geographic inaccuracies. This type of Canadian, if he does travel to a tropical
country, will ensure that he remains at all times within the safe confines of his
hotel and that he returns to Canada with all his preconceived ideas intact.

4   Foreign students should not be upset by the Cool Canadian; they should
ignore his chilliness. Besides, like a heat wave in March, an unexpected thaw

can occur and create extraordinary warmth. Likewise, a Warm Canadian may become a little frosty sometimes, but, like a cold spell in June, this condition won't last. And when the weather changes, foreign students will find an opportunity to display their own qualities of understanding, tolerance, and acceptance of others as they are.

Reprinted by permission of the author.

Questions for Discussion

1. What are the main points of contrast in "The Canadian Climate"?
2. Which method of contrast has the author chosen for the subject, block or point by point?
3. Why did the author choose this approach? Would the essay work as well if it were organized the other way? Outline the main points of contrast as they would look in the other format.
4. What other points of contrast between the two kinds of Canadians can you think of?
5. What audience does the author have in mind? How do you think Canadians would respond to this essay? Foreign students?

SHOPPING AROUND

Aniko Hencz

1 The word "shopping" inspires visions of crowded, airless malls, aggressive salespeople, whining children, and weary feet. Some consumers embrace the ritual chaos while others recoil in horror. For the mall-weary shopper, help has arrived in the form of the Internet. Online shopping has exploded in recent years and now offers a viable alternative to the bricks-and-mortar experience. However, as my partner and I discovered recently, when it comes to selection, service, pricing, and convenience, there are significant differences between the two options. Which should you choose? It depends on your priorities.

2 Sometimes too much choice leads to confusion, but having a wide selection to choose from is generally considered a good thing. Online shopping makes available millions of products at the click of a mouse. When we explored dozens of sites in our search for a digital video camera, national borders didn't limit us, and we found models with all the latest features and functions. In contrast, when we visited a number of electronics stores—after wasting half an hour looking for a parking space—we found a limited selection of models and options in our price range.

3 While we are not exactly Luddites, we needed the intricacies and features of the latest generation of video cameras explained to us. Most electronics

stores are staffed with knowledgeable salespeople who are only too happy to explain technical jargon, demonstrate a product's features, and offer an opinion on its relative merits. On the other hand, if you are willing to spend time on your computer, online information may well serve your needs. You can do all your research and decision-making electronically by visiting manufacturers' and retail outlets' websites, and even by consulting the opinions of other consumers at product comparison and review sites.

4   "Where can I get the best deal?" is something every consumer wants to know. Ask happy customers the reason for their satisfaction, and the answer invariably involves price. Online merchants can often offer lower prices because they can avoid the overhead (rent, inventory, heat and light, wages, etc.) of conventional stores. Not surprisingly, we found that in-store prices for digital video cameras were routinely higher than those posted by online merchants. Electronics stores have responded to the online competition by routinely offering coupons and special discounts.

5   Shopping online is undoubtedly convenient. As long as you have a credit card, you can shop anywhere, anytime. There are no salespeople to pressure you, and you never have to deal with parking or crowds. However, these advantages are countered by the major inconvenience of returning a damaged or unsatisfactory product, especially if you have to repackage the item and ship it across borders. We were disconcerted by the possibility that we would have to return our video camera, a fragile item that could be easily damaged during shipping. Offsetting the limitations of the bricks-and-mortar experience is the relative speed with which items can be returned or exchanged.

6   So where did we buy our camera? We weighed the pros and cons of the alternative selections, services, prices, and convenience of the two shopping environments, and decided that service—both before and after our purchase—was more important to us than saving money and time by shopping online. While we chose the local electronics store as the supplier that best met our needs, other consumers have different priorities, as the increasing popularity of online shopping demonstrates. Bricks and mortar or mouse and monitor? North Americans should consider themselves fortunate to enjoy the advantages of both—for now.

Questions for Discussion

1. Draft a rough outline for this essay. How is the information organized: in blocks or point by point? Why do you think the author chose this organizational pattern?
2. In your own words, combine the thesis and the main points of this essay in a single sentence. Is it an effective thesis statement? Why?

3. This piece is told from the first-person plural point of view. Consider how the effect on the reader would change if it had been written from either the first-person singular point of view (personal) or from the third-person point of view (impersonal). Did the author choose her point of view wisely? Why?

4. Identify three or four transitional techniques the author has employed to enhance her essay's coherence. (See pages 102–04 for a review of transition strategies.)

5. Early in the essay, the author provides clues as to which shopping option she and her partner chose. Do these hints spoil the conclusion for the reader? Why?

6. Search InfoTrac to find two or three articles that present evidence of the rapid growth of online shopping and its negative effects on the profitability of bricks-and-mortar stores.

7. Does it matter to you who wins the battle of the shopping options? Why?

THE GAS-ELECTRIC HYBRID DEMYSTIFIED

Sara R. Howerth

1   A hybrid is a cross between two established varieties of plant, animal, . . . or technology. The hybrid bicycle, for example, combines the features of a road bike with those of an off-road bike to produce a comfortable and efficient bicycle for short distance cycling. For most people today, the word "hybrid" signifies a fuel-efficient, low-emission automobile. Hybrid car technology combines a gasoline or diesel internal combustion engine with a battery-powered electric motor. Its objective is to maximize the best properties of both the gas engine and the electric motor.

2   A gasoline engine is powerful enough for the pickup, torque, and speed any driver requires. Because of the petroleum infrastructure that has developed over the past 100 years, gas-powered vehicles are also easy to refuel and can travel 400 km to 800 km between fill-ups. On the other hand, they are expensive to operate and are becoming even more so as fuel prices rise. More importantly, they are a major cause of the pollution that contributes to smog, environmental degradation, and global warming.

3   Battery-powered electric motors are quiet, efficient, and relatively clean— depending, of course, on how the electricity that charges them is produced. However, they cannot yet travel very far on a charge (some can go 200 km), and most need to be recharged 12 hours or overnight. The technology is evolving rapidly, however, and these limitations of distance and time will probably be significantly reduced in the coming years.

4   The hybrid vehicle uses both types of motors and exploits the advantages of each. A gasoline engine provides the power and torque, while an electric engine adds power and thus reduces the amount of gasoline required. There are two types of hybrid vehicle; the difference between them consists of their approach to the twinning of the two engines.

5   The "mild hybrid" uses a small electric motor that boosts the capability of the gas engine, thus enabling a smaller gas engine to get the same performance as a larger power plant. Small engines consume less gas and produce fewer emissions, so the smaller the gas engine, the more cost and environmental benefit, so long as the electric motor can deliver the performance equivalent of a more powerful engine. Another way the mild hybrid saves fuel is by allowing the gas engine to shut down when the vehicle is stopped, even for a few seconds at a stoplight. The electric engine starts instantly when the accelerator is touched, and it acts as a starter for the gas motor.

6   The "full hybrid" uses the two motors quite differently. Like the mild hybrid, the full hybrid allows the gas engine to shut down when the vehicle is stopped, but it stays off at low speeds (under about 40 km/h), since the vehicle is powered only by the electric motor until more power is required. As speed increases, the gas or diesel motor kicks in automatically and the two work in tandem to provide the power needed for highway driving, acceleration, and climbing. This arrangement means that cars equipped with full-hybrid engines get better mileage in stop-and-start city driving than they do in long-distance highway conditions.

7   Both hybrid models use the power produced by the gas engine to recharge the onboard batteries, so they never need to be recharged by plugging the vehicle into an outlet. In addition, both models use the electric motor as a generator during deceleration; therefore, power that is normally lost as heat when a conventional car brakes is recaptured and sent to the batteries, keeping them charged. This process is called "regenerative braking."

8   Each year, the marketplace offers more hybrid technology models to cost-conscious and environmentally aware consumers. This trend will continue so long as gas prices rise, and so long as people are concerned about the pollution caused by petroleum-powered vehicles. Perhaps the hybrid will be a stepping stone to even more efficient, less polluting technologies, such as hydrogen fuel-cell powered cars. But for now and into the foreseeable future, the hybrid automobile is a technology whose time has arrived.

Questions for Discussion

1. "The Gas-Electric Hybrid Demystified" has a more complex structure than the first two essays in this chapter. To understand how the piece is put together, write an outline for it.

2. What audience did the author have in mind as she wrote this essay? Are her intended readers car enthusiasts? Auto mechanics? Use examples from the essay to support your answer.

3. What methods of paragraph development does Howerth use to help her readers understand her explanation of her subject? Support your answer with specific examples.

4. Search InfoTrac to find another article that discusses the differences between the "full hybrid" and the "mild hybrid." Compare that article to Howerth's essay. Consider level of language, target audience, and the purpose of the two pieces. Which was easier for you to understand? Why?

5. In the last decade, the word "hybrid" has come to signify the type of car that is the subject of this essay. Using the resources of InfoTrac, identify five applications of the word "hybrid" that have nothing to do with automobiles. List the meanings in order of your familiarity with them, from most to least.

JUSTICE AND JOURNALISM
Victor Chen

1   "Justice must not only be done, it must be seen to be done." This principle, in part, accounts for the news media's appetite for stories about our justice system. It is the principle that news organizations always cite when their access to information about the courts, criminals, or police is limited, or when they are prevented from distributing that information. Given the media's apparent concern for the public's knowledge about Canadian justice, it is troubling to learn that what we read, hear, and see is often distorted. The reality of our justice system and what we learn about it from our media are, all too often, two different things. Two aspects of our justice system will serve to illustrate this contrast: the incidence of violent crime and the sentencing of criminals.

2   Occurrences of violent crime have declined steadily in Canada over the past decade. While this fact has occasionally been reported, it doesn't sell newspapers or advertising nearly as well as juicy stories about murder, mayhem, assault, or aggression. The news media are in business to attract an audience, and the pressure to sensationalize is relentless. Hence, while murders constitute about 1% of violent crime committed in Canada, in our news media more than 25% of crime stories are about killings. Since virtually all of our information about crime comes to us from newspapers and news broadcasts, is it any wonder that we have the impression that murders are far more common than they really are? Furthermore, violent crime itself represents about 12% of all crime that is dealt with by our police and courts. Yet, in the media, 50% of

the coverage of criminal activity is devoted to violent crime. We have two societies: an imaginary one, created by the news media, that most of us live in, and the real, less violent one that few of us know about.

3   As well as a distorted view of violent crime, the media give us false impressions about proceedings in the criminal courts. Except in a few notable cases, reporters are not assigned to cover an entire trial; instead, they attend the courtroom only for the sensational opening addresses and for the verdict and sentencing. Very little of what goes on for most of the trial—the evidence, the arguments, the painstaking detail, and the finer points of courtroom procedure—ever appears in the news. What effect does this omission have on our understanding of law and order? In a recent study, J. Roberts and A. Doob demonstrate that the public's understanding of the justice system is distorted. Half of the participants in the study read the newspaper accounts of a trial. The other half read the court documents—transcripts of what had actually taken place during the trial. Of those who read the newspapers, the vast majority (over 60%) thought that the sentence handed down by the judge was too lenient. Less than 15% felt the sentence was too harsh. However, of those who read the court proceedings without the slant provided by reporters and editors, the majority felt the punishment was too harsh. Less than 20% believed that a more severe sentence was warranted, while more than 50% thought the sentence given for the crime was too long (508–12). What does this experiment tell us about how Canadians form their often strongly held opinions about the justice system?

4   The contrast between what our news media tell us about our justice system and the reality of what is going on in the police departments and courtrooms of the nation is an indictment of the sensationalist media. Even more important, this contrast is a sobering reminder that our opinions can be based on a superficial understanding of the issues. The news media will not change; the pressures for sensational reporting are too great. Public opinion will, therefore, be based on distorted impressions. We can only hope that our lawmakers will form their opinions and base their decisions not on media reports and not on the popular opinion which those reports create, but on a careful, researched study of the reality behind the headlines.

Work Cited

Roberts, J., and A. Doob. "Sentencing and Public Opinion: Taking False Shadows for True Substances." *Osgoode Hall Law Journal* 27.3 (1989): 491–515.

Reprinted by permission of the author.

Questions for Discussion

1. Which method of contrast has Chen used to organize this essay? Using the information given in the essay, write a point-form outline for an essay organized according to the alternate method. Which organization do you think is more effective? Why?

2. What purpose—other than contrasting the image and reality of our justice system—does the author of this piece have in mind? Does he achieve his purpose?

3. Statistics do not often make very interesting reading. How has the author tried to make the statistics in this essay readable as well as meaningful? Is he successful?

4. So long as they are not overused, rhetorical questions (questions asked for effect rather than to elicit an answer) can be effective in capturing and holding readers' attention. Identify two rhetorical questions in this essay and rephrase them as statements. Which version—question or statement—has more impact on the reader? Why?

5. Parallelism (see Chapter 26) is often used by writers to reinforce the seriousness of a subject or the weight of an argument. Identify four examples of parallel structure that you think contribute effectively to the solemn tone of this essay.

FOR MINORITIES, TIMING IS EVERYTHING
Olive Johnson

1   Left-handedness and homosexuality both tend to run in families. As my husband's family and mine have some of each, it is not surprising that one of our children is left-handed and another homosexual. Both my left-handed daughter and my homosexual son turned out to be bright, funny, talented people with loving friends and family. But their experience of growing up in different minority groups was a striking contrast and an interesting illustration of how societal attitudes change as sufficient knowledge accumulates to make old beliefs untenable.

2   By the time my daughter was growing up, left-handedness was no longer regarded as a sign of immorality or mental deficiency. Almost everybody knew "openly" left-handed friends, teachers and relatives and viewed them as normal people who wrote differently. Except for a little awkwardness in learning to write at school, my daughter's hand preference was simply never an issue. If people noticed it at all, they did so with a shrug. Nobody called her nasty names or banned school library books about left-handed families, as

school trustees in Surrey, B.C., recently banned books about gay families. Nobody criticized her left-handed "lifestyle" or suggested that she might be an unfit role model for young children. Nobody claimed that she *chose* to be left-handed and should suffer the consequences.

3   My gay son did not choose to be different either, but when he was growing up, homosexuality was still too misunderstood to be accepted as just another variant of human sexuality. Because gay people still felt unsafe revealing their sexual orientation, he was deprived of the opportunity of knowing openly gay teachers, friends and relatives. He grew up hearing crude jokes and nasty names for people like him, and he entered adulthood knowing that being openly gay could prevent you from getting a job or renting an apartment. It could also get you assaulted.

4   Bigotry has never been reserved for homosexuality, of course. I am old enough to remember the time when bigotry directed toward other minorities in Canada was similar to that which is still sometimes aimed at homosexuals. In my Vancouver childhood, Chinese were regularly called "Chinks" (the boys in my high school wore black denim "Chink pants" tailored for them in Chinatown). Black people were "niggers," prohibited from staying in most Vancouver hotels. Kids in the special class were "retards" or "morons." Jews were suspected of all sorts of crazy things, and physically disabled people were often regarded as mental defectives.

5   Left-handed children were still being punished for writing with their left hand, particularly in the more religious parts of Canada. (When I was a graduate psychology student in Newfoundland doing research on handed-ness, I discovered that several of my "right-handed" subjects were actually left-handers; at school their left hands had been tied behind their backs by zealous nuns.)

6   The gay children and teachers of my childhood were simply invisible. Two female teachers could live together without raising eyebrows, chiefly because women in those days (especially women *teachers*) were not generally thought of as sexual persons. Two male "bachelors" living together did tend to be sus-pect, and so gay men brave enough to live together usually kept their living arrangements quiet. "Sissy" boys and "boyish" girls took a lot of teasing, but most people knew too little about homosexuality to draw any conclusions. These boys and girls were expected to grow up and marry people of the oppo-site sex. Some of them did, divorcing years later to live with one of their own.

7   Many of the teachers and parents of my childhood who tried to convert left-handed children into right-handers probably believed they were helping children avoid the stigma of being left-handed, just as many misguided ther-apists tried to "cure" patients of their homosexuality to enable them to avoid the stigma of being gay in a heterosexual world.

8   Thanks to advances in our understanding, left-handedness gradually came to be seen as a natural and innate trait. We know now that people do not

choose to be more skillful with one hand than the other; they simply are. While researchers are still debating the precise mechanisms that determine hand preference, there is general agreement that left- and right-handedness are just two different (and valid) ways of being. Left-handers are a minority in their own right, not "deviants" from normal right-handedness.

9   The same is true for sexual orientation. Although we do not yet clearly understand the mechanisms that determine sexual orientation, all indicators point to the conclusion that it results from interactions between genetic, hormonal and possibly other factors, all beyond the individual's control. Like left-handedness, sexual orientation is an innate trait, not a choice or "lifestyle." Like left-handedness, homosexuality is a valid alternative sexuality, not a deviance from "normal" heterosexuality.

10   As with other minorities, attitudes toward homosexuality are inevitably becoming more liberal, at least in Canada. A recent poll, commissioned by the B.C. Teachers' Federation, found that almost 70 per cent of B.C. residents think students should be taught in school to accept homosexuals and treat them as they would other people. (Twenty per cent said homosexuality should be discouraged, 9 per cent said they didn't know and 3 per cent refused to answer.) These results indicate that overt bigotry toward homosexuality is increasingly limited to religious extremists. The Surrey school trustees who voted against having gay and lesbian resource materials in schools are probably at about the same stage of cultural evolution as were the Newfoundland nuns who tied children's left hands behind their backs 40 years ago.

11   Even so, I'm grateful that they're further along the path of enlightenment than their predecessors in medieval Europe, who burned many left-handers and homosexuals at the stake. Being born in the late 20th century was a wise move on the part of my son and daughter. In some things, timing is everything.

Johnson, Olive. "For Minorities, Timing Is Everything." *Globe and Mail* 7 July 1997: A14.

Questions for Discussion

1. To develop the main points of this essay, the author uses her own children as examples. Would the essay have been more effective had she supported her argument with less personal examples? Why?
2. Under what points does the author compare the treatment of left-handedness and homosexuality in Canada in the last century?
3. Comparing two groups is not the purpose of this essay; it is the means the author has chosen to accomplish her purpose. What is the main purpose of this piece? How effective do you think the author is in achieving it?

4. What is the topic sentence of paragraph 10? How is the topic developed? Do you agree with the statement the author makes in the fourth sentence of that paragraph? Why?

5. Consider the final paragraph of this essay. What function does it serve, other than to conclude the piece? What is its effect on readers?

Exercise 15.1

List eight to ten characteristics of two people, or jobs, or courses. Examine your lists and choose characteristics of each that would make a basis for a comparison between the two. Then go back over the lists and choose characteristics that would make a basis for contrast.

Exercise 15.2

Write a comparison or contrast essay on one of the following subjects. Be sure to follow the guidelines for essay development, from selecting a subject, through managing your main points, to outlining your paper and writing your paragraphs.

Two fast-food restaurants
Two magazines with the same target audience (e.g., *Maclean's* and *Time*, *People* and *Us*, *Shift* and *Wired*)
Two approaches to child-rearing
College and university
Two political leaders
Two management styles
Your generation and that of your parents (or grandparents)

Exercise 15.3

 Contrast papers often turn persuasive, but they don't have to. When you are presenting a contrast, try not to be influenced by your own opinion. List the arguments on both sides of three of these controversial issues.

Single-sex schools
Gay marriage
The use of animals in medical research
Nuclear power
Physician-assisted suicide

For one of the topics you worked on in Exercise 15.3, write an essay contrasting the views held by the two sides. Some research may be necessary to find out exactly what the opposing arguments are and to explain those arguments to your reader.

Construct a comparison essay or a contrast essay, using one of the suggestions given below. Develop a thesis statement that reflects the relationship of the two subjects. Before you begin, write an outline of your thoughts, using either the block or the point-by-point method.

Quebec and TROC (the rest of Canada)

Your spouse and the fantasy you had of a spouse before you were married

Two newspapers' coverage of a news event

Your life now with your life five (or ten or twenty) years ago

Working in an office and working at home

Television advertisements for one of these pairs of consumer products: new cars and beer; home-care and personal-care products; financial services and travel services, a fast-food chain and muffler repairs

16

Cause and Effect

- What are the consequences of dropping out of school?
- What are some of the effects of low interest rates?
- What are the major causes of global warming?
- What are the causes of addiction?
- Why is interest in alternative medicine growing so rapidly?

These are the kinds of subjects often discussed in **causal analysis**. On some occasions, cause and effect may be combined in one paper or report, but its length and complexity would put it out of the range of our introductory discussions here. In short papers, writers usually concentrate either on causes or on effects.

The most common problem found in causal analysis is oversimplification. In the absence of solid facts, figures, or evidence, inexperienced writers have a tendency to generalize and to substitute unsupported opinions for reasons. One cause of this problem is choosing a topic that is too big for the length of the paper. For example, one student decided to analyze the effects of Canada's immigration policy, a subject so big and so complicated that he could do nothing more than give vague and unsupported opinions. The result made him seem not only ignorant but also racist. You can avoid this pitfall by choosing your subject carefully, focusing it into a limited topic, and supporting each main point with lots of evidence.

Tips on Writing Causal Analysis

1. Your thesis statement should clearly indicate whether you are tackling cause or effect, and it should present your main points in order. Consider these examples.

The chief causes of complaint among the workers in this office are low wages, health hazards, and boredom.

The benefits effects of a long canoe trip include reduced stress and increased fitness.

2. Avoid three common logical fallacies: oversimplification, faulty causal relation, and leaping to a conclusion.
   - An oversimplified analysis is one that ignores the complexities of an issue. If, for example, you claim that "men deliberately keep women down" and base this conclusion on the fact that, on average, the annual salary of women is lower than that of men, you are over-simplifying because the two groups are not identical. To take just one difference, there are more part-time workers among females than among males, and the salaries of part-timers cannot be compared to the earnings of full-time workers. (And even if the two wage groups were identical in all respects except one—annual income—that one difference is not proof of male conspiracy.)
   - Just because one event occurs along with or after another event does not mean that the first *caused* the second. For example: on Tuesday, your little brother swallowed a nickel. On Wednesday, he broke out in a rash. To conclude that the nickel caused the rash is a faulty causal relation. He may be allergic to something; he may have measles. As a writer, you must carefully examine all possible causes before determining that Y is the result of X.
   - Leaping to a conclusion (sometimes called hasty generalization) results when you do not consider enough data before forming a judgment. This is a common error: we commit it every time we form an opinion based on one or two instances. For example, the sponsorship scandal is not proof of the assertion, "the Liberal government is full of crooks."

3. Fully support your statements. You must provide proof of what you say in the form of examples, facts, statistics, quotations, anecdotes, etc. (see Chapter 7). If you begin with the assumption that your reader disagrees with you, you will be more likely to provide adequate support for your points.

The following five essays demonstrate writing that discusses causes and effects. In the first essay, the writer uses examples to explain effects; in the second essay, specific details and narrative are used to identify causes and illustrate effects; in the third and fourth essays, the writers use facts, examples, statistics, and paraphrases to develop their causal analyses; in the fifth essay, all seven developmental strategies are used to explore both cause and effect.

LIGHTWEIGHT LIT.

Brian Green

1   [1]I really enjoy literary discussions. [2]I love it when people at trendy restaurants smack their lips in appreciation of the latest South American novelist, Egyptian poet, or Armenian essayist. [3]By eavesdropping on these discussions, I can find out what's going on in the world of "great literature" so that when people ask me what I've read lately I can pretend that I, too, am devoted to highbrow literature. [4]I'm ashamed to admit my secret vice, but, because we're friends, I can tell you . . . I *love* "trash." [5]I'm embarrassed about it, and I know that my intellectual friends would ridicule me if they found out. [6]Still, I have very good reasons for enjoying light literature. [7]I find it educates, relaxes, and entertains in a way that more cerebral reading doesn't—at least, not for me.

2   [8]The educational nature of popular or junk literature is often overlooked. [9]From reading countless police novels, I know the workings of the Los Angeles and New York police departments inside out. [10]I have a thorough grounding in the operations of the CIA, the KGB, MI5, and any number of less illustrious spy agencies. [11]I'm eagerly awaiting the first novel about a hero from Canada's CSIS. [12]Science-fiction books have detailed for me the ways of life, war, travel, and even agriculture in outer space. [13]My education even includes the laws of nature in alternative universes: I know about the society of Gor, the politics of Fionavar, and the nature of good and evil in a hundred other worlds.

3   [14]Acquiring all this knowledge may sound tiring, but light novels are actually extremely relaxing. [15]The way I read this kind of literature is slouched in my favourite chair with my feet up and a comforting drink close at hand, and, because I can't do anything else while I read, the overall effect is complete physical relaxation. [16]Also, an absorbing novel will take me away from the concerns and stresses of everyday life, allowing me to escape to a world created by the writer. [17]Because I can have no effect on this world, I can, with a completely clear conscience, let things unfold as they may and assume the relaxing role of observer.

4   [18]Although education and relaxation are important, most of us read light novels to be entertained. [19]Entertainment means different things to different people. [20]Some enjoy being frightened half to death by the books of Stephen King or his colleagues; others get satisfaction from the sugary romance of Harlequin novels; many people find science fiction absorbing and devour the works of Isaac Asimov or Jerry Pournelle. [21]Whatever subject or style appeals to you, there are literally thousands of novels to suit your taste. [22]I'm lucky because—with the exception of popular romance—I can find enjoyment in almost any type of reasonably well-written light novel.

5   [23]None of the novelists I read will ever win the Nobel prize for literature, and few of them will be studied in university literature courses. [24]However, many writers have become wealthy from selling their fantasies to those millions of readers like me who seek entertainment, relaxation, and education from the novels they enjoy—even if they have to enjoy them in secret.

Questions for Discussion

1. What is the main topic identified in "Lightweight Lit.," and what are its three effects?

   The effects of _____ are _____,

   _____, and _____.

2. What is the author's role in this essay?
3. Who are the intended readers? Will they be convinced of the causes for the author's literary preferences?
4. What purpose is served by the author's supposed embarrassment? How does this device affect you as a reader?
5. The author uses specific examples to support the main points. List the examples used to illustrate each point.

PRIDE *VERSUS* PREJUDICE

David Geiss

1   "Why did God make me gay?" "Why can't I just go through life passing as straight?" These are questions I was asking myself just a short time ago. In the span of little more than a year, I have gone from a confused, lonely, and fashion-impaired gay boy to a comfortable, "out," and energetic gay man. My thoughts on gay life, culture, and responsibility have been completely turned around. I attribute this transformation mainly to my involvement with GBLUR (Gays, Bisexuals, and Lesbians at the University of Regina).

2   One question I was *not* asking myself was "Where do I find other people like me?" but the answer presented itself anyway. I had suspected for a while that Tim, a fellow film student, "played for my team," and out of the blue one night, he told me to give him a call. I hesitated, but after a brief lecture from my friend April on "Why I Should Meet New People," I decided to make the call. Tim changed my life forever. Meeting someone who was so much like me on the inside, yet obviously more comfortable with himself and confident on the outside, forced me to take a step back and look at who *I* was. Through

Tim, I soon met more gay people and realized that many of them were just like me. It was very exciting and comforting to know that others [were] going through the same conflicts and challenges. At around the time I met him, Tim was in the process of organizing GBLUR and he needed a secretary. I hesitantly volunteered for the position, and the metamorphosis of my social and cultural life began.

3   One of our first tasks was to organize a fundraiser so our group would have the money to actually operate. To my dismay, Tim decided that a drag show at the Lazy Owl campus bar would be a fabulous fundraiser. Since dressing in drag was not even close to being an option for me at that time, and, frankly, I had no idea what a drag show was all about anyway, I decided just to help out here and there with the organizational tasks. Even making decorating decisions was a big step for me. But the night of the show, when I suddenly realized that there was a crowd of 500 smiling, supportive faces in the audience, I started to get this funny feeling inside. I realize now that it was that emotion everyone talked about so much it made me cringe: Pride. Pride in entertaining so many people, pride in raising money for a charity, and pride in being myself. For the next drag show, six months later, I took sole charge of the decorating duties, and also dressed in silver from head to toe.

4   I used to be on the outside looking in; I knew I was gay, but I was stuck in a straight world and willing to let myself continue to be stuck there. I was by no means comfortable, but I was content enough to assume that the rest of my life would be like this, so I accepted it. I refused to believe that I had any reason or responsibility to appreciate, [let alone] celebrate what I was. I used to think Gay Pride Week, and especially the accompanying parade, was just a way for attention-seekers to dance around on a float and get their pictures in the paper or on the nightly television news. What I failed to realize was that apathy breeds oppression, and my indifference was working against me. As a gay man, I am limited, in some cases by law, to less freedom than everyone else: I'm shunned by some potential employers, I've had doctors refuse me as a patient, I can't donate blood, and I sure as hell can't kiss my boyfriend in public without repercussions. Until recently, I couldn't get married. But now I am on the inside looking out; I see the gay world as *my* world, and I no longer feel uncomfortable inside it.

5   I own a rainbow pride flag, but it sits unopened in my closet (there must be a metaphor in that!) Actually, I just haven't taken the time to hang it up; I don't think I even have room to hang it anywhere. I'm not out to change the world. I just want to be comfortable in my own skin and I want everyone else to be comfortable around me. I've learned that, contrary to what some extremists believe, the inequalities between straight people and gay people will never entirely disappear. But instead of hiding or condemning our differences, we should celebrate them. GBLUR hasn't turned me into a ranting

raving, equality-obsessed activist. But it has opened my eyes to a world that I can finally call my own, a world I can be *proud* of.

Questions for Discussion

1. In "Pride *versus* Prejudice," the author credits an external agent (GBLUR) for the transformation of his life. Is this essay an analysis of causes or of effects? Which sentences in the first paragraph identify the author's thesis and suggest his main points?
2. Identify the topics of paragraphs 2, 3, and 4.
3. The conclusion consists of a subtle (rather than obvious) restatement of the author's main points. Identify the links between the first seven sentences of paragraph 5 and the three topics you identified in question 2.
4. What do you think of the attention-getter and memorable statement in this essay? Are they effective? Why?
5. This piece confronts the issue of a gay person taking pride in his orientation, despite the fact that his upbringing and cultural experiences have trained him to feel ashamed of what he is. Find out the significance of this issue in the gay world by searching the InfoTrac database, limiting your search to gay journals (use the browse function to identify suitable magazines). Find two or three articles that confirm or reinforce the observations Geiss makes in "Pride *versus* Prejudice."

THE SLENDER TRAP

Trina Rys

> Starvation is not a pleasant way to expire. In advanced stages of famine, as the body begins to consume itself, the victim suffers muscle pain, heart disturbances, loss of hair, dizziness, shortness of breath, extreme sensitivity to cold, physical and mental exhaustion. The skin becomes discoloured. In the absence of key nutrients, a severe chemical imbalance develops in the brain, inducing convulsions and hallucinations. (Krakauer 198)

1 Every day, millions die of hunger. The symptoms of starvation are so horrific that it seems unthinkable anyone would choose this way of death. How is it possible that in the Western world, one in two hundred young women from upper- and middle-class families practises starvation as a method of weight control? How do young women become so obsessed with being thin that they develop anorexia nervosa? To cause such a fearsome and potentially fatal condition, the influencing factors must be powerful indeed. And they are

powerful: the psychological pressures of adolescence, the inescapable expectations of family and peers, and the potent influence of the media.

2   A tendency to perfectionism, lack of identity, and feelings of helplessness are three aspects of a young woman's psychology that can contribute to the development of anorexia nervosa. Young women who exhibit perfectionism are particularly susceptible to the disease because they often have unrealistic expectations about their physical appearance. These expectations can lead to feelings of helplessness and powerlessness, and some young women with these feelings see starving themselves as a means to empowerment. Their diet is often the only thing they can control, and they control it with a single-mindedness that astonishes and horrifies their families and friends. As well as the need for control, anorexia in young women can be caused by a weak or unformed identity. Confused about who they are, many young women define themselves by how closely they approximate our society's notion of the ideal woman. Unfortunately, for the past half-century, Western society's ideal female image has been that of an unrealistically thin young woman. When women focus on this impossible image as the ideal and strive to starve their bodies into submission, they suffer emotional and physical damage.

3   In addition to an unstable psychological state, family and peer pressure can contribute to a fragile young woman's development of anorexia nervosa. By emphasizing physical appearance, by criticizing physical features, and even by restricting junk food, family members can push a young woman over the cliff edge that separates health from illness. A home environment in which physical appearance is overvalued can be destructive for young women. Surrounded by family members and friends who seem to be concerned primarily about appearance, a young woman can begin to feel insecure about how she looks. This uncertainty can produce the desire—and then the need—to look better. And better means thinner. This flawed logic underlies the disease in many young women. A family or peer group that overvalues physical appearance is often also critical of physical flaws. Critical comments about weight and general appearance, even when spoken jokingly, can be instrumental in a young woman's desire to be thin. Ironically, food restrictions imposed by parents can also contribute to anorexia in young women. Restricting the consumption of junk food, for example, has been known to cause bingeing and purging, a condition associated with anorexia.

4   While a young woman's developing psyche and the pressures of those close to her can exert tremendous influence, the root cause of the "thin is beautiful" trap is a media-inspired body image. Television, fashion magazines, and stereotypical Hollywood images of popular stars provide young women with an unrealistic image of the ideal female body. While only 5 percent of North American females are actually underweight, 32 percent of female television and movie personalities are unhealthily thin (ANRED sec. 6). The media's unrealistic portrayal of a woman's ideal body can cause a young

woman to develop a sense of inadequacy. To be considered attractive, she feels she must be ultra-thin. Television's unrealistic portrayal of the way young women should look is reinforced on the pages of fashion magazines. Magazine ads feature tall, beautiful, *thin* women. Media images also perpetuate the stereotype that a woman must be thin in order to be successful. Thanks to television and movies, when we think of a successful woman, the image that comes to mind is that of a tall, well-dressed, *thin* woman. This stereotypical image leads impressionable young women to associate success with body weight and image. When internalized by young women, these artificial standards can result in the development of anorexia nervosa.

5   If the media do not begin to provide young women with a positive and healthy image of femininity, we will see no lessening in the numbers of anorexia victims. If our cultural ideal of female beauty does not change to reflect a range of healthy body types, the pressures to realize idealized and unhealthy physical standards will continue, and young women's feelings of helplessness and inadequacy will persist. In order for anorexia to become less prominent among young women, healthier associations must replace the existing connections among beauty, success, and thinness. Young women must realize that self-inflicted starvation is not a means to empowerment, but a process of self-destruction.

Works Cited

ANRED: Anorexia and Related Eating Disorders Inc. 2004. 13 June 2004.
     <http://www.anred.com/causes.html>.
Krakauer, Jon. *Into the Wild.* New York: Villard, 1996.

Questions for Discussion

1. Identify the author's thesis statement and plan of development. Compose a single sentence combining both the thesis statement and the main points Rys uses to develop her thesis.
2. What two supporting points does the author use to develop the main point of paragraph 2? (See sentence 5, which serves as a transition between the two supporting ideas.)
3. What kind of development does Rys use in paragraph 3?
4. Study the concluding paragraph carefully. The author's treatment of her summary and memorable statement is unusual and interesting. Sentence 2 of the conclusion summarizes the three main points that have been developed in the essay, but in an original, unpredictable way. Underline the clauses of this sentence, and write above each clause the number of the main point it reinforces.
5. What audience did Rys have in mind when she wrote this essay? How do you know?

LABOURING THE WAL-MART WAY

Deenu Parmar

1   *Always low prices. Always.* This is the slogan of the world's largest corporation, a U.S.-based retailer whose big-box stores offer a one-stop shop, from groceries to garments to garden hoses. The secret of Wal-Mart's success is to give consumers the lowest prices—14 percent lower than its competitors (Greenhouse, 2003)—by increasing the efficiency of the supply chain, the productivity of the labour force, and the use of labour-saving technology. Competitors must adopt a similar business plan, offer something Wal-Mart does not, or go out of business—as Woolco, Eaton's, Simpsons, and Woodwards have in Canada (Moore & Pareek, 2004). The influence of the Wal-Mart model is not likely to wane in the near future. With over 235 stores in Canada and plans for rapid expansion, Wal-Mart and its effects on labour are worth considering. Are its offers of jobs, its attitude toward unionization, and its influence on industry labour practices worth the low price on the shelf?

2   One of the most frequent complaints about Wal-Mart, which employs 1.4 million people worldwide, is its failure to pay workers a living wage. Store employees are paid 20–30 percent less than the industry average, making many of them eligible for social assistance. It is estimated that American taxpayers fork out $2.5 billion a year in welfare payments to Wal-Mart employees (Head, 2004). Because the retailer hires hard-to-place workers, like recent immigrants, seniors, and single mothers, its employees are often afraid they will not find work elsewhere. The kind of work Wal-Mart does offer is gruelling: stores are intentionally understaffed—the strategy behind the company's legendary productivity gains—so that existing employees will work harder (Head, 2004). It is alleged that systemic discrimination against women within the corporation has denied the majority of Wal-Mart workers the chance at promotion, a charge that is now the subject of the largest civil-rights suit in U.S. history.

3   The corporation's staunch anti-unionism is its main defence in keeping workers' wages down and profits up. Without a union to give them collective clout, the store's employees suffer not only lower wages and benefits but abuses like being forced to work overtime without pay. The hiring process is designed to weed out union sympathizers; however, if organizing activity is reported in the store, an anti-union team is flown out from the headquarters in Bentonville, Arkansas, to break it up (Featherstone, 2004). The recent unionizing of the first Wal-Mart store in Canada (Jonquière, Quebec) exposed the company's strategy in the event that its anti-union efforts fail: condemn the store as unprofitable and announce a closing date. Although Wal-Mart's methods of keeping its workforce union-free have been ruled illegal in the

United States, the company often finds it cheaper to pay labour violations than abide by labour rules (Featherstone, 2004). As a result, litigation is a common but costly form of redress for Wal-Mart workers whose rights have been violated.

4   One of the main reasons retail workers at other stores want to see Wal-Mart unionized is to preserve the gains their own unions have made. The necessity of competing with Wal-Mart has already been used as an excuse for supermarkets all over the United States to lower the wages and benefits of their employees (Featherstone, 2004). In early 2004, unionized grocery workers in southern California were forced to accept cuts to their benefits so their employers could compete with a soon-to-open Wal-Mart Supercenter. Wal-Mart's reputation for putting local stores out of business also means that employees of the competition may find themselves working at Wal-Mart for less.

5   Although Wal-Mart's record of paying low wages, crushing unionizing efforts, and lowering industry employment standards bodes ill for Canadian labour, it is unlikely that Canadians will refrain from shopping there. The lure of good prices is hard to resist, and the company's widely admired business model would continue to thrive, even if Wal-Mart were to vanish tomorrow. In the interest of justice and fairness—and in avoiding pitting the customer's savings against the worker's ability to make a living—it falls on the government to pass laws that balance the interests of big business with the protection of labour, environmental, and community rights (Golden, 2004). This kind of legislation will require pressure from organized citizens acting not as consumers but as workers and concerned members of a community. The price on the shelf might rise as a result, causing Wal-Mart supporters to point out that the poor can no longer afford to shop there. However, the ability to buy at rock-bottom prices does not address the systemic causes of poverty— though it may contribute to them.

References

Featherstone, L. (2004, June 28). Will Labor take the Wal-Mart challenge? *The Nation.* Retrieved December 30, 2004, from http://www.thenation.com/doc.mhtml?i=20040628&s=featherstone

Golden, A. (2004, October 7). Productivity, but not at any price [Comment section]. *The Globe and Mail,* p. A23.

Greenhouse, S. (2003, October 19). Wal-Mart, driving workers and supermarkets crazy. *The New York Times,* p. D3.

Head, Simon. (2004, December 16). Inside the leviathan. *The New York Review of Books, 51*(20). Retrieved December 30, 2004, from http://www.nybooks.com/articles/17647

Moore K., & Pareek N. (2004, August 19). A whole new take on shock and AWE: There's BWE (Before Wal-Mart Entered), and there's AWE (After Wal-Mart Entered). *The Globe and Mail,* p. A17.

Questions for Discussion

1. In this essay, is the author addressing Wal-Mart, Wal-Mart's customers, or Wal-Mart itself? What effect does she hope the essay will have on her target audience?
2. Consider the essay's attention-getter and memorable statement. Given the author's purpose and target audience, are they effective? Why?
3. What are the main kinds of evidence the author uses to support her causal analysis?
4. Why do you think the author uses documented sources to support her thesis? How would the effect of the essay change if the sources were omitted?
5. The author says that even if Canadians are aware of the effects of Wal-Mart's policies and practices, they will continue to shop there. Has this essay reduced your desire to shop at Wal-Mart?
6. Use InfoTrac to do a keyword search of "Wal-Mart." Limit your search to three business journals (use the Browse button to select the journals). Note the kind of article that InfoTrac lists in these journals. Now do the search again, looking for articles from general-interest magazines such as *Maclean's*, *Time*, the *New York Times*, and *People*. What are the main differences between the articles taken from the two categories of print sources?

THE TELEPHONE

Anwar F. Accawi

1   When I was growing up in Magdaluna, a small Lebanese village in the terraced, rocky mountains east of Sidon, time didn't mean much to anybody, except maybe to those who were dying, or those waiting to appear in court because they had tampered with the boundary markers on their land. In those days, there was no real need for a calendar or a watch to keep track of the hours, days, months, and years. We knew what to do and when to do it, just as the Iraqi geese knew when to fly north, driven by the hot wind that flew in from the desert, and the ewes knew when to give birth to wet lambs that stood on long, shaky legs in the chilly March wind and baaed hesitantly, because they were small and cold and did not know where they were or what to do now that they were here. The only timepiece we had need of then was the sun. It rose and set, and the seasons rolled by, and we sowed seed and harvested and ate and played and married our cousins and had babies who got whooping cough and chickenpox—and those children who survived

grew up and married *their* cousins and had babies who got whooping cough and chickenpox. We lived and loved and toiled and died without ever needing to know what year it was, or even the time of day.

2   It wasn't that we had no system for keeping track of time and of the important events in our lives. But ours was a natural—or, rather, a divine—calendar, because it was framed by acts of God. Allah himself set down the milestones with earthquakes and droughts and floods and locusts and pestilences. Simple as our calendar was, it worked just fine for us.

3   Take, for example, the birth date of Teta Im Khalil, the oldest woman in Magdaluna and all the surrounding villages. When I first met her, we had just returned home from Syria at the end of the Big War and were living with Grandma Mariam. Im Khalil came by to welcome my father home and to take a long myopic look at his foreign-born wife, my mother. Im Khalil was so old that the skin of her cheeks looked like my father's grimy tobacco pouch, and when I kissed her (because Grandma insisted that I show her old friend affection), it was like kissing a soft suede glove that had been soaked with sweat and then left in a dark closet for a season. Im Khalil's face got me to wondering how old one had to be to look and taste the way she did. So, as soon as she had hobbled off on her cane, I asked Grandma, "How old is Teta Im Khalil?"

4   Grandma had to think for a moment; then she said, "I've been told that Teta was born shortly after the big snow that caused the roof on the mayor's house to cave in."

5   "And when was that?" I asked.

6   "Oh, about the time we had the big earthquake that cracked the wall in the east room."

7   Well, that was enough for me. You couldn't be more accurate than that, now, could you? Satisfied with her answer, I went back to playing with a ball made from an old sock stuffed with other, much older socks.

8   And that's the way it was in our little village for as far back as anybody could remember: people were born so many years before or after an earthquake or a flood; they got married or died so many years before or after a long drought or a big snow or some other disaster. One of the most unusual of these dates was when Antoinette the seamstress and Saeed the barber (and tooth puller) got married. That was the year of the whirlwind during which fish and oranges fell from the sky. Incredible as it may sound, the story of the fish and oranges was true, because men—respectable men, like Abu George the blacksmith and Abu Asaad the mule skinner, men who would not lie even to save their own souls—told and retold that story until it was incorporated into Magdaluna's calendar, just like the year of the black moon and the year of the locusts before it. My father, too, confirmed the story for me. He told me that he had been a small boy himself when it rained fish and oranges from

heaven. He'd gotten up one morning after a stormy night and walked out into the yard to find fish as long as his forearm still flopping here and there among the wet navel oranges.

9   The year of the fish-bearing twister, however, was not the last remarkable year. Many others followed in which strange and wonderful things happened: milestones added by the hand of Allah to Magdaluna's calendar. There was, for instance, the year of the drought, when the heavens were shut for months and the spring from which the entire village got its drinking water slowed to a trickle. The spring was about a mile from the village, in a ravine that opened at one end into a small, flat clearing covered with fine gray dust and hard, marble-sized goat droppings, because every afternoon the goatherds brought their flocks there to water them. In the year of the drought, that little clearing was always packed full of noisy kids with big brown eyes and sticky hands, and their mothers—sinewy, overworked young women with protruding collar-bones and cracked, callused brown heels. The children ran around playing tag or hide-and-seek while the women talked, shooed flies, and awaited their turns to fill up their jars with drinking water to bring home to their napping men and wet babies. There were days when we had to wait from sunup until late afternoon just to fill a small clay jar with precious, cool water.

10   Sometimes, amid the long wait and the heat and the flies and the smell of goat dung, tempers flared, and the younger women, anxious about their babies, argued over whose turn it was to fill up her jar. And sometimes the arguments escalated into full-blown, knockdown-dragout fights; the women would grab each other by the hair and curse and scream and spit and call each other names that made my ears tingle. We little brown boys who went with our mothers to fetch water loved these fights, because we got to see the women's legs and their colored panties as they grappled and rolled around in the dust. Once in a while, we got lucky and saw much more, because some of the women wore nothing at all under their long dresses. God, how I used to look forward to those fights. I remember the rush, the excitement, the sun dancing on the dust clouds as a dress ripped and a young white breast was revealed, then quickly hidden. In my calendar, that year of drought will always be one of the best years of my childhood, because it was then, in a dusty clearing by a trickling mountain spring, I got my first glimpses of the wonders, the mysteries, and the promises hidden beneath the folds of a woman's dress. Fish and oranges from heaven . . . you can get over that.

11   But, in another way, the year of the drought was also one of the worst in my life, because that was the year that Abu Raja, the retired cook who used to entertain us kids by cracking walnuts on his forehead, decided it was time Magdaluna got its own telephone. Every civilized village needed a telephone, he said, and Magdaluna was not going to get anywhere until it had one. A telephone would link us with the outside world. At the time, I was too young

to understand the debate, but a few men—like Shukri, the retired Turkish-army drill sergeant, and Abu Hanna the vineyard keeper—did all they could to talk Abu Raja out of having a telephone brought to the village. But they were outshouted and ignored and finally shunned by the other villagers for resisting progress and trying to keep a good thing from coming to Magdaluna.

12   One warm day in early fall, many of the villagers were out in their fields repairing walls or gathering wood for the winter when the shout went out that the telephone company truck had arrived at Abu Raja's *dikkan*, or country store. There were no roads in those days, only footpaths and dry steambeds, so it took the telephone-company truck almost a day to work its way up the rocky terrain from Sidon—about the same time it took to walk. When the truck came into view, Abu George, who had a huge voice and, before the telephone, was Magdaluna's only long-distance communication system, bellowed the news from his front porch. Everybody dropped what they were doing and ran to Abu Raja's house to see what was happening. Some of the more dignified villagers, however, like Abu Habeeb and Abu Nazim, who had been to big cities like Beirut and Damascus and had seen things like telephones and telegraphs, did not run the way the rest did; they walked with their canes hanging from the crooks of their arms, as if on a Sunday afternoon stroll.

13   It did not take long for the whole village to assemble at Abu Raja's *dikkan*. Some of the rich villagers, like the widow Farha and the gendarme Abu Nadeem, walked right into the store and stood at the elbows of the two important-looking men from the telephone company, who proceeded with utmost gravity, like priests at Communion, to wire up the telephone. The poorer villagers stood outside and listened carefully to the details relayed to them by the not-so-poor people who stood in the doorway and could see inside.

14   "The bald man is cutting the blue wire," someone said.

15   "He is sticking the wire into the hole in the bottom of the black box," someone else added.

16   "The telephone man with the mustache is connecting two pieces of wire. Now he is twisting the ends together," a third voice chimed in.

17   Because I was small and unaware that I should have stood outside with the other poor folk to give the rich people inside more room (they seemed to need more of it than poor people did), I wriggled my way through the dense forest of legs to get a first-hand look at the action. I felt like a barefoot Moses, sandals in hand, staring at the burning bush on Mount Sinai. Breathless, I watched as the men in blue, their shirt pockets adorned with fancy lettering in a foreign language, put together a black machine that supposedly would make it possible to talk with uncles, aunts, and cousins who lived more than two days' ride away.

18   It was shortly after sunset when the man with the mustache announced that the telephone was ready to use. He explained that all Abu Raja had to do was lift the receiver, turn the crank on the black box a few times, and wait for an operator to take his call. Abu Raja, who had once lived and worked in Sidon, was impatient with the telephone man for assuming that he was ignorant. He grabbed the receiver and turned the crank forcefully, as if trying to start a Model T Ford. Everybody was impressed that he knew what to do. He even called the operator by her first name: "Centralist." Within moments, Abu Raja was talking with his brother, a concierge in Beirut. He didn't even have to raise his voice or shout to be heard.

19   If I hadn't seen it with my own two eyes and heard it with my own two ears, I would not have believed it—and my friend Kameel didn't. He was away that day watching his father's goats, and when he came back to the village that evening, his cousin Habeeb and I told him about the telephone and how Abu Raja had used it to speak with his brother in Beirut. After he heard our report, Kameel made the sign of the cross, kissed his thumbnail, and warned us that lying was a bad sin and would surely land us in purgatory. Kameel believed in Jesus and Mary, and wanted to be a priest when he grew up. He always crossed himself when Habeeb, who was irreverent, and I, who was Presbyterian, were around, even when we were not bearing bad news.

20   And the telephone, as it turned out, was bad news. With its coming, the face of the village began to change. One of the first effects was the shifting of the village's center. Before the telephone's arrival, the men of the village used to gather regularly at the house of Im Kaleem, a short, middle-aged widow with jet-black hair and a raspy voice that could be heard all over the village, even when she was only whispering. She was a devout Catholic and also the village *shlikki*—whore. The men met at her house to argue about politics and drink coffee and play cards or backgammon. Im Kaleem was not a true prostitute, however, because she did not charge for her services—not even for the coffee and tea (and, occasionally, the strong liquor called arrack) that she served the men. She did not need the money; her son, who was overseas in Africa, sent her money regularly. (I knew this because my father used to read her son's letters to her and take down her replies, as Im Kaleem could not read and write.) Im Kaleem was no slut either—unlike some women in the village—because she loved all the men she entertained, and they loved her, every one of them. In a way, she was married to all the men in the village. Everybody knew it—the wives knew it; the itinerant Catholic priest knew it; the Presbyterian minister knew it—but nobody objected. Actually, I suspect the women (my mother included) did not mind their husband's visits to Im Kaleem. Oh, they wrung their hands and complained to one another about their men's unfaithfulness, but secretly they were relieved, because Im Kaleem took some of the pressure off them and kept the men out of their hair while they attended to their endless chores. Im Kaleem was also

a kind of confessor and troubleshooter, talking sense to those men who were having family problems, especially the younger ones.

21   Before the telephone came to Magdaluna, Im Kaleem's house was bustling at just about any time of day, especially at night, when its windows were brightly lit with three large oil lamps, and the loud voices of the men talking, laughing, and arguing could be heard in the street below—a reassuring, homey sound. Her house was an island of comfort, an oasis for the weary village men, exhausted from having so little to do.

22   But it wasn't long before many of those men—the younger ones especially—started spending more of their days and evenings at Abu Raja's *dikkan*. There, they would eat and drink and talk and play checkers and backgammon, and then lean their chairs back against the wall—the signal that they were ready to toss back and forth, like a ball, the latest rumors going around the village. And they were always looking up from their games and drinks and talk to glance at the phone in the corner, as if expecting it to ring any minute and bring news that would change their lives and deliver them from their aimless existence. In the meantime, they smoked cheap, hand-rolled cigarettes, dug dirt out from under their fingernails with big pocketknives, and drank lukewarm sodas that they called Kacula, Seffen-Ub, and Bebsi. Sometimes, especially when it was hot, the days dragged on so slowly that the men turned on Abu Saeed, a confirmed bachelor who practically lived in Abu Raja's *dikkan*, and teased him for going around barefoot and unshaven since the Virgin had appeared to him behind the olive press.

23   The telephone was also bad news for me personally. It took away my lucrative business—a source of much-needed income. Before the telephone came to Magdaluna, I used to hang around Im Kaleem's courtyard and play marbles with the other kids, waiting for some man to call down from a window and ask me to run to the store for cigarettes or arrack, or to deliver a message to his wife, such as what he wanted for supper. There was always something in it for me: a ten- or even a twenty-five-piaster piece. On a good day, I ran nine or ten of those errands, which assured a steady supply of marbles that I usually lost to Sami or his cousin Hani, the basket weaver's boy. But as the days went by, fewer and fewer men came to Im Kaleem's, and more and more congregated at Abu Raja's to wait by the telephone. In the evenings, no light fell from her window onto the street below, and the laughter and noise of the men trailed off and finally stopped. Only Shukri, the retired Turkish-army drill sergeant, remained faithful to Im Kaleem after all the other men had deserted her; he was still seen going into or leaving her house from time to time. Early that winter, Im Kaleem's hair suddenly turned gray, and she got sick and old. Her legs started giving her trouble, making it hard for her to walk. By spring she hardly left her house anymore.

24   At Abu Raja's *dikkan*, the calls did eventually come, as expected, and men and women started leaving the village the way a hailstorm begins: first one,

then two, then bunches. The army took them. Jobs in the cities lured them. And ships and airplanes carried them to such faraway places as Australia and Brazil and New Zealand. My friend Kameel, his cousin Habeeb, and their cousins and my cousins all went away to become ditch diggers and mechanics and butcher-shop boys and deli owners who wore dirty aprons sixteen hours a day, all looking for a better life than the one they had left behind. Within a year, only the sick, the old, and the maimed were left in the village. Magdaluna became a skeleton of its former self, desolate and forsaken, like the tombs, a place to get away from.

25   Finally, the telephone took my family away, too. My father got a call from an old army buddy who told him that an oil company in southern Lebanon was hiring interpreters and instructors. My father applied for a job and got it, and we moved to Sidon, where I went to a Presbyterian missionary school and graduated in 1962. Three years later, having won a scholarship, I left Lebanon for the United States. Like the others who left Magdaluna before me, I am still looking for that better life.

Accawi, Anwar F. "The Telephone." *Canadian Content*. Ed. Sarah Norton and Nell Waldman. 4th ed. Toronto: Harcourt, 2000. 236–42.

Questions for Discussion

1. Does this essay focus primarily on cause or on effect? Of what?
2. "The Telephone" is divided into two parts: paragraphs 1 to 10 and 11 to 25. Summarize the content of the two halves of the piece.
3. Explain the irony in paragraph 11, the turning point of the essay.
4. In addition to causal analysis, this essay contains strong elements of description and narration. Identify two paragraphs that you think are particularly effective examples of each.
5. The first effect of the telephone on the village community is told through the story of Im Kaleem, "the village *shlikki*" (paragraphs 20 to 22). What is this consequence, and why do you think the author chooses Im Kaleem's story to communicate it?
6. In paragraph 24, we are told that "the calls did eventually come." What happens then? Where do people go? What happens to Magdaluna itself? Do you think that these effects are all due to the arrival of the telephone in the village?
7. In your own words, describe how the author feels about the changes that swept through his world. Refer to specific details from paragraphs 24 and 25.

Develop each of the following thesis statements by adding three good main points.

1. Obesity, a common problem in North America, is the result of three major causes: _____

   _____,

   _____, and

   _____.

2. The positive effects of professional day care upon preschool children are

   _____,

   _____, and

   _____.

3. Some major effects on Canada of the 9/11 terrorism attack have been

   _____,

   _____, and

   _____.

4. The major causes of air pollution are _____

   _____,

   _____, and

   _____.

5. The fitness craze was prompted by these causes: _____

   _____,

   _____, and

   _____.

6. There are several causes for the increase in numbers of full-time workers returning to college for part-time study: _____

_____,

_____, and

_____.

7. Three common effects of emotional stress are _____

_____,

_____, and

_____.

Exercise 16.2

Begin with the question "What are the causes of _____?" and fill in five career-related topics that you know enough about to identify at least three causes.

If possible, work with a partner who shares your career interests.

Examples: What are the causes of the widespread frustration among nurses?
What are the causes of public school teachers' unhappiness with their jobs?

Exercise 16.3

Repeat Exercise 16.2, using the question "What are the effects of _____?"

Examples: What are the effects of understaffing in our hospitals?
What are the effects of large classes (30–35 children) in grades 1 to 3?

Exercise 16.4

Choose one of the topics that you have developed in either Exercise 16.2 or Exercise 16.3 and work that topic into a full essay, taking care to select a subject about which you know enough to support your ideas.

Exercise 16.5

Write a cause essay or an effect essay on one of the following subjects. If you don't know enough to fully support your ideas, be prepared to do some research.

Causes

Adjusting to college was not as easy as I'd thought it would be.

Many people look forward to early retirement.

My first job was a good (or bad) experience.

Vandalism is a symptom of adolescent frustration.

Self-employment is the best option for many college grads.

Many workers have unrealistic expectations of their employers.

Eating a balanced diet is a challenge for many young people.

Homelessness is increasingly widespread in large cities.

Many runaways prefer the street to a dysfunctional home life.

Effects

Technology is making us lazy.

A poor manager can have a devastating influence on morale.

Credit cards can be dangerous.

Being an only child is a difficult way to grow up.

Poor driving skills are a hazard to everyone.

Caffeine is a harmful substance.

Injuries resulting from overtraining are common among athletes.

Worrying can age you prematurely.

Losing your job can be a positive experience.

17

Argument and Persuasion

How many times have you won an argument? If you're like most of us, not very often. Getting people to understand what you say is hard enough; getting them to agree with you is the most difficult task any writer faces.

In the context of writing, the terms *argument* and *persuasion* have specific meanings, slightly different from their meanings in general conversation.

- An **argument** is a piece of writing that is intended to convince readers that the writer's opinion about an issue is reasonable and valid. An **issue** is an opinion or belief, something that not all people agree on; it is *controversial*, a word that literally means "having two sides."

    Factual reports, memos, and analyses are not likely to be arguments, although some writing intended primarily to inform may also be intended to influence the reader's thinking: "Pucker Up"(page 195), "The Slender Trap" (page 221), and "Justice and Journalism" (page 209) are just three examples.
- **Persuasion** is intended to change the way readers think or feel about an issue, perhaps even to act in some way that supports the writer's point of view (e.g., buy a product, donate to a charity, vote for a particular candidate).

Drafting, revising, and editing argument and persuasion are much the same as for other kinds of writing. Planning, however, requires a slightly different approach.

Choose Your Issue Carefully

Assuming that you have not been assigned a topic, you will need to choose one. Your choice is even more critical for an argument or a persuasive paper than it is for a factual analysis. You can argue only matters of opinion, not fact. Facts can be interpreted in different ways—that's what an argument is: an interpretation of a set of facts. No one can dispute the fact that Canada has ten provinces and three territories. An appropriate subject for your paper is one that can be disputed. Someone has to be able to say, "No. You are not right. That's not what these facts mean." For example, "Canada should be reorganized into five regional provinces and one territory."

You cannot argue matters of taste, either. Taste is personal preference: there is no point in arguing that Thai food is better than pizza, or that green is more flattering than blue. Even if you could argue these assertions, they are not significant enough to bother with. Choose your subject carefully. It must pass the 4-S test (see page 39), and it should be one you know and care about. Ideally, it should be one your reader cares about, too.

GO TO WEB

EXERCISE 17.1

Next, consider the scope of your subject. How much time do you have to prepare? How long is your paper expected to be? Throughout this book, we have recommended that when you choose a subject, you should limit your focus. This recommendation is even more important when you are preparing an argument than when you are proposing to explain something. Even subjects that look narrowly focused can require surprising amounts of development when you are composing an argument for or against them.

Avoid large, controversial issues: abortion, for example, or capital punishment, or religious faith. There are two reasons for this caution. First, they are hugely complex issues; and, second, they are issues on which virtually everyone already has an opinion. It is difficult enough to convince readers about an issue on which they have not already formed an opinion; it's practically impossible to get them to change their minds when they hold an entrenched belief.

Consider Your Audience

When you are trying to get readers to agree with you, you must know (or be able to make an educated guess about) what opinions they already hold and how likely they are to disagree with your views. If, for example, you want to convince your readers that music broadcasters should be required to adhere strictly to Canadian content regulations, the approach you take will depend on your readers' level of knowledge, their interest in the subject, even their age. What do they think about the issue? Do they care about it, one way or the other? What beliefs do they hold that would make them inclined to agree or disagree with you? If you know the answers to these questions, you'll know how to approach your subject: what points to argue, which to emphasize, and which to downplay.

Identify Your Purpose

Do you want your readers simply to understand and respect your opinion on an issue? Or do you want to change their thinking or their behaviour in some way? If your primary purpose is to get them to agree with you, your argument will rely on solid evidence and sound, logical reasoning.

If your primary purpose is to get your readers to do something, to act in some way, your argument will need to appeal not only to their sense of what is reasonable, but also to their feelings, loyalties, ambitions, or desires.

State Your Thesis

Before you begin your first draft, write out your opinion in the form of a proposition (opinion statement). You may or may not use this statement in your paper, but you need it in front of you as you (1) identify your reasons for holding the opinion you do, (2) list the evidence you intend to use, and (3) decide on the order of presentation. If you have ever heard a formal debate, you know what a proposition is. It is the statement of opinion that one side argues in favour of and the other side argues against. Here are three examples:

> Few cities in the world offer the affordable living, student amenities, and cultural dynamism that Montreal does. (thesis of "A City for Students," pages 242–43)

> . . . I cannot deny that by catching a fish, I am in a sense torturing it for my pleasure. (thesis of "Of Pain, Predators, and Pleasure," pages 246–47)

> A liberal arts education is a sound investment of time and money. (thesis of "Arts Education Does Pay Off," pages 248–49)

The test of a satisfactory proposition is that it is arguable—i.e., someone could defend the contrary point of view. (A statement that includes the word *should* or *must* is likely to be a proposition.) You could argue that fishing is a cruel, unjustifiable sport, or that a liberal arts education is a waste of time and money, or that to anglophone students, Montreal offers decrepit housing, poor amenities, and few cultural opportunities.

Once you have a clear statement of a specific opinion, you are ready to identify your reasons for holding it and evidence to support your reasons. It is possible to support an argument entirely from personal experience, but you are more likely to convince your readers if you provide a variety of kinds of evidence (see Chapters 7 and 18).

Identify Your Reasons and Evidence

Readers are not likely to be convinced of anything unless the concept is first clearly explained to them. Whether your purpose is to argue or to persuade, you need to provide reasons for believing your opinion. Your reasons, which are your main points, must be significant, distinct, and relevant (see Chapter 4). To support each reason, you need to provide lots of accurate evidence: facts, concrete details, statistics, events or experiences your readers are familiar with or can relate to, authorities you can refer to or quote. To engage your readers' hearts as well as their minds, at least some of your evidence should be emotionally "loaded"; that is, it should arouse the readers' compassion, or anger, or sense of justice, or any other feeling that supports your side of the issue.

Decide on an Approach: Direct or Indirect?

If you think your readers are likely to argue with your view or even slightly inclined to oppose it, it is best to build your case with definitions, examples, and other evidence before stating your own opinion. Readers who are confronted early by a statement they disagree with are often not open to argument or persuasion. Instead, they are inclined to read the rest of the paper trying to pick holes in your argument and thinking of rebuttals. A potentially hostile audience would respond best to an indirect, or inductive, approach:

Before we decide how to vote, we should consider the candidates' records, their platforms, and their characters.

On the other hand, if your readers are sympathetic to your point of view, you can state your opinion up front and then identify your reasons and the evidence that supports those reasons. This is called the direct, or deductive, approach:

> Based on her record, her platform, and her character, Julie Kovac is the candidate who deserves your vote.

For an explanation of inductive and deductive reasoning, together with some of the common logical fallacies that can damage your argument, see "Making the Argument" on the *Essay Essentials* website (http://www.essayessentials4e.nelson.com).

Arrange Your Reasons and Evidence

An argument or a persuasive paper can be developed in several ways. It is possible, as you will see in the readings for this chapter, to use a number of different structural patterns to convince your readers. A cause–effect analysis might be an effective way to urge action to lower the carbon monoxide and carbon dioxide emissions that contribute to global warming. You might choose comparison to discuss the efficiency of Canada's regulated airline industry as opposed to the deregulated industry in the United States and to argue in favour of one approach over the other.

Two patterns are specific to argument and persuasion. One is the classic "their side–my side" strategy, which is particularly useful when you are arguing a controversial position that may provoke serious dispute. This pattern involves your presenting the "con" (or "against") points of an argument, then refuting them with the "pro" (or "for") side of the argument. For instance, if a writer were to argue that women in the Canadian Armed Forces should participate in combat, she might choose to present the opposing position and then counter each point with well-reasoned arguments of her own.

Like a comparison, the "their side–my side" strategy can be presented either in block form or in point-by-point form, depending on how many points there are to discuss. Be sure to arrange your points in the order in which they will be most effective (see the list of possible arrangements discussed in Chapter 4).

If you are a skilled debater, you can often dismiss the opposing side's argument by identifying and exposing flaws in their reasoning or evidence. If you are an inexperienced writer, however, you will probably find it easier to use one or more of the following techniques:

- Identify any irrelevant or trivial points.
- Show that a point covers only part of the issue.
- Show that a point is valid only some of the time.
- Show that a point may have immediate advantages, but that its long-term results will be negative.
- Acknowledge the validity of the opposition's point(s), but provide a better alternative.

Carefully presented, the "their side–my side" pattern impresses readers with its fairness and tends to neutralize opposition.

The second structural pattern specific to argument and persuasion makes use of the familiar thesis statement. Add carefully worded reasons to your proposition, and you have a thesis statement that can appear near the beginning of your paper, in a direct approach, or near the end, if you are treating your subject indirectly. Be sure you have arranged your reasons in the most effective order. Usually, writers present their reasons in climactic order, saving their most compelling reason for the end of the paper.

The keys to good argumentation and persuasion are to think carefully about your opinion and to present fairly your reasons for believing it—*after* you have analyzed your reader's possible biases or prejudices and degree of commitment to one side or the other.

To argue or persuade successfully, you need to be not only well organized, informative, and thorough, but also honest and tactful, especially if your readers are not already inclined to agree with you.

Tips on Writing Argument and Persuasion

1. Choose an issue that you know and care about and can present with enthusiasm.
2. Select your reasons and evidence with your audience in mind. You are already convinced; your task is to convince your readers.
3. Decide whether your audience can be approached directly or if they should be approached indirectly—gently and with plenty of evidence before receiving your "pitch."
4. Arrange your argument in whatever structural pattern is most appropriate for your issue and your audience.
5. Remember that there is another side to the issue. You can help your own cause by presenting the opposing viewpoint and refuting it. Present the other side tactfully and fairly. You will only antagonize readers by unfairly stating or belittling the case for the other side. Opinions are as sensitive as toes: tread carefully to avoid causing pain.

The five essays that follow illustrate a variety of approaches to argument and persuasion. Read the essays and answer the questions that follow each one.

A CITY FOR STUDENTS
Aliki Tryphonopoulos

1   It is hard to think of a city more exhilarating for a student to live in than Montreal. Where else can you hear a conversation shift between two or even three languages with ease and playfulness at the local coffee shop? Cosmopolitan and cultured, *la belle ville* is unique in North America for its intersection of two historically established language groups with a large and growing immigrant population. Montrealers have translated this rich cultural diversity into a vibrant civic life with world-renowned festivals, a well-established art scene, lively café culture, and acclaimed international cuisine and fashion. Few cities in the world offer the affordable living, student amenities, and cultural dynamism that Montreal does.

2   Long-standing socioeconomic factors make Montreal an affordable city for students—no small consideration given that Canadian undergraduate tuition has risen by 111 percent since 1990 ("Bottom Line," 2004). Naysayers point out that although Quebec has the lowest tuition rates in Canada (frozen since 1994), out-of-province students must pay roughly twice as much as Quebec residents, placing them in the higher bracket of national tuition payers. Some students get around this disadvantage by working and taking part-time classes for a year in order to qualify for the in-province tuition rates. For those who are required to pay the higher rates, however, the financial burden is more than offset by the relatively low cost of rental housing in Montreal (Canada Mortgage, 2004, table 2). One of the best ways for students to economize is by living close to the university. Montreal is a walking city, so it is possible for students to conduct all of their business within a five-block radius.

3   Pedestrian-friendly urban planning plays a large part in Montreal's reputation as a festival city that hosts over 40 events annually. In the sultry summer months, streets shut down for the Jazz Festival, the Montreal Grand Prix, and Just for Laughs, while the Fête des Neiges and the Montreal High Lights Festival provide outdoor activities and culinary delights in the winter. Students find plenty of ways to keep active—cycling, jogging, skating, skiing, dancing and drumming at Montreal's sexy Tam-Tams in Mount Royal Park—and gain

an appreciation of the city's vibrant arts scene, from the numerous galleries in Old Montreal to fine art cinemas such as Cinema du Parc and Ex-Centris. Students can argue the merits of the latest Denys Arcand film in one of the many cafés along St. Denis frequented by their compatriots from Concordia, McGill, Université de Montréal, and Université du Québec à Montréal. As for ambience, the eclectic mix of old European limestone mansions and North American glass towers lends this oldest of Canadian cities a unique architectural allure.

4   Montreal's cultural dynamism, whose historic roots draw comparisons to such international cities as Barcelona and Brussels, is not only the city's most attractive attribute, but sadly, what scares many students away. Bill 101, meant to protect the French language in Quebec, contributed to the exodus of nonfrancophones from Montreal during the 1980s and 1990s. That trend is slowly reversing (DeWolf, 2003). A recent study reveals what Montrealers already know: the unique interaction of francophone, anglophone, and allophone (languages other than French or English) cultures in Montreal is characterized by mutual respect, accommodation, and even a sense of fun (Lamarre, 2002). Students can absorb and appreciate the international flavour of the various boroughs and contribute to the daily cultural exchange. With the city's high rates of bilingualism and trilingualism, anglophone students do not need to know French in order to function, but their social and cultural life will be far richer if they do. And what better place to learn *la langue française* than in the second-largest French-speaking city in the world!

5   Education is as much about what goes on outside the classroom as in it. Those students who are willing to embrace Montreal's vibrant cultural milieu will find their worldviews challenged and broadened. In a global environment fraught with the dangers of intercultural miscommunication and ignorance, that kind of education is vital.

References

The bottom line. (2004, November 15). *Maclean's*, p. 72.

Canada Mortgage and Housing Corporation. (2004, December 1). *Average rents in privately initiated apartment structures of three units and over in metropolitan areas* (table 2). Retrieved December 22, 2004, from http://www.cmhc.ca/en/News/nere/2004/2004-12-21-0715.cfm

DeWolf, C. (2003, May 25). The road to Montreal. *The Gazette* [Montreal]. Retrieved December 20, 2004, from http://maisonneuve.org/about_media.php?press_media_id=21

Lamarre, P. (2002). Multilingual Montreal: Listening in on the language practices of young Montrealers. *Canadian Ethnic Studies, 34*(3), 47–75.

Questions for Discussion

1. This essay's introduction establishes the author's thesis and previews her main points. What other purposes does it serve?
2. In an argument, it is often necessary to address the opposition's point of view. The writer can choose either to turn a negative into a positive, or to present the opposition's arguments and then refute them. Find examples of both techniques in this essay.
3. The acknowledgment of source material is a standard feature of academic research papers. Why do you think the author of this general-interest essay uses and documents source material?
4. Use InfoTrac to do a keyword search of "Montreal." How many hits did you get? Narrow your search to find information that supports the key points of this essay. What keyword gave you the best results?

"HIRE" LEARNING
Editorial[1]

1   Ideally, at the core of our education system lies the desire to inculcate those talents and attitudes that prepare the young for the obligations of citizenship and open them to greater intellectual and spiritual life. What, then, should we make of suggestions that children be paid to get good grades? "Kids are growing up in a lean and mean environment," says psychologist Robert Butterworth, president of Los Angeles-based International Trauma Associates. "If adults don't work for free, why should kids?" Mr. Butterworth says governments should consider rewarding students with a $50 cheque for every A grade.

2   Right off the bat, we're flunking Mr. Butterworth—for promoting even more government interference in our lives (with the extra taxation that implies). But his cash for grades idea should also be condemned for its reductionist view of education and human psychology.

3   Don't get us wrong. Rewarding children for getting good grades with money is a common practice in many families, and there's nothing wrong with it as long as the money is not an end in itself. But that is precisely what Mr. Butterworth is proposing. He effectively makes money the "end" of education by saying, implicitly at least, that the only reason to get good grades is for cash. To our mind, that's the same as saying that money is the only standard by which people's accomplishments are to be judged, that without the money they have accomplished nothing. In short, money becomes the cause, not the effect. It becomes the only measure of human worth.

[1] *Ottawa Citizen*, August 13, 1999.

4   It is a measure. Certainly, many people go to school—particularly college and university—so that they'll be able to get good jobs. But that is not the deepest purpose of education. A good education may be essential to job success, but at the same time, it is also the best route for availing us of those spiritual satisfactions that give our practical success wider significance. Education, ultimately, opens our psyche to the possibility of being better than we might otherwise be.

5   Consider the student who spends weeks on some project and wins the plaudits of his teacher and classmates. Sure, a bit of cash might be nice; heck, the plaudits are nice. But the real reward is psychological. It comes from knowing that you have done something, accomplished something, learned something, that wasn't yours yesterday. Such recognition reinforces those talents that push a student to greater achievements in a cycle that, hopefully, leads to a modicum of wisdom. In that sense, intellectual endeavour is its own reward.

6   Mr. Butterworth's proposals, if instituted, would forego this spiritual dimension of education, turning a child's schooling into a "job." Indeed, his prescription would reduce education to the functional task of gaining "competitive advantage" or "enhancing productivity" (this sounds a bit like the debate over teaching liberal arts in universities).

7   But what about the school years as a time of playfulness, discovery, risks, and failures? In a world where your "income" depends on your grades, who'd want to waste time on some difficult intellectual effort? Why savour Shakespeare if a scan of Coles Notes will win the paycheque?

8   Yes, parents reward their children for good performance. Sometimes that includes a bit of cash. But, first, we hope, it includes sharing the excitement of learning. Mr. Butterworth gets an F.

Questions for Discussion

1. Is this editorial intended to be an argument or a persuasive piece? Support your answer with evidence from the piece.
2. Review the discussion of the "their side–my side strategy" and "the proposition + supporting reasons" structures on pages 240–41. Which of these structural patterns does the author use in this piece?
3. Paragraph 7 contains three rhetorical questions (questions to which no answer is expected). Why do you think the writer chose rhetorical questions rather than declarative sentences? Rewrite the three questions as statements and then describe the different effects the two versions have on the reader.
4. As a postsecondary student, do you think that education should be exclusively about learning how to earn a living? Or do you believe that postsecondary education should include the study of subjects

that contribute to your learning how to live the life that you earn? Did reading this editorial influence your opinion in any way? How?

5. It is said that most newspapers are aimed at a grade 8 reading level. Cite evidence that suggests " 'Hire' Learning" was written for a higher-level reader. Why do you think this editorial is aimed at a more-educated audience than the newspaper norm?

6. Use InfoTrac to find another article by or about California child psychologist Robert R. Butterworth. (Be careful! The database contains articles by several Robert Butterworths.) Read the article and then, using both the article and " 'Hire' Learning" for support, summarize your opinion of Mr. Butterworth's ideas about child psychology.

OF PAIN, PREDATORS, AND PLEASURE

Walter Isaacs

1   The issue of whether fish feel pain when hooked by an angler has been widely debated in a number of publications recently. Scientific studies arguing that the fish's mouth does or does not have pain receptors have supported both sides of this debate. It seems to me that this squabble is as irrelevant as the medieval debates about how many angels can dance on the head of a pin. Of course we cause the fish distress, mortal distress! Like any animal, the fish is programmed to survive and procreate. Any predatory threat to that primal function—from a bear, an osprey, a bigger fish, or an angler—must cause extreme stress; whether that stress can be called "pain" through anthropomorphism, it's certainly more dire to the fish than the prick of a hook in its jaw (felt as "pain" or not). To argue that we aren't distressing a fish by catching it is to hand opponents of fishing proof that fishers are either in denial or just plain stupid.

2   I admit that I love tricking fish. I take as much pleasure as anyone in catching them, and my pleasure is increased when I've been especially clever or skillful in fooling the creature into taking my fly. I do everything that I can to minimize the pain and stress on any fish I catch, but I cannot deny that by catching the fish, I am in a sense torturing it for my pleasure. How can I justify my actions?

3   First, I acknowledge that I am a predator and something somewhere in me loves the idea of taking a wild animal through stealth or guile, even when (as I almost always do) I release it unharmed. Whether this instinct comes from a gene somewhere in my DNA or a gland buried in the folds of my brain, there's no denying that it's there. Just as I enjoy sex, laughter, anchovies on pizza, warm fall days, a Bach concerto, and a good Riesling, I enjoy catching fish on

a fly. Some pleasures are instinctive, some are learned, but the fact that they are pleasures cannot be denied. Yes, I could give up any of these pleasures if the motivation were sufficient, but so far I haven't had sufficient motivation to relinquish any of them.

4   Second, let's acknowledge that, as predators go, anglers are relatively benign. When you compare the millions of fish that are hatched to the number that live long enough to be the prey of anglers, it's clear that other predators are more efficient and more dangerous than fly fishers. I suppose the case could be made that for every salmon killed by an angler, thousands of eels and other sea creatures are saved. If we can anthropomorphize the fish's pain, let's go another step and ask the fish which predator it would rather be caught by: that female osprey gliding over the river, or Walter Isaac. Both predators will cause it the immediate fear/stress/pain of being caught, but in the first case, the osprey will feed its catch alive to its chicks; in the second, the fish will survive to procreate.

5   Finally, because of my love of fishing, I contribute both time and money to support such activities as the restoration and maintenance of stream habitat, stocking programs, and the development of a cleaner, wilder environment in which fish can thrive. In other words, my conservation efforts help to produce more and healthier fish at the end of each season than there would be if I didn't love tricking them.

6   If I could fish without harming the creatures in any way, I'd do it in a heart-beat. But since I must hurt the fish somewhat to pursue an activity that gives me such pleasure, these justifications serve to let me do it in good conscience, while recognizing and respecting the stress I cause. I know that what I've said won't convince those who are fundamentally opposed to angling, and I understand their viewpoint. But such people just don't seem to have that gene or gland that makes fishing such a pleasure for me. Heck, I even know people who don't like sex.

Questions for Discussion

1. The argument that is the basis for this essay is supported by three points. What are they? In what order has the author arranged his sup-porting evidence?

2. This essay was first published in a fly-fishing magazine. Identify clues that indicate the piece was written for a sympathetic audience.

3. How would the essay differ if it had been written for an audience of animal-rights activists? Draft a rough outline for such an essay.

4. The essay's concluding sentence seems to have been tossed off for the purpose of ending on a light note. What more serious purpose does it serve in supporting the author's argument?

5. This essay is, among other things, the author's response to contradictory findings about whether or not fish feel pain the way humans do. Use InfoTrac to find articles on this subject. Be sure to choose articles that reflect both sides of the argument. After reading a few of these articles, decide which side of the debate you support. In a sentence or two, summarize your opinion and identify three or four reasons that support it.

ARTS EDUCATION DOES PAY OFF

Livio Di Matteo

1   Canada's universities—particularly the humanities and social sciences—face a major challenge. The current approach to education emphasizes immediate tangible benefits. This has led to government funding initiatives in science and technology that fail to recognize the importance of a liberal arts education. Yet supporting a humanities and social science education is justified on sound economic grounds, not just on the civic and academic grounds usually used.

2   The humanities and social sciences provide social benefits that private market mechanisms do not count. Just as a vaccination benefits people other than those inoculated by reducing disease transmission, the humanities and social sciences have spill-over benefits by transmitting wisdom to society. The inability to attach a market price to a literate and civil society of educated citizens does not make this type of education valueless.

3   The humanities and social sciences complement scientific and technical training, and provide innovative strategies for meeting future challenges. While science graduates can provide technical solutions to problems, only individuals trained in human science can deal with the economic, ethical, cultural and social implications of these solutions. For example, we are told that advances in genetics are making a vastly extended human lifespan possible in the not-so-distant future. How will this affect the distribution of income and employment, and the quality of life in our society? Is this type of analysis not of economic benefit to society?

4   Market benefits to humanities and social science graduates translate into jobs, as economist Robert Allen of the University of British Columbia recently demonstrated in a study. Prof. Allen found that unemployment rates for humanities and social science graduates did not substantially differ from those of graduates in other fields. Moreover, these graduates' age–income profiles can actually be steeper than those in the sciences or technical programs, where the latest technical knowledge depreciates quickly. Like fine wine, humanities and social science graduates appreciate with age as their skills deepen, generating a steeply rising income over their working life. Some uni-

versities, such as Dalhousie, are beginning to [issue transcripts that list] skills such as collaborative work, oral communication, and analytical work to their liberal arts graduates. This communicates what was once obvious, but now has to be marketed: Liberal arts graduates are prized because of their ability to think creatively and laterally, using skills acquired in analysis, synthesis, research and communication.

5   Having reduced their market intervention on the grounds that private forces work best, governments are now replicating that interventionist role in post-secondary education by targeting funding increases to programs in science and technology. These programs are worthy of funding, but for universities to function according to a private-sector model, governments should provide universities with block increases in funding and allow them to pursue those programs they are best at. Targeted funding distorts resource allocation decisions by inducing universities to expand government-favoured programs. This leaves governments selecting educational winners and losers when the economy's future needs are uncertain.

6   Other issues present themselves, too. What about the long-run cost structure of universities, given that the per-student cost of producing science and engineering graduates is higher than in other fields? Who is responsible if such funding generates a graduate glut in any one discipline? Will government be accountable, or will the buck be passed to the universities for once again "failing" in their role to society?

7   Humanities and social sciences students make up approximately half of university enrolments. If you believe that "voting with your feet" is a test of market demand, this enrolment share should be sending a clear message to educational policy-makers as to how the public values these programs. Humanities and social science students should be entitled to adequate research and teaching facilities, and to professors who conduct leading-edge research. When it comes to resource allocation, why should half of university students be placed on a path to second-rate treatment when they are indeed "paying customers"?

8   It is time to restore some balance. The current targeted funding approach ignores the obvious demand for humanities and social science training. Governments can best serve the university system by ensuring adequate general funding and allowing universities, in consultation with government and the public, to make the resource allocation decisions. In neglecting the humanities and social sciences, governments have not fully consulted all constituencies, and their funding decisions implicitly attach a negative value to these disciplines. Canadian society will pay huge economic and cultural costs if such myopic policies are continued.

Di Matteo, Livio. "Arts Education Does Pay Off." *Financial Post* 31 May 1999: 3.

Questions for Discussion

1. Does the author approach his argument directly or indirectly? Where is the thesis statement? Identify the reasons the author cites to support his opinion.
2. Who is the target audience for this essay? How do you know?
3. What is the author's purpose: to win his readers' agreement, or to move them to action? What sort of action could they take to support the author on this issue?
4. Identify the various kinds of evidence the author uses in this essay.
5. The author uses a number of rhetorical questions (questions to which no answer is expected). Are they effective in supporting his argument? Why?
6. In your own words, explain why the author thinks targeted funding is a poor idea. (See paragraphs 5 and 6.)
7. Do you agree with the author? Why or why not?

STUPID JOBS ARE GOOD TO RELAX WITH

Hal Niedzviecki

1 Springsteen kicked off his world tour at Toronto's Massey Hall a while back. Along with record company execs and those who could afford the exorbitant prices scalpers wanted for tickets, I was in attendance. As Bruce rambled on about the plight of the itinerant Mexican workers, I lolled in the back, my job, as always, to make myself as unapproachable as possible—no easy feat, trapped as I was in paisley vest and bow-tie combo. Nonetheless, the concert was of such soporific proportions and the crowd so dulled into pseudo-reverence, I was able to achieve the ultimate in ushering—a drooping catatonia as close as you can get to being asleep while on your feet at a rock concert.

2 But this ushering nirvana wouldn't last long. For an usher, danger takes many forms, including vomiting teens and the usher's nemesis: the disruptive patron. And yes, to my semi-conscious horror, there she was: well-dressed, blond, drunk and doped up, swaying in her seat and . . . clapping. Clapping. In the middle of Springsteen's solo dirge about Pancho or Pedro or Luisa, she was clapping.

3 Sweat beaded on my forehead. The worst was happening. She was in my section. Her clapping echoed through the hall, renowned for its acoustics. The Boss glared from the stage, his finger-picking folksiness no match for the drunken rhythm of this fan. Then, miracle of miracles, the song ended. The woman slumped back into her seat. Bruce muttered something about how he didn't need a rhythm section. Placated by the adoring silence of the well-to-

do, he launched into an even quieter song about an even more desperate migrant worker.

4   I lurked in the shadows, relaxed the grip I had on my flashlight (the usher's only weapon). Springsteen crooned. His guitar twanged. It was so quiet you could hear the rats squirrelling around the ushers' subterranean change rooms. The woman roused herself from her slumber. She leaned forward in her seat, as if suddenly appreciating the import of her hero's message. I wiped the sweat off my brow, relieved. But slowly, almost imperceptibly, she brought her arms up above her head. I stared, disbelieving. Her hands waved around in the air until . . . boom! Another song ruined, New York record execs and L.A. journalists distracted from their calculations of Bruce's net worth, the faint cry of someone calling, "Usher! Do something!"

5   For several years now, I have relied on stupid jobs to pay my way through the world. This isn't because I am a stupid person. On the contrary, stupid jobs are a way to avoid the brain-numbing idiocy of full-time employment. They are the next best thing to having no job at all. They will keep you sane, and smart.

6   I'm lazy sometimes. I don't always feel like working. On the stupid job, you're allowed to be lazy. All you have to do is show up. Hey, that's as much of an imposition on my life as I'm ready to accept. Does The Boss go to work every day? I don't think so. He's The Boss.

7   Understanding the stupid job is the key to wading your way through the muck of the working week and dealing with such portentous concepts as The Youth Unemployment Crisis and The Transformation of the Workplace. So sit back and let me explain. Or, as I used to say behind the scowl of my shining grin: "Hi, how are you this evening? Please follow me and I will show you to your seat."

8   "Out of Work: Is There Hope for Canada's Youth?" blurted the October 1997 issue of *Canadian Living.* My answer? There is more hope than ever. I'm not talking about ineffectual governments and their well-intentioned "partners," the beneficent corporations, all banding together to "create" jobs. After all, what kind of jobs do you think these corporations are going to create? Jobs that are interesting, challenging and resplendent with possibilities? Hardly. These are going to be stupid jobs. Bring me your college graduates, your aspiring business mavens, your literature lovers and we will find them rote employment where servility and docility are the best things they could have learned at university.

9   But hope, hope is something altogether different. Hope is the process whereby entire generations learn to undervalue their work, squirm out of the trap of meaningless employment, work less, consume less and actually figure out how to enjoy life.

10 I hope I'm right about this, because the reality of the underemployed, overeducated young people of Canada is that the stupid job is their future. As the middle-aged population continues to occupy all the "real" jobs, as the universities continue to hike tuition prices (forcing students to work and study part time), as the government continues to shore up employment numbers with make-work and "retraining," there will be more stupid jobs than ever. And these stupid jobs won't be reserved for the uneducated and poor. The fertile growth of the stupid job is already reaping a crop of middle-class youngsters whose education and upbringing have, somehow, given way to (supposedly) stalled prospects and uncertain incomes.

11 These are your grandchildren, your children, your sisters, your cousins, your neighbours. Hey, that might very well be a multicoloured bow-tie wrapped around your neck.

12 I took a few tenuous steps down the aisle. All around me, luxurious people hissed in annoyance and extended their claws. Clapping woman was bouncing in her seat. She was smiling. Her face was flushed and joyous. The sound of her hands coming together was deafening. I longed for the floor captain, the front-of-house manager, the head of security, somebody to come and take this problem away from me. I hit her with a burst of flashlight. Taking advantage of her momentary blindness, I leaned in: "Excuse me Miss," I said. "You can't do that." "What?" she said. "That clapping," I said. "Listen," she slurred. "I paid $300 to see this. I can do what I want."

13 My flashlight hand wavered. Correctly interpreting my silence for defeat, she resumed her clapping. Springsteen strummed louder, unsuccessful in his attempt to drown out the beat of luxury, the truth of indulgence. I faded away, the darkness swallowing me up. For a blissful moment, I was invisible.

14 A lot of young people think their stupid jobs are only temporary. Most of them are right, in a way. Many will move on from being, as I have been, an usher, a security guard, a delivery boy, a data co-ordinator, a publishing intern. They will get marginally better jobs, but what they have learned from their stupid jobs will stay with them forever. Hopefully.

15 If I'm right, they will learn that the stupid job—and by extension, all jobs— must be approached with willing stupidity. Set your mind free. It isn't neces- sary, and it can be an impediment. While your body runs the maze and finds the cheese, let your mind go where it will.

16 Look at it this way: you're trading material wealth and luxury for freedom and creativity. To simplify this is to say that while you may have less money to buy things, you will have a lot more time to think up ways to achieve your goals without buying things. It is remarkable how quickly one comes to value time to just sit and think. Oddly, many of us seem quite proud of having

absolutely no time to think about anything. The words "I'm so busy" are chanted over and over again like a mantra, an incantation against some horrible moment when we realize we're not so busy. In the stupid job universe, time isn't quantifiable. You're making so many dollars an hour, but the on-job perks include daydreams, poems scribbled on napkins, novels read in utility closets and long conversations about the sexual stamina of Barney Rubble. How much is an idea worth? An image? A moment of tranquillity? A bad joke? The key here is to embrace the culture of anti-work.

17   Sometime after the Springsteen debacle, I was on a delivery job dropping off newspapers at various locales. I started arguing with my co-worker, the van driver, about work ethic. I suggested we skip a drop-off or two, claiming that no one would notice and even if they did, we could deny it and no one would care. He responded by telling me that no matter what job he was doing, if he accepted the work, he was compelled to do it right. I disagreed. Cut corners, I argued. Do less for the same amount of pay. That's what they expect us to do, I said. Why else would they pay us so little? Not that day, but some weeks later, he came to see things my way.

18   What am I trying to tell you? To be lazy? To set fire to the corporation?

19   Maybe. Our options might be limited, but they are still options. Somewhere in the bowels of Massey Hall it has probably been noted in my permanent record that I have a bad attitude. That was a mistake. I wasn't trying to have a bad attitude. I was trying to have no attitude. . . .

20   What I should have told my friend in the delivery van was that when working the stupid job, passivity is the difference between near slavery and partial freedom. It's a mental distinction. Your body is still in the same place for the same amount of time (unless you're unsupervised), but your mind is figuring things out. Figuring out how many days you need to work to afford things like hard-to-get tickets to concerts by famous American icons. Or figuring out why it is that at the end of the week, most people are too busy or too tired to do anything other than spend their hard-earned dollars on fleeting moments of cotton candy ecstasy as ephemeral as lunch hour. Personally, I'd take low-level servitude over a promotion that means I'll be working late the rest of my life. You want me to work weekends? You better give me the rest of the week off. . . .

21   Montreal has one of the highest unemployment rates of any city in Canada. Young people in that city are as likely to have full-time jobs as they are to spend their nights arguing about Quebec separation. Not coincidentally, some of the best Canadian writers, comic artists and underground periodicals are from that city. We're talking about the spoken-word capital of North America here. Creativity plus unemployment equals art.

22   The burgeoning stupid job aesthetic is well documented in another youth culture phenomenon, the vaunted 'zine (photocopied periodicals published by individuals for fun, not money). Again, it doesn't take a genius to make the connection between the youth culture of stupid jobs and the urgency and creativity 'zine publishers display when writing about their lives. "So why was I dishonest and subversive?" asks Brendan Bartholomew in an article in the popular Wisconsin 'zine *Temp Slave*. "Well, I've been sabotaging employers for so long, it's become second nature. It's in my blood. I couldn't stop if I wanted to."

23   Slacking off, doing as little as possible, relishing my lack of responsibility, this is what the workplace has taught me to do. This is the stupid job mantra. It isn't about being poor. The stupid job aesthetic is not about going hungry. Canada is a country of excess. You cannot have a stupid job culture when people are genuinely, truly, worried that they are going to starve in the streets.

24   Nevertheless, the tenets of the stupid job revolution are universal: work is mainly pointless; if you can think of something better to do, you shouldn't have to work; it's better to have a low-paying job and freedom than a high-paying job and a 60-hour workweek. It was Bruce's drunken fan who highlighted the most important aspect of what will one day be known as the stupid job revolution: with money, you think you can do whatever you want, but you rarely can; without money, you can be like Bartholomew—a postmodern rat, a stowaway writing his diaries from the comfort of his berth at the bottom of the sinking ship.

25   My father's plight is a familiar one. He started his working life at 13 in Montreal. He's 55 now. His employer of 12 years forced him to take early retirement. The terms were great, and if he didn't own so much stuff (and want more stuff) he could live comfortably without ever working again. But he feels used, meaningless, rejected.

26   On his last day, I helped him clean out his office. The sight of him stealing staplers, blank disks and Post-it note pads was something I'll never forget. It was a memo he was writing to his own soul (note: they owe me).

27   But the acquisition of more stuff is not what he needs to put a life of hard work behind him. I wish that he could look back on his years of labour and think fondly of all the hours he decided not to work, those hours he spent reading a good book behind the closed door of his office, or skipping off early to take the piano lessons he never got around to. Instead of stealing office supplies, he should have given his boss the finger as he walked out the door. Ha ha. I don't care what you think of me. And by the way, I never did.

28   Despite his decades of labour and my years of being barely employed (and the five degrees we have between us), we have both ended up at the same place. He feels cheated. I don't.

Questions for Discussion

1. Which paragraph states the thesis of the essay?
2. What strategy does the author use in his conclusion (see paragraphs 25 to 28)? Do you think it's effective? Why?
3. What were your expectations of the author when you read the title of the essay? Were you surprised to find words such as "exorbitant," "soporific," and "catatonia" in the first paragraph? What other elements of style and structure tell us that the author is far from "stupid"?
4. Is this essay primarily argument or persuasion?
5. What is the basis of the author's argument with the van driver as they're dropping off newspapers? (See paragraphs 17 to 20.) Whom do you agree with? Who has the right attitude toward the job?
6. What proof does the author offer to support his point that art and creativity are likely to flourish among people who are unemployed or have "stupid jobs"?
7. What is the author's attitude toward consumerism? Does he think we buy too much or not enough? Where in the essay is his attitude most clearly revealed? Do you agree with him? Why?

Exercise 17.1

Read through the following list of propositions. With a partner, select one that you are both interested in, but do not discuss it. Working individually, write down two or three points both for and against the issue. Then exchange papers and read each other's work. Which points appear on both lists? Why? Can you judge from the points presented whether your partner is for or against the issue?

Canada should (should not) increase its level of immigration.
The salaries of professional athletes should (should not) be capped.
Music lyrics should (should not) be monitored and censored.
Technology is (is not) improving the workplace.
Courses in physical education should (should not) be required throughout high school.
Smokers should (should not) receive the same medical coverage as non-smokers.

Exercise 17.2

Most people have firm convictions, yet few are willing to take action to uphold them. Everyone agrees, for example, that a cure for cancer should be found, but not everyone participates in fundraising events or supports the Cancer Society. With a partner, choose a charitable cause in which you believe and list all the reasons why people should give money to support it. Then list all the reasons people might give for not donating.

Decide which of you will take the "pro" side and which the "con," and write a short essay arguing your position. You will know from your discussion whether your partner is sympathetic or hostile, so you will know whether you should approach your subject directly or indirectly. Then exchange papers and critique each other's work.

Exercise 17.3

Together with a partner, select a *small*, controversial, local issue (one involving your community, college, or profession, for example). Choose sides, and write an argument using the "their side–my side" pattern of organization.

Exercise 17.4

With a partner, develop a questionnaire and survey at least 20 students in your college, from different programs and different years, to determine their attitude toward one of the following:

food services
class sizes
professors' teaching ability
required (or general education) courses
tutorial (or counselling) services

Both of you should take notes during these interviews.

When you and your partner have gathered enough information, it's time to work independently. Compose an indirect argument that arrives at a conclusion about the issue and makes a recommendation based on the evidence you have gathered. Compare your paper with your partner's. What are the main similarities and differences between your two compositions? What conclusions can you draw from your comparative analysis?

Exercise 17.5

Choose an issue with which you are familiar and about which you feel strongly. If you don't feel strongly about anything, choose a proposition from the list below. Draft a statement of thesis and outline your reasons and evidence. Then write a persuasive paper, making sure that your points are well supported and that the paper is clearly structured. Assume that your reader is not hostile, but is not enthusiastically supportive, either.

Forty percent of the college curriculum should/should not be devoted to liberal arts (general education) courses.
Marijuana should/should not be available for sale through government-controlled retail outlets.
Grades in college courses should/should not take effort into consideration, not just results.
Parents of underage youth should/should not be financially responsible for damages their offspring may cause to other people's property.

PART 5

The Research Paper

Introduction

A **research paper** is an essay that presents the results of a writer's investigation of a topic in print, electronic, or multimedia formats. The skills involved—finding, evaluating, and assimilating the ideas of other writers—are essential in any field of study. They will also be useful to you in your career. Much of the writing you do on the job, especially if you are in management, requires you to express in your own words the facts, opinions, and ideas of others.

Writing a research paper follows the same process as other kinds of writing, from planning through drafting to revising. The difference is that instead of relying exclusively on what you already know about a topic, you include source material—facts, data, knowledge, or opinions of other writers—to support your thesis. Chapter 18 explains the different kinds of source material you can choose from and tells you the strengths and weaknesses of each. Chapter 19 shows you how to integrate the information you have found into your paper.

A research paper is not simply a collection of what other people have said about a subject. It is your responsibility to shape and control the discussion, to make sure that what you include from your sources is interesting and relevant to your thesis, and to comment on its validity or significance. It is *your* paper, *your* subject, *your* main points; ideas from other writers should be included as support for *your* topic sentences.

One of the challenges of writing a research paper is differentiating between your ideas and those you took from sources. Readers cannot hear the different "speakers," so you have to indicate who said what. To separate your sources from your own ideas, research papers require **documentation**—a system of acknowledging source materials. Chapter 20 shows you how to provide your readers with a guide to the information contained in your paper—a play-by-play of who is "speaking."

Research papers are usually longer than essays, and the planning process is more complex. For these reasons, the time you are given to complete a research assignment is usually longer than the time allowed for an essay. Don't fool yourself into thinking you can put the assignment off for a few weeks. You will need all the time you've been given to find the sources you need, decide what you want to say, and then draft, revise, and polish your paper. Instructors assign research papers so that they can assess not only your research skills but also your writing skills.

Tips on Writing a Research Paper

1. Even though your instructor may be your only reader, think of your potential audience as your fellow students—those taking the course with you, those who took it in recent years, and those who will take it in the near future. This way, you can count on a certain amount of shared knowledge. For a course in economics, for example, you can assume your audience knows what the Phillips Curve relationship is; a definition would be superfluous. For a course in literature, you won't need to inform your readers that Jonathan Swift was an 18th-century satirist. Think of your readers as colleagues who want to see what conclusions you have reached and what evidence you have used to support them.

2. Manage your time carefully. Divide the work into a number of tasks, develop a schedule that leaves lots of time for revision, and stick to your schedule.

3. Choose a subject that interests you. Define it as precisely as you can before beginning your research, but be prepared to modify, adapt, and revise it as you research and write your paper.

4. If you cannot find appropriate sources, ask a reference librarian for help.

5. When making notes, *always* record the author, title, publication data, and page numbers of the source. For electronic sources, note also the URL and the date you accessed the site.

6. Use your source material to support your own ideas, not the other way around.

7. Document your sources according to whatever style your instructor prefers.

8. Revise, edit, and proofread carefully. If you omit this step, the hours and weeks you have spent on your assignment will be wasted, not rewarded.

18

Researching
Your Subject

Your first step in writing a research paper is the same as your first step in any writing task: select a suitable subject, preferably one you are curious about. Whether you are assigned a topic or choose your own, don't rush off to the library or log onto the Internet right away. A little preparation up front will save you a lot of time and possibly much grief later on.

First of all, if you're not sure what your instructor expects, clarify what is required of you. Next, even if your subject is tentative, check it with the 4-S test: is it significant, single, specific, and supportable (researchable)? If not, refine it by using the techniques discussed in Chapter 3. Finally, consider what approach you might take in presenting your subject. Does it lend itself to a comparison? Process? Cause or effect? If the topic is assigned, often the wording of the assignment will suggest how your instructor wants you to develop it. Deciding up front what kind of paper you are going to write will save you hours of time, both in the library and at your desk.

Exercise 18.1

In the workplace, people rarely have the opportunity to select a research topic without consultation. In some cases, the subject is assigned or approved by a board of directors; in others, a committee is responsible for ensuring that a research project meets the company's needs.

Before you start your own research project, take some time to ensure that your proposed subject is appropriate for the time and space you have been given. The class should be divided into "committees" of four or five people. Each committee should be given four or five pieces of coloured paper, a different colour for each group.

- Each committee identifies a chairperson and a note-taker. At the direction of the chair, each member of the committee presents an idea for a research paper. After each presentation, discuss the subject in terms of its significance to the target audience (the whole class, including the instructor). If the committee feels a subject requires revision to be significant, make these revisions as a group. It is important that the committee come to a consensus regarding any revisions.
- Once each subject is agreed upon as significant, record it on a slip of the coloured paper assigned to your committee.
- Repeat this procedure until your committee has identified at least one significant subject for each of its members.
- Toss your committee's subjects into the company's think tank (a container), along with the subjects submitted by the other committees in the class.
- The chair of each committee draws out of the think tank four or five proposed research subjects. Be sure to draw a representative sampling of colours from other committees.
- As a committee, discuss each subject that has been drawn from the think tank. Since each has already been approved as significant by another committee, your task is to determine whether each proposed subject is single and specific.
- For each subject, record any revisions that the committee deems necessary and briefly explain why.
- Return the revised subjects to their appropriate committees according to the corresponding coloured paper.
- When every committee has received its original proposed research subjects, each group discusses the suggested revisions until everyone understands them.
- Next, as a committee, discuss whether each proposed subject is supportable. What sorts of research materials would you look for to help you explain and defend each subject?
- Record the final version of the proposed research subjects on a flip chart, ready to present to a board of directors. (You should have one subject for each member of the committee.)
- Present your committee's proposed research subjects before the board of directors (the whole class). Discuss the revisions and decide whether each proposal now meets the criteria of the 4-S test.

When you're sure your subject is appropriate and you've decided, at least tentatively, on the approach you're going to take, you are ready to focus on the kind of information you need to look for in your research. For example, if you've been asked to apply four theories of conflict to a case study, you won't waste time discussing the major schools of conflict theory or their development over the last few decades. You can restrict your investigation to sources that contain information relevant to your specific subject.

Once you have an idea of the kind of information you need in order to develop your topic, it's time to find the best sources you can. But how will you know if what you've found is "good" information?

Selecting Your Sources

Not all sources are created equal. There's no point in wasting time making notes on a source unless the information is relevant, current, and reliable. Evaluating the quality of source material before you use it is a key step in the research process.

To evaluate a print source, first check it over closely. Scan the table of contents, the headings, and chapters or articles to ensure the book or periodical contains information relevant to your topic. ("Periodicals" are publications that are produced at regular "periods," such as daily newspapers or monthly magazines.) Then check to see where the information comes from: its author, the date it was published, and the organization or company that published it. Most traditional print sources—newspapers, magazines, and scholarly journals—have fact-checkers and editorial boards to ensure that the information they publish is reliable.

Print sources are easier to assess for reliability than electronic sources. Yet the Internet and the World Wide Web have vastly increased the amount of potential research material, and it is essential to learn how to evaluate it. For example, if you are doing a report on a recent business venture or medical breakthrough, the most current information will be online. How do you decide, given the millions of pieces of information out there in cyberspace, what is useful for your specific purpose? Of course, when you use online editions of traditional print sources (e.g., electronic versions of newspapers, magazines, and books), you can assume the same standards of credibility and reliability. The CD-ROM full-text versions of *The Globe and Mail* or the *Financial Times* are no less (and no more) accurate than the printed versions.

With electronic sources that have no hard-copy equivalent, the domain name is one place to begin your evaluation. Does the source's URL end with .com (commercial), .gov (government), or .edu (educational institution)? Sites from these different sources will present data on a topic in different ways. A commercial site will probably attempt to influence consumers as well as to inform them. A .edu suffix suggests the credibility of a recognized college or university, but offbeat student web pages or the informal musings of faculty members at the institution may share the suffix as well.

Another difference between print and electronic sources is authorship. There is seldom any doubt about who wrote a particular book or article. In online material, however, often no author (or date) is identified. Sometimes the person who compiles ("comp") or maintains ("maint") the website is the only one named. For academic research, it's wise to be cautious of "no-name" sources. If you wish to use information from one of these sources, be sure the organization or institution where it originated is reliable. You wouldn't want to be researching the history of discrimination in Canada, for example, and find yourself quoting from the disguised website of a hate organization.

Recognizing that much online work is collaborative and that several writers may have contributed to a potential source, it is a good idea to check out the people who are involved in producing it. Powerful online search engines such as Google make checking the author's reliability easier for electronic sources than it is for print sources. Simply key the author's name into the search engine and then evaluate the results to see if he or she is a credible person in the field. Often you'll be able to check the author's biography, credentials, other publications, and business or academic affiliation. If no author's name is given, you can check out the company, organization, or institution in the same way. Cyber-sleuthing is a useful skill to learn!

In the end, however, with both print and electronic sources, you must apply your own critical intelligence. Is the information timely, accurate, and reliable? Is there evidence of any inherent bias? How can you best make use of the findings to support and enhance your own ideas? The answers to these questions are critical to producing a good research paper.

Taking Good Research Notes

Once you've found a useful source, record the information you need. You'll save time and money by taking notes directly from your sources rather than photocopying everything. Most often, you will need a summary of the information. Follow the instructions on summarizing given on pages 272–75. Alternatively, you can paraphrase (see pages 277–79). Sometimes a quotation is appropriate; when this is the case, it's wise to make a copy of your source. Whenever you take notes—in any form—from a source, be sure to record the information you will need about the source itself. For each published source that you use in your paper, you should write down the following information.

For Books

1. Author(s)' or editor(s)' full name
2. Full title and edition number (if any)
3. City of publication
4. Name of publisher
5. Year of publication
(You will find all this information on the front and back of the title page.)
6. Page(s) from which you took notes

For Journal Articles

1. Author(s)' full name
2. Title of the article
3. Name of the journal
4. Volume number of the journal
5. Year of publication
6. Inclusive page numbers of the article
7. Page(s) from which you took notes

For Internet Sources

1. Author(s)' full name
2. Title of the document
3. Title of the database, periodical, or site
4. Name of the editor (if any)
5. Date of publication or last update
6. Name of the institution or organization sponsoring the site (if any)
7. Network address, or URL
8. Date you accessed the source

For Newspaper or Magazine Articles

1. Author(s)' full name
2. Title of the article
3. Title of the newspaper or magazine
4. Date of publication
5. Inclusive page numbers of the article
6. Page(s) from which you took notes

Some researchers record each piece of information on a separate index card. Others write their notes on sheets of paper, being careful to keep their own ideas separate from the ideas and words taken from sources. (Using a highlighter or a different colour of ink will help you to tell at a glance which ideas you have taken from a source.) Use the technology available to help you record, sort, and file your notes. You can record and file information by creating a database, and you can use a photocopier (usually available in the library) to copy relevant pages of sources for later use. Whatever system you use, be sure to keep a separate record for each source and to include the documentation information. If you don't, you'll easily get your sources confused. The result of this confusion could be inaccurate documentation, which could lead your reader to suspect you of plagiarizing.

Avoiding Plagiarism

Plagiarism is presenting someone else's ideas as your own. It's a form of stealing (the word comes from the Latin word *plagiarius*, which means "kidnapper"). There have been famous cases of respected journalists and academics who have been accused of plagiarizing the articles or books they have written. Suspected plagiarists who are found guilty often lose their jobs. Sometimes the accusation alone is enough to compromise an author's reputation and thus prevent him or her from continuing to work as a scholar or writer.

Students who copy essays or parts of essays from source material, download them from the Internet, or pay someone else to write them are cheating. And, in so doing, they commit a serious academic offence. Sometimes, however, academic plagiarism is accidental. It can result from careless note-taking or an incomplete understanding of the conventions of documentation. It is not necessary to identify the sources of common knowledge (e.g., *The solstice occurs twice a year; B.C. is Canada's westernmost province*) or proverbial sayings (e.g., *Love is blind*), but when you are not sure whether to cite a source, it's wise to err on the side of caution and provide documentation. Statistics should always be cited because the meaning of numbers tends to change, depending on who is using them and for what purpose.

If, after you have finished your first draft, you are not sure which ideas need documenting and which don't, take your research notes and your outline to your instructor and ask. It's better to ask before submitting a paper than to try to explain a problem afterward. Asking saves you potential embarrassment as well as time.

Using the Library

The electronic age has transformed the library—traditionally a warehouse of information contained within print sources—into a Learning Resource Centre: a portal to sources of information such as databases, e-books, e-journals, and the Internet, together with the traditional print and audio-visual resources. With new technology, information retrieval is faster, easier, and more efficient than ever before. However, this fact does not make the library any less intimidating to inexperienced users. Many students are overwhelmed by what at first appears to be a vast and confusing array of collections. Using the library becomes a less daunting prospect when you realize that all of its contents are organized and classified in such a way as to make finding information easy, if not simple. First, you need to know the organizational system used by your library. In this section, we will describe the collections found in most academic libraries, give you tips on how to access them, and summarize their strengths and weaknesses as sources. We will also decode some of the terminology used by library staff to describe and arrange collections.

THE ONLINE CATALOGUE (OPAC)

All but the smallest libraries today use automated catalogue systems to access collections. These online catalogues are commonly called OPACs (Online Public Access Catalogues). They may be stand-alone computer terminals within the library or accessible via the library's website. OPAC search options usually include title, author, subject, or keyword. How you search the catalogue will depend on what you are looking for and on what you already know.

Along with books, the OPAC may list other resources available in the library, such as periodical titles. If a periodical title is available in full-text format from one of the library's subscription databases, there may be a link to the title and, possibly, the text from the OPAC. Many of today's OPACs allow the library to link to several useful online sources of information. Your library's OPAC should be the first place you check for resources when beginning your research paper.

BOOKS

Book collections are represented in the online catalogue and may be searched in a variety of ways: by author, title, subject, keyword, and sometimes call number.

If you know of a particular book by title, choose that option and enter the **title**—*English Online*, for example. If your search is successful, write down the call number of the book. Alternatively, if you know that Eric Crump wrote a book on using the Internet, but you aren't sure of the title, do an **author** search, using the last name first: Crump, Eric. If you don't know of any books or authors in your field of research, begin by doing a **subject** or **subject keyword** search, such as "online English composition instruction." Most systems will respond by identifying relevant holdings and listing instructions to follow at the bottom of the computer screen. One of the biggest advantages of automated systems is that they identify the **status** of the book, letting you know if the book is in or when it is due back. Many systems allow you to place a **hold** on a book that is out. This means that when the book is returned to the library, it will be set aside for a period of time to allow you to go in and pick it up.

In order to find a book on the shelves, you must match the **call number** as it appears on the screen or catalogue card with the number taped on the spine of the book. Every book has a unique call number, and books are arranged on the shelves according to their call numbers. Guide signs are usually posted on the ends of shelving units (sometimes called **stacks**). Most colleges and universities use the **Library of Congress (LC)** system of classification, which uses a letter or combination of letters to begin the call number. The LC system is generally more suitable to academic collections than the Dewey decimal system used by public and smaller libraries.

A title keyword search is often the fastest way of retrieving books on your topic. If the library carries a book on your subject of research, chances are the topic will appear somewhere in the title.

Strengths	Weaknesses
• Author may be an authority on the subject • Information is usually reliable (if published by a respected publisher) • Several aspects of the topic may be covered in the book	• Information cannot be as current as other sources

PERIODICALS

Your library's collection of **periodicals**—publications that are issued at regular intervals, such as magazines, newspapers, and scholarly or technical journals—may contain useful articles on the subject you are researching.

To locate specific articles, you need to use one or more of the databases and periodical indexes available from your library. Before you begin, read the description of the database to determine if it includes periodicals on your topic. Each database has specific strengths and will allow you to search a subject in a wide variety of periodicals. From the selection offered in your library, you may be able to search databases such as EBSCOhost, ProQuest, LexisNexis, or InfoTrac.[1] These databases are delivered using the Internet, but are paid for by the library; their use is limited by licence agreements to students and staff of the institution that pays for them. It may be possible to access them from home, but you will need a log-in or other means of identifying yourself as a student. Check with the library staff at your institution to find out more about access from your Internet service provider.

Databases have been created with users in mind; they have search interfaces that make finding information relatively simple. Once you have found the database you wish to use, you will be presented with a search box similar to those found on Internet search engines. Here you type in a word or phrase that relates to your research topic. For example, if you were researching the art movement known as Impressionism, you would enter this word in the text box. The search mechanism of the database would look for this term, and all articles containing the word "Impressionism"

---

[1]Your purchase of *Essay Essentials,* Fourth Edition, entitles you to free access to InfoTrac.

would be displayed on the screen. From the list, you would select those you think may be useful to you.

Most databases allow you to e-mail the results of your search. If you are pressed for time, do a quick search, e-mail the results to yourself, and check them later for relevancy. You can always delete them and start over.

Increasingly, full-text articles are included with each new release of these databases. This means you can print or download the text of an article without having to retrieve the actual magazine or journal. If you find a reference to a magazine article for which the full text is not available, be sure to note the title and date of the periodical in which it appeared; then check to see if your library subscribes to this periodical.

Strengths	Weaknesses
• Contain current information • Articles in databases are easy to retrieve • Databases are accessible 24/7	• Some articles may be opinion pieces but presented as factual

ENCYCLOPEDIAS

A useful source of general information on a topic is an encyclopedia; it is often a good place to begin your research. There are many types of encyclopedias, and several are now available online or on CD-ROM. Information is easy to find, usually through a user-friendly search screen, and CD versions of encyclopedias often include sound or video clips to enhance the text. You might begin your search with a general encyclopedia such as *Britannica*, *Colliers*, or the *World Book* and then move on to a specialized encyclopedia related to your subject. Look in the reference collection for a call number area that matches the one in which you found books on your topic (for example, medical encyclopedias are in the R section), or ask the reference librarian if a specialized encyclopedia exists on your subject.

Strengths	Weaknesses
• Provide a good overview of a subject • Often list titles of major books on the subject • Online editions are convenient, easy to use, and updated regularly	• Information in print versions may be dated

THE INTERNET

Most students today have grown up with the Internet and are accustomed to using it to meet their information needs. They turn to the Net for news reports, weather updates, and maps to destinations near and far; to find phone numbers and addresses, purchase theatre tickets, shop online, and plan vacations. They use search engines to locate information about topics ranging from medical disorders to building a deck. Canada is one of the world's leaders in per capita Internet use.

When you are gathering material to write a research paper, however, you should keep in mind that the Internet is not necessarily a reliable source of information. (Some instructors will not accept websites as legitimate resources for research papers, so be sure you have permission to use them before you spend hours on Google or Yahoo.) Evaluating Internet information for reliability is not a simple matter. We've already mentioned checking the domain name as one place to begin. A good guide to evaluating websites can be found at http://www.lib.berkeley.edu/TeachingLib/Guides/Internet/Evaluate.html.

The number of results called up by a keyword search can be overwhelming. All search engines offer advice on effective searching from the home page. Here are four ways you can limit and focus the results of an initial query:

- Use one or more of the shortcuts available on most search engines.
- Use an Advanced Search screen that allows you to combine concepts. For example, the Advanced Search screen at Google allows you to search for an exact phrase such as "breast cancer" and include the word "treatment" without the word "chemotherapy." You can also limit the type of domain you'd like returned (.edu) as an example, choose the language you'd like for your results, and decide where you'd like the search engine to look for your terms (in the title only, for example).
- Put quotation marks around your search term(s). Doing so turns your keyword search into a search for a phrase ("breast cancer treatment," for example).
- Use the tilde sign (~) or plus and minus signs to add or eliminate concepts. Plus and minus signs add or subtract words from your search word or phrase ("breast cancer" + treatment – chemotherapy). Google interprets the tilde as a signal to search for variations of a word. For example, "~treatment" would include the plural, "treatments," in your results list.

Get in the habit of using more than one search engine to vary results. A subject directory search engine, such as Yahoo, may be a better starting point for your topic than a general keyword search.

Librarians regularly scour the Internet for exceptional websites as good sources of information. Look for these recommendations on your library's website, or look for links to government websites or sources such as the Internet Public Library (http://www.ipl.org) from your library's OPAC.

Strengths	Weaknesses
• Fast and convenient	• Number of results can be daunting
• Excellent resource for directory-type information	• Reliability and authority can be difficult to determine
• Websites of leading experts are sometimes available	• Amount of information is staggering (most users will not browse past the first two or three pages of results, so valuable information may be missed)
• Increasingly, authoritative information sources are posted on the Net (e.g., government documents, databases of scholarly journals)	• Questionable content may appear to be valid

OTHER SOURCES

Most libraries contain other collections that may help you in your research. Don't overlook the possibility of finding useful information in the **audio-visual collection**, which normally includes videotapes, films, audiotapes, DVDs, and slide presentations. **Government publications** are another good source of information. The government, as one of the country's largest publishers, may have produced documents related to your topic. Many of these documents are available on the Internet.

Finally, the library is not the only source of information you can use. Interviews with people familiar with your subject are excellent sources because they provide a personal view, and they ensure that your paper will contain information not found in any other paper the instructor will read. It is perfectly acceptable to e-mail a question or set of questions to an expert in a field of study. **Original research**, such as surveys or questionnaires that you design, distribute, and analyze can also enhance your paper. Doing your own research is time-consuming and requires some knowledge of survey design and interpretation, but it has the advantage of being original and current.

A good research paper will contain references to material from a variety of sources. Some instructors require a minimum number of references from several types of sources: books, periodicals, encyclopedias, interviews, etc. Most, but not all, institutions will allow you to use Internet sources, but use them with caution. Be mindful that anyone can place information, reliable or not, on any subject at a website. For this reason, it is best to use research gathered from reliable sources such as books, encyclopedias, scholarly journals, and reputable magazines.

As you conduct your research and think about your paper, keep your reader in mind. Every teacher faced with a pile of papers hopes to find some that are not simply a rehash of known facts. Before anything else, teachers are learners; they like nothing better than discovering something new. If you cannot find new information about your subject, be sure to provide an original interpretation of the evidence you find.

Exercise 18.2

This exercise will quickly familiarize you with your school's library: the variety and extent of its holdings; the different ways you and your library can communicate with each other; and basic library policies you should know about.

1. Does your library provide handouts or other documents on how to conduct research? On how to format electronic source citations?
2. Check your library's OPAC (online catalogue) for a video that deals with study skills. Make a note of the title and call number.
3. How many newspapers does the library subscribe to? Name two and note how long the library keeps them.
4. What is the URL for the library's website? Find two unique resources or services listed there.
5. Is it possible to contact the library staff by e-mail? If yes, note the e-mail address.
6. What is the loan period for books? What is the fine charged for an overdue video?
7. What does it mean when a book is "on reserve"?
8. Using one of your library's subscription databases, search for an article on smoking-cessation programs. Give the title of the article, the author's name, and the name and date of the publication in which it appeared.
9. Using a different database from the one you searched in question 8, find a Canadian newspaper article that deals with genetically modified (GM) foods. Provide the article title and the name of the newspaper it appeared in.
10. Can you access your library's databases from your home Internet service provider? If so, what procedure do you follow?

19

Summarizing, Paraphrasing, and Quoting

Once you have identified and evaluated your research sources, you must make accurate notes of the information you think you might use in your paper. There are many ways to take notes, ranging from jotting down single words or phrases to photocopying entire articles. You will save time if you remember that there are three ways of incorporating source information into your own writing: **summary**, **paraphrase**, and **direct quotation**. When you summarize or paraphrase, you restate in your own words the idea(s) of another speaker or writer. When you quote, you reproduce the exact words of another speaker or writer. Before we examine those three techniques, it is worthwhile to review what plagiarism is and how to avoid it.

PREVENTING PLAGIARISM

You can avoid plagiarism—the single biggest problem faced by students writing research papers and the instructors who mark them—by acknowledging (citing) all information you found in the sources you used for your paper. Cite your sources in an approved documentation style (usually MLA or APA).

Here are some guidelines to follow:

- Facts or sayings that are common knowledge do not have to be attributed; that is, you need not give sources for them. Examples: "Quebec City is the capital of Quebec"; "Sir John A. Macdonald was Canada's first prime minister"; "Beauty is in the eye of the beholder."

- Any passage, long or short, taken word for word from a source must be marked as a quotation, and you must cite its source. (See below, pages 280–86, and Chapter 20.)
- Facts, opinions, or ideas that you discovered on the Internet, found in a book or article, or learned from any other source—even if you express the information in your own words—must be acknowledged. (See below, pages 280–86, and Chapter 20.)
- Facts, opinions, or ideas that you remember reading or hearing somewhere cannot be presented as your own. If you cannot find and acknowledge the source, you should not use the information.
- If you are not sure whether a fact, opinion, or idea should be acknowledged, err on the side of caution and cite it. It's better to be safe than sorry.

Summarizing

When you summarize information, you find the main ideas in an article, essay, report, or other document, and rephrase them. You shorten (condense) the most important idea or ideas in the source material and express your understanding of them in your own words. The purpose of summarizing is to give the reader an overview of the article, report, or chapter. If the reader is interested in the details, he or she will read the original.

It's hard to overstate how valuable the ability to summarize is. Note-taking in college is one form of summarizing. Abstracts of articles, executive summaries of reports, market surveys, legal decisions, research findings, and records (called "minutes") of meetings, to name only a few kinds of formal documents, are all summaries. Thesis statements and topic sentences are essentially summaries; so, often, are conclusions. In committee, group, or teamwork, imagination and creativity are valuable, but the ability to summarize is even more so. There is no communication skill that you will need or use more than summarizing.

As a matter of fact, you summarize for yourself and others in every conversation you have. With friends, you may summarize the plot of a movie you've just seen or what happened in class this morning. When your mother calls, you'll summarize the events of the past week that you want her to know about. But most of us are not very good at summarizing effectively, especially in writing. It is a skill that doesn't come naturally. *You need to practise it.* You'll improve very quickly, however, if you think about what you're doing—that is, if you are conscious rather than unconscious of the times and the circumstances in which you call upon your summarizing skills. The following exercise will get you started.

1. In groups of three or four, choose a movie you have all seen, a course you have all taken, a party or concert you have all attended, or a book you have all read. Then, without discussing your topic first, spend five minutes each writing a one-paragraph summary. After you have written your summary, use a highlighter to accent your main points.

2. Read and compare your summaries. What similarities and differences do you notice? Can you all agree that one summary is both complete and accurate? If not, spend another five or ten minutes discussing which are the main ideas and which are secondary to a discussion of your topic.

3. Now revise your one-paragraph summary to include all the main ideas and no secondary details.

4. Once again, read and compare each other's paragraphs. Which paragraph summarizes the topic best? What features does this paragraph have that the others lack?

HOW TO WRITE A SUMMARY

The work you summarize can be as short as a paragraph or as long as a book, as the following passage demonstrates:

One of Edward de Bono's books is called *Six Thinking Hats*. [In it] he proposes that you adopt six different mind sets by mentally putting on six different coloured hats. Each hat stands for a certain way of thinking about a problem. By "putting on the hat" and adopting a certain role, we can think more clearly about the issues at hand. Because we're only "playing a role," there is little ego riding on what we say, so we are more free to say what we really want to say. De Bono likens the process of putting on the six hats one at a time to that of printing on a multicoloured map. Each colour is not a complete picture in itself. The map must go through the printing press six times, each time receiving a new colour, until we have the total picture.

Perrin, Timothy. "Positive Invention." *Better Writing for Lawyers.* Toronto: Law Society of Upper Canada, 1990. 51.

Notice that Perrin is careful to tell his readers the source of the ideas he is summarizing: both the author and the book are identified up front.

Before you can summarize anything, you need to *read* and *understand* it. The material you need to summarize is usually an article, essay, or chapter (or some portion of it). Depending on how much of the piece you need, your summary will range from a few sentences to one or two paragraphs.[1] Here's how to proceed:

1. Read through the piece carefully, looking up any words you don't understand. Write their meanings between the lines, above the words they apply to.

2. Now read the article or essay again. Keep rereading it until you have grasped the main ideas and formed a mental picture of their arrangement. Highlight the title, subtitle, and headings (if there are any). The title often identifies the subject of the piece, and a subtitle usually indicates its focus. If the article is long, the writer will often divide it into a number of smaller sections, each with its own heading. These headings usually identify the main points. If there are no headings, pay particular attention to the introduction—you should find an overview of the subject and a statement of the thesis—and the conclusion, which often summarizes the information and points to the significance of the topic.

3. In point form, and in your own words, write out a bare-bones outline of the piece. Your outline should consist of the controlling idea (thesis) of the article and the main ideas, in the order in which they appear. Do not include any supporting details (statistics, specific facts, examples, etc.).

4. Working from your outline, draft the summary. In the first sentence, identify the article or essay you are summarizing (by title, enclosed in quotation marks) and the author (by name, if known). Complete the sentence by stating the author's controlling idea. Here's an example:

In his essay "The Canadian Climate," D'Arcy McHale divides Canadians into two types: warm and cool.

Then state, in order, the author's main points. After each sentence in which you identify a main point, include any necessary explanation or clarification of that point. (The author, remember, developed each idea in the supporting details.) Try to resist going back to the article for your explanation. If you have truly understood the article, you should be

---

[1]This restriction applies only to the kind of research paper we are discussing in this part: one prepared for a college course. Other kinds of summary are longer. A précis, for example, is one-third the length of the source document. An abstract, which is a summary of a dissertation, academic paper, or public presentation, can be several paragraphs long.

able to explain each point from memory. If the author's conclusion contains any new information (i.e., is more than a summary and memorable statement), briefly state that information in your conclusion.

5. Revise your draft until it is coherent, concise, and makes sense to someone who is unfamiliar with the original work. It's a good idea to get someone to read through your summary to check it for clarity and completeness.

6. Don't forget to acknowledge your source. (Chapter 20 will show you how.)

The paragraph below summarizes the essay found on pages 204–05. Read it first, before you read the summary that follows.

In his essay "The Canadian Climate," D'Arcy McHale divides Canadians into two types: "warm" and "cool." The first category includes people who are enthusiastic about Canada's scenery, climate, and recreational activities, which they encourage newcomers to enjoy. Warm Canadians are also sincerely interested in learning about what life is like in the visitor's country of origin. In contrast, Cool Canadians are negative about their country and find it hard to believe that anyone from a warm climate would choose to endure the cold, bleak Canadian winters. Cool Canadians are not interested in detailed information about the visitor's country of origin, either; they are comfortable with their stereotypes. Finally, McHale acknowledges that the two types are mixed: each can at times behave like the other. Canadians, like the weather, are unpredictable, and newcomers are encouraged to accept them as they are and for themselves.

This seven-sentence paragraph (140 words) captures the gist of McHale's 600-word essay. Admittedly, it isn't very interesting. It lacks the flavour of the original. Summaries are useful for conveying an outline or a brief overview of someone else's ideas, but by themselves they are not very memorable. Details and specifics are what stick in a reader's mind; these are what your own writing should provide.

A summary should be entirely in your own words. Your ability to identify and interpret the author's meaning is evidence of your understanding of the article or essay. If you must include a short phrase from the source because there is no other way to word it, enclose the quoted material in quotation marks.

When writing a summary, do not

- introduce any ideas not found in the original
- change the proportion or emphasis of the original
- introduce your own opinion of the material

Exercise 19.2

Following the first five steps of the process outlined above, summarize "Ready, Willing . . . and Employable," which appears on pages 74–75. When you have completed your work, exchange papers with a partner. Use the following checklist to critique each other's summary.

	Good	Adequate	Try Again
1. The first sentence gives the title and the author's name.			
2. The essay's thesis is clearly and concisely reworded.			
3. Each main point (topic sentence) is restated in a single sentence.			
4. Each main point is briefly explained.			
5. The summary includes no secondary details that could be eliminated without diminishing the reader's understanding.			
6. The summary is balanced and objective.			
7. The paragraph flows smoothly; there are no obvious errors in sentence structure, grammar, spelling, or punctuation.			

Exercise 19.3

Select an article from a professional journal in your field. Summarize it by following the six steps given on pages 274–75. Assume your reader is a professional in the field.

Exercise 19.4

Choose an article that interests you from one of the regular sections (e.g., business, medicine, education, music, art) of a general news magazine such as *Maclean's*, *Time*, *Newsweek*, or the *Economist*. Summarize the article for a friend who is not an expert in the field and who has not read it. Do not evaluate the article or give your opinion about it. In a paragraph of approximately 150 to 200 words, simply inform your friend of its contents. Don't forget to cite your source!

Paraphrasing

When you paraphrase, you restate someone else's ideas in your own words. Unlike a summary, a paraphrase includes both the main and supporting ideas of your source. The usual purpose of a paraphrase is to express someone else's ideas more clearly and more simply—to translate what may be complex in the original into easily understandable prose. A paraphrase may be longer than the original, it may be about the same length, or it may be shorter. Whatever its length, a good paraphrase satisfies three criteria:

1. It is clear, concise, and easy to understand.
2. It communicates the idea(s) of the original passage.
3. It doesn't contain any idea(s) not found in the original passage.

Occasionally, you may need to clarify technical language or explain an aphorism, a proverb, or other saying that states a principle, offers an insight, or teaches a point. Statements that pack a lot of meaning into few words can be explained only at greater length. For example, one of the principal tenets of modern biology is "ontogeny recapitulates phylogeny." It simply isn't possible to paraphrase this principle in three words. (It means that as an embryo grows, it follows the same pattern of development that the animal did in the evolutionary process.)

Exercise 19.5

Working with a partner or a small group, discuss the meaning of the following expressions. When you are sure you understand them, write a paraphrase of each one.

1. A picture is worth a thousand words.
2. Money talks.
3. More haste, less speed.
4. Birds of a feather flock together.
5. Too many cooks spoil the broth.

To paraphrase a passage, you need to dig down through your source's words to the underlying ideas and then reword those ideas as clearly and simply as you can. Like summarizing, the ability to paraphrase is not an inborn talent; it takes patience and much practice to perfect it. But the rewards are worth your time and effort. First, paraphrasing improves your reading skill as well as your writing skill. Second, it improves your memory. In order to paraphrase accurately, you must thoroughly understand what you've read—and once you understand something, you're not likely to forget it.

First, let's look at how *not* to paraphrase. Assume we are writing an essay on designing an energy-efficient home, and we want to use the information given in the following paragraph.

> The site and how the building relates to it is a critical determinant in the calculation of energy consumption. The most profound effects, and the ones the individual has least control over, are the macro-climatic (regional) factors of degree days, design temperature, wind, hours of bright sunshine, and the total solar insolation. Other factors which can have an enormous effect on the energy consumption of a house are micro-climatic. These include the topography of a site, the sun path, specific wind regime, vegetation, soil, and the placement of other buildings.

Argue, Robert. *The Well-Tempered House: Energy-Efficient Building for Cold Climates.* Toronto: Renewable Energy, 1980. 14.

There are two pieces of information in this paragraph that we want to include in our essay:

1. Some of the factors influencing energy consumption relate to the climate and weather patterns of the region (macro-climatic factors).
2. Some of the factors influencing energy consumption relate to the specific characteristics of the building site (micro-climatic factors).

If we are not careful, or if we don't have much experience with paraphrasing, our paragraph might look something like this:

> In *The Well-Tempered House*, Robert Argue explains that a designer must consider two critical determinants in building an energy-efficient home. The most important factors, and the ones the individual has least control over, are the macro-climatic (regional) factors of degree days, design temperature, wind, hours of sunshine, and the total solar insolation. The other significant factors are the micro-climatic ones, which include the topography of the site, the sun path, wind regime, vegetation, soil, and the location of other buildings on or near the site.

This is plagiarism. Although we have indicated the source of the information, we have not indicated that the wording is almost identical to that of the original. Of the total 90 words, 50 come from the source. There are no visual or verbal cues to alert the reader that these are Argue's words, not ours. Let's try again.

In *The Well-Tempered House*, Robert Argue identifies two significant influences the cost-conscious home builder must consider in designing an energy-efficient house. The first and strongest influence is the typical weather of the region. The designer must be familiar with such "macro-climatic factors" as "degree days" (the difference between the indoor comfort temperature and the average daily outdoor temperature), "design temperature" (the lowest temperature to be expected during the heating season), wind, and the total effect of the sun. The other influences are called "micro-climatic factors" and include the site's topography (elevation and slope of the land), sun path, prevailing wind pattern, and the presence or absence of vegetation and nearby buildings.

Although this draft is technically a paraphrase rather than plagiarism, it doesn't demonstrate very much work on our part. We have replaced the source's words with synonyms and added explanations where the original is too technical to be easily understood by a general reader, but our paragraph still follows the original too closely. A paraphrase should not be used to pass off someone else's ideas as your own by changing a few words and sentences. A good paraphrase goes further. It uses source information but rearranges it, rephrases it, and combines it with the writer's own ideas to create something new. Let's try once more:

The cost-conscious home builder must consider a number of factors that will affect the energy consumption of his or her new home. The exterior design of the house should take advantage of the natural slope of the land, the presence of sheltering vegetation, prevailing wind patterns, the path of the sun, and other characteristics of the building site (Argue 14). In addition to sufficient insulation, the interior should feature appropriate heating and cooling devices to keep the family comfortable during the coldest winter days and the hottest summer days. To keep costs down, these devices should take advantage of the natural energy sources available: wind, sun, and seasonal fluctuations in temperature can all be used to harness and conserve energy. With careful planning, a new home can be designed to maximize the advantages of even an apparently unlikely site, minimize the negative effects of temperature and weather, and cost surprisingly little to maintain at a comfortable temperature year-round.

Here we have used paraphrase to incorporate information from a published source into a paragraph whose topic and structure are our own. This is how paraphrase can be used both responsibly and effectively. If you want to take ideas more directly from a source, retaining the original arrangement and some of the wording, you should use quotations.

Quoting

Of the three ways to introduce ideas from a source into your research paper, direct quotation is the one you should use least. (The exception is the literary essay, in which quotations from the original work are the evidence in your argument; see, for example, Jess Friedland's essay on pages 320–24.) If you use too many quotations, your paper will be a patchwork of the ideas of others, in their words, and very little of your own thinking will be communicated to the reader. Remember that the main reason teachers assign research papers is to test your ability to find, digest, and make sense of specific information about a topic. If what you hand in consists of a string of quotations, your paper will demonstrate only one of these three capabilities.

In most research papers, the ideas, facts, and statistics are the important things, not the wording of an idea or the explanation of facts or statistics. Occasionally, however, you will find that someone else—an expert in a particular field, a well-known author, or a respected public figure—has said what you want to say eloquently, vividly, more memorably than you could ever hope to say it. In such cases, quotations, *as long as they are short and not used too frequently*, are useful in developing your topic. Carefully woven into your paragraphs, they help convince the reader of the validity of what you have to say. Use quotations in writing the way you use salt in cooking: sparingly.

You can quote from two kinds of sources—

- people you know, or have heard speak, or have interviewed
- print, electronic, or recorded materials (e.g., books, articles, CD-ROMs, websites, films, tapes)

—and your quotation may be long or short.

BLOCK AND SPOT QUOTATIONS

If the material you are quoting is more than 40 words or four typed lines, it is a long—or **block**—quotation. After you have introduced it, you begin the quoted passage on a new line and indent all lines of the quotation 10 spaces or 2.5 cm from the left margin. *Do not put quotation marks around a block quotation.* The ten-space indentation is the reader's visual cue that this portion of the paragraph is someone else's words, not yours. Here's an example:

> Committees put a lot of thought into the design of fast foods. As David Bodanis points out with such good humour in *The Secret House*, potato chips are

an example of total destruction foods. The wild attack on the plastic wrap, the slashing and tearing you have to go through is exactly what the manufacturers wish. For the thing about crisp foods is that they're louder than non-crisp ones. . . . Destructo-packaging sets a favourable mood. . . . Crisp foods have to be loud in the upper register. They have to produce a high-frequency shattering; foods which generate low-frequency rumblings are crunchy, or slurpy but not crisp. . . .

Companies design potato chips to be too large to fit into the mouth, because in order to hear the high-frequency crackling, you need to keep your mouth open. Chips are 80 percent air, and each time we bite one we break open the air-packed cells of the chip, making that noise we call "crispy." Bodanis asks:

How to get sufficiently rigid cell walls to twang at these squeaking harmonics? Starch them. The starch granules in potatoes are identical to the starch in stiff shirt collars. . . . [In addition to starch,] all chips are soaked in fat. . . . So it's a shrapnel of flying starch and fat that produces the conical air-pressure wave when our determined chip-muncher finally gets to finish her chomp.

Ackerman, Diane. *A Natural History of the Senses.* New York: Random House, 1990. 142–43.

Notice that Ackerman is careful to tell her readers the source of her quotations. To introduce the first one, she gives the author's full name and the title of his book. To introduce the second quotation, which is from the same book, she simply identifies the author by surname. Thus, she doesn't waste words by repeating information, nor does she leave readers wondering where the quotation came from. (The only information missing is the publication data—city, publisher, and date—which is provided in the list of sources. See Chapter 20 for information on how to document your sources.)

A **spot quotation** is a word, a phrase, or a short sentence that is incorporated into one of your own sentences. *Put quotation marks before and after a spot quotation.* The quotation marks are a signal to the reader that these aren't your words; a new voice is speaking. The following paragraph contains several spot quotations.

"You are what you quote," in the words of the American essayist Joseph Epstein, himself a heavy user of quotations and the writer who introduced "quotatious" into my vocabulary. Winston Churchill understood the value of a well-aimed quotation: as a young man he read a few pages of *Bartlett's Familiar Quotations* every day to spruce up his style and compensate for his lack of a university education. [Gradually,] he transformed himself from a quotatious writer into the most quoted politician of the western world. . . . Fowler's *Modern English Usage* warns against quoting simply to demonstrate knowledge: "the discerning reader detects it and is contemptuous," while the undiscerning reader finds it tedious. A few years ago Garry Trudeau made fun of George Will's compulsive quoting by inventing a researcher who served as "quote boy" in Will's office: "'Quote boy! Need something on the banality of contemporary society.' 'Right away, Dr. Will!'" . . . As for me, I say don't judge, because you might get judged, too. That's how the quotation goes, right?

Fulford, Robert. "The Use and Abuse of Quotations." *Globe and Mail* 11 Nov. 1992: C1.

HOW TO MODIFY A QUOTATION

In addition to illustrating how to introduce and format block quotations and how to punctuate spot quotations, the examples above also show how to modify a quotation to fit your space and suit your purpose. Although *you must quote exactly and never misrepresent or distort your source's intention*, you may, for reasons of conciseness or smoothness, omit or add a word or phrase or even a sentence or two.

- To leave out a word or words, indicate the omission by replacing the word(s) you've omitted with three spaced dots called **ellipses** (. . .). If the omission comes at the end of your sentence, add a fourth dot as the period.
- If you need to add or change a word or words to make the quoted passage more readable within your paragraph, use **square brackets** around your own words, as we did when we added "[In addition to starch,]" in Ackerman's second block quotation from Bodanis and "[Gradually,]" to Fulford's paragraph.

  If you have omitted some words from a source, you may need to add a transitional phrase or change the first letter of a word to a capital: [T]hus. Another reason for changing words in a quoted passage is to keep the verb tenses consistent throughout your paragraph. If you are writing in the present tense and the passage you are quoting is in the past tense, you can change the verbs to present tense (so long as the change doesn't distort the meaning) and put square brackets around them so the reader knows you have made these changes.

Modifying short quotations to make them fit smoothly into your own sentences without altering the source's meaning takes practice. Reread the paragraph that we have quoted on pages 281–82. Notice that to make Fulford's original slightly shorter and easier to read, we made a couple of minor alterations to the original. The signals to the reader that something has been added or left out are the same as those used in a block quotation: square brackets and ellipses.

HOW TO INTEGRATE QUOTATIONS INTO YOUR WRITING

When you decide to quote source material, you should introduce it so that it will blend as seamlessly as possible into your writing. Don't simply park someone else's words in the middle of your paragraph; you'll disrupt the flow of thought. If Diane Ackerman were not so skillful a writer, she might have "dumped" quotations into her paragraph instead of integrating them. Contrast the readability of the paragraph below with that of Ackerman's second paragraph (on page 281).

Companies design potato chips to be too large to fit into the mouth because, in order to hear the high-frequency crackling, you need to keep your mouth open. Chips are 80 percent air, and each time we bite one, we break open the air-packed cells of the chip, making that crispy noise. "The starch granules in potatoes are identical to the starch in stiff shirt collars." Starch is just one of the ingredients that contribute to the crispiness of potato chips. "All chips are soaked in fat." "So it's a shrapnel of flying starch and fat that produces the conical air pressure wave when our determined chip-muncher finally gets to finish her chomp."

Without transitional phrases, the paragraph lacks coherence and doesn't make sense. Not convinced? Try reading the two paragraphs aloud.

Every quotation should be introduced and integrated into an essay in a way that makes clear the relationship between the quotation and your own argument. There are four ways to integrate a spot quotation.

1. You can introduce it with a phrase such as "According to X," or "Y states" (or *observes*, or *comments*, or *writes*), followed by a comma. Different verbs suggest different attitudes toward the quoted material. For example, "Fulford *suggests* that writers should not overuse quotations" is more tentative than "Fulford *warns* that writers should not overuse quotations." Other verbs you can use to introduce quotations are *asserts*, *notes*, *points out*, *maintains*, *shows*, *reports*, and *claims*. Choose your introductory verbs carefully, and be sure to use a variety of phrases. The repetitive "X says," "Y says," and "Z says," is a sure way to put your reader to sleep.

2. If your introductory words form a complete sentence, use a colon (:) to introduce the quotation.

   George Bernard Shaw's poor opinion of teachers is well known: "Those who can, do; those who can't, teach."

Oscar Wilde's opinion of teachers is less famous than Shaw's but even more cynical: "Everybody who is incapable of learning has taken to teaching."

3. If the passage you are quoting is a couple of words, a phrase, or anything less than a complete sentence, do not use any punctuation to introduce it.

Oscar Wilde defined fox hunters as "the unspeakable in full pursuit of the uneatable."

Wilde believed that people "take no interest in a work of art until they are told that the work in question is immoral."

4. If you insert your own words into the middle of a quotation, use commas to separate the source's words from yours.

"It is a truth universally acknowledged," writes Jane Austen at the beginning of *Pride and Prejudice*, "that a single man in possession of a good fortune must be in want of a wife."

In general, periods and commas are placed inside the quotation marks (see the examples above). Unless they are part of the quoted material, colons, semicolons, question marks, exclamation marks, and dashes are placed outside the quotation marks. Use single quotation marks to mark off a quotation within a quotation.

According to John Robert Colombo, "The most widely quoted Canadian aphorism of all time is Marshall McLuhan's 'The medium is the message.'"

Block quotations are normally introduced by a complete sentence followed by a colon (for example, "X writes as follows:"). Then you copy the quotation, beginning on a new line and indenting 10 spaces or 2.5 cm. If your introductory statement is not a complete sentence, use a comma or no punctuation, whichever is appropriate. The passage by Diane Ackerman on pages 280–81 contains examples of both ways to introduce block quotations. Turn to it now. Can you explain why Ackerman has used no punctuation to introduce the first block quotation and a colon to introduce the second one?

Exercise 19.6

For each of the following quotations, make up three different sentences as follows:

a. Introduce the complete quotation with a phrase followed by a comma.
b. Introduce the complete quotation with an independent clause followed by a colon.
c. Introduce a portion of the quotation with a phrase or statement that requires no punctuation between it and the quotation. Use ellipses and square brackets, if necessary, to signal any changes you make in the original wording.

Example: Education is the ability to listen to almost anything without losing your temper or your self-confidence. (Robert Frost)

a. According to Robert Frost, "Education is the ability to listen to almost anything without losing your temper or your self-confidence." (complete quotation introduced by phrase + comma)
b. Robert Frost had a peculiar notion of higher learning: "Education is the ability to listen to almost anything without losing your temper or your self-confidence." (complete quotation introduced by independent clause + colon)
c. Robert Frost defined education as "the ability to listen to . . . anything without losing [one's] temper or [one's] self-confidence." (partial quotation introduced by phrase requiring no punctuation; changes indicated with ellipses and square brackets)

1. I find the three major administrative problems on a campus are sex for the students, athletics for the alumni, and parking for the faculty. (Clark Kerr, former president of the University of California)
2. Education is not a *product*: mark, diploma, job, money—in that order; it is a *process*, a never-ending one. (Bel Kaufman, author of *Up the Down Staircase*)
3. School days, I believe, are the unhappiest in the whole span of human existence. (H. L. Mencken, American humorist)
4. In the first place, God made idiots. This was for practice. Then he made school boards. (Mark Twain)
5. Education makes a people easy to lead, but difficult to drive; easy to govern, but impossible to enslave. (Lord Brougham, founder of the University of London, 1825)

TIPS ON USING QUOTATIONS IN YOUR WRITING

1. **Use quotations sparingly and for a specific purpose,** such as *for emphasis* or *to reinforce an important point.* Avoid the temptation to produce a patchwork paper—one that consists of bits and pieces of other people's writing stuck together to look like an original work. Far from impressing your readers, overuse of quotations will give them the impression you have nothing of your own to say.

2. **Be sure every quotation is an accurate reproduction of the original passage.** If you need to change or omit words, indicate those changes with square brackets or ellipses, as appropriate.

3. **Be sure every quotation is relevant.** No matter how interesting or well worded, a quotation that does not clearly and directly relate to your subject does not belong in your essay. An irrelevant quotation will either confuse readers or annoy them (they'll think it's padding), or both.

4. **Make clear the link between the quotation and your controlling idea.** Don't assume readers will automatically see the connection you see between the quotation and your topic sentence. Comment on the quotation so they will be sure to make the connection you intend. If you have used a block quotation, your explanatory comment can sometimes form the conclusion of your paragraph.

5. **Always identify the source of a quotation.** This can be done by mentioning in your paragraph the name of the author and, if appropriate, the title of the source of the quotation. Include the page number(s) in a parenthetical citation. See Chapter 20 for details, and follow the format your instructor prefers.

Exercise 19.7

Read the passages below and then, with your partner, discuss and answer the questions that follow.

1.   Whenever college teachers get together informally, sooner or later the conversation turns to students' excuses. The stories students tell to justify absences or late assignments are a source of endless amusement among faculty. These stories tend to fall into three broad thematic categories.

Accident, illness, and death are at the top of the list. If the stories were true, such incidents would be tragic, not funny. But how could any instructor be expected to keep a straight face at being told, "I can't take the test on Friday because my mother is having a vasectomy"? Or "I need a week's extension because my friend's aunt died"? Or—my personal favourite—"The reason I didn't show up for the final exam was because I have inverse testosterone"?

Problems with pets rank second in the catalogue of student excuses. Animals take precedence over tests: "I can't be at the exam because my cat is having kittens and I'm her coach"; and they are often responsible for a student's having to hand in an assignment late. The age-old excuse "My dog ate my homework" gets no more marks for humour than it does for originality, but occasionally a student puts a creative spin on this old chestnut. Would you believe "My paper is late because my parrot crapped in my computer"?

In third place on the list of students' tales of extenuating circumstances are social commitments of various sorts. "I was being arraigned in Chicago for arms dealing"; "I had to see my fence to pick out a ring for my fiancée"; and "I can't take the exam on Monday because my Mom is getting married on Sunday and I'll be too drunk to drive back to school" are just three examples collected by one college teacher in a single semester.

An enterprising computer programmer could easily compile an "excuse bank" that would allow students to type in the code number of a standard explanation and zap it to their professors. I suspect, however, that there would be little faculty support for such a project. Electronic excuses would lack the humour potential of live ones. Part of the fun comes from watching the student confront you, face to face, shamelessly telling a tale that would make Paul Bunyan blush.

1. Are all the quotations relevant to the subject of this brief essay? Are they sufficiently limited, or could the essay be improved by leaving any out?
2. Underline the specific connections the writer makes between her quotations and her controlling idea.
3. What purpose does the concluding sentence serve? Would the essay be equally effective without it? Why?

2. U.S. federal drug policy, especially the mandatory minimum sentences for drug offenders enacted by Congress in 1987, has so distressed federal judges that approximately 10 percent of them will not hear drug trials. Judge Jack B. Weinstein of Brooklyn, N.Y., is a case in point. In an April 1993 memo to all the judges in his district, he announced that he would no longer preside over trials of defendants charged with drug crimes:

> One day last week I had to sentence a peasant woman from West Africa [with four dependent children] to forty-six months. . . . On the same day I sentenced a man to thirty years as a second drug offender—a heavy sentence mandated by the Guidelines and statute. These two cases confirm my sense of frustration about much of the cruelty I have been party to in connection with the "war on drugs" that is being fought by the military, police, and courts rather than by our medical and social institutions.

I myself am unsure how this drug problem should be handled, but I need a rest from the oppressive sense of futility that these cases leave. Accordingly, I have taken my name out of the wheel for drug cases. This resolution leaves me uncomfortable since it shifts the "dirty work" to other judges. At the moment, however, I simply cannot sentence another impoverished person whose destruction can have no discernible effect on the drug trade. I wish I were in a position to propose a solution, but I am not. I'm just a tired old judge who has temporarily filled his quota of remorse-lessness.

The sentencing guidelines that Congress requires judges to follow are so harsh they cause, in Weinstein's words, "overfilling [of] our jails and . . . unneccessary havoc to families, society, and prisons." As a senior judge, Weinstein can choose the cases he hears. But 90 percent of judges are not so fortunate. After they have imposed on a low-level smuggler or a poverty-stricken "mule" a sentence far harsher than those mandated for someone convicted of rape or manslaughter, one wonders how—or if—judges can sleep at night.

"The War on Drugs: A Judge Goes AWOL." *Harper's Magazine* Dec. 1993: 18.

1. This writer uses both block and spot quotations to develop her point. Where does she make clear the connection between the block quotation and her topic?
2. The original passage from which the writer extracted her spot quotation reads as follow: "Most judges today take it for granted, as I do, that the applicable guideline for the defendant before them will represent an excessive sentence. The sentencing guidelines result, in the main, in the cruel imposition of excessive sentences, overfilling our jails and causing unnecessary havoc to families, society, and prisons." Why did the writer modify the quotation the way she did?
3. In tip 4 (see page 286), we advise you not to introduce a quotation and just leave it hanging but to comment on it. Where does this writer comment on the quotations she has used?

Additional Suggestions for Writing

1. Interview someone two generations removed from you (e.g., a grandparent, an elderly neighbour) about his or her life as a young person. What were the sources of entertainment? Leisure activities? Work? Family responsibilities? Major challenge or concerns? Goals? Write an essay in which you tell this person's story, using summary, paraphrase, and quotation to develop your main points.

2. Interview a friend, classmate, or relative on one of the following topics. Then write an essay using summary, paraphrase, and quotation to help tell your reader how your interviewee answered the question.
   a. If you were to live your life over knowing what you know now, what would you do differently?
   b. Explain what being a Canadian (or a parent, or childless, or unemployed, or successful, or a member of a particular religious group) means to you.
   c. "Once I was _____; now I am _____."
3. Research a topic of particular interest to you and write an essay using summary, paraphrase, and quotation to develop your main points.
4. Select a news article or a group of articles dealing with a current issue in your career field. In a paragraph of approximately 200 to 300 words, summarize the issue for your instructor, who has just returned from spending six months in the wilderness without access to either print or electronic media.

20

Documenting
Your Sources

Documentation is the process of acknowledging source material. When you document a source, you provide information that

1. tells your readers that the ideas they are reading have been borrowed from another writer, and
2. enables your readers to find the source and read the material for themselves.

When acknowledging your sources in a research paper, you need to follow a system of documentation. There are many different systems, but one of the most widely used is that of the Modern Language Association (MLA). The instructions and examples in this chapter are a slightly simplified version of the principles outlined by Joseph Gibaldi in the *MLA Handbook for Writers of Research Papers*, 6th ed. (New York: MLA, 2003. http://www.mla.org). Most instructors in English and the humanities require students to use MLA style.

Instructors in the social sciences (psychology, sociology, political science, and economics) usually expect papers to conform to the principles of APA style, based on the *Publication Manual of the American Psychological Association*, 5th ed. (Washington, DC: APA, 2001. http://www.apa.org). You will find instruction and examples of APA style in Appendix B.

For research papers in the biological sciences, your instructor may require Council of Biology Editors (CBE) style, presented in *Scientific Style and Format: The CBE Manual for Authors, Editors, and Publishers* (http://www.councilscienceeditors.org).

Many academic institutions publish their own style guides, which are available in college and university libraries and bookstores. Be sure to ask your instructor which documentation style he or she prefers.

Introduction: The Two-Part Principle of Documentation

Documentation styles vary in their details, but all styles require authors to

- identify in a parenthetical reference any information taken from a source, and
- list all sources for the paper on a separate page at the end.

A **parenthetical reference** (called a **parenthetical reference citation** in APA style) tells the reader that the information preceding the parentheses[1] is borrowed from a source and provides a key to the full identification of that source. For the most part, footnotes are no longer used to document source material; they are used to give additional information that cannot be conveniently worked into the body of your paragraph. (Note the example in this paragraph.)

A **Works Cited** list (called **References** in APA style) is a list of all the sources from which you have borrowed words, ideas, data, or other material in your paper.[2] Preparing and presenting a Works Cited list requires paying close attention to the details of presenting the information required in each entry. The format—including the order of information, capitalization, and punctuation—prescribed by your style guide must be followed *exactly*. This requirement may sound picky, but there is a good reason to abide by it.

Every kind of source you use requires a particular format. If entries are formatted correctly, an experienced reader can tell by glancing at them what kinds of sources you have used: books, journal articles, newspaper articles, Web documents, etc. If you use the wrong style, or leave something out, or scramble the elements in a citation, you will mislead or confuse your reader. Fortunately, technology is available to help you make the task of documenting much less onerous than it once was. Before you begin taking notes, find a reference manager program such as EndNote or ProCite. (See http://www.isiresearchsoft.com for these and other managers.) Some programs offer a 30-day free trial. Different programs have different features, but most will help you keep track of the notes you've taken from various sources, and all will format your Works Cited or References list for you.

---

[1]A punctuation note: *parentheses* means the pair of curvy punctuation marks: ( ). *Brackets* are the pair of square marks that surround altered words or phrases in a quotation: [ ].
[2]Formerly, this list was called a *Bibliography*.

How to Punctuate Titles in MLA Style

Depending on your instructor's preference, you may *italicize* or <u>underline</u> titles and subtitles of any work that is published as a whole—e.g., the names of books, plays, periodicals (newspapers, magazines, and journals), films, radio and television programs, compact discs—or underline them if you are using a pen. Put quotation marks around the titles of works published within larger works—e.g., the names of articles, essays, poems, songs, and individual episodes of television or radio programs. Also put quotation marks around the titles of unpublished works, such as lectures and speeches. Use capital letters for the first, the last, and all main words in a title and subtitle even if your source capitalizes only the first word in a title.

Parenthetical References in MLA Style

Every time you include in your paper a quotation, paraphrase, summary, fact, or idea you have borrowed from another writer, you must identify the source in parentheses immediately following the borrowed material. The parenthetical reference tells your reader that what he or she has just read comes from somewhere else, and it points your reader to the complete information about the source in your Works Cited list. Parenthetical references should be as short and simple as possible while still fulfilling these two purposes.

The standard practice in MLA style is to provide the surname of the author of the source material and the page number where the material was taken from. Once your reader has the author's name and page number, he or she can find complete bibliographic information about the source in your Works Cited list at the end of your paper. Of course, electronic sources present a challenge to this author-based citation method because they often lack an identifiable author, and they rarely include page numbers. More on this later.

You need to include a piece of source information only once; don't repeat information unnecessarily. For example, if you've already mentioned the author's name in your paragraph, you only need to give the page reference in the parentheses.

On page 293 is an excerpt from a research paper. The writer uses summary, paraphrase, and quotation, and gives the necessary source information in parentheses immediately following each borrowing. This excerpt also demonstrates how to omit a word or words from a source, using ellipses, and how to add or change a word or words, using square brackets.

The Works Cited list that follows the excerpt gives the reader full bibliographic information about each source.

The attractive young people who are portrayed in tobacco advertising make it easy for viewers to forget the terrible consequences of tobacco addiction. Cigarette advertisements routinely portray happy, energetic young people engaging in athletic activities under invariably sunny skies. The implication of these ads is that smoking is not a deterrent to an active lifestyle; in fact, it may even be a prerequisite (Cunningham 67).

Full parenthetical citation

It is difficult to overstate the impact of tobacco advertising on young people. As Cunningham points out,

> Few teenagers begin smoking for cigarettes' inherent physical qualities. Instead, teens are attracted to smoking for its image attributes, such as the five S's: sophistication, slimness, social acceptability, sexual attractiveness, and status. Marketing gives a cigarette a false "personality." (66)

Block quotation

Is it any wonder that young people continue to take up the habit?

Abbreviated parenthetical citation

In an effort to reverse the trend of teenage tobacco addiction, the federal government sponsors awareness campaigns to demonstrate how the tobacco industry dupes and manipulates young people. According to Robert Sheppard, the industry plays on teenagers' "need [for] something to rebel against . . . [which] is exactly how cigarette manufacturers market their wares" (20). To counteract the image of smoking as a symbol of rebellion, government anti-tobacco campaigns present smoking as a symbol of conformity.

Short quotation with
- *word changed*
- *words left out*
- *parenthetical citation*

Yielding to pressure from the government and the community, the tobacco industry has begun to sponsor programs aimed at restricting youth access to tobacco products. In a comprehensive review, however, the Ontario Medical Association (OMA) concludes that these programs are ineffective and makes several recommendations to strengthen youth reduction initiatives (OMA).

Parenthetical citation of paraphrase

The OMA recommends that all parties interested in reducing tobacco use endorse a comprehensive tobacco control program. The Association offers to work with the Canadian Medical Association and other interested parties to ensure that its position statement is published as widely as possible. And finally, the OMA recommends that all tobacco industry-sponsored programs be carefully monitored in the future (OMA).

Parenthetical citation of summary

Works Cited

Cunningham, Rob. *Smoke and Mirrors: The Canadian Tobacco War*. Ottawa: IDRC, 1996.

Ontario Medical Association. "More Smoke and Mirrors: Tobacco Industry-Sponsored Youth Prevention Programs in the Context of Comprehensive Tobacco Control Programs in Canada." A Position Statement. Feb. 2002. 3 Feb. 2005 <http://www.oma.org/phealth/ smokeandmirrors.htm>.

Sheppard, Robert. "Ottawa Butts Up against Big Tobacco." *Maclean's* 6 Dec. 1999: 20–24.

Study the way the excerpt on page 293 uses parenthetical references to identify information sources. The introductory paragraph ends with a paraphrase, which is immediately followed by a full parenthetical reference. Because the author's name is not mentioned in the writer's paragraph, it is given in parentheses, together with the number of the page on which the information was found. For more details, the reader would turn to the Works Cited list, reproduced at the bottom of page 293.

The second paragraph includes a block quotation from the same source. The author's name is given in the statement that introduces the quotation, so the parentheses contain only the page number on which the quotation can be found.

The third paragraph includes a short quotation integrated into the writer's own sentence. The introductory phrase gives the author's name, so the parenthetical reference provides only the page number of the article on which this partial quotation is found. Complete bibliographic information for this source appears in the Works Cited list.

In the fourth paragraph, the writer includes both a paraphrase and a summary of information found in an unsigned article posted on the website of the Ontario Medical Association. The source document is not paginated, so no page number is given. Complete information about this source appears in the alphabetical list of Works Cited under Ontario Medical Association, the sponsor of the site.

EXAMPLES OF PARENTHETICAL REFERENCES: TRADITIONAL PRINT SOURCES

1. If you name the source author in your paragraph, give just the page number in parentheses.

Isajiw asserts that the twentieth century "has produced more refugees and exiles than any other preceding period since the fall of the Roman Empire"(66).

The Works Cited entry for this book is on page 298.

2. If you do not name the source author in your paragraph, give the author's surname and the page number.

The effect of "status drop" on the psychological well-being of immigrants can be substantial: "Especially among those more highly educated, this experience can cause feelings of bitterness or hostility. . . ." (Isajiw 97).

3. If no author is named in the source, give the first few words of the Works Cited entry.

Legislation to reduce the amount of pollution generated by large-scale vehicles has been on the federal agenda for some time: "Canada has said it will toughen pollution-emission rules for all new vehicles, ending a loophole that allowed less stringent standards for popular sport-utility vehicles and minivans" ("Canada to Toughen" A6).

The Works Cited entry for this source is on page 300.

4. If your source was published in more than one volume, give the volume number before the page reference.

Only once in his two-volume work does Erickson suggest conspiracy (2: 184).

The Works Cited entry for this source is on page 298.

5. If you are quoting from a literary classic or the Bible, use Arabic numerals separated by periods to identify act, scene, and lines from a play or a biblical chapter and verse.

In Shakespeare's play, the duke's threat to give "measure for measure" (5.1.414) echoes the familiar passage in the Bible (Matthew 7.1–2).

EXAMPLES OF PARENTHETICAL REFERENCES: ELECTRONIC SOURCES

Parenthetical references for print sources in MLA style usually include the author's surname and the page number of the source. This principle is problematic for electronic sources since many of them lack one or both of these elements. Give enough information to guide your reader to the source listed in your Works Cited list.

1. If the electronic source lists an author, give the surname in your parenthetical reference.

Planespotting is a popular hobby, even an obsession, for growing numbers of people who are fascinated with aviation: "Some spotters take photographs. Others make videotapes. But the majority flock to airports around the world, equipped with scanners and notepads, with one goal in mind--recording the registration numbers painted on airplane tails" (Bourette).

> This quotation comes from *Shift*, an online magazine. The Works Cited entry for this quotation is on page 302.

2. If the electronic source does not list an author, give the document title (or a shortened version of the title) in italics or quotation marks as appropriate, instead of the author's name.

New websites are available to help students navigate their way through the challenging works of William Shakespeare:

> There are some people who don't even attempt to learn Shakespeare because they think that Shakespeare is . . . only for English scholars. But that's not true! Shakespeare can be FUN. That's right—Shakespeare can actually be something you want to learn about. ("William Shakespeare")

> This quotation comes from a website called *Shakespeare: Chill with Will*. The Works Cited entry for this quotation is on page 303.

3. You do not usually find page numbers or other navigation devices in an electronic source. If there are page, paragraph, or section numbers that could guide your reader to the specific material being quoted, include them. If the author's name is included in the parenthetical reference, put a comma after it and include the section or paragraph numbers. Use the abbreviations *sec.* and *par.*

Even Margaret Atwood must endure the editing process before her books are published:

> Being edited is like falling face down into a threshing machine. Every page gets fought over, back and forth, like WWI. Unless the editor and the writer both have in mind the greater glory of the work, . . . blood will flow and the work will suffer. Every comma, every page break, may be a ground for slaughter. (sec. 6)

This quotation comes from an article posted on Atwood's website. The Works Cited entry is found on page 303.

If there are no page, paragraph, or section numbers to identify the quotation, simply give the author's name or the title in parentheses. If your reader wants to locate the information, web browser search engines can often find it through a keyword search.

The Works Cited List

The Works Cited list appears at the end of your essay. It includes detailed bibliographical information for all the sources you have summarized, paraphrased, or quoted in your paper. The information listed in the Works Cited list enables your reader to assess the extent of your research and to find and check every source you used.

Begin the list on a new page and number each page, continuing the page numbers of your paper. (The page number appears in the upper right-hand corner, 1.25 cm from the top and lined up with the right margin.) Centre the heading, Works Cited, an inch from the top of the page. Double-space the entire list, including the title and the first entry. Begin each entry at the left margin. If an entry runs more than one line (and most do), indent the subsequent line or lines five spaces or 1.25 cm. This format is called a "hanging indent"[3] and can be found in most word-processing packages.

Arrange the entries alphabetically, beginning with the first word of the entry, which is often the author's surname. If no author is identified in your source, alphabetize by the first word in the title, ignoring *A*, *An*, and *The*. For example, *The Canadian Encyclopedia* would be listed under *C*, for *Canadian*. Separate the main parts of each entry with periods. Do not number your entries.

Below you will find instruction and examples for four different kinds of Works Cited entries: books, periodical articles, audiovisual sources, and electronic sources.

BOOKS, ENCYCLOPEDIAS, AND GOVERNMENT PUBLICATIONS

Here is the basic model for a book entry in a Works Cited list.

> Last name of author, First name. *Title of Book.* City of publication:
>   Publisher, year of publication.

Note the spacing, capitalization, and punctuation as well as the order of the information. If several cities are listed, use the first one. Shorten the publisher's name. For example, McGraw-Hill, Inc. is abbreviated to McGraw. If the publisher is a well-known university press, use the abbreviation UP: e.g., Oxford UP, U of Toronto P. The year the book was published is usually found on the back of the title page; if it is not given, use the latest copyright date.

---

[3]Hanging indents help readers locate authors' names in the alphabetical listing. If you have only one source to acknowledge, you do not need to indent the second line. For example, see the source citation for Robert Argue's book on page 278.

- **Book by one author or editor**

  Isajiw, Wsevolod W. *Understanding Diversity: Ethnicity and Race in the Canadian Context.* Toronto: Thompson, 1999.

  Barnes, Wendy, ed. *Taking Responsibility: Citizen Involvement in the Criminal Justice System.* Toronto: Centre of Criminology, University of Toronto, 1995.

- **Book by two or three authors or editors**

  Strange, Carolyn, and Tina Loo. *True Crime, True North: The Golden Age of Canadian Pulp Magazines.* Vancouver: Raincoast Books, 2004.

  France, Honoré, Maria del Carmen Rodriguez, and Geoffrey Hett, eds. *Diversity, Culture and Counselling: A Canadian Perspective.* Calgary: Detselig, 2004.

- **Book by more than three authors or editors**

  Beebe, Steven A., et al. *Interpersonal Communication: Relating to Others.* Scarborough: Allyn and Bacon, 1997.

- **Edition other than the first**

  Cooperman, Susan H. *Professional Office Procedures.* 3rd ed. Upper Saddle River, NJ: Prentice, 2002.

- **Recent edition of a classic text**

  Shakespeare, William. *The Tempest.* Ed. S. Orgel. Oxford: Oxford UP, 1994.

- **Multivolume work**

  Erickson, Edward W., and Leonard Waverman, eds. *The Energy Question: An International Failure of Policy.* 2 vols. Toronto: U of Toronto P, 1974.

- **Article, essay, story, or poem in a collection**

  Kliewer, Gregory. "Faking My Way through School." *Canadian Content.* Ed. Nell Waldman and Sarah Norton. 4th ed. Toronto: Harcourt, 2000. 311–12.

- **Encyclopedia reference**

  Driedger, Leo. "Ethnic Identity." *Canadian Encyclopedia.* 2000 ed.

- **Book published by a corporation (company, commission, or agency)**

  International Joint Commission. *Protection of the Waters of the Great Lakes: Final Report to the Governments of Canada and the United States.* Ottawa: The Commission, 2000.

- **Government publication**
  If the author is not named, identify the government first, then the agency, then the title, city of publication, publisher, and date.

  Canada. Canadian Heritage. *Canadian Content in the 21st Century: A Discussion Paper about Canadian Content in Film and Television Productions.* Hull, QC: Canadian Heritage, 2002.

  Ontario. Ministry of Training, Colleges and Universities. *Employment Profile: A Summary of the Employment Experience of 1999–2000 College Graduates Six Months after Graduation.* Toronto: Ministry of Training, Colleges and Universities, 2001.

ARTICLES IN JOURNALS, MAGAZINES, AND NEWSPAPERS

As with a book, information for an article begins with the author's name, if available, includes the title of the article, and ends with the details of publication, including the date, and the complete pages of the article. For a periodical that is published weekly or every two weeks, provide the day, month, and year, in that order. Abbreviate all months except for May, June, and July (Jan., Feb., Mar., Apr., Aug., Sept., Oct., Nov., Dec.). If the periodical is published monthly, provide month and year.

Works Cited entries for newspapers include the name as it appears on the masthead (top front page of the paper) but omit *The* (e.g., *Globe and Mail*). If the name of the city is not included in a locally published paper, add the city in square brackets—not underlined—after the name so that readers will know where it was published; for instance, *Comox Valley Record* [Campbell River].

Give the complete page span for each article in your Works Cited list. For example, if an article begins on page 148 and concludes on page 164, put a colon and the pages after the date: 5 June 2006: 148–64. If the article begins on page 36, then skips to page 40 and concludes on page 41, give only the first page and a plus sign: 36+. In a newspaper, the sections are usually numbered separately, so include the section number as well as the page number: *Calgary Herald* 16 Aug. 2005: S1+.

Note the order, punctuation, and capitalization of the information in the model below.

Author's last name, First name. "Title of Article." *Title of Periodical* Volume no. [if any] Issue no. [if any] Date: pages.

- **Article in a scholarly journal**

Lemire, Judith A. "Preparing Nurse Leaders: A Leadership Model." *Nursing Leadership Forum* 6.3 (2001): 39–44.

Some scholarly journals publish a number of issues each year; together, these issues make up an annual volume. Give the volume number (in this example, 6) right after the periodical title, add a period, and then give the issue number (here, 3) immediately before the date, which is given in parentheses in this type of entry, but not in those that follow.

- **Article in a monthly magazine**

Reece, Erik. "Death of a Mountain: Radical Strip Mining and the Leveling of Appalachia." *Harper's* Apr. 2005: 41–60.

- **Signed article in a newspaper**

Edwards, Steven. "Teenagers Told to Turn Off the Sun." *National Post* 18 Mar. 2005: A19.

- **Unsigned newspaper article**

"Canada to Toughen Auto-Emissions Rules." *Wall Street Journal* 5 Apr. 2002: A6.

- **Review**

Houpt, Simon. "Spamalot a Spoof to End All Spoofs." Rev. of *Monty Python's Spamalot,* by Eric Idle. Dir. Mike Nichols. Shubert Theatre, New York. *Globe and Mail* 19 Mar. 2005: R7.

AUDIOVISUAL SOURCES

- **Television show**

Remembering Peter Gzowski. Host Mark Kelley. CBC Newsworld. 30 Jan. 2002.

- **Radio show**

  "Hallway Confidential." *Outfront.* CBC Radio One, Toronto. 23 Mar.
      2005.

- **Recording**

  Chiarelli, Rita. *Breakfast at Midnight.* NorthernBlues, 2001.

- **Film, videocassette, laser disc, or DVD**

  Bowling for Columbine. Dir. Michael Moore. 2002. DVD. United
      Artists/Alliance Atlantis. 2002.

  If you wish to give credit to the contribution of a particular individual
  to a film or recording, begin with that person's name.

  Hitchcock, Alfred, dir. *Rear Window.* Perf. Jimmy Stewart, Grace Kelly,
      and Raymond Burr. 1954. DVD. Universal, 2001.

ELECTRONIC SOURCES

Documentation guidelines for electronic publications are now fairly standardized. Check with your Resource Centre to see if it provides handouts to
help you cite these sources accurately. Works Cited entries should identify
the source and provide enough information to enable a reader to locate it—
author, title, publication information, and date. However, providing all this
information is not always possible for online materials. Include as much
information as you can, and remember that the key element in citing an
electronic source is its electronic address or URL (uniform resource locator).

Do not use a hyphen to divide a URL over two lines; otherwise, you will
make it invalid. Record the URL on a single line, or break it after a slash (/),
and enclose it within angle brackets (<...>). Because the symbols, letters, and
numbers that make up a URL are complex and must be recorded accurately,
some recent guidelines suggest that angle brackets be omitted. Be sure to use
the format your instructor prefers.

Along with the URL, other essential information includes the date of
publication (if it is available) and the date that you, as the researcher,
accessed the information. The access date is important because online documents can be altered at any time. (Use the abbreviation conventions provided in the guidelines for periodicals: e.g., Mar. for March.)

Download and print online material so that you can verify it if, at a later
date, it is revised, unavailable, or inaccessible.

Follow this basic model for online source entries in a Works Cited list:

Author's last name, First name [if known]. "Title of Document or File."
Title of Complete Work or Site. Date of document or of last revision.
Date of access <URL, including protocol[4]>.

Several of your sources should come from the subscription databases available at your library. These databases provide access to full-text articles in reputable journals, magazines, newspapers, and other reliable research resources. When you use an online subscription service to retrieve articles, MLA style requires that you include the name of the library in the reference citation:

Author's last name, First name (if known). "Title of Article." *Title of Journal/Newspaper/Magazine.* Date of publication. Name of database. Name of library, City in which library is located. Date of access <URL of the subscription database>.

Many subscription databases will keep track of your citations and format them in various documentation styles (MLA, APA, Turabian, etc.). Look for this feature on the results page of the database, or ask a librarian if the database you are using offers this service. Databases, like humans, can make mistakes. Be sure to consult the style handbook or website to confirm that the citations generated by a database are correctly formatted.

- **Magazine article from an online (library subscription) database**

  Wahl, Andrew. "Emission Impossible." *Canadian Business* 28 Feb. 2005: 24. *eLibrary Canada.* Niagara College Library, Welland, ON. 21 Mar. 2005 <http://elibrary.bigchalk.com>.

- **Newspaper article from an online (library subscription) database**

  Claudia H. Deutsch. "Are Women Responsible for Their Own Low Pay?" *New York Times* 27 Feb. 2005, Late Edition (East Coast): 3.7. *National Newspaper Abstracts* (3). ProQuest. Niagara College Library. Welland, ON. 22 Mar. 2005 <http://www.proquest.com/>.

- **Article in an online periodical**

  Bourette, Susan. "Planespotting." *Shift* Mar. 2002: 20–24. 8 June 2005 <http://www.shift.com/content/10.1/53/1.html>.

---

[4]"Protocol" refers to a particular set of rules for performing tasks on the Internet, such as http (hypertext transfer protocol), nntp (network news transfer protocol), ftp (file transfer protocol), and so on.

- **Government publication**

  Canada. Health Canada. Health Products and Food Branch. *Natural Health Products in Canada—A History*. June 2003. 4 April 2005 <http://www.hc-sc.gc.ca/hpfb-dgpsa/nhpd-dpsn/ history_e.html#top>.

- **Online encyclopedia**

  "Art Deco." *Encyclopedia Britannica Online*. Encyclopaedia Britannica. 27 May 2005 <http://search.eb.com/eb/article?eu=9778>.

- **Online news service**

  MSNBC News Services. "Images Show Wide Rifts in Tsunami Seabed." MSN.Com 10 Feb. 2005. 1 Mar. 2005 <http:// www.msnbc.msn.com/id/6946276/>.

- **Personal or professional website**

  Atwood, Margaret. "The Rocky Road to Paper Heaven." *Margaret Atwood Reference Site*. N.d. 10 June 2005 <http:// www.owtoad.com/>.

  "William Shakespeare." *Shakespeare: Chill with Will*. N.d. 8 June 2005 <http://library.thinkquest.org/19539/front/htm>.

- **Personal e-mail communication**
  Follow this format:

  Author's surname, First name [or alias]. "Title of Message [from subject line]." E-mail to First name and Last name of recipient. Date of message.

  Note: Never give the writer's e-mail address.

  Zacharatos, Phil. "The Forest or the Trees?" E-mail to Caroline Bouffard. 1 Apr. 2005.

- **Online posting, listserv, or discussion group**

  Ballard, Rex. "Re: Windows vs. Linux." Online posting. 22 Apr. 2005. 2 May 2005 <news:comp.os.linux.advocacy>.

  Wincapaw, Celeste. "Cyber-Fem: New Perspectives on Midwifery." Online posting. 27 Mar. 2005. 5 June 2005. <http:// www.hsph.harvard.edu/rt21/talk/frame1.html>.

- **CD-ROMs**

Follow this basic model, including as many elements as are given in the source:

Author's surname, First name. "Title of Article, Song, or Poem [if relevant]." *Title of the Publication.* CD-ROM. Edition, release, or version [if relevant]. Place of publication: Name of publisher, date.

Delmar's Community Health Nursing: A Case Study. CD-ROM. Clifton Park, NY: Delmar, 2003.

Ward, Al. *Photoshop for Right-Brainers: The Art of Photo Manipulation.* CD-ROM. San Francisco: Sybex, 2004.

Below, you will find a sample Works Cited list to show you what the final page of your paper should look like.

Author Name 15

Works Cited

Newspaper article from library database
> Chang, Kenneth. "Nanoparticles." *Edmonton Journal.* 6 Mar. 2005. *eLibrary Canada.* Mohawk College Library. Hamilton, ON. 14 Apr. 2005 <http://elibrary.bigchalk.com>.

Online encyclopedia
> Drexler, Eric. "Nanotechnology." *AccessScience.* 10 Apr. 2003. McGraw-Hill Encyclopedia of Science and Technology Online. Niagara College Library, Welland, ON. 15 May 2005 <http://www.accessscience.com>.

Posting to online forum
> Fox, Fiona. "Nanotech—The Next Controversy alike GM?" Online posting. Mar. 2004. EuroScience.Net. 22 Mar. 2005 <http://www.euroscience.net/article6.html>.

Book
> Hall, J. Storrs. *Nanofuture: What's Next for Nanotechnology.* New York: Prometheus, 2005.

Print interview from internet
> Harris, Charles E. Interview. Nanotechnology Now. Mar. 2002. 14 Apr. 2005 <http://nanotech-now.com/charles-harris-interview-032002.htm>.

Magazine article
> "Nanotech." *Technology Review* Dec. 2004: 31.

Website
> *National Institute for Nanotechnology.* 2002. National Research Council Canada. 30 Mar. 2005 <http://nint-innt.nrc-cnrc.gc.ca/home/index_e.html>.

For each of the following quotations, write a short paragraph in which you use all or a portion of the quotation and credit it in a parenthetical citation. Be sure to punctuate titles correctly.

1. From a book entitled Getting it done: the transforming power of self-discipline by Andrew J. Dubrin, published by Pacesetter Books in Princeton in 1995. This sentence appears on page 182: "Stress usually stems from your interpretation and perception of an event, not from the event itself."

2. From a journal article by Linda A. White that appeared on pages 385 to 405 of Canadian Public Policy, a journal with continuous paging: "If a clear connection exists between the presence of child care and high levels of women's labour market participation, that would provide good reasons for governments and employers to regard child care as part of an active labour market policy." White's article is entitled Child Care, Women's Labour Market Participation and Labour Market Policy Effectiveness in Canada. The quotation appears on page 389 of the fourth issue of the 27th volume, published in 2001.

3. From the American Institute of Stress website, found on May 2, 2005, at http://www.stress.org: "Increased stress results in increased productivity—up to a point."

4. From a newspaper article that appeared on page A2 in the March 30, 2005 issue of The Vancouver Sun by Nancy Cleeland and found on the elibrary Canada database at your college library. The article is entitled As jobs heat up, workers' hearts take a beating. "For years, occupational health researchers have struggled to come up with formulas for measuring job stress and determining its effect on health."

5. From an interview with Hans Selye, conducted on Jan 1, 1982, shortly before his death, on the topic of his pioneering work on stress and illness: "Stress is the non-specific response of a human body to any demand made upon it."

6. From an e-mail message on the subject of time management from your friend, Janet Ford, on March 5, 2005: "Using a daily planner and checking e-mail only once a day are two ways I've found to manage my stress during the school year."

Prepare a Works Cited list in MLA style for the sources in Exercise 20.1 above.

21

Formatting a Research Paper

The appearance of your paper makes an impression on your reader. A correctly formatted paper reflects the care and attention to detail that instructors value in students' work.

Ask your instructor if he or she has any special requirements for the format of your research assignment. If so, follow them carefully. Otherwise, follow the guidelines in this chapter to prepare your paper for submission. These guidelines are based on MLA style. (You will find instruction on formatting in APA style on our website at http://www.essayessentials4e.nelson.com.) After the guidelines, you will find two model research papers, both formatted according to the MLA principles of documentation. The first, "Uncertain Future: Potential Dangers of Genetically Modified Crops," is an essay on a topic of general interest. The second, "The Evolution of Moral Balance in Charlotte Brontë's *Jane Eyre*," is an essay on a literary topic. Together, they provide examples of most of the possibilities you are likely to encounter when writing and formatting your own research paper.

Paper

Compose your final draft on 22 × 28 cm (8.5 × 11 inch) white bond paper. Be sure to use a fresh cartridge in your printer. If your instructor will accept a handwritten document, make sure it adheres to all of the guidelines that follow, including those regarding ink colour, margins, spacing, etc. Print out or write your research paper on *one side* of the paper only.

Fasten your paper together with a paper clip or a single staple in the upper left-hand corner. Unless your instructor specifically requests, don't bother with plastic or paper covers; most teachers find it annoying to disentangle your essay for marking.

Printing/Typing

Choose a standard, easily readable typeface, such as Times New Roman, in a 12-point font. Use black ink (or dark blue, if you are writing by hand).

Spacing and Margins

Unless you are instructed otherwise, double-space throughout your essay, including quotations and the Works Cited list. In a handwritten paper, write on every other line of a ruled sheet of white paper.

Adequate white space on your pages makes your paper more attractive and easier to read. It also allows room for instructors' comments. Leave margins of 2.5 cm at the top, bottom, and both sides of your paper. If you are using a word processor, click on the "justify left" formatting command.

Indent the first line of every paragraph five spaces or 1.25 cm; use the tab default setting in your word-processing program. Indent all lines of a block quotation ten spaces or 2.5 cm from the left margin.

Title Page

Do not prepare a separate title page unless your instructor requires it. Instead, at the top of the left margin of the first page of your essay, on separate lines, type your name, your instructor's name, the course number, and the date. Leave a double space and centre the title of your essay. Capitalize main words (see Chapter 40, page 478), but do not underline, italicize, or put quotation marks around your title (unless it contains the title of another author's work, which you should punctuate in the usual way).

Header and Page Numbers

Number your pages consecutively throughout the paper, including the Works Cited list, in the upper right-hand corner, 1.25 cm from the top and 2.5 cm from the right edge of the page. Type your last name before the page number. Use a word processor to create a running head consisting of your last name, a single space, and the page number—no punctuation or *p*. See the student papers at the end of this chapter for examples.

Copy

Always keep a copy of your paper for your files!

Projecting an Image

As well as presenting your understanding of the topic, a research paper demonstrates your writing skills and your ability to follow specific requirements of documentation and format. Meeting your instructor's submission requirements is as important as any other aspect of the preparation of your paper. This may be the last stage of your writing task, but it is the first impression your reader will have of your work.

The paper that follows is an example of a properly formatted, documented essay. Before writing her paper, Soraya prepared an outline. Notice that she included in her outline the sources she wanted to refer to in each section. This technique saves hours of paper shuffling when you sit down to write.

Uncertain Future: Potential Dangers
of Genetically Modified Crops

Attention-Getter: Most people eat genetically modified foods every day, but few of stop to consider their potential dangers.

Thesis Statement: Genetically modified crops may have disastrous health, environmental, and sociopolitical effects.

I.   GM foods pose incalculable risks to human health.
  A. GM foods may contain toxic proteins. (Commoner; Mellon)
  B. Despite the testing that goes on during the genetic engineering process, allergic reactions to GM foods are likely. (Hopkin; Humphrys)
  C. The spread of antibiotic resistant bacteria is also a possibility. (Hopkin)

II. GM crops may have a catastrophic and unpredictable impact on the environment.
  A. Built-in pesticides have benefits, but they kill creatures other than agricultural pests, destroying the balance of ecosystems. (Brown; Suzuki)
  B. Pests develop tolerance to built-in pesticides. (Brown)

    C. The transfer of pollen from genetically modified plants to weeds creates superweeds. (Randerson)

III.   The social, economic, and political effects of GM crops may be harmful or even disastrous.

    A. Biotechnology corporations use patents and "terminator technology" to control GM seeds; people become dependent on these companies. (Kneen)

    B. GM crops won't feed the world. (Suzuki; Mellon)

Summary: The health, environmental, and sociopolitical effects of GM crops may be dreadful.

Memorable Statement: More research needs to be done before we can evaluate the impact of GM technology. Right now, the risks are largely unknown and unpredictable.

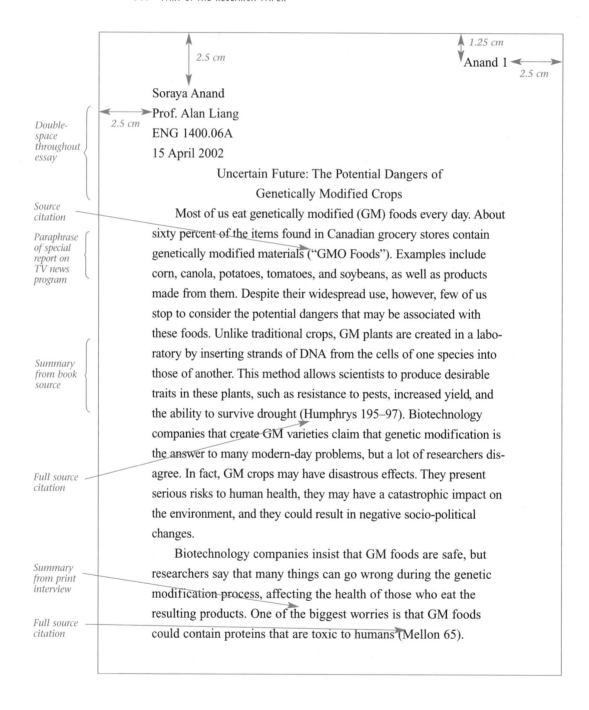

Double-space throughout essay

2.5 cm

2.5 cm

1.25 cm

2.5 cm

Anand 1

Soraya Anand

Prof. Alan Liang

ENG 1400.06A

15 April 2002

Uncertain Future: The Potential Dangers of

Genetically Modified Crops

Source citation

Paraphrase of special report on TV news program

Most of us eat genetically modified (GM) foods every day. About sixty percent of the items found in Canadian grocery stores contain genetically modified materials ("GMO Foods"). Examples include corn, canola, potatoes, tomatoes, and soybeans, as well as products made from them. Despite their widespread use, however, few of us stop to consider the potential dangers that may be associated with these foods. Unlike traditional crops, GM plants are created in a labo-ratory by inserting strands of DNA from the cells of one species into those of another. This method allows scientists to produce desirable traits in these plants, such as resistance to pests, increased yield, and the ability to survive drought (Humphrys 195–97). Biotechnology companies that create GM varieties claim that genetic modification is the answer to many modern-day problems, but a lot of researchers dis-agree. In fact, GM crops may have disastrous effects. They present serious risks to human health, they may have a catastrophic impact on the environment, and they could result in negative socio-political changes.

Summary from book source

Full source citation

Biotechnology companies insist that GM foods are safe, but researchers say that many things can go wrong during the genetic modification process, affecting the health of those who eat the resulting products. One of the biggest worries is that GM foods could contain proteins that are toxic to humans (Mellon 65).

Summary from print interview

Full source citation

Anand 2

Barry Commoner, a senior scientist at City University of New York, *Quotation from magazine article*
points out that recent discoveries prove that the results of DNA
transfer are unpredictable. Transferring genes from one organism to
another, he says, "might give rise to multiple variants of the intended *Abbreviated citation*
protein--or even to proteins bearing little structural relationship to
the original one" (45). Margaret Mellon notes that "as scientists
manipulate systems that they don't completely understand, one of the *Summary from article, with full citation*
unexpected effects could be turning on genes for toxins" (65).

Allergic reactions are also a concern (Hopkin 60). In the mid-
1990s, scientists tried to genetically improve soybeans with a gene
from brazil nuts. The beans caused allergic reactions in people
allergic to brazil nuts, so development was stopped (Humphrys
219–20). Supporters of GM technology cite this case as an example *Author and title of book source*
of the effectiveness of the testing process, but John Humphrys, the
author of *The Great Food Gamble,* says that we may not be so lucky
in the future:

> *10 sp*   The brazil nut allergen was well known and could be
> specifically tested for . . . . In other cases, of course, the
> allergen might not be known. It is entirely possible that
> its effects might appear only over a period of time. It
> might produce a form of allergy of which we have no *Block quotation from book*
> experience. It might simply not be identified. Far from
> exonerating the industry, what this little tale tells is that
> the risks exist. (220–21)

The spread of antibiotic resistant bacteria--bacteria that cannot
be killed by known antibiotics--is another potential problem. Food
engineers often use antibiotic resistant genes when designing GM *Paraphrase from website*
crops (Greenpeace). The possibility that "resistance genes might

Abbreviated book citation

Full citation for website

Anand 3

somehow jump from GM foods to bacteria in a consumer's gut" is small, but it cannot be ignored (Hopkin 61). If such a jump occurs, antibiotic resistant bacteria could quickly spread, adding to the already serious medical problem of antibiotic resistance.

Paragraph topic developed by paraphrase and block quotation

Genetically modified crops may also harm the environment. Most GM plant varieties are engineered to be resistant to pests such as insects. Supporters of GM crops point out that the farmers who plant them do not have to spray chemical pesticides on their fields, which is good for the environment (Brown 52). Yet there are other consequences as well. Studies indicate that insect-resistant GM crops may kill not only agricultural pests but also other creatures that happen to be exposed to them, such as monarch butterflies and green lacewing caterpillars (Brown 53–54). Long-term effects could be unpredictable but significant enough to affect whole ecosystems. David Suzuki warns readers:

Block quotation from article on website (no page, paragraph, or section numbers given)

> If we grow fields of crops that are toxic to all organisms except humans, what will that do to beneficial insects, or to the important microorganisms that live in our soils? This could have serious repercussions because depletion of insect numbers, for example, would lead to fewer birds and small mammals, and could have other implications up and down the food chain.

Paraphrase of idea found in two sources

In addition, even the defenders of GM crops are realizing that insect pests will develop a tolerance to built-in insecticides (Brown 54; McHughen 108). When this occurs, entire crops may suddenly fail, causing enormous losses. To prevent this disaster, farmers in the United States and elsewhere are now required to set aside a part of their farmland for crops that have not been genetically modified. In

Anand 4

these areas, "insects that have acquired some resistance . . . breed with those that have not, diluting the resistance trait" (Brown 57). Many environmentalists question the effectiveness of this strategy. They claim that the areas set aside "are either too small or too poorly designed to keep insect resistance at bay for long" (57). As resistance develops, another form of chemical control will have to be used or food engineers will have to develop new GM crop varieties, causing more environmental devastation.

Short quotation integrated into sentence

The transfer of pollen from a genetically modified species to other plants nearby can also lead to environmental damage. The main reason is that many GM crops are designed to be resistant to herbicides--chemical substances that kill plants. As a result, farmers can spray their fields with herbicides to eliminate weeds without damaging their own crops ("Herbicide"). The problem starts when pollen from one of these GM plants is carried to another plant species, such as a weed. The weed obtains the herbicide-resistant gene and can then grow unchecked, since it can no longer be killed by herbicides. It becomes a so-called superweed (Brown 55). According to a study commissioned by English Nature, the advisory body on conservation for the government of the United Kingdom, many superweeds already exist in Canada. Consequently, farmers are often forced to use older, stronger herbicides to kill them (Randerson).

Summary of encyclopedia article

Summary of online magazine article

The social, economic, and political implications of GM crops are also worrying. One problem often cited by critics is that a few large corporations control the industry. Because GM seeds can be patented, these companies not only dictate the price of seeds but also hold "intellectual property" rights for their products

Anand 5

(Humphrys 197–98). Brewster Kneen, the author of *Farmageddon: Food and the Culture of Biotechnology*, explains the results:

Words left out

> To say the seed is sold . . . is misleading, because in a sense the owners of the technology, the seed companies, do not sell it at all; they rent it out to the farmer for a season. The farmer is not allowed to keep any of the crop for replanting or to share it with a neighbor because the technology [is] owned and patented by one or another major transnational corporation. (107)

Word changed

To protect its interests, one company uses what has been called "terminator technology," which makes plants sterile (Robbins). As a result, farmers cannot save seeds from their plants to produce another harvest; they must buy new seeds instead. Kneen argues that as GM crops become more popular, control of the global food supply shifts dangerously. Eventually, he says, corporate ownership of seeds "will end the ability of the majority of the world's people to feed themselves and will make them dependent on corporate seed suppliers" (61).

Paragraph topic developed by quotations and paraphrase

In light of such practices, many people question what Bill Lambrecht, the author of *Dinner at the New Gene Café*, calls "the grand promise by some of the companies . . . that they will be able to more capably feed the world" with GM crops. Increased productivity will not solve the problem of starvation in developing countries because, as David Suzuki says, "most food shortages are caused by political and social issues, not an overall lack of food production capacity." There is more than enough food in the world, but it doesn't get to those in need (Mellon 64). Drought-tolerant GM crops could potentially benefit people in many countries, but

Anand 6

chances are that these people will not be able to afford them (Mellon 64).

The jury is out on GM foods. Scientists, corporations, governments, and the public continue to debate their pros and cons. In the meantime, most of us unknowingly eat products containing genetically modified ingredients every day. As we reach for the corn chips, we should realize that GM crops may have dreadful and unexpected health, environmental, and socio-political consequences. More research and testing need to be done before we can evaluate this technology and its impact on our lives and on the world. Right now, the risks are still largely unknown and unpredictable.

Anand 7

Works Cited

Brown, Kathryn. "Seeds of Concern." *Scientific American*
    Apr. 2001: 52–57.

Commoner, Barry. "Unravelling the DNA Myth: The Spurious
    Foundation of Genetic Engineering." *Harper's* Feb. 2002:
    39–47.

"GMO Foods." *The National*. CBC-TV. Toronto. 23 Aug. 2001.
    Transcript.

Greenpeace. "The Secret Ingredient." 10 Apr. 2002
    <http://www.greenpeace.ca/e/resource/publications/gmo/
    secret_ingredient.pdf>.

"Herbicide." *The Columbia Encyclopedia*. 2001 ed. 10 Apr. 2002
    <http:// www.bartleby.com/65/he/herbicid.html>.

Hopkin, Karen. "The Risks on the Table." *Scientific American*
    Apr. 2001: 60–61.

Humphrys, John. *The Great Food Gamble*. London: Hodder and
    Stoughton, 2001.

Kneen, Brewster. *Farmageddon: Food and the Culture of
    Biotechnology*. Gabriola Island: New Society Publishers, 1999.

Lambrecht, Bill. Interview. Canada AM. CTV. 1 Oct. 2001.
    Transcript.

McHughen, Alan. *Pandora's Picnic Basket: The Potential and
    Hazards of Genetically Modified Foods*. New York: Oxford
    UP, 2000.

Mellon, Margaret. Interview. *Scientific American* Apr. 2001: 64–65.

Randerson, James. "Genetically-modified Superweeds 'Not
    Uncommon.'" *New Scientist* 5 Feb. 2002. 10 Apr. 2002
    <http://www.newscientist.com/news/news.jsp?id=ns99991882>.

Anand 8

Robbins, John. Interview. *Times-Herald 13* Jan. 2002: 3.

Suzuki, David. "Genetically Modifying Our Food." Science Matters series. 3
    Nov. 1999; 10 Nov. 1999. 10 Apr. 2002 <http://www
    .davidsuzuki.org/Dr_David_Suzuki/Article_Archives/>.

The following essay won the Sydney Singh Memorial Award at Grant MacEwan College in 2000. This award is given annually to the student who has written the best essay analyzing a work of literature in an English 101 class.

The Evolution of Moral Balance
in Charlotte Brontë's *Jane Eyre*

Introduction: Brontë's use of balancing elements contributes to the impact of *Jane Eyre*.

Thesis statement: Jane is pulled in opposing directions: between the values of Helen Burns and those of Bertha Mason; between the spirituality of St John Rivers and the sensuality of Rochester. Through her struggles with these opposing elements, Jane eventually finds a position on the moral continuum that satisfies her.

I.   Helen Burns and Bertha Mason represent the externalization of "the division of the Victorian female psyche into its extreme components of mind and body." (Showalter 68)

  A. Helen is an asexual child, focused on her spirituality to the point of physical self-denial.

  B. Bertha is a highly sexual woman, whose excessive indulgence has caused her to lose her reason.

  C. Brontë destroys the two "polar personalities" to make way for the integration of Jane's physical and spiritual beings. (Showalter 68)

  D. The values represented by Helen and Bertha influence Jane's moral development.

  E. The lessons she has learned are most clearly evident when she rejects Rochester's proposition.

II.   One of Rochester's arguments for an affair is that nobody will be harmed by it because Jane has no family to offend.

  A. Jane initially seems to accept his reasoning. (356)

  B. Helen's indoctrination about the value of one's good conscience (81) prevents her from acquiescing.

  C. She cannot live without self-respect. (356)

  D. Bertha's story shows her that if she were to become Rochester's mistress, she would share that fate: madness and estrangement from Rochester.

  E. Jane's moral position between the two extremes offered by Bertha and Helen is tested both by Rochester's proposition and by St John's proposal.

III. St John Rivers and Rochester are two characters who balance each other on many levels, from looks to lifestyle. The extremes they represent push her toward middle ground.

    A. Description of Rochester: 129–30.

    B. Description of St John: 386.

    C. Rochester's past: 355.

    D. St John's past: 393.

    E. Jane is offered contrasting choices: a passionate, illicit affair vs. a pious marriage of convenience.

    F. On the surface, the proposals are in contrast, but both would force her to suppress a part of her nature.

    G. Both proposals threaten the fulfillment Brontë has in mind for Jane. (Eagleton 33)

    H. Jane resists temptation; Brontë saves her for a transformed Rochester.

IV. *Jane Eyre* ends with Jane no longer having to compromise herself in order to be with Rochester.

    A. The humbled Rochester is no longer asking Jane to abandon her conscience to live in sin.

    B. Rochester and Jane are now a perfect match because he has moved away from his earlier extremes.

    C. Rochester's physical mutilation is a "symbolic castration" (Chase, qtd. in Gilbert and Gubar 368), but more than his masculinity, his spirit has been transformed.

    D. Humility has taught him wisdom. (495)

    E. Their "perfect concord" (500) is made possible by Rochester's movement away from his earlier extreme to become Jane's ideal mate.

    F. Their blissful marriage is contrasted with the life and death of St John in India.

    G. Brontë pays tribute to St John (417), while still validating Jane's choice.

    H. Jane has achieved an ideal moral balance; she can live a full life on earth and still earn the reward of heaven.

Summary: Jane's refusal to reject the demands of either her mind or her body is the essence of the novel. She is alternately taught and tested by Helen Burns and Bertha Mason, by St John Rivers and Rochester, and ultimately comes to reconcile the two extremes.

Memorable statement: Jane's journey to her own satisfying moral code and a life that celebrates it are intensified by Brontë's use of balancing elements.

Friedland 1

Jess Friedland
Professor MacDonald
EN101-354X
1 December 2000

The Evolution of Moral Balance in
Charlotte Brontë's *Jane Eyre*

A profusion of balancing elements contribute to the impact of
Charlotte Brontë's novel, *Jane Eyre*. Brontë uses these balances to
convey the maturation of Jane's value system. The diametrically
opposed characters of Helen Burns and Bertha Mason represent the
duality of Jane's nature, and ultimately influence her moral choices.
The proposals of Rochester and St John Rivers seem antithetical,
but display an underlying similarity. Jane is pulled in opposite
directions throughout the novel, but her final address to the reader
shows that she has found a position on the moral continuum that
satisfies her. The balances utilized to demonstrate her journey
enhance both our view of Jane's internal struggle and our understanding of her choices.

According to Elaine Showalter, Helen Burns and Bertha
Mason represent the externalization of "the division of the
Victorian female psyche into its extreme components of mind and
body" (68). Brontë's characterizations support this observation.
Helen is an unequivocally asexual child, focused solely on her spirituality to the point of physical self-denial. Bertha is an unequivocally sexual woman, who has seemingly lost her mind through
excessive indulgence in bodily pleasure. Showalter goes on to say:

> Brontë gives us not one but three faces of Jane, and she
> resolves her heroine's psychic dilemma by literally and
> metaphorically destroying the two polar personalities to make

Friedland 2

way for the full strength and development of the central consciousness, for the integration of the spirit and the body. (68)

Jane's rejection of either extreme validates this statement on a
metaphorical level. In the literal sense, however, both Bertha and
Helen influence Jane's morality in more relevant ways than merely
dying. Jane is neither an angel nor a demon, but she certainly ends
up closer to Helen's end of the spectrum than to Bertha's. Their lessons are most apparent during Jane's rejection of Rochester's
proposition.

One of Rochester's main arguments for an affair is that nobody
will be harmed by it as Jane has no family to offend. Jane pleads
with herself to "tell him you love him and will be his. Who in the
world cares for you? or who will be injured by what you do?"
(Brontë 356; ch. 27). Helen's indoctrination of the intrinsic value of
one's own good conscience prevents her from acquiescing. "If all the
world hated you, and believed you wicked, while your own conscience approved you, and absolved you from guilt, you would not
be without friends" (Brontë 81; ch. 8). The opposite must also hold
true: if Jane's conscience does not approve her, Rochester's love will
not matter. Jane will be without her own self-respect. Therefore, she
cannot stifle the "indomitable [. . .] reply--'I care for myself'"
(Brontë 356; ch. 27). Bertha's lesson is more subtle, but equally
effective. Her sexual nature has led her to madness and estrangement
from Rochester. Once her story is told to Jane, the implications are
clear. She must reject a life as Rochester's mistress or potentially
face similar consequences. Jane's moral position between the two
extremes offered by Bertha and Helen is more a function of their
lives than of their deaths. This moral position is tested most notably
by the aforementioned proposition and by the proposal of her cousin.

Friedland 3

St John Rivers and Rochester balance each other on many levels, from looks to lifestyle. Again, these extreme options, which are more literally presented to Jane, push her toward middle ground. Jane's first description of Rochester is of "a dark face, with stern features and a heavy brow"; she implies that he is far from being "a handsome, heroic-looking young gentleman" (Brontë 129–30; ch. 12). St John, on the other hand, is "young [. . .] tall, slender," with "a Greek face, very pure in outline: quite a straight, classic nose; quite an Athenian mouth and chin" (Brontë 386; ch. 29). Rochester's past is riddled with "lust for a passion--vice for an occupation" (Brontë 355; ch. 27), whereas St John is called "blameless in his life and habits [. . .] pure-lived, conscientious" (Brontë 393–94; ch. 30). Jane is offered a passionate, illicit affair by one, and a pious marriage of convenience by the other. These proposals are superficially contrary, but if Jane accepted either one, she would be forced to suppress part of her nature.

As Terry Eagleton states in his study of the novel, "Jane [. . .] must refuse Rivers as she has refused Rochester: loveless conventionalism and illicit passion both threaten the kind of fulfilment the novel seeks for her" (33). Fulfillment involves being accepted and loved without moral modification. Jane is sorely tempted, first to turn her back on her conscience for Rochester, and later to turn her back on her heart for St John. Brontë does not allow her to give in to either man at these crucial points, saving her instead for a revised Rochester.

The conclusion of *Jane Eyre* has Jane and Rochester married at last. Jane no longer needs to compromise herself in order to be with him, and his first wife is not the only obstacle that has been removed. The man who insisted that she abandon her conscience to live in sin has changed significantly. Rochester now complements

Friedland 4

Jane as never before. His mutilation has been referred to as a "symbolic castration" by Richard Chase (qtd. in Gilbert and Gubar 368), but it is his spirit rather than his masculinity that seems to have been honed. Rochester has been humbled, and the taste of humility has taught him wisdom. He is able to admit to Jane, "I did wrong: I would have sullied my innocent flower--breathed guilt on its purity" (Brontë 495; ch. 37). During their first engagement, Jane was unsure and often uncomfortable about her place in Rochester's life. In her description of their marriage however, she says that "we are precisely suited in character--perfect concord is the result" (Brontë 500; ch. 38). Such a perfect fit is only made possible by Rochester's movement away from his earlier extreme. He has become a close match for Jane on every level, and therefore becomes her ideal mate.

The final three paragraphs of the novel throw this blissful marriage into sharp contrast with the life and imminent death of St John in India. He is greeting his death at the end of ten years of martyrdom with eagerness, while Jane and Rochester are living life to its fullest. Brontë is giving respectful tribute to St John, but there remains a sense of validation for Jane's choices. St John's reason for clinging solely to his spirituality and rejecting his body is that he will not relinquish his "foundation laid on earth for a mansion in heaven" (Brontë 417; ch. 32). There can be no doubt, however, that Jane will be worthy of heaven upon her death. Jane's moral balance is thus portrayed as ideal; she can live a happy, full life on earth and yet not fear eternal damnation.

Jane's refusal to discount entirely either her mind or her body is the essence of the story. The course by which she comes to reconcile the two is compellingly wrought. She is alternately taught and tested by Helen Burns and Bertha Mason, by St John Rivers and Rochester. Jane's journey to her own satisfying moral code, and a life that celebrates it, are intensified by Brontë's use of balancing elements.

Friedland 5

Works Cited

Brontë, Charlotte. *Jane Eyre*. Harmondsworth, England: Penguin,
  1996.

Eagleton, Terry. "*Jane Eyre*: A Marxist Study." *Charlotte Brontë's*
  Jane Eyre: *Modern Critical Interpretations*. Ed. Harold
  Bloom. New York: Chelsea House Publishers, 1987. 29–45.

Gilbert, Sandra M., and Susan Gubar. *The Madwoman in the Attic*.
  New Haven: Yale UP, 1984.

Showalter, Elaine. "Charlotte Brontë: Feminine Heroine." Jane
  Eyre: *Contemporary Critical Essays*. New Casebooks. Ed.
  Heather Glen. New York: St. Martin's Press, 1997. 68–77.

PART 6

A Review of the Basics

How to Use This Section

This part of *Essay Essentials* is a workbook designed to improve the correctness of your writing. In Chapters 22 to 41, we look at the errors that give many writers trouble, whether they are writing student papers, professional reports, PowerPoint presentations, or office memoranda.

In each chapter, we do three things: explain a point, illustrate it with examples, and provide exercises in the text and on the website to help you master the point. The exercises are arranged in sets that get more difficult as you go along. By the end of the last set in each chapter, you should have a good grasp of the skill. You will lose that grasp, however, if you do not practise. To maintain and reinforce your mastery of the skills you are learning, make a conscious effort to apply them every time you write.

You should work your way through this part of the book while you are working on Parts 1 through 5. If you have been out of school for some time, or if your basic skills are not as strong as you'd like them to be, you may find it helpful to set up a schedule, matching a section of the workbook with a unit of the text. For example, while you are learning how to plan an essay in Part 1, you could set yourself the goal of working through Chapters 22 to 27, on sentence structure; while learning how to write an essay in Part 2, you could work through Chapters 28 to 30, on grammar. You would then cover Chapters 31 to 36, on punctuation, along with Part 3, revising the essay. Finally, as you learn about the different kinds of essays in Part 4, you could cover Chapters 37 through 41, on spelling.

Alternatively, you could go through this workbook section by section, addressing in order the errors your instructor identifies in your writing. Whichever approach you choose, we recommend that you complete every chapter of the workbook. If you do so conscientiously, we guarantee that as your papers improve in organization and effectiveness, your writing will also improve in correctness and clarity.

Here's how to proceed in each chapter.

1. Read the explanation. Do this even if you think you understand the point being discussed.
2. Study the highlighted rules and the examples that follow them.
3. Now turn to the exercises. Try at least one set even if you are confident that you understand the principle.
4. Always check your answers to each set of exercises before going on to the next. Only if you check your answers after every set can you avoid repeating your mistakes and—worse—possibly reinforcing your errors. For those exercises marked with an asterisk (*), you will find the answers in the back of the book. For those on the website, the answers are marked automatically, so you will know instantly whether or not you have understood the material.
5. When you make a mistake, go back to the explanation and examples and study them again. Try making up some examples of your own to illustrate the rule. If you are truly stuck, check with your instructor. You can reinforce your understanding by doing the practice tests that you will find on the More Practice page of the *Essay Essentials* website.

6. At the end of each chapter, there is a mastery test marked with the icon shown in the margin. Your instructor can provide you with the answers for these tests. Use these tests to help track your progress as you master basic writing skills.

On the inside front cover, you will find a Quick Revision Guide. Use it to ensure that you have covered all the essentials before handing in your paper.

On the inside back cover, you will find a list of correction marks commonly used by instructors to draw your attention to specific errors. Use this list to be sure you've eliminated any errors your instructor has previously identified in your writing.

22

Cracking the Sentence Code

There is nothing really mysterious or difficult about sentences; you've been speaking them since you were two. The difficulty arises when you try to write—not sentences, oddly enough, but paragraphs. Most college students, if asked to write 10 sentences on 10 different topics, could do so without error. However, when those same students write paragraphs, then fragments, run-ons, and other sentence faults appear.

The solution to sentence-structure problems has two parts.

Be sure every sentence you write
1. has both a subject and a verb
2. expresses a complete thought

If English is your first language, your ear may be the best instrument with which to test your sentences. If you read a sentence aloud, you may be able to tell by the sound whether it is complete and clear. Sometimes, however, your ear may mislead you, so this chapter will show you, step by step, how to decode your sentences to find their subjects and verbs. When you know how to decode sentences, you can make sure that every sentence you write is complete.

Read these sentences aloud.

Snowboarding is one of the world's newest sports.
Although snowboarding is still a young sport.

The second "sentence" doesn't sound right, does it? It does not make sense on its own and is in fact a sentence fragment.

Testing your sentences by reading them aloud won't work if you read your paragraphs straight through from beginning to end. The trick is to read from the end to the beginning. That is, read your last sentence aloud and *listen* to it. If it sounds all right, then read aloud the next-to-last sentence, and so on, until you have worked your way back to the first sentence you wrote.

Now, what do you do with the ones that don't sound correct? Before you can fix them, you need to decode each sentence to find out if it has both a subject and a verb. The subject and the verb are the bare essentials of a sentence. Every sentence you write must contain both. There is one exception:

In a **command**, the subject is suggested rather than stated.

Consider these examples.

Sign here. = [You] sign here. (The subject you is implied or understood.)
Charge it. = [You] charge it.
Play ball! = [You] play ball!

Finding Subjects and Verbs[1]

A sentence is about *someone* or *something*. That someone or something is the **subject**. The word (or words) that tells what the subject *is* or *does* is the **verb**. In the following sentences, the subject is underlined once and the verb twice.

Snow falls.
Kim dislikes winter.
We love snowboarding.
Mt. Whistler offers excellent opportunities for winter sports.
In Canada, winter is six months long.
Some people feel the cold severely.

The subject of a sentence is always a **noun** (the name of a person, place, thing, or concept) or a **pronoun** (a word such as *I, you, he, she, it, we,* or *they* used in place of a noun). In the examples above, the subjects include persons (*Kim, we, people*); a place (*Mt. Whistler*); a thing (*snow*); and a concept (*winter*). In one sentence, a pronoun (*we*) is the subject.

Find the verb first.

---

[1]If you have forgotten (or have never learned) the parts of speech and the basic sentence patterns, you will find this information on the student page of the *Essay Essentials* website, http://www.essayessentials4e.nelson.com

One way to find the **verb** in a sentence is to ask what the sentence says about the subject. There are two kinds of verbs.

- **Action verbs** tell you what the subject is doing. In the examples above, *falls*, *dislikes*, *love*, and *offers* are action verbs.
- **Linking verbs** link or connect a subject to a noun or adjective describing that subject. In the examples above, *is* and *feel* are linking verbs.

    Linking verbs tell you the subject's condition or state of being. (For example, "Tadpoles *become* frogs," "Frogs *feel* slimy.") The most common linking verbs are forms of *to be* (*am, is, are, was, were, have been*, etc.) and verbs such as *look, taste, feel, sound, appear, remain, seem*, and *become*.

Another way to find the verb in a sentence is to put a pronoun (*I, you, he, she, it,* or *they*) in front of the word you think is the verb. If the result makes sense, it is a verb. For example, you could put *it* in front of *falls* in the first sentence listed above: "it falls" makes sense, so you know *falls* is the verb in this sentence. Try this test with the other five example sentences.

    Keep this guideline in mind as you work through the exercises below.

To find the subject, ask <u>who</u> or <u>what</u> the sentence is about.
To find the verb, ask what the subject <u>is</u> or <u>is doing</u>.

Exercise 22.1*

In each of the following sentences, underline the <u>subject</u> with one line and the <u>verb</u> with two. Answers for exercises in this chapter begin on page 523. If you make even one mistake, go to the website and do the exercise listed beside the Web icon that follows this exercise. Be sure you understand this material thoroughly before you go on.

1. I bought a used car.

2. The used car was cheap.

3. It needed some repairs.

4. Unfortunately, the repairs were expensive.

5. Insurance for the car was expensive, too.

6. Buying a car is costly.

7. According to the salesman, the car was not overpriced.

8. Always get a second opinion.

9. After 10 years, cars sometimes develop serious problems.

10. Paying for repairs compensates for the cheap price.

GO TO WEB

EXERCISE 22.1

Usually, but not always, the subject comes before the verb in a sentence.

Occasionally, we find the subject after the verb:

- In sentences beginning with *Here* + a form of *to be* or with *There* + a form of *to be*

  Here and *there* are never the subject of a sentence.

  Here <u>are</u> the test <u>results</u>. (Who or what <u>are</u>? <u>Results</u>.)
  There <u>is</u> a <u>fly</u> in my soup. (Who or what <u>is</u>? A <u>fly</u>.)

- In sentences that are deliberately inverted for emphasis

  Finally, at the end of the long, boring joke <u>came</u> the pathetic <u>punch line</u>.
  Out of the stadium and into the pouring rain <u>marched</u> the <u>parade</u>.

- In questions

  <u>Are</u> <u>we</u> there yet?
  <u>Is</u> <u>she</u> the one?

  But notice that in questions beginning with *who, whose, what, where,* or *which*, the subject and verb are in "normal" order: subject followed by verb.

  <u>Who</u> <u>ate</u> my sandwich?   <u>Whose</u> <u>horse</u> <u>came</u> first?
  <u>What</u> <u>caused</u> the accident?   <u>Which</u> <u>car</u> <u>runs</u> best?

Exercise 22.2*

Underline the subject with one line and the verb with two. Watch out for inverted sentences. If you make an error, do the Web exercises that follow.

1. Here is an idea to consider.

2. William Lyon Mackenzie led a rebellion against the Government of Canada.

3. He later became the mayor of Toronto.

4. Who wants the last piece?

5. Eat slowly.

6. There, beyond the swimming pool, is the gym.

7. A moving chicken is poultry in motion.

8. Far behind the leaders trailed the main group of cyclists.

9. Here are the results of your examination.

10. Irish coffee contains ingredients from all four of the essential food groups: caffeine, fat, sugar, and alcohol.

GO TO WEB

EXERCISES 22.2, 22.3, 22.4

More about Verbs

The verb in a sentence may be a single word, as in the exercises you've just done, or it may be a group of words. When you are considering whether or not a word group is a verb, there are two points you should remember.

1. No verb preceded by *to* is ever the verb of a sentence.[2]
2. **Helping verbs**[3] are often added to main verbs.

---

[2] The form *to* + verb—e.g., *to speak, to write, to help*—is an infinitive. Infinitives can act as subjects or objects, but they are never verbs.

[3] If you are familiar with technical grammatical terms, you will know these verbs as **auxiliary verbs**.

The list below contains the most common helping verbs.

be (all forms of *to be* can act as helping verbs: e.g., *am, are, is, was, were, will be, have/had been*, etc.)	can could/could have do/did have/had may/may have might/might have	must/must have ought shall/shall have should/should have will/will have would/would have

> The complete verb in a sentence consists of the main verb together with any helping verbs.

Here are a few of the forms of the verb *write*. Notice that in questions the subject may come between the helping verb and the main verb.

You <u>may write</u> now.   You <u>ought to write</u> to him.
He certainly <u>can write</u>!   We <u>will have written</u> by then.
We <u>should write</u> home more often.   He <u>had written</u> his apology.
I <u>shall write</u> tomorrow.   I <u>will write</u> to the editor.
He <u>could have written</u> yesterday.   The proposal <u>has been written</u>.
She <u>is writing</u> her memoirs.   Orders <u>should have been written</u>.
<u>Did</u> he <u>write</u> to you?   <u>Could</u> you <u>have written</u> it in French?

One verb form *always* takes a helping verb. Here is the rule.

> A verb ending in *-ing* MUST have a helping verb (or verbs) before it.

Here are a few of the forms an *-ing* verb can take:

I <u>am writing</u> the report.
<u>Is</u> she <u>writing</u> the paper for him?
You <u>are writing</u> illegibly.
I <u>was writing</u> neatly.
You <u>will be writing</u> a report.
They <u>must have been writing</u> all night.
<u>Have</u> you <u>been writing</u> on the wall?

Beware of certain words that are often confused with helping verbs.

> Words such as *not, only, always, often, sometimes, never, ever*, and *just* are NOT part of the verb.

These words sometimes appear in the middle of a complete verb, but they are modifiers, not verbs. Do not underline them.

I <u>have</u> just <u>won</u> a one-way ticket to Moose Factory.
She <u>is</u> always <u>chosen</u> first.
Most people <u>do</u> not <u>welcome</u> unasked-for advice.

Exercise 22.3*

Underline the subject once and the complete verb twice. Check your answers, and if you made even one mistake, try the Web exercises that follow.

1. He has talked nonstop for three hours.

2. I am not going to drive.

3. Could they return the goods tomorrow?

4. You cannot eat your birthday cake before dinner.

5. Carla should have been filing the letters and memos.

6. I will be the first member of my family to graduate from college.

7. Paula's lawsuit should never have been allowed to proceed this far.

8. Have you ever been to the Zanzibar tavern?

9. There has never been a better time to travel to Greece.

10. How are the club members identified?

GO TO WEB

EXERCISES 22.5, 22.6, 22.7, 22.8

More about Subjects

Often groups of words called **prepositional phrases** come before the subject in a sentence or between the subject and the verb. When you're looking for the subject in a sentence, prepositional phrases can trip you up unless you know the following rule.

The subject of a sentence is never in a prepositional phrase.

You must be able to identify prepositional phrases so that you will know where *not* to look for the subject.

A prepositional phrase is a group of words that begins with a preposition and ends with a noun or a pronoun that answers the question *what* or *when.*

The noun or pronoun is called the object of the preposition. It is this word that, if you're not careful, you might think is the subject of the sentence.

Below is a list of prepositional phrases. The italicized words are prepositions; the words in regular type are objects of the prepositions.

about the book	*between* the desks	*near* the wall
above the desk	*by* the book	*of* the typist
according to the book	*concerning* the memo	*on* the desk
after the meeting	*despite* the policy	*onto* the floor
against the wall	*down* the hall	*over* a door
along the hall	*except* the staff	*to* the staff
among the books	*for* the manager	*through* the window
among them	*from* the office	*under* the book
around the office	*in* an hour	*until* the meeting
before lunch	*in* front *of* the desk	*up* the hall
behind the desk	*inside* the office	*with* a book
below the window	*into* the elevator	*without* the book
beside the book	*like* the book	*without* them

Before you look for the subject in a sentence, cross out all prepositional phrases.

The keyboard ~~of your computer~~ should be cleaned occasionally.

What <u>should be cleaned</u>? The <u>keyboard</u> (not the computer).

Regardless ~~of the expense~~, one ~~of us~~ should go ~~to the IT conference in Las Vegas~~.

Who <u>should go</u>? <u>One</u> (not the group).

Exercise 22.4*

In the following sentences, first cross out the prepositional phrase(s), then underline the subject once and the verb twice. Check your answers before going on to the Web exercises that follow.

1. Among English teachers, Santa's helpers are known as subordinate clauses.

2. After his death, Terry Fox became a national symbol of heroic courage.

3. In the state of Florida, it is illegal for single, divorced, or widowed women to parachute on Sunday afternoons.

4. In Kentucky, no woman may appear in a bathing suit on any highway in the state unless escorted by two officers or armed with a club.

5. In my wildest imaginings, I cannot understand the reason for these laws.

6. During a break in the conversation, Darryl's embarrassing comment could be heard in every corner of the room.

7. In my lawyer's dictionary, a will is defined as a dead giveaway.

8. To the staff and managers of the project, I extend my congratulations for an excellent job.

9. Against all odds, and despite their shortcomings, the St. John Miners made it into the playoffs of the Southern New Brunswick Little League.

10. Walk a mile in my shoes at high noon with your head held high in order to avoid clichés like the plague.

GO TO WEB

EXERCISES 22.9, 22.10

Multiple Subjects and Verbs

So far, you have been decoding sentences containing a single subject and a single verb, even though the verb may have consisted of more than one word. Sentences can, however, have more than one subject and one verb.

Multiple subjects are called **compound subjects**; multiple verbs are **compound verbs**.

Here is a sentence with a compound subject:

Esquimalt and Oak Bay border the city of Victoria.

This sentence has a compound verb:

She groped and stumbled her way down the dark aisle of the movie theatre.

And this sentence has a compound subject and a compound verb:

The detective and the police sergeant leaped from their car and seized the suspect.

The parts of a compound subject or verb are usually joined by *and* (sometimes by *or*). Compound subjects and verbs may contain more than two elements, as in the following sentences:

Careful planning, organization, and conscientious revision are the keys to good essay writing.

I finished my paper, put the cat outside, took the phone off the hook, and crawled into bed.

Exercise 22.5*

In the following sentences, cross out any prepositional phrases, then underline the subjects once and the verbs twice. Be sure to underline all the elements in a compound subject or verb. Check your answers before continuing.

1. Management and union met for a two-hour bargaining session.

2. They debated and drafted a tentative agreement for a new contract.

3. The anesthetist and the surgeon scrubbed for surgery and hurried to the operating room.

4. Frederick Banting and Norman Bethune are known around the world as medical heroes.

5. Kevin and Sandra hiked and cycled across most of Newfoundland.

6. My son or my daughter will meet me and drive me home.

7. Knock three times and ask for Stan.

8. In the 17th and 18th centuries, the French and the English fought for control of Canada.

9. Buy the base model and don't waste your money on luxury options.

10. Ragweed, golden rod, and twitch grass formed the essential elements in the bouquet for his English teacher.

GO TO WEB

EXERCISES   22.11, 22.12, 22.13, 22.14

Here's a summary of what you've learned in this chapter. Keep it in front of you as you write the mastery test.

Summary

- The subject is *who* or *what* the sentence is about.
- The verb tells what the subject *is* or *does*.
- The subject normally comes before the verb (exceptions are questions and sentences beginning with *there* or *here*).
- The complete verb = a main verb + any helping verbs.
- By itself, a word ending in *-ing* is not a verb.
- An infinitive (a phrase consisting of *to* + a verb) is never the verb of a sentence.
- The subject of a sentence is never in a prepositional phrase.
- A sentence can have more than one subject and/or verb.

Exercise 22.6

This challenging exercise will test your ability to find the main subjects and verbs in sentences. In each sentence below, first cross out any prepositional phrases, and then underline each subject with one line and each verb with two lines. Be sure to underline all elements in a multiple subject or verb.

1. The politicians of all parties try in vain to change the world, but they seldom try to change themselves.

2. In the past, men and women had clearly defined roles and seldom broke away from them.

3. Police, firefighters, and paramedics comforted, rescued, and treated my aunt and uncle after their car accident.

4. Among the many kinds of cheese made in Canada are Camembert, Fontina, and Quark.

5. French fries, gravy, and cheese curds are the ingredients in traditional Quebec poutine.

6. Increasingly, in high-end restaurants, chefs are experimenting with Canadian foods like elk meat, fiddlehead greens, and Saskatoon berries.

7. On the Lovers' Tour of Lake Louise were two elderly women with walkers, a couple of elderly gentlemen with very young wives, half a dozen middle-aged divorcées, and me.

8. Negotiate in English, swear in German, argue in Spanish, and make love in French.

9. After the rain, the sun came out, the birds sang, and the tourists returned to their chairs by the pool.

10. According to its campaign literature, the incoming government will provide jobs for all Canadians, eliminate the national debt, find a cure for cancer, land a Canadian on Mars, and reduce income tax by 50 percent, all in its first year in office!

23

Solving Sentence-Fragment Problems

Every complete sentence has two characteristics. It contains a subject and a verb, and it expresses a complete thought. Any group of words that is punctuated as a sentence but lacks one of these characteristics is a **sentence fragment**. Fragments are appropriate in conversation and in some kinds of writing, but normally they are unacceptable in college, technical, and business writing.

There are two kinds of fragments you should watch out for: the "missing piece" fragment and the dependent clause fragments.

"Missing Piece" Fragments

Sometimes a group of words is punctuated as a sentence but is missing one or more of the essential parts of a sentence: a subject and a verb. Consider these examples.

1. Found it under the pile of clothes on your floor.

   Who or what <u>found</u> it? The sentence doesn't tell you. The subject is missing.

2. Their arguments about housework.

   The sentence doesn't tell you what the arguments <u>were</u> or <u>did</u>. The verb is missing.

3. During my favourite TV show.

<u>Who</u> or <u>what</u> <u>was</u> or <u>did</u> something? Both subject and verb are missing.

4. The programmers working around the clock to trace the hacker.

Part of the verb is missing. Remember that a verb ending in *-ing* needs a helping verb to be complete.

Finding fragments like these in your work when you are revising is the hard part. Fixing them is easy. There are two ways to correct sentence fragments. Here's the first one.

To change a "missing piece" fragment into a complete sentence, add whatever is missing: a subject, a verb, or both.

1. You may need to add a subject:

Your <u>sister</u> found it under the pile of clothes on your floor.

2. You may need to add a verb:

Their arguments <u>were</u> about housework. (linking verb)
Their arguments about housework eventually <u>destroyed</u> their relationship. (action verb)

3. You may need to add both a subject and a verb:

My <u>mother</u> always <u>calls</u> during my favourite TV show.

4. Or you may need to add a helping verb:

The programmers <u>have been</u> working around the clock to trace the hacker.

Don't let the length of a fragment fool you. Students sometimes think that if a string of words is long, it must be a sentence. Not so. No matter how long the string of words, if it doesn't contain both a subject and a verb, it is not a sentence. For example, here's a description of children going from door to door for treats on Halloween:

In twos and threes, dressed in the fashionable Disney costumes of the year, as their parents tarried behind, grownups following after, grownups bantering about the schools, or about movies, about local sports, about their marriages, about the difficulties of long marriages, kids sprinting up the next driveway, kids decked out as demons or superheroes or dinosaurs . . . beating back the restless souls of the dead, in search of sweets.

Moody, Rick. *Demonology*. New York: Little, Brown, 2001. 291.

At 68 words, this "sentence" is long, but it is a fragment. It lacks both a subject and a verb. If you add "The <u>children</u> <u>came</u>" at the beginning of the fragment, you would have a complete sentence.

In the following exercises, decide whether each group of words is a complete sentence or a "missing piece" fragment. Put *S* before each complete sentence and *F* before each fragment. Make each fragment into a complete sentence by adding whatever is missing: the subject, the verb, or both. Then compare your answers with our suggestions. Answers for exercises in this chapter begin on page 524.

Exercise 23.1*

1. _____ About historical events.

2. _____ To decide on the basis of rumour, not facts.

3. _____ Trying to be helpful, I offered to check the files.

4. _____ Cooking my famous tuna casserole.

5. _____ The party members gathering in the campaign office.

6. _____ We won.

7. _____ Hands over your head.

8. _____ To go anywhere without my iPod.

9. _____ Having worked hard all her life.

10. _____ Wanting to please them, she had coffee ready on their arrival.

GO TO WEB

EXERCISES 23.1, 23.2, 23.3, 23.4

Exercise 23.2*

_____ Professional athletes making millions of dollars a year. _____ At the same time, owners of sports franchises growing fantastically rich from the efforts of their employees, the players. _____ The fans being the forgotten people in the struggle for control over major league sports. _____ The people who pay the money that makes both owners and players rich. _____ I have an idea that would protect everyone's interests. _____ Cap the owners' profits. _____ Cap the players' salaries. _____ And, most important, the ticket prices. _____ A fair deal for everyone. _____ Fans should be able to see their teams play for the price of a movie ticket, not the price of a television set.

Dependent Clause Fragments

Any group of words containing a subject and a verb is a **clause**. There are two kinds of clauses. An **independent clause** is one that makes complete sense on its own. It can stand alone, as a sentence. A **dependent clause**, as its name suggests, cannot stand alone as a sentence; it depends on another clause to make complete sense.

Dependent (also known as **subordinate clauses**) begin with **dependent-clause cues** (subordinating conjunctions).

Dependent-Clause Cues

after	if	until
although	in order that	what, whatever
as, as if	provided that	when, whenever
as long as	since	where, wherever, whereas
as soon as	so that	whether
because	that	which, whichever
before	though	while
even if, even though	unless	who, whom, whose

Whenever a clause begins with one of these words or phrases, it is dependent.

A dependent clause must be attached to an independent clause. If it stands alone, it is a sentence fragment.

Here is an independent clause:

I am a poor speller.

If we put one of the dependent-clause cues in front of it, it can no longer stand alone:

Because I am a poor speller.

We can correct this kind of fragment by attaching it to an independent clause:

Because I am a poor speller, I have a spell checker in my PDA.

Exercise 23.3*

Put an *S* before each clause that is independent and therefore a sentence. Put an *F* before each clause that is dependent and therefore a sentence fragment. Circle the dependent-clause cue in each sentence fragment.

1. _____ Although she practised it constantly.

2. _____ Since the horse stepped on her.

3. _____ As soon as the troops arrived, the fighting stopped.

4. _____ Whichever route the bikers choose.

5. _____ Before Biff bought his bike.

GO TO WEB

EXERCISES 23.5, 23.6, 23.7, 23.8

Exercise 23.4*

Identify the sentence fragments in the paragraph below by highlighting the dependent-clause cue in each fragment you find.

Although many companies are experiencing growth, thanks to a healthy economy. Middle managers are not breathing easy. As long as there is a surplus of junior executives. Middle managers will continue to look over their shoulders, never sure when the axe will fall. Whether through early retirement, buyout, or termination. Their positions are being eliminated by cost-conscious firms whose eyes are focused on the bottom line. Because the executive branch of many businesses expanded rapidly during the years of high growth. Now there is a large block of managers who have no prospects of advancement. As one analyst observed, when he examined this block of largely superfluous executives and their chances of rising in the company hierarchy, "You cannot push a rectangle up a triangle."

Most sentence fragments are dependent clauses punctuated as sentences. Fortunately, this is the easiest kind of fragment to recognize and fix. All you need to do is join the dependent clause either to the sentence that comes before it or to the one that comes after it—whichever linkage makes better sense.

Read the following example to yourself; then read it aloud (remember, last sentence first).

Montreal is a sequence of ghettos. Although I was born and brought up there. My experience of French was a pathetically limited and distorted one.

The second "sentence" sounds incomplete, and the dependent-clause cue at the beginning of it is the clue you need to identify it as a sentence fragment. You could join the fragment to the sentence before it, but then you would get "Montreal is a sequence of ghettos, although I was born and brought up there," which doesn't make sense. The fragment should be linked to the sentence that follows it, like this:

Montreal is a sequence of ghettos. Although I was born and brought up there, my experience of French was a pathetically limited and distorted one. (Mordecai Richler)

If, as in the example above, your revised sentence *begins* with the dependent clause, you need to put a comma after it. If, however, your revised sentence *ends* with the dependent clause, you don't need a comma between it and the independent clause that precedes it.

My experience of French was pathetically limited although I was born and brought up [in Montreal].

See Chapter 31, Rule 3 (page 419).

Exercise 23.5*

Turn back to Exercise 23.4 and revise it by joining each dependent clause fragment to an independent clause that precedes or follows it, whichever makes better sense.

GO TO WEB

EXERCISE 23.9

Exercise 23.6*

The following paragraph contains both independent and dependent clauses (fragments), all punctuated as if they were complete sentences. Letting meaning be your guide, join each dependent clause fragment to the independent clause that comes before or after it—whichever makes better sense. Be careful to punctuate correctly between clauses.

In spite of what everyone says about the weak economy and the scarcity of jobs, especially for young people. I have financed my college career with a variety of part-time and seasonal jobs. Right now, for instance, while completing my third year at college. I have not one, or two, but three part-time jobs. I am a short-order cook three nights a week for a local bar and diner. And a telemarketer for a cable company after school. Or whenever I have free time. I'm also a server at a specialty coffee store on weekends. To maintain any kind of social life. While juggling three jobs and the requirements of my third-year program is not exactly easy, but I find it hard to turn down the opportunity for experience. Not to mention cash. I'm willing to put my social life on hold. For a while.

Exercise 23.7

As a final test of your skill in finding and correcting sentence fragments, try this exercise. Make each fragment into a complete sentence.

1. I had never eaten curry. But the first time I tasted it. I decided I liked it.
2. In France, they say that an explosion in the kitchen could have disastrous results. Such as linoleum blown apart.
3. Our family thinks my sister is too young to get married. Since she and her boyfriend want to be registered at Toys "R" Us.
4. It may surprise you to know that Canadians have made significant contributions to world cuisine. Two of the best known being baby pabulum and frozen peas.
5. Bathing the family cat. It's an activity that carries the same risks as tap dancing in a minefield. Or juggling with razor blades.
6. After working for three nights in a row trying to make my essay perfect so that I would get a high grade in my course. I lost my entire project when my brother crashed the computer while playing Grand Theft Auto.
7. I decided to take swimming lessons for two reasons. The first is fitness. Second, water safety.
8. There is good news. The man who was caught in an upholstery machine has fully recovered.
9. All of us are more aware of the effects of pollution now than we were 10 years ago. Because we are continually bombarded with information about the environment and our impact on it. In school, on television, and in newspapers.
10. My second favourite household chore is ironing. The first being hitting my head on the top bunk bed until I faint. (Erma Bombeck)

24

Solving Run-On Problems

Some sentences lack certain elements and thus are fragments. Other sentences contain two or more independent clauses that are incorrectly linked together. A sentence with inadequate punctuation between clauses is a **run-on**. Run-ons tend to occur when you write in a hurry, without first organizing your thoughts. If you think about what you want to say and punctuate carefully, you shouldn't have any problems with them.

There are two kinds of run-on sentences to watch out for: comma splices and fused sentences.

Comma Splices and Fused Sentences

As its name suggests, the **comma splice** occurs when two complete sentences (independent clauses) are joined together with only a comma between them. Here's an example:

I stayed up all night, I am exhausted.

Tea may be good for you, coffee is not.

A **fused sentence** occurs when two complete sentences are joined together with no punctuation at all:

I stayed up all night I am exhausted.

Tea may be good for you coffee is not.

There are four ways to fix run-on sentences.

1. Make the independent clauses into separate sentences.

I stayed up all night. I am exhausted.
Tea may be good for you. Coffee is not.

2. Separate the independent clauses with a comma followed by one of these words: *and, but, or, nor, for, so,* or *yet.*[1]

I stayed up all night, and I am exhausted.

You can insert one of the dependent-clause cues listed in Chapter 23, on page 342.

Because I stayed up all night, I am exhausted.

3. Make one clause dependent on the other by adding one of the dependent-clause cues listed on page 342.

Because I stayed up all night, I am exhausted.
I am exhausted because I stayed up all night.
Tea may be good for you although coffee is not.

4. Use a semicolon, either by itself or with a transitional word or phrase, to separate the independent clauses. (See Chapter 32.)

I stayed up all night; I am exhausted.
Tea may be good for you; on the other hand, coffee is not.

Note: All four solutions to comma splices and fused sentences require you to use a word or punctuation mark strong enough to come between two independent clauses. A comma by itself is too weak, and so is a dash.

The sentences in the following exercises will give you practice in fixing comma splices and fused sentences. Correct the sentences where necessary and then check your answers, beginning on page 525. Since there are four ways to fix

---

[1]These words are called **coordinating conjunctions** because they are used to join equal (or coordinating) clauses. If you are not sure how to punctuate sentences with coordinating conjunctions, see Chapter 31, Rule 2 (page 418).

each sentence, your answers may differ from our suggestions. If you find that you're confused about when to use a semicolon and when to use a period, be sure to read pages 427–31 before going on.

Exercise 24.1*

1. This is strong coffee, it has dissolved my spoon!
2. Just let me do the talking, we're sure to get a ticket if you open your mouth.
3. I keep buying lottery tickets, but I have won only free tickets.
4. If you have never tried it, hitting a golf ball may look easy, it's not.
5. As long as you smile when you speak, you can get away with saying almost anything.
6. Montreal used to be known as Ville St. Marie, before that it was known as Hochelaga.
7. Students today really need summer jobs and part-time employment, their tuition and living costs are too high for most families to subsidize.
8. Because I'm not very good at calculating odds, I'm afraid to play poker with you.
9. It's very windy, a ball hit deep to centre field will likely go into the stands.
10. "I was married by a judge, I should have asked for a jury." (Groucho Marx)

GO TO WEB

EXERCISES 24.1, 24.2

Exercise 24.2*

1. I use a keyboard all the time and my handwriting has become illegible.
2. Despite my parents' objections, I enjoy having long hair, it makes me feel attractive.
3. Casual meetings are fine for small groups, more formal settings are appropriate for larger groups.
4. I'd be happy to help you, just call when you need me, I'll be here all day.
5. In Canada, winter is more than a season it's a bad joke.
6. Perfection is probably impossible to achieve, but that doesn't mean you should stop trying your best.
7. For students in most technology programs, the future looks bright, however a diploma does not guarantee job security.

8. A Canadian who speaks three languages is called multilingual, one who speaks two languages is called bilingual, one who speaks only one language is called an English Canadian.
9. Skilled people are needed in specialized fields, currently, the top three are geriatrics, hospitality, and environmental technology.
10. I believe in a unified Canada, I believe that in 1867 the Fathers of Confederation were right, a federation of provinces can make a strong nation.

Exercise 24.3

As a final test of your ability to identify and correct run-on sentences, find and correct the 10 errors in the following paragraphs.

According to a news report, a private girls' school in Victoria was recently faced with an unusual problem, they solved it in a way that can only be described as creative, it is also a good example of effective teaching. Some of the grade 10 girls, forbidden by their parents to wear lipstick at home, began to apply it at school, in the second-floor washroom. That was the first problem, the second was that after applying the lipstick, they would press their lips to the mirror, leaving dozens of perfect lip prints. Every night, the maintenance crew would remove the prints, the next day the girls would reapply them and finally the principal decided that something had to be done.

She called the girls into the washroom where she met them with one of the maintenance men and he stood by while the principal addressed the girls. She explained that the lip prints on the mirrors were causing a problem for the maintenance crew, they had to clean the mirrors every night instead of doing other work. To demonstrate how difficult the cleaning job was and how much time was wasted on this needless chore, the principal asked the maintenance man to clean one of the mirrors, the girls watched with interest he took out a long-handled squeegee and began scrubbing at the lipstick prints. When he had scrubbed for a while, he turned, dipped his squeegee into one of the toilets, and continued to work on the mirrors and since then, there has not been another set of lip prints on the washroom mirror.

25

Solving Modifier Problems

Felix was complimented on a great game and a fine job of goaltending *by his mother.*

Snarling furiously and baring his teeth, Maurice crawled through a basement window only to confront an angry watchdog.

When she was a first-year student, the English professor told Mara she would *almost* write all her assignments in class.

These sentences show what can happen to your writing if you aren't sure how to use modifiers. A **modifier** is a word or phrase that adds information about another word in a sentence. In the examples above, the italicized words are modifiers. Used correctly, modifiers describe, explain, or limit another word, making its meaning more precise. Used carelessly, however, modifiers can cause confusion or, even worse, amusement.

You need to be able to recognize and solve two kinds of modifier problems: **misplaced modifiers** and **dangling modifiers**.

Misplaced Modifiers

Modifiers must be as close as possible to the words they apply to. Usually, readers will assume that a modifier modifies whatever it's next to. It's important to remember this, because, as the following examples show, changing the position of a modifier can change the meaning of your sentence.

Jason walked (only) as far as the corner store. (He didn't walk any farther.)

Jason (only) walked as far as the corner store. (He didn't jog or run.)

(Only) Jason walked as far as the corner store. (No one else went.)

Jason walked as far as the (only) corner store. (There were no other corner stores.)

To make sure a modifier is in the right place, ask yourself "What does it apply to?" and put it beside that word or word group.

When a modifier is not close enough to the word it refers to, it is said to be misplaced. A misplaced modifier can be a single word in the wrong place.

The supervisor told me they needed someone who could use both Word and WordPerfect (badly.)

Is some company really hiring people to do poor work? Or does the company urgently need someone familiar with word processing programs? Obviously, the modifier *badly* belongs next to *needed*.

The supervisor told me they (badly) needed someone who could use both Word and WordPerfect.

Be especially careful with these words: *almost, nearly, just, only, even, hardly, merely, scarcely.* Put them right before the words they modify.

Misplaced: She (nearly) answered every question.

Correctly placed: She answered (nearly) every question.

Misplaced: After driving all night, we (almost) arrived at 7:00 a.m.

Correctly placed: After driving all night, we arrived at (almost) 7:00 a.m.

A misplaced modifier can also be a group of words in the wrong place.

> Bundled up in down clothing to keep warm, the dog team waited for the driver.

The modifier, *bundled up in down clothing to keep warm*, is too far away from the word it is supposed to modify, *driver*. In fact, it seems to modify *dog team*, making the sentence ridiculous. We need to rewrite the sentence.

> The dog team waited for the driver, bundled up in down clothing to keep warm.

Look at this one:

> I drove my mother to Saskatoon, where my aunt lives in a rental car.

In a rental car applies to *drove* and should be closer to it.

> I drove my mother in a rental car to Saskatoon, where my aunt lives.

Notice that a modifier need not always go right next to what it modifies; it should, however, be as close as possible to it.

Occasionally, as in the examples above, the modifier is obviously out of place. The writer's intention is clear, and the sentences are easy to correct. But sometimes modifiers are misplaced in such a way that the meaning is not clear, as in the following example:

> Raj said after the game he wanted to talk to the press.

Did Raj *say* it after the game? Or does he want to *talk to the press* after the game? To avoid confusion, we must move the modifier and, depending on which meaning we want, write either

> After the game, Raj said he wanted to talk to the press.

> or

> Raj said he wanted to talk to the press after the game.

In Exercises 25.1 and 25.2, rewrite the sentences that contain misplaced modifiers, positioning them closely as possible to the words they modify. Check your answers to the first set before continuing. Answers for this chapter begin on page 526.

Exercise 25.1*

1. Trevor left the can of Pet Grrmet out for the dog that he had opened.

2. Our supervisor told us on the first day that no one takes coffee breaks.

3. I enthusiastically recommend this candidate with no experience whatever.

4. Professor Green told us in September he thought our class was a hopeless case.

5. We almost enjoyed the whole movie; only the ending was a disappointment.

6. Leo and Annie found an apartment in a highrise within walking distance of the campus with two bedrooms and a sunken living room.

7. There just are enough pieces to go around.

8. It almost seems there is a game every day during baseball season.

9. A charming, intelligent companion is sought by a vertically challenged but wealthy gentleman who looks good in evening gowns and diamonds.

10. One of us could only go because there was enough money just to buy one ticket.

Exercise 25.2*

1. One finds the best Chinese food in those restaurants where the Chinese eat usually.

2. He caught sight of a canary and several finches using his new binoculars.

3. Using my new camera, I can take professional-quality pictures with automatic functions.

4. The football practices have been organized for players who are not with a team in the summertime as a keep-fit measure.

5. Vancouver is a wonderful city for anyone who likes rain and fog to live in.

6. Some games are less demanding in terms of time and equipment, such as tiddlywinks.

7. The Human Rights Code prohibits discrimination against anyone who is applying for a job on the basis of race, religion, sex, or age.

8. We looked for a birthday present for our boss in a golf store.

9. Each year, 500,000 Canadian men almost have a vasectomy.

10. We hope to improve our students' performance using cash as a motivator.

Dangling Modifiers

A dangling modifier occurs when there is no appropriate word in the sentence for the modifier to apply to. That is, the sentence does not contain a specific word or idea to which the modifier could sensibly refer. With no appropriate word to modify, the modifier seems to apply to whatever it's next to, often with ridiculous results.

(After a good night's sleep,) my teachers were impressed with my unusual alertness.

This sentence seems to say that the teachers had a good night's sleep.

(Trying desperately to finish an essay,) my roommate's stereo made it impossible to concentrate.

The *stereo* was writing an essay?

Dangling modifiers are harder to correct than misplaced ones; you can't simply move danglers to another spot in the sentence. There are, however, two ways in which you can fix them. One way requires that you remember the following rule.

When a modifier comes at the beginning of a sentence, it modifies the subject of the sentence.[1]

This rule means that you can avoid dangling modifiers by choosing the subjects of your sentences carefully.

---

[1] The rule has exceptions, called adverbial modifiers, but they won't give you any trouble. Example: (Quickly) she did as she was told.

1. Ensure the subject is an appropriate one for the modifier to apply to.

Using this method, we can rewrite our two examples by changing the subjects.

After a good night's sleep, I impressed my teachers with my unusual alertness.

Trying desperately to finish an essay, I found it impossible to concentrate because of my roommate's stereo.

2. Another way to correct a dangling modifier is by changing it into a dependent clause.

After I had had a good night's sleep, my teachers were impressed with my unusual alertness.

When I was trying desperately to finish an essay, my roommate's stereo made it impossible to concentrate.

Sometimes a dangling modifier comes at the end of a sentence:

A Smart is the car to buy when looking for efficiency and affordability.

Can you correct this sentence? Try it; then look at the suggestions at the foot of the page.

Here is a summary of the steps to follow in solving modifier problems.

Summary

1. Ask "What does the modifier apply to?"
2. Be sure there is a word or group of words *in the sentence* for the modifier to apply to.
3. Put the modifier as close as possible to the word or word group it applies to.

Here are two suggestions.
1. Add a subject: Looking for efficiency and affordability, I decided a Smart was the car to buy.
2. Change the dangler to a dependent clause: A Smart is the car to buy since I am looking for efficiency and affordability.

Exercise 25.3*

Most of the following sentences contain dangling modifiers. Correct each sentence by using whichever solution given on page 357 best suits your purpose. There is no one right way to correct these sentences; our answers are only suggestions.

1. Driving recklessly and without lights, the police stopped Gina at a road block.

2. My supervisor gave me a lecture about punctuality after being late twice in one week.

3. After criticizing both my work and my attitude, I was fired.

4. With enough memory to store her favourite movies and more than 10,000 songs, Hannah knew that the iBook was the computer she needed.

5. After spending two weeks quarrelling over money, their relationship was over.

6. As a dedicated fan of Alice Munro, her last book is her best.

7. In less than a minute after applying the ointment, the pain began to ease.

8. Making her first formal presentation to her colleagues and her supervisor, Jake was probably more nervous than Allison was.

9. When handling hazardous waste, the safety manual clearly outlines the procedures to follow.

10. After spending the day in the kitchen preparing a gourmet meal, the guests drank too much wine to appreciate Kendra's effort.

Exercise 25.4*

In the following sentences, correct the misplaced and dangling modifiers in any way you choose. Our answers are only suggestions.

1. Only she was the baker's daughter, but she could loaf all day.

2. Being horribly hung over, the only problem with a free bar is knowing when to quit.

3. Rearing and kicking, Sam finally got the terrified horse under control.

4. In a hurry to get to the interview on time, my résumé was left lying on my desk at home.

5. As a college student constantly faced with new assignments, the pressure is sometimes intolerable.

6. Listening to the rumours, the newlyweds are already on the road to separation.

7. As a nondrinker, the display of liquor in the duty-free outlet held no interest.

8. Quartetto Gelato receives enthusiastic acclaim for its original arrangements and witty presentations from Vancouver to St. John's.

9. Rolling on her back, eager to have her tummy scratched, Queen Elizabeth couldn't resist the little Corgi puppy.

10. Wearing a small Canadian flag on a backpack or lapel, your reception abroad will be warm and enthusiastic.

GO TO WEB

EXERCISES 25.1, 25.2, 25.3, 25.4

Exercise 25.5

As a final test of your ability to use modifiers, correct the misplaced and dangling modifiers in the sentences below, using any solution you choose.

1. Obviously having drunk too much, I drove poor Tanya to her apartment, made her a pot of coffee, and called her mother.

2. When trying for your Red Cross bronze medal, your examiner will evaluate your speed, endurance, and resuscitation techniques.

3. The Riel Rebellion this month will be featured in *Canadian History* magazine.

4. Sinking like a ball of fire below the horizon, our sailboat was the perfect vantage point from which to watch the setting sun.

5. Not being reliable about arriving on time, I can't hire her to supervise others who are expected to be punctual.

6. While they were in my pocket, my children managed to break my glasses by leaping on me from behind.

7. Combining comfortable accommodation and economical travel, my wife and I find a camper van ideal for travelling both here and abroad.

8. The only used motorcycles we could find had been ridden by bikers that were in pretty bad shape.

9. After submitting the lowest bid that met all the developer's criteria, not being awarded the contract was bitterly disappointing.

10. "This bus has a seating capacity of 56 passengers with a maximum height of four metres." (Sign on a double-decker bus in Charlotte-town)

26

The Parallelism Principle

Brevity, clarity, and force: these are three characteristics of good writing style. **Parallelism** will reinforce these characteristics in everything you write.

When your sentence contains a series of two or more items, they must be grammatically parallel. That is, they must be written in the same grammatical form. Consider this example:

Sophie likes *swimming, surfing,* and *to sail.*

The three items in this series are not parallel. Two are nouns ending in *-ing*, but the third, *to sail*, is the infinitive form of the verb. To correct the sentence, you must put all the items in the same grammatical form. You have two choices. You can write

Sophie likes *swimming, surfing,* and *sailing.* (all nouns)

Or you can write

Sophie likes *to swim, to surf,* and *to sail.* (all infinitives)

Now look at this example with two nonparallel elements:

Most people seek happiness in *long-term relationships* and *work that provides them with satisfaction.*

Again, you could correct this sentence in two ways. You could write "Most people seek happiness *in relationships that are long-term* and *in work that provides them with satisfaction*," but that solution produces a long and clumsy sentence. The shorter version works better: "Most people seek happiness in *long-term relationships* and *satisfying work*." This version is concise, clear, and forceful.

> Correct faulty parallelism by writing all items in a series in the same grammatical form; that is, all words, or all phrases, or all clauses.

One way to tell whether the items in a series are parallel is to write them out in list form, one below the other. That way, you can see at a glance if all the elements are in the same grammatical form.

Not Parallel	Parallel
My brother is *messy,* *rude,* and *an obnoxious person.*	My brother is *messy,* *rude,* and *obnoxious.*
(This list has two adjectives and a noun phrase.)	(This list has three adjectives.)
I support myself by *delivering pizza,* *poker,* and *shooting pool.*	I support myself by *delivering pizza,* *playing poker,* and *shooting pool.*
(This list has two phrases and one single word as objects of the preposition *by*.)	(This list has three phrases as objects of the preposition *by*.)
Jules wants a job that *will interest him,* *will challenge him,* and *pays well.*	Jules wants a job that *will interest him,* *(will) challenge him,* and *(will) pay him well.*
(This series of clauses contains two future tense verbs and one present tense verb.)	(All three subordinate clauses contain future tense verbs.)

As you can see, achieving parallelism is partly a matter of developing an ear for the sound of a correct list. A parallel sentence has a smooth, unbroken rhythm. Practice and the exercises in this chapter will help. Once you have mastered parallelism in your sentences, you will be ready to develop ideas in parallel sequence—in thesis statements, for example—and thus to write clear, well-organized prose. Far from being a frill, parallelism is a fundamental characteristic of good writing.

Correct the sentences where necessary in the following exercises. As you work through these sentences, try to spot parallelism errors from the change in rhythm that the faulty element produces. Then revise the sentence to bring the faulty element into line with the other elements in the series. Check your answers to each set of 10 before going on. Answers for this chapter begin on page 528.

Exercise 26.1*

1. This program is easy to understand and using it is not difficult, either.

2. We were told that we would have to leave and to take nothing with us.

3. We organized our findings, wrote the report, and finally our PowerPoint presentation was prepared.

4. Both applicants were unskilled, unprepared, and lacked motivation.

5. Elmer's doctor advised that he should be careful with his back and not to strain his mind.

6. The company is looking for an employee who has a car and knowledge of the city would be a help.

7. If consumers really cared, they could influence the fast-food industry to produce healthy, delicious food that didn't cost very much.

8. When I want to get away from it all, there are three solitary pleasures I enjoy: a walk in the country, reading a good book, and fine music.

9. A recent survey of female executives claims that family responsibilities, being excluded from informal networks, and lacking management experience are the major factors keeping them from advancement.

10. If it is to be useful, your report must be organized clearly, written well, and your research should be thorough.

GO TO WEB

EXERCISES 26.1, 26.2

Exercise 26.2*

1. For my birthday, I requested either a Roots jacket or a scarf from Dior.

2. In my community, two related crimes are rapidly increasing: drug abuse and stealing things.

3. Bodybuilding has made me what I am today: physically perfect, very prosperous financially, and practically friendless.

4. After reading all the explanations and all the exercises have been completed, you'll be a better writer.

5. Bruce claimed that, through repetition and giving rewards, he had trained his centipede to be loyal and demonstrate obedience.

6. During their vacation in New Brunswick, Tracy and Jane visited many beautiful locations and wonderful seafood was eaten.

7. I'm an average tennis player; I have a good forehand, my backhand is average, but a weak serve.

8. The problem with being immortalized as a statue is that you will be a target for pigeon droppings and artists who write graffiti.

9. Never disturb a sleeping dog, a baby that is happy, or a silent politician.

10. I'd like to help, but I'm too tired, and my time is already taken up with other things.

GO TO WEB

EXERCISES 26.3, 26.4, 26.5, 26.6

Exercise 26.3*

Make the following lists parallel. In each case, you can make your items parallel with any item in the list, so your answers may differ from ours.

Example:	Wrong:	report writing	program a computer
	Right:	report writing	computer programming
	Also right:	write a report	program a computer

1. Wrong: wine   women   singing
   Right:

2. Wrong: doing your best   don't give up
   Right:

3. Wrong: lying about all   to do whatever I
   morning   please
   Right:

4. Wrong: information   education   entertaining
   Right:

5. Wrong: individually   as a group
   Right:

6. Wrong: privately   in public
   Right:

7. Wrong: happiness   healthy   wisdom
   Right:

8. Wrong: employers   people working   workers on
   full-time for an employer   contract
   Right:

9. Wrong: insufficient time   too little money   not enough
   staff
   Right:

10. Wrong: French is the   English is used   profanity
   language of love   in business   sounds best
   in German
   Right:

Exercise 26.4*

Correct the faulty parallelism in these sentences.

1. Not being able to speak the language causes confusion, is frustrating, and it's embarrassing.

2. Trying your best and success are not always the same thing.

3. The first candidate we interviewed seemed frightened and to be shy, but the second was a composed person and showed confidence.

4. To lick one's fingers and picking one's teeth in a restaurant are one way to get attention.

5. Our CEO claims his most valuable business assets are hitting a good backhand and membership at an exclusive golf club.

6. In order to succeed in this economy, small businesses must be creative and show innovation and flexibility.

7. Lowering our profit margin, raising prices, and two management lay-offs will enable us to meet our budget.

8. After an enjoyable dinner, I like to drink a cappuccino, a dark choco-late mint, and, occasionally, a good cigar.

9. Lying in the sun, consumption of high-fat foods, and cigarette smoking are three dangerous activities that were once thought to be healthy.

10. Business travellers complain of long delays at airports, they are paying higher costs for services, and tighter restrictions on their freedom of movement.

Exercise 26.5

As a test of your mastery of parallel structure, correct the six errors in the following paragraph.

The dictionary can be both a useful resource and an educational enter-tainment. Everyone knows that its three chief functions are to check spelling, for finding out the meanings of words, and what the correct pro-nunciation is. Few people, however, use the dictionary for discovery as well as learning. There are several methods of using the dictionary as an aid to discovery. One is randomly looking at words, another is to read a page or two thoroughly, and still another is by skimming through words until you find an unfamiliar one. It is by this last method that I discovered the word *steatopygous*, a term I now try to use at least once a day. You can increase your vocabulary significantly by using the dictionary, and of course a large and varied vocabulary can be used to baffle your colleagues, employers will be impressed, and your English teacher will be surprised.

27

Refining by Combining

To reinforce what you've learned about sentence structure, try your hand at **sentence combining**, a technique that enables you to avoid a choppy, monotonous, or repetitious style while at the same time producing correct sentences. Sentence combining accomplishes three things: it reinforces your understanding of sentence structure; it helps you to refine and polish your writing; and it results in a style that will keep your reader alert and interested in what you have to say.

Let's look at two short, technically correct sentences that could be combined:

I prefer champagne.

My budget allows only beer.

There are several ways of combining these two statements into a single sentence.

1. You can connect them with an appropriate linking word, such as *and, but, or, nor,* or *for* (the FANBOYS words).

I prefer champagne, *but* my budget allows only beer.

2. You can change one of the sentences into a subordinate clause.

Although I prefer champagne, my budget allows only beer.

My budget allows only beer *even though I prefer champagne.*

3. You can change one of the sentences into a modifying phrase.

(Living on a beer budget,) I still prefer champagne.

4. Sometimes it is possible to reduce your sentences to single-word modifiers.

I have (champagne) tastes and a (beer) budget.

In sentence combining, you are free to move parts of the sentence around, change words, add or delete words, or make whatever other changes you find necessary. Anything goes, so long as you don't drastically alter the meaning of the base sentences. Remember that your aim in combining sentences is to create effective sentences, not long ones. Clarity is essential, and brevity has force.

In the following exercises, try your solutions aloud before you write them. You may also want to refer to Chapters 31 and 32 for advice on using the comma and the semicolon, respectively.

Exercise 27.1*

Combine each pair of sentences using a FANBOYS connecting word *and, but, or, nor, for, so,* or *yet*. Suggested answers for the exercises in this chapter begin on page 529.

1. We cannot sell our cottage.
   We will live there instead.

2. There are three solutions given for this problem.
   All of them are correct.

3. The people in our firm work very hard.
   They wouldn't want it any other way.

4. We could spend our day off shopping at the mall.
   We could spend the day fishing.

5. Great leaders do not bully their people.
   They do not deceive them.

6. I will not be able to finish my report by the deadline.
   There are only two hours before the deadline.

7. Jennifer knows that she will probably not get the vice-president's job.
   She wants the experience of applying for it.

8. Finish the estimate.
   Do not begin work until the estimate has been approved.

9. Today has been the worst day of my life.
   My horoscope was right today.

10. The government did not offer me a job.
    It did not even reply to my letter.

Exercise 27.2

Using dependent-clause cues (see Chapter 23, page 342), combine the following sentences into longer, more interesting units.

Hint: Read each set of statements through to the end before you begin to combine them, and try out several variations aloud or in your head before writing down your preferred solution.

1. Leonardo da Vinci was a great artist and inventor.
   He invented scissors, among other things.

2. Cats can produce over 100 vocal sounds.
   Dogs can make only 10 vocal sounds.

3. It is said that men don't cry.
   They do cry while assembling furniture.

4. The name Wendy was made up for a book.
   The book was called *Peter Pan*.

5. Ten percent of Canadians are heavy drinkers.
   Thirty-five percent of Canadians abstain from alcohol.

6. Travel broadens the mind.
   Travel flattens the bank account.

7. We are seeking an experienced and innovative director.
   The candidate should be fluent in French.

8. One hundred thousand Vietnam veterans have taken their own lives.
   This is twice the number who were killed in action.

9. My cooking class went on a field trip to gather greens for a salad.
   We discovered that what we thought was watercress was not watercress.
   It was poison ivy.

10. The classmates ate the salad.
    Eight were hospitalized.
    No one was seriously affected.

Exercise 27.3

Combine the following sentences, using the connecting words listed in Exercise 27.1 and the dependent-clause cues listed on page 342.

1. Mario loses a girlfriend.
   He goes shopping for new clothes.

2. Failure breeds fatigue, according to Mortimer Adler.
   There is nothing more energizing than success.

3. We won't have enough stock to fill our orders.
   A shipment arrives today.

4. Friends may come, and friends may go.
   Enemies accumulate.

5. Marriage is for serious people.
   I have not considered it an option.

6. Divorce is an acknowledgement.
   There was not a true commitment in the first place.
   Some people still believe this.

7. In his essay "A Modest Proposal for a Divorce Ceremony," Pierre Berton proposed that Canada institute a formal divorce ceremony.
   The divorce ceremony would be like a formal wedding ceremony.
   All the symbolism would be reversed.

8. The bride, for example, would wear black.
   Immediately after the ceremony, the newly divorced couple would go into the vestry.
   They would scratch their names off the marriage register.

9. Twenty percent of adults in Canada are illiterate.
   Fifty percent of the adults who can read say they never read books.
   This is an astonishing fact.

10. Canada is a relatively rich country.
    Most of us brush up against hunger and homelessness almost daily.
    We encounter men, and less often, women begging.
    They are on downtown street corners.

After you have combined a number of sentences, you can evaluate your work. Read your sentences out loud. How they *sound* is important. Test your work against these six characteristics of successful sentences:

Summary

1. **Meaning:** Have you said what you mean?
2. **Clarity:** Is your sentence clear? Can it be understood on the first reading?
3. **Coherence:** Do the parts of your sentence fit together logically and smoothly?
4. **Emphasis:** Are the most important ideas either at the end or at the beginning of the sentence?
5. **Conciseness:** Is the sentence direct and to the point? Have you cut out all redundant or repetitious words?
6. **Rhythm:** Does the sentence flow smoothly? Are there any interruptions in the development of the key idea(s)? Do the interruptions help to emphasize important points, or do they distract the reader?

If your sentences pass all six tests of successful sentence style, you may be confident that they are both technically correct and pleasing to the ear. No reader could ask for more.

28

Mastering Subject–Verb Agreement

Singular and Plural

One of the most common writing errors is lack of agreement between subject and verb. Both must be singular, or both must be plural. If one is singular and the other plural, you have an agreement problem. You have another kind of agreement problem if your subject and verb are not both in the same "person" (see Chapter 30, pages 396–415).

Let's clarify some terms. First, it's important to distinguish between **singular** and **plural**.

- "Singular" means one person or thing.
- "Plural" means more than one person or thing.

Second, it's important to know what we mean when we refer to the concept of **person**:

- "First person" is the person(s) speaking or writing: *I, me; we, us*
- "Second person" is the person(s) being addressed: *you*
- "Third person" is the person(s) being spoken or written about: *he, she, it; they, them*

Here's an example of the singular and plural forms of a regular verb in the present tense.

	Singular	Plural
first person	I win	we win
second person	you win	you win
third person	she wins (*or* he, it, the horse wins)	they win (*or* the horses win)

The form that most often causes trouble is the third person because the verb endings do not match the subject endings. Third-person singular present-tense verbs end in *-s,* but their singular subjects do not. Third-person plural verbs never end in *-s,* while their subjects normally do. Look at these examples.

A <u>fire</u> <u>burns</u>.
The <u>car</u> <u>skids</u>.
The <u>father</u> <u>cares</u> for the children.

The three singular verbs, all of which end in *-s* (*burns, skids, cares*), agree with their singular subjects (*fire, car, woman*), none of which ends in *-s.* When the subjects become plural, the verbs change form, too.

Four <u>fires</u> <u>burn</u>.
The <u>cars</u> <u>skid</u>.
The <u>fathers</u> <u>care</u> for the children.

Now all of the subjects end in *-s,* and none of the verbs does.
To ensure **subject–verb agreement**, follow this basic rule:

Subjects and verbs must both be either singular or plural.

This rule causes difficulty only when the writer doesn't know which word in the sentence is the subject and so makes the verb agree with the wrong word. As long as you decode the sentence correctly (see Chapter 22), you'll have no problem making every subject agree with its verb.

If you have not already done so, now is the time to memorize this next rule:

The subject of a sentence is NEVER in a prepositional phrase.

Here's an example of how errors occur.

Only one of the 2,000 ticket buyers are going to win.

What is the subject of this sentence? It's not *buyers,* but *one.* The verb must agree with *one,* which is clearly singular. The verb *are* does not agree with *one,* so the sentence is incorrect. It should read

Grammar

Only <u>one</u> ~~of the 2,000 ticket buyers~~ <u>is</u> going to win.

Pay special attention to words that end in *-one, -thing,* or *-body.* They cause problems for nearly every writer.

> Words ending in *-one, -thing,* or *-body* are always singular.

When used as subjects, these pronouns require singular verbs.

anyone	anything	anybody
everyone	everything	everybody
no one	nothing	nobody
someone	something	somebody

The last part of the pronoun subject is the tip-off here: every*one*, any*thing*, no*body*. If you focus on this last part, you'll remember to use a singular verb with these subjects. Usually, these words cause trouble only when modifiers crop up between them and their verbs. For example, you would never write "Everyone are here." The trouble starts when you insert a group of words in between the subject and the verb. You might, if you weren't careful, write this: "Everyone involved in implementing the company's new policies and procedures are here." The meaning is plural: several people are present. But the subject (*everyone*) is singular, so the verb must be *is*.

More subject–verb agreement errors are caused by violations of this rule than any other. Be sure you understand it. Memorize it, and then test your understanding by doing the following exercise before you go any further.

Exercise 28.1*

Rewrite each of the following sentences, using the alternative beginning shown. Answers for this chapter begin on page 530.

Example: <u>She</u> <u>wants</u> to make a short documentary.
<u>They</u> <u>want</u> to make a short documentary.

1. He sells used essays to other students.
   They

2. That new guideline affects all the office procedures.
   Those

3. Everyone who shops at Pimrock's receives a free can of tuna.
   All those

4. The woman maintains that her boss has been harassing her.
   The women

5. That girl's father is looking for a rich husband for her.
   Those

So far, so good. You can match up singular subjects with singular verbs and plural subjects with plural verbs. Now let's take a look at a few of the complications that make subject–verb agreement such a disagreeable problem.

Five Special Cases

Some subjects are tricky. They look singular but are actually plural, or they look plural when they're really singular. There are six kinds of these slippery subjects, all of them common, and all of them likely to trip up the unwary writer.

> 1. Compound subjects joined by *or; either . . . or; neither . . . nor;* or *not . . . but*

Most of the compound subjects we've dealt with so far have been joined by *and* and have required plural verbs, so agreement hasn't been a problem. But watch out when the two or more elements of a compound subject are joined by *or; either . . . or; neither . . . nor;* or *not . . . but.* In these cases, the verb agrees in number with the nearest subject. That is, if the subject closest to the verb is singular, the verb will be singular; if the subject closest to the verb is plural, the verb must be plural too.

Neither <u>the coach</u> nor <u>the players</u> <u>are</u> ready to give up.

Neither <u>the players</u> nor <u>the coach</u> <u>is</u> ready to give up.

Exercise 28.2*

Circle the correct verb in each of the following sentences.

1. Not your physical charms but your honesty (is are) what I find attractive.

2. Either your job performance or your school assignments (is are) going to suffer if you continue your frantic lifestyle.
3. The college has decided that neither final marks nor a diploma (is are) to be issued to students who owe library fines.
4. Not unemployment but the rising cost of medical care (is are) Canadians' chief concern.
5. Neither the compensation nor the benefits (tempt tempts) me to accept your offer.

2. Subjects that look like compound subjects but really aren't

Don't be fooled by phrases beginning with words such as *with*, *like*, *together with*, *in addition to*, or *including*. These prepositional phrases are NOT part of the subject of the sentence. Since they do not affect the verb, you can mentally cross them out.

Mario's <u>brother, ~~together with three of his buddies,~~ is going</u> to the Yukon to look for work.

Obviously four people are looking for work. Nevertheless, the subject (<u>brother</u>) is singular, and so the verb must be singular (<u>is going</u>).

All my <u>courses, ~~except economics,~~ are</u> easier this term.

If you mentally cross out the phrase *except economics*, you can easily see that the verb (<u>are</u>) must be plural to agree with the plural subject (<u>courses</u>).

Exercise 28.3*

Circle the correct verb in each of the following sentences.

1. Some meals, like tagine, (is are) best enjoyed in a large group.
2. Our city, along with many other North American urban centres, (register registers) a dangerous level of carbon monoxide pollution in the summer months.
3. The Tour de France, like the Olympic Games, (is are) a world-class athletic competition.
4. Lori's mother, along with her current boyfriends, (wonder wonders) when she'll decide to settle down.
5. My English instructor, in addition to my math, biology, and even my learning skills instructor, (put, puts) a lot of pressure on me.

3. Each (of), either (of), neither (of)

Used as subjects, these words (or phrases) take singular verbs.

Either is acceptable to me.

Each wants desperately to win.

Neither of the stores is open after six o'clock. (Remember, the subject is never in a prepositional phrase.)

Exercise 28.4

Circle the correct verb in each of the following sentences.

1. Unless we hear from the coach, neither of us (is are) playing this evening.
2. Each of these courses (involve involves) field placement.
3. When my girlfriend asks if she has lost weight, I know that either of my answers (is are) bound to be wrong.
4. Each of the women (want wants) desperately to win the Ms. Nanaimo bodybuilding competition.
5. Strict discipline is what each of our teachers (believe believes) in.

---

4. Collective nouns

A **collective noun** is a word that names a group. Some examples are *company*, *class*, *committee*, *team*, *crowd*, *band*, *family*, *audience*, *public*, and *jury*. When you are referring to the group acting as a *unit*, use a *singular* verb. When you are referring to the *members* of the group acting *individually*, use a *plural* verb.

The team is sure to win tomorrow's game. (Here *team* refers to the group acting as a whole.)

The team are getting into their uniforms now. (The members of the team are acting individually.)

Exercise 28.5

Circle the correct verb in each of the following sentences.

1. The whole gang (plan plans) to attend the bikers' rally.

Grammar

2. The wolf pack (has have) been almost wiped out by local ranchers.
3. By noon on Friday, the whole dorm (has have) left their rooms and headed for the local pubs and coffeehouses.
4. After only two hours' discussion, the committee (was were) able to reach consensus.
5. The majority of Canadians, according to a recent survey, (is are) not so conservative about sex and morality as we had assumed.

5. Units of money, time, mass, length, and distance

When used as subjects, they all require singular verbs.

Four kilometres <u>is</u> too far to walk in this weather.

Remember that <u>2.2 pounds equals</u> a kilogram.

<u>Three weeks is</u> a long time to wait to get your paper back.

Exercise 28.6*

Circle the correct verb in each of the following sentences.

1. No wonder you are suspicious if $70 (was were) what you paid for last night's pizza.
2. Tim told his girlfriend that nine years (seem seems) like a long time to wait.
3. Forty hours of classes (is are) too much in one week.
4. When you are anxiously looking for a gas station, 30 km (is are) a long distance.
5. Ninety cents (seems seem) very little to tip, even for poor service.

In Exercises 28.7 and 28.8, correct the errors in subject–verb agreement. (Some rephrasing may be required.) Check your answers to each exercise before going on.

Exercise 28.7*

1. Neither of the following two sentences are correct.

2. The teachers, with the full support of the college administration, treats plagiarism as a serious offence.

3. Either good looks or intelligence run in our family, but never at the same time.

4. None of these computer programs are able to streamline our billing procedures.

5. The enjoyment of puns and jokes involving plays on words are the result of having too little else on your mind.

6. Anyone who jumps from one of Paris's many bridges are in Seine.

7. It is amazing how much better the orchestra play now that the conductor is sober.

8. The number of layoffs reported in the headlines seem to be rising again.

9. Her supervisors all agree that Emily need further training to be effective.

10. Canada's First Nations population are thought to have come to this continent from Asia thousands of years before the Europeans arrived in North America.

Exercise 28.8 *

Quebec City, along with Montreal, Toronto, and Vancouver, are among Canada's great gourmet centres. Whereas Toronto is a relative latecomer to this list, neither Quebec City nor Montreal are strangers to those who seeks fine dining. Indeed, travel and food magazines have long affirmed that the inclusion of these two cities in a Quebec vacation are a "must." Montreal is perhaps more international in its offerings, but Quebec City provides exquisite proof that French-Canadian cuisine and hospitality is second to none in the world. Amid the Old World charm of the lower city is to be found some of the quaintest and most enjoyable traditional restaurants; the newer sections of town boasts equally fine dining in more contemporary surroundings. The combination of the wonderful food and the city's fascinating charms are sure to make any visitor return frequently. Either the summer, when the city blooms and outdoor cafés abound, or the winter, when Carnaval turns the streets into hundreds of connecting parties, are wonderful times to visit one of Canada's oldest and most interesting cities.

GO TO WEB

EXERCISES 28.1, 28.2, 28.3, 28.4

Summary

- Subjects and verbs must agree: both must be singular, or both must be plural.
- The subject of a sentence is never in a prepositional phrase.
- Pronouns ending in *-one, -thing,* or *-body* are singular and require singular verbs.
- Subjects joined by *and* are always plural.
- When subjects are joined by *or; either . . . or; neither . . . nor;* or *not . . . but*, the verb agrees with the subject that is closest to it.
- When looking for the subject in a sentence, ignore phrases beginning with *as well as, including, in addition to, like, together with,* etc. They are prepositional phrases.
- When *each, either,* and *neither* are used as subjects, they require singular verbs.
- Collective nouns are usually singular.
- Units of money, time, mass, length, and distance are always singular.

Exercise 28.9

As a final check of your mastery of subject–verb agreement, correct the following sentences as necessary.

1. Each of the options you outlined in your concluding remarks are worth examining further.

2. My opinion of the college's accounting programs are that neither of them are what I need.

3. Every one of the dozen people we interviewed qualify for the position.

4. My whole family, with the exception of the cat, dislike anchovies on pizza.

5. The applause from a thousand enthusiastic fans were like music to the skaters' ears.

6. Neither of your decisions are likely to improve sales, let alone morale.

7. Three thousand dollars per term, the students agree, are too much to pay for their education.

8. Neither age nor illness prevents Uncle Alf from leering at the nurses.

9. The birth of triplets, after six other children in eight years, were too much for the parents to cope with.

10. Everything you have accomplished in the last three years are wasted if you fail this assignment.

Grammar

29

Using Verbs Effectively

Good writers pay especially careful attention to verbs. A verb is to a sentence what an engine is to a car: it's the source of power—but it can also be a source of trouble. Now that you've conquered subject–verb agreement, it's time to turn to the three remaining essentials of correct verb use: **form**, **consistency**, and **voice**.

Choosing the Correct Verb Form

Every verb has four forms, called its **principal parts**:

1. The **infinitive** form: used with *to* and with *can, may, might, shall, will, could, should, would, must*
2. The **simple past** (also called the **past tense**)
3. The **present participle** (the **-ing**) form
4. The **past participle** form: used with *has* or *have*

Here are some examples:

Infinitive	Simple Past	Present Participle	Past Participle
dance	danced	dancing	danced
learn	learned	learning	learned
play	played	playing	played
seem	seemed	seeming	seemed

To use verbs correctly, you must be familiar with their principal parts. Knowing three facts will help you.

- The present participle, the *-ing* form, is always made up of the base form of the verb + *ing*.
- Your dictionary gives you the principal parts of all **irregular** verbs. Look up the base form, and you'll find the simple past and the present and past participles given beside it, usually in parentheses. For example, if you look up *sing* in your dictionary, you will find *sang* (simple past), *sung* (past participle), and *singing* (present participle) listed immediately after the verb itself. If the past tense and past participle are not given, the verb is **regular**.
- To form the simple past and the past participle of regular verbs: add *-ed* to the base form. The examples listed above—*dance, learn, play, seem*—are all regular verbs.

Unfortunately, many of the most common English verbs are irregular. Their past tenses and past participles are formed in unpredictable ways. The verbs in the list that follows are used so often that it is worth your time to memorize their principal parts. (We have not included the *-ing* form because, as we have noted above, it never causes any difficulty.)

The Principal Parts of Irregular Verbs

Infinitive	Simple Past	Past Participle
(Use with *to* and with helping/ auxiliary verbs)		(Use with *have, has, had*)
awake	awoke/awaked	awaked/awoken
be (am, is)	was/were	been
bear	bore	borne
beat	beat	beaten
become	became	become
begin	began	begun
bid (offer to pay)	bid	bid
bid (say, command)	bid/bade	bid/bidden
bite	bit	bitten
bleed	bled	bled
blow	blew	blown
break	broke	broken
bring	brought (*not* brang)	brought (*not* brung)

Grammar

Infinitive	Simple Past	Past Participle
(Use with *to* and with helping/ auxiliary verbs)		(Use with *have, has, had*)
broadcast	broadcast	broadcast
build	built	built
burst	burst	burst
buy	bought	bought
catch	caught	caught
choose	chose	chosen
come	came	come
cost	cost	cost
cut	cut	cut
deal	dealt	dealt
dig	dug	dug
dive	dived/dove	dived
do	did (*not* done)	done
draw	drew	drawn
dream	dreamed/dreamt	dreamed/dreamt
drink	drank (*not* drunk)	drunk
eat	ate	eaten
fall	fell	fallen
feed	fed	fed
feel	felt	felt
fight	fought	fought
find	found	found
fling	flung	flung
fly	flew	flown
forget	forgot	forgotten/forgot
forgive	forgave	forgiven
freeze	froze	frozen
get	got	got/gotten
give	gave	given
go	went	gone (*not* went)
grow	grew	grown
hang (suspend)	hung	hung
hang (put to death)	hanged	hanged
have	had	had
hear	heard	heard
hide	hid	hidden

Infinitive	Simple Past	Past Participle
(Use with *to* and with helping/ auxiliary verbs)		(Use with *have, has, had*)
hit	hit	hit
hold	held	held
hurt	hurt	hurt
keep	kept	kept
know	knew	known
lay (put or place)	laid	laid
lead	led	led
leave	left	left
lend	lent (*not* loaned)	lent (*not* loaned)
lie (recline)	lay	lain (*not* layed)
light	lit/lighted	lit/lighted
lose	lost	lost
mean	meant	meant
meet	met	met
pay	paid	paid
raise (lift up, increase, bring up)	raised	raised
ride	rode	ridden
ring	rang	rung
rise	rose	risen
run	ran	run
say	said	said
see	saw (*not* seen)	seen
sell	sold	sold
set (put or place)	set	set
shake	shook	shaken (*not* shook)
shine	shone	shone
sing	sang	sung
sink	sank	sunk
sit	sat	sat
sleep	slept	slept
slide	slid	slid
speak	spoke	spoken
speed	sped	sped
steal	stole	stolen
stick	stuck	stuck
strike (hit)	struck	struck

Grammar

Infinitive	Simple Past	Past Participle
(Use with *to* and with helping/ auxiliary verbs)		(Use with *have, has, had*)
strike (affect)	struck	stricken
swear	swore	sworn
swim	swam	swum
swing	swung (*not* swang)	swung
take	took	taken
teach	taught	taught
tear	tore	torn
tell	told	told
think	thought	thought
throw	threw	thrown
wake	woke/waked	waked/woken
wear	wore	worn
weave	wove	woven
win	won	won
wind	wound	wound
wring	wrung	wrung
write	wrote	written

Exercise 29.1*

Find and correct the verbs in the following sentences. When you have finished, check your answers on page 532.

1. Once I laid down, I found it very hard to get up again.

2. The staff have ate all the sandwiches that were ordered for the board's lunch.

3. Have you ever rode in a Porsche?

4. Having finished his presentation, Greg set down to answer questions.

5. After spending all day in class, I need to lay down for an hour or two.

6. The contractor who was eventually chose was the one who submitted the lowest bid.

7. My computer has print the document in a font so small I can't read it.

8. When will I get back the money I loaned you last month?

9. After three years of constant use, our copier is practically wore out.

10. I should have knew that all generalizations are false.

GO TO WEB

EXERCISES 29.1, 29.2, 29.3, 29.4

Exercise 29.2

As a final test of your mastery of verb forms, correct the errors in the following sentences.

1. We swum in the pool until my toes were almost froze.

2. The stars shined like diamonds the night I told Emmy-Lou how I feeled about her and gave her the ring that costed me a week's pay.

3. Dan had drove very slowly on the gravel road, but once he reached the highway he speeded away into the night.

4. She had forgot how much I dislike the green dress and weared it at the wedding rehearsal.

5. If only we had knew then what we know now, we wouldn't have spoke so quickly.

6. We have never forgave her for the time when her cell rung during the scariest part of the movie.

7. It finally sunk in that he had stole my heart.

8. After the band had sang "The Lion Sleeps Tonight" seven times, we realized that they had been payed too much because they only knowed four tunes.

9. The priest has spoke with the condemned man who will be hung in the morning unless the governor gives him a stay of execution.

10. I played the guitar they loaned me and sung an old tune that I had wrote when I was much younger.

Keeping Your Tenses Consistent

Verbs are time markers. Changes in tense express changes in time: past, present, or future.

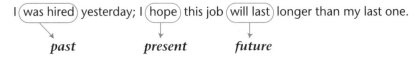

Sometimes, as in the example above, it is necessary to use several different tenses in a single sentence to get the meaning across. But most of the time, whether you're writing a sentence or a paragraph, you use one tense throughout. Normally, you choose either the past or the present tense, depending on the nature of your topic. (Few paragraphs are written completely in the future tense.) Here is the rule to follow.

Don't change tense unless meaning requires it.

Readers like and expect consistency. If you begin a sentence with "I worried and fretted and delayed," your readers will tune in to the past-tense verbs and expect any other verbs in the sentence to be in the past tense too. Therefore, if you finish the sentence with ". . . and then I decide to give it a try," your readers will be jolted abruptly out of one time frame and into another. This sort of jolting is uncomfortable, and readers don't like it.

Shifting tenses is like shifting gears: it should be done smoothly and only when necessary. Avoid causing verbal whiplash: keep your tenses consistent.

Wrong: Monika starts the car and revved the engine.
Right: Monika started the car and revved the engine.
Also right: Monika starts the car and revs the engine.

Wrong: Carrie flounces into the room and sat down. Everyone stares.
Right: Carrie flounced into the room and sat down. Everyone stared.
Also right: Carrie flounces into the room and sits down. Everyone stares.

Exercise 29.3*

In this exercise, most of the sentences contain unnecessary tense shifts. Use the first verb in each sentence as your time marker and change the tense(s) of the other verb(s) in the sentence to agree with it. Answers are on page 532.

1. After he accused me, I call him a liar.

2. Hank Aaron broke Babe Ruth's record of 714 home runs in a lifetime when he hits number 715 in 1974.

3. Children are quite perceptive and will know when you are lying to them.

4. She went up to the counter and asks for a refund.

5. When Brad Pitt walked into the room, the girls go crazy.

6. You should not go into that building until the police arrive.

7. Tim walked into the room, took one look at Leroy, and smashes him right through the wall.

8. First you will greet the guests; then you show them to their rooms.

9. The largest cheese ever produced took 43 hours to make and weighs a whopping 15,723 kg.

10. He watches television until he finally went to sleep.

Exercise 29.4*

Correct the 15 faulty tense shifts in this passage.

For some reason, when mistakes or accidents happen in radio or television, they were often hilariously funny. If, in the course of a conversation, someone said, "Here come the Duck and Doochess of Kent," listeners would probably be mildly amused. But many years ago, when an announcer makes that slip on a live radio broadcast, it becomes one of the most famous blunders in radio history. Tapes of the slip will be filed in "bloopers" libraries all over the world. This heightened sense of hilarity is the reason that so many people who work in radio dedicated their creativity to making the on-air announcer laugh while reading the news. To take one example, Lorne Greene's is the deeply serious voice that is heard on the CBC news during World War II. He is the victim of all kinds of pranks aimed at getting him to break up while reading the dark, often tragic, news of the combat overseas.

The pages of his news script are set on fire while he reads. He is even stripped naked as he reads, calmly, and apparently without strain. Lorne Greene will be a true professional. Many other newscasters, however, will have been highly susceptible to falling apart on air at the slightest provocation. And there were always people around a radio station who cannot resist giving them that little push.

GO TO WEB

EXERCISE 29.5

Exercise 29.5

To test and reinforce your mastery of correct verb forms and tense consistency, correct the 10 errors in the following paragraph. Use the italicized verb as your time marker.

The art of writing *is* not dead. Thanks to the use of computers in homes and businesses, it will now be more important than ever to be able to write competently. Not everyone agrees with this statement. Many people will continue to think that electronic technology has eliminated the need to learn how to write, but it will be clear that reports of the death of the written word were premature. Computer networking, bulletin boards, e-mail, and electronic forums made it more important than ever to write well. In the past, when letters were written on paper, writers could have checked their messages over before mailing them to ensure that there were no errors or embarrassing miscommunications. Now, however, communication is instantaneous, and any writing faults will be immediately apparent. The exposure of writing flaws, however, is not the only reason electronic communication links require the ability to write clear, unambiguous prose. Paper letters were normally mailed to a few people, at most.

Electronic mail, on the other hand, will often be sent to dozens, even hundreds, of receivers; therefore, the message will need to be carefully composed if all recipients are to understand what the writer intended. In today's world of electronic communication, good writing skills will be more important than ever before.

Choosing between Active and Passive Verbs

Verbs have another quality besides tense (or time). Verbs also have what is called "voice," which means the quality of being either active or passive. In sentences with **active voice** verbs, the "doer" of the action is the grammatical subject of the sentence.

Active voice: Good parents <u>support</u> their children.
A car <u>crushed</u> the cat.
Someone <u>will show</u> a movie in class.

In sentences with **passive voice** verbs, the grammatical subject of the sentence is the "receiver" of the action (that is, the subject is passively acted upon), and the "doer" becomes an object of the preposition *by* or is absent from the sentence entirely, as in the third example below.

Passive voice: Children <u>are supported</u> by good parents.
The cat <u>was crushed</u> by a car.
A movie <u>will be shown</u> in class.

Always use an active verb unless you have a specific reason to choose a passive one.

You probably use the passive voice more often than you think you do. To be a better writer, you need to know the distinction between active and passive, to understand their different effects on the reader, and to use the passive voice only when it is appropriate to your meaning.

Grammar

There are three good reasons for choosing a passive verb rather than an active one.

1. The person or agent that performed the action is unknown (or the writer does not wish to disclose the identity).

My books <u>were stolen</u> from my locker this morning.

Giovanna's father <u>was killed</u> in Bosnia.

Unlike the streets of a typical prairie city, which <u>are laid out</u> on a grid, Vancouver's streets <u>are laid out</u> to follow the curves and bends of the harbour and the Fraser River.

2. You want to place the emphasis on the person, place, or object that was acted upon rather than on the subject that performed the action.

Early this morning, the Bank of Montreal at 16th and Granville <u>was robbed</u> by four men wearing nylon stockings over their heads and carrying shotguns.

This sentence focuses the reader's attention on the bank rather than on the robbers. A quite different effect is produced when the sentence is reconstructed in the active voice:

Four men wearing nylon stockings over their heads and carrying shotguns <u>robbed</u> the Bank of Montreal at 16th and Granville early this morning.

3. You are writing a technical or scientific report or a legal document.

Passive verbs are the appropriate choice when the focus is on the facts, methods, or procedures involved rather than on who discovered or performed them. Passive verbs also tend to establish an impersonal tone that is appropriate in these kinds of writing. Contrast the emphasis and tone of the following sentence pairs:

Passive: The heat <u>was increased</u> to 200°C and <u>was maintained</u> at that temperature.

Active: My lab partners and I <u>increased</u> the heat to 200°C and <u>maintained</u> it at that temperature.

Passive: Having been found guilty, the accused <u>was sentenced</u> to two years.

Active: The jury <u>found</u> the accused guilty, and the judge <u>sentenced</u> him to two years.

In general, because active verbs are more concise and forceful than passive verbs, they add vigour and impact to your writing. The distinction between active and passive is not something you should worry about during the drafting stage, however. The time to focus on verbs and decide whether active or passive would best serve your purpose is during revision. When you find a passive verb in your draft, think about who is doing what. Ask yourself why the "who" is not the subject of the sentence. If there's a good reason, then use the passive verb. Otherwise, choose an active verb.

Grammar

Exercise 29.6*

Rewrite the sentences below, changing their verbs from passive to active. Note that you may have to add a word or word group to identify the "doer" of the action of the verb.

Example: Matt's two front teeth <u>were knocked out</u> by Clark's shot.

Clark's shot <u>knocked out</u> Matt's two front teeth.

1. A meeting was called by the department head.
2. The espresso will be made by the server in a few minutes.
3. When it gets cold, the block heater is plugged in overnight.
4. For many years, steroids have been used by professional athletes to improve speed and endurance.
5. The dough must not be kneaded, or your pastry will be tough.
6. This postcard was written by my parents while they were hiking in Nepal.
7. This movie was made for less than $900,000 by a crew of students.
8. While our neighbours were vacationing in the Caribbean, their house was broken into by thieves.
9. An error was made in the code you wrote for this program.
10. The Red Sox and the White Sox have been replaced as the stupidest team names in sports by the Mighty Ducks.

Exercise 29.7*

Rewrite each of the sentences below, changing the verbs from active to passive or vice versa, and then decide which sentence is more effective.

1. Sarah McLachlan won another Juno.
2. Carl spiked the ball after scoring the winning points.
3. City council passed a bylaw forbidding smoking in bars and restaurants.
4. Forty-eight hours later, 2 mL of sterile water was added to the culture in the petri dish.
5. By standing in line all night, Courtenay managed to get four tickets for the concert.
6. The 10 p.m. news revealed the truth behind the famous Doobie Brothers scandal.
7. The judgment was finally announced today, almost a year after the environmental hearings were concluded.
8. After a long debate, the committee finally agreed to endorse Yasmin's fundraising proposal.
9. A computer program that analyzes speech patterns has been developed by psychologist Dr. Hans Steiner of Stanford University.
10. After years of research among college students, it has been concluded by Dr. Steiner that people who frequently use passive-voice constructions tend to be maladjusted.

Exercise 29.8

Rewrite the following paragraphs, changing the 15 misused passive verbs to active verbs. (Remember, passive voice verbs are sometimes appropriate.)

The last time Glenn had his hair cut by the barber at the local mall was the day of the big high-school graduation dance. One of the prettiest girls in the school had been invited to the prom by Glenn, and to make a good impression was what was wanted. The barber was thought to be talented, if a little unconventional: he had long hair and a vaguely dreamy smile. It was well known by everybody that he had been a hippie back in the 1970s; it was thought by some that his youthful excesses might be responsible for his soft voice and mumbling speech.

Glenn settled into the chair, and a few inaudible words were muttered by the barber. Glenn made a guess at what had been said and replied that the weather was fine. Another mumble from the barber. This time, Glenn thought he'd been asked which college he planned to attend in the fall, and he answered politely. At this point, the conversation was stopped, and the barber got on with his work.

Half an hour later, the sheet was swept away, and the chair was spun so that Glenn could see his image in the mirror. To his horror, it was discovered that he was practically bald, except for an 8 cm high strip of hair running from his forehead to the nape of his neck. Glenn's scream was heard through the entire mall. After the excitement died down, it was learned by the crowds of curious shoppers that when Glenn had been asked what kind of haircut he wanted, Glenn had replied, "Mohawk."

So the prom was attended by Glenn in a tux, a startling haircut, and with a very unsympathetic date. The following week, Glenn left for Hamilton and Mohawk College. His high-school sweetheart was never seen by him again.

Grammar

30

Solving
Pronoun Problems

Look at the following sentences. Can you tell what's wrong with them?

"Dev must choose between you and I," Miranda said.

When you are on a diet, it is a good idea for one to avoid Bagel World.

We had invited everybody to come with their partner, so we were a little surprised when Marcel showed up with his Doberman.

Everyone is expected to do their duty.

Mohammed's nose was badly sunburned, but it has now completely disappeared.

Most of the students that were protesting tuition increases were ones which had been elected to council.

These sentences all contain pronoun errors. After verbs, pronouns are the class of words most likely to cause problems for writers. In this chapter, we will look at the three aspects of pronoun usage that can trip you up if you're not careful: pronoun form, agreement, and consistency. We'll also look at the special problems of usage that can lead to sexist language.

Choosing the Correct Pronoun Form

First you need to be sure you are using the "right" pronouns—that is, the correct pronoun forms—in your sentences. Here are some examples of incorrect pronoun usage:

Her and me can't agree on anything.

The reason for the quarrel is a personal matter between he and I.

How do you know which form of a pronoun to use? The answer depends on the pronoun's place and function in your sentence.

SUBJECT AND OBJECT PRONOUNS

There are two forms of personal pronouns: one is used for subjects, and the other is used for objects. Pronoun errors occur when you confuse the two. In Chapter 22, you learned to identify the subject of a sentence. Keep that information in mind as you learn the following basic rule.

When a subject or a complement is a pronoun, the pronoun must be in **subject form**. Otherwise, use the **object form**.

Subject Pronouns

Singular	Plural
I	we
you	you
he, she, it, one	they

She and *I* tied for first place. (The pronouns are the subject of the sentence.)

The lucky winners of the all-expenses-paid weekend in Paris are *they*. (The pronoun is the complement and refers to the subject of the sentence, *winners*.)

The student who regularly asks for extra help is *he*. (The pronoun is the complement and refers to the subject of the sentence, *student*.)

Object Pronouns

Singular	Plural
me	us
you	you
him, her, it, one	them

Between you and *me*, I think he's cute. (*Me* is not the subject of the sentence; it is one of the objects of the preposition *between*.)

Omar asked *him* and *me* for help. (*Him* and *me* are not the subject of the verb *asked*; Omar is, so the pronouns need to be in the object form.)

Be especially careful when using pronouns in compound subjects or after prepositions. If you can remember the following two rules, you'll be able to eliminate most potential errors.

1. A pronoun that is part of a compound subject is *always* in subject form.
2. A pronoun that follows a preposition is *always* in object form.

Examples:

She and *I* had tickets to U2. (The pronouns are used as a compound subject.)

It is up to *you* and *her* to pay for the damage. (The pronouns follow the preposition *to*.)

When you're dealing with a pair of pronouns and can't decide which form to use, try this test.[1] Mentally cross out one pronoun at a time, then read aloud the sentence you've created. Applying this technique to the first example above, you get "*She* has tickets" and "*I* have tickets." Both sound right and are correct. In the second sentence, if you try the pronouns separately, you get "It is up to *you*" and "It is up to *her*." Again, you know by the sound that these are the correct forms. (You would never say "*Her* had tickets," or "*Me* had tickets," or "It is up to *she*.") If you deal with paired pronouns one at a time, you are unlikely to choose the wrong form.

Note, too, that when a pair of pronouns includes "I" or "me," that pronoun comes last. For example, we write "between *you* and *me*" (not

---

[1] This test is reliable only for those who are fluent in English. ESL students must rely on memorizing the rules.

"between *me* and *you*"); we write "*she* and *I*" (not "*I* and *she*"). There is no grammatical reason for this rule. It's based on courtesy. Good manners require that you speak of others first and yourself last.

Exercise 30.1*

Correct the pronouns in these sentences as necessary. Answers for the exercises in this chapter begin on page 534.

1. No one except you and I would go camping in this weather.
2. Him and I can't figure out this problem set any better than you and her could.
3. George and him fell asleep in class, as usual.
4. Do you want to work with Emma and she?
5. We can use the film passes all week, and you and her can use them on the weekend, when Biff and me are going skiing.
6. Thanks to the recommendations provided by your math instructor and I, you and her got the tutorial jobs.
7. As we were going to class, Karl and me heard that there had been an explosion in the lab.
8. If it hadn't been for Hassan and he, the only ones to show up would have been you and I.
9. Quentin and him agreed to split the price of a case with Stan and I.
10. Only two students passed the midterm: Nadia and me.

GO TO WEB

EXERCISES 30.1, 30.2

Using Pronouns in Contrast Constructions

Choosing the correct pronoun form is more than just a matter of not wanting to appear ignorant or careless. Sometimes the form you use determines the meaning of your sentence. Consider these two sentences:

Stefan is more interested in his new car than *I*.

Stefan is more interested in his new car than *me*.

There's a world of difference between the meaning of the subject form ("Stefan is more interested in his new car than *I* [am]") and the object form ("Stefan is more interested in his new car than [in] *me*").

When using a pronoun after *than*, *as well as*, or *as*, decide whether you mean to contrast the pronoun with the subject of the sentence. If you do, use the subject form of the pronoun. If not, use the object form.

Jay would rather watch television than I. (*I* is contrasted with the subject, *Jay*.)

Jay would rather watch television than me. (*Me* is contrasted with the object, *television*.)

To test your sentence, try putting a verb after the pronoun. If the sentence makes sense, then the subject form is the form you want.

Jay would rather watch television than I [would].

Some writers prefer to leave the added verb in place, a practice that eliminates any possibility of confusion.

Exercise 30.2*

Correct the following sentences where necessary.

1. At 14, my younger brother is already taller than me.

2. No one likes partying more than him and Anne.

3. Would you like to join Daniel and I for dinner and a movie?

4. Only one person in this firm could manage the department as well as him.

5. At last I have met someone who enjoys grilled liver as much as me!

6. We can skate as well as them, but they are much better at shooting and defending than us.

7. More than me, Serge uses the computer to draft and revise his papers.

Exercise 30.3[*]

Revise the following paragraph to correct the errors in pronoun form.

(1) My boyfriend and me have different opinions when it comes to food. (2) I like fast food better than him. (3) He likes vegetables better than me. (4) In fact, between you and I, he is a vegetarian, though he would deny it. (5) When we go out with friends, it is difficult for they to know where to take him and I because our tastes are so different. (6) The only type of restaurant where us and them can all have what we like is Italian. (7) There, him and his friends can sample pasta primavera and eggplant parmigiana while my friends and I tuck into spaghetti and meatballs and pepperoni pizza. (8) We are probably not as healthy as they, but they don't seem to enjoy their food as much as us.

Now that you know how to choose the correct form of pronouns within a sentence, let's turn to the problems of using pronouns consistently throughout a sentence and a paragraph.

Pronoun–Antecedent Agreement

The name of this pronoun problem may sound difficult, but the idea is simple. Pronouns are words that substitute for or refer to the name of a person, place, or thing mentioned elsewhere in your sentence or your paragraph. The word(s) that a pronoun substitutes for or refers to is called the **antecedent**.

Hannibal had his own way of doing things. (The pronoun *his* refers to the antecedent *Hannibal*.)

Grammar

Chantal respects *her* boss. (The pronoun *her* refers to the antecedent *Chantal*.)

The *computer* is processing as fast as *it* can. (The pronoun *It* substitutes for the antecedent *computer*.)

Usually, as in these three examples, the antecedent comes before the pronoun that refers to it. Here is the rule to remember.

A pronoun must agree with its antecedent in
- number (singular or plural)
- person (first, second, or third)
- gender (masculine, feminine, or neuter)

Most of the time, you follow this rule without even realizing that you know it. For example, you would never write

Hannibal had *your* own way of doing things.

Chantal respects *its* boss.

The computer is processing as fast as *she* can.

You know these sentences are incorrect even if you may not know precisely why they are wrong.

There are three kinds of pronoun–antecedent agreement that you do need to learn about. They lead to errors that, unlike the examples above, are not obvious, and you need to know them so you can watch out for them. The rules you need to learn involve **indefinite pronouns ending in -one, -body, or -thing; vague references; and relative pronouns.**

1. INDEFINITE PRONOUNS: PRONOUNS ENDING IN *-ONE*, *-BODY*, OR *-THING*

The most common pronoun–antecedent agreement problem involves **indefinite pronouns:**

anyone	anybody	anything
everyone	everybody	everything

no one	nobody	nothing
someone	somebody	something
each (one)		

In Chapter 28, you learned that when these words are used as subjects they are singular and take singular verbs. So it makes sense that the pronouns that stand for or refer to them must also be singular.

> Antecedents ending in *-one*, *-body*, or *-thing* are singular and must be referred to by singular pronouns: *he, she, it; his, her, its.*

Please put everything back in *its* place.

Anybody can retire comfortably if *he* or *she* begins planning now.

Everyone is expected to do *his* share.

No one in *his* right mind would claim *he* enjoys living in this climate.

Now take another look at the last two sentences. Until about 30 years ago, the pronouns *he, him,* and *his* were used with singular antecedents to refer to both men and women. In order to appeal to the broadest possible audience, most writers today are careful to avoid this usage and other examples of what may be seen as sexist language.

In informal speech, it has become acceptable to use plural pronouns with *-one*, *-body*, or *-thing* antecedents. Although these antecedents are grammatically singular and take singular verbs, they are often plural in meaning, and in conversation we find ourselves saying

Everyone is expected to do *their* share.

No one has to stay if *they* don't want to.

This usage is acceptable in speech, but it is not acceptable in academic or professional writing.

Writers sometimes make errors in pronoun–antecedent agreement because they are trying to write without indicating whether the person referred to is male or female. A sentence such as "Everyone is required to do *their* oral presentation" is incorrect, as we have seen, but it does avoid making "everyone" male. It also avoids the awkwardness of "Everyone is required to do *his* or *her* oral presentation." There are two better ways to solve this problem.

1. Revise the sentence to leave the pronoun out.

Everyone is required to deliver an oral presentation in the last week of class.

or

An oral presentation is required of everyone in the last week of class.

Such creative avoidance of gender-specific or incorrect constructions can be an interesting challenge. The results often sound a little artificial, however. The second method is easier to accomplish.

2. Revise the sentence to make both the antecedent and the pronoun plural.

You are all required to deliver an oral presentation in the last week of class.

or

All students are required to deliver an oral presentation in the last week of class.

Here are two more examples for you to study.

Problem: Everybody has been given his or her assignment.
Revision 1: Everybody has been given an assignment.
Revision 2: All of the students have been given their assignments.

Problem: No one wants his copy edited.
Revision 1: No one wants copy editing.
Revision 2: Most writers object to having their copy edited.

Exercise 30.4*

In the following sentences, identify the most appropriate word(s) from the choices given in parentheses. (Note: the options may not be the best choices stylistically; just select the one that is grammatically correct in each case.) Check your answers on page 534 before continuing.

1. Everyone who enjoys a thrilling match will reserve (his their) seat for today's chess club meeting.

2. Despite the inconvenience, everyone climbed to the fourth floor to hand in (her their) course evaluation.
3. Each of her sons has successfully completed (his their) diploma.
4. Someone with a lot of cash left (her their) purse in the women's washroom.
5. Every reporter must decide for (himself themselves) how far (he they) will go in pursuit of a story.

Exercise 30.5*

Rewrite the sentences in Exercise 30.4 to eliminate sexist language.

Exercise 30.6*

Correct the following sentences where necessary, being careful to avoid awkward repetition and sexist language.

1. Virginia claims that every one of her male friends has a room of their own.
2. Almost everyone I know is concerned about finding a job that will be suitable for him or her.
3. Anybody who applies for a job with this institution can expect to spend a lot of their time in selection committee interviews.
4. Taking a picture of someone when they are not looking can produce interesting results.
5. Nearly every man who can cook will tell you that they enjoy preparing food.

2. VAGUE REFERENCE

Avoiding the second potential difficulty with pronoun–antecedent agreement requires common sense and the ability to think like your readers. If you look at your writing from your readers' point of view, it is unlikely that you will break the following rule.

Every pronoun must have a clearly identifiable antecedent.

The mistake that occurs when you fail to follow this rule is called **vague reference.**

Chris told his brother that he was losing his hair.

Who is going bald? Chris or his brother?

Grammar

Here's another example:

The faculty are demanding higher salaries and fewer teaching hours, but the administration does not support them.

What does the administration not favour: higher salaries, fewer classes, or the faculty themselves?

In sentences like these, you can only guess the meaning because you don't know who or what is being referred to by the pronouns. You can make such sentences less confusing by using either more names or other nouns and by using fewer pronouns. For example:

Chris told his brother Sam that Sam was losing his hair.

The faculty are demanding higher salaries and fewer teaching hours, but the administration does not support their demands.

Another type of vague reference occurs when there is no antecedent at all in the sentence for the pronoun to refer to.

I sold my skis last year and can't even remember how to do it anymore. (Do what?)

Reading is Sophia's passion, but she says she doesn't have a favourite. (A favourite what?)

My roommate smokes constantly, *which* I hate. (There is no noun or pronoun for *which* to refer to.)

I hate homework; this is my downfall. (*This* refers to homework, but homework is not my downfall. My hatred of doing it is.)

How would you revise these sentences? Try it, then see our suggestions in the footnote below.[2]

Be sure that every pronoun has a clear antecedent with which it agrees in number, person, and gender. Once you have mastered this principle, you'll have no further trouble with pronoun–antecedent agreement.

---

[2]I sold my skis last year and can't even remember how to *slalom* anymore.

Reading is Sophie's passion, but she says she doesn't have a favourite *writer*.

My roommate is constantly smoking, *which* I hate.

She hates doing homework; *this* is her downfall.

Exercise 30.7*

Correct the following sentences where necessary. There are several ways to fix these sentences. In some cases, the antecedent is missing, and you need to supply one. In other cases, the antecedent is so vague that the meaning of the sentence can be interpreted in more than one way. You need to rewrite these sentences to make the meaning clear.

1. I know that smoking is bad for me and everyone else, but I can't give them up.

2. If your pet rat won't eat its food, feed it to the kitty.

3. Our cat is a picky eater, which is inconvenient and expensive.

4. Whenever Stefan and Matt played poker, he stacked the deck.

5. The gorilla was mean and hungry because he had finished it all in the morning.

6. Madonna has transformed herself at least four times in her career, which makes her unique.

7. Dani backed her car into a garbage truck and dented it.

8. Rocco was suspicious of handgun control because he thought everyone should have one for late-night subway rides.

9. Get your ears pierced during this week's special and take home an extra pair free.

10. Our car is in the shop, but this won't keep us from going to the party.

Exercise 30.8

To test your understanding of the pronoun problems we have covered so far, try this exercise, which contains all three kinds of pronoun–antecedent agreement errors. Correct the following sentences where necessary.

1. Each of her suitors had their faults, but Denise decided to overlook the shortcomings of the one that had the most money.

2. Embezzling is what he does best, but he hasn't been able to pull one off lately.

3. Everyone may pick up their exams in my office on Tuesday after 9:00 a.m.

4. None of the candidates came with their résumé, so we had to reject them all.

5. Every applicant must submit their portfolio of work, their essay on why they want to enter the program, and a neatly folded $50 bill.

6. When I go fishing, I expect to catch at least a few.

7. Every secretary knows that their boss is someone that could not survive for 15 minutes without competent secretarial assistance.

8. All the women in this beauty pageant are treated like a sister even though the competition is fierce.

9. Everybody that joins the tour will receive their own souvenir hat.

10. Before a Canadian votes, it is their responsibility to make themselves familiar with the candidates and the issues.

---

3. RELATIVE PRONOUNS

The third potential difficulty with pronoun–antecedent agreement is how to use relative pronouns—*who/whoever, whom/whomever, which,* and *that*—correctly. Relative pronouns refer to someone or something already mentioned in the sentence or paragraph. Here is the guideline to follow.

> Use *who/whom* and *whoever/whomever* refer to people.
> Use *that* and *which* to refer to everything else.

The student *who* won the Governor General's Academic Medal decided to go to Dalhousie.

For *whom* are you voting: the Liberals or the New Democrats?

The moose *that* I met looked hostile.

Her car, *which* is imported, is smaller than cars *that* are built here.

Tips:

1. Whether you need *who* or *whom, whoever* or *whomever*, depends on the pronoun's place and function in your sentence. Apply the basic rule of pronoun usage: if the pronoun is acting as, or refers to, the subject or the complement, use *who/whoever*. Otherwise, use *whom/whomever*.

   My husband was the idiot *who* entered a contest to win a trip to Moose Factory. (The pronoun refers to the subject of the sentence, *husband*.)

   The trip's promoters were willing to settle for *whomever* they could get. (The pronoun does not refer to the sentence's subject, *promoters*; it is the object of the preposition *for*.)

   An even simpler solution to this problem is to rewrite the sentence so you don't need either *who* or *whom*.

   My husband entered a contest to win a trip to Moose Factory.

   The trip's promoters were willing to settle for anyone they could get.

2. *That* is required more often than *which*. You should use *which* only in a clause that is separated from the rest of the sentence by commas. (See Comma Rule 4 on page 420.)

   The moose *that* I met looked hostile.

   The moose, *which* was standing right in front of my car, looked hostile.

(**Exercise 30.9***)

Correct the following sentences where necessary.

1. The actress that saw her first grey hair thought she'd dye.

2. I am a longtime fan of David Cronenberg, a director that began his career in Canada.

3. I wonder why we are so often attracted to people which are completely opposite to us.

4. I'm one of those people that should stay out of the sun.

5. People that take afternoon naps often suffer from insomnia as a result.

6. The vacuum-cleaner salesperson which came to our door was the sort of person that won't take no for an answer.

7. This is the brilliant teacher that helped me achieve the grades which I had thought were beyond me.

8. Marathon runners that wear cheap shoes often suffer the agony of defeat.

9. The math problems which we worked on last night would have baffled anyone that hadn't done all the problem sets.

10. We took the ancient Jeep, that we had bought from a friend that had lost his licence, to a scrapyard who paid us $200 for it.

GO TO WEB

EXERCISES 30.3, 30.4, 30.5, 30.6

Person Agreement

So far, we have focused on using pronouns correctly and clearly within a sentence. Now let's turn to the problem of **person agreement**, which means using pronouns consistently throughout a sentence or a paragraph. There are three categories of person that we use when we write or speak:

	Singular	Plural
First person	I; me	we; us
Second person	you	you
Third person	she, he, it, one; her, him *and all pronouns ending in* -one, -thing, -body	they; them

Here is the rule for person agreement.

Do not mix "persons" unless meaning requires it.

In other words, be consistent. If you begin a sentence using a second-person pronoun, you must use second person all the way through. Look at this sentence:

If *you* wish to succeed, *one* must work hard.

This is the most common error—mixing second-person *you* with third-person *one*.

Here's another example:

One can live happily in Vancouver if *you* have a sturdy umbrella.

1. We can correct this error by using the second person throughout:

You can live happily in Vancouver if *you* have a sturdy umbrella.

2. We can also correct it by using the third person throughout:

a. *One* can live happily in Vancouver if *one* has a sturdy umbrella.

or

b. *One* can live happily in Vancouver if *he* or *she* has a sturdy umbrella.

These examples raise two points of style that you should consider.

Grammar

1. Don't overuse *one*.

All three revised sentences are grammatically correct, but they make different impressions on the reader, and impressions are an important part of communication.

- The first sentence, in the second person, sounds the most informal—like something you would say. It's a bit casual for general writing purposes.
- The second sentence, which uses *one* twice, sounds the most formal— even a little pretentious.
- The third sentence falls between the other two in formality. It is the one you'd be most likely to use in writing for school or business.

Although it is grammatically correct and nonsexist, this third sentence raises another problem. Frequent use of *he or she* in a continuous prose passage, whether that passage is as short as a paragraph or as long as a paper, is guaranteed to irritate your reader.

2. Don't overuse *he or she*.

He or she is inclusive, but it is a wordy construction. If used too frequently, the reader cannot help shifting focus from what you're saying to how you're saying it. The best writing is transparent—that is, it doesn't call attention to itself. If your reader becomes distracted by your style, your meaning gets lost. Consider this sentence:

> A student can easily pass this course if he or she applies himself or herself to his or her studies.

Readers deserve better. A paper—or even a single paragraph—filled with this clumsy construction will annoy even the most patient reader. There are two better solutions to the problem of sexist language, and they are already familiar to you because they are the same as those for making pronouns ending in -*one*, -*body*, or -*thing* agree with their antecedents.

- You can change the whole sentence to the plural.

  > Students can easily pass this course if they apply themselves to their studies.

- You can rewrite the sentence without using pronouns.

  > A student can easily pass this course by applying good study habits.

Exercise 30.10*

In each of the following sentences, select the correct word from the choices given in parentheses. Check your answers before continuing.

1. If you want to make good egg rolls, I advise (them her you) to buy the ready-made wrappings.

2. If you win tonight's lottery, will (one he you) tell (one's his your) friends?

3. Anyone who wants to swim should bring (their your his her a) bathing suit and towel.

4. Every person working in this office should know that (they she) helped to finish an important project.

5. When we toured the House of Commons, (you we he one) didn't see a single MP.

Exercise 30.11

Correct the following sentences where necessary.

1. When a person lives in a glass house, they shouldn't throw stones.

2. Experience is something one acquires just after you need it.

3. Anyone who enjoys snowboarding can have your best holiday ever in western Alberta.

4. When she asked if Peter Tchaikovsky played for the Canucks, you knew she wasn't the woman for me.

5. From time to time, most of us think about the opportunities we've missed even if you are happy with what you have.

6. Managers who are concerned about employee morale should think about ending your policy of threats and intimidation and consider other means to improve your efficiency.

7. If you are afraid of vampires, one should wear garlic around one's neck and carry a silver bullet.

8. Any woman who wears a garlic necklace probably won't have to worry about men harassing them, either.

9. Can you really know another person if you have never been to their home?

10. A sure way to lose one's friends is to eat all the ice cream yourself.

Exercise 30.12

Revise the following passage to make the nouns and pronouns agree in person (first, second, or third) and number (singular or plural). Use the italicized word in the first sentence of each paragraph as your marker.

When *people* see a dreadful occurrence on television, such as a bombing, an earthquake, or a mass slaughter, it does not always affect one. It is one thing for people to see the ravages of war oneself and another thing to see a three-minute newscast of the same battle, neatly edited by the CBC. Even the horrible effects of natural catastrophes that wipe out whole populations are somehow minimized or trivialized when I see them on TV. And though viewers may be horrified by the gaunt faces of starving children on the screen, you can easily escape into your familiar world of Egg McMuffins, Shake'n Bake, and Labatt Blue that is portrayed in commercial messages.

Thus, the impact of television on *us* is a mixed one. It is true that one is shown terrible, sometimes shocking, events that you could not possibly have seen before television. In this way, one's world is drawn together more closely. However, the risk in creating this immediacy is that one may become desensitized and cease to feel or care about one's fellow human beings.

GO TO WEB

EXERCISES 30.7, 30.8

Exercise 30.13

Revise the following paragraph, which contains 15 errors representing the three different kinds of pronoun–antecedent agreement error. If you change a subject from singular to plural, don't forget to change the verb to agree. Some of your answers may differ from our suggestions and still be correct. Check with your instructor.

Everyone that has been to Newfoundland knows that an outport is a small fishing community along the coast of that vast island province. Ladle Cove, for example, is a tiny outport with fewer than 200 residents that live there all year. Despite its small population, Ladle Cove is a village which enjoyed a nation-wide moment of fame when a man that lives there met the Queen. Fred had left Ladle Cove, as just about every man does when they need to find work, and gone to St. John's. Fred wanted to work, but he had few marketable skills to help him get one. Fortunately, he had relatives in St. John's that helped him find a place to stay and eventually found him a job at Purity Foods, a company famous for their baked goods—and for Newfoundland's favourite treat, Jam Jam cookies.

During Queen Elizabeth's visit to St. John's, the officials that organized her tour decided it would be a good idea for her to visit a local industry which had a national reputation. Purity Foods was the logical choice. While touring the plant, the Queen stopped to talk to a few of the men and women that were on the production line. Near the end of the tour, that was being filmed by the national media, the Queen stopped by one of the workers that were making the famous Jam Jams: Fred. As the television lights glared and each reporter held their pencil poised over their notebook, the Queen leaned toward Fred and asked, "And what are we making here?" With a courteous bow in Her Majesty's direction, Fred replied, "Ten-fifty an hour, Ma'am. Ten-fifty an hour."

Grammar

31

The Comma

Many writers-in-training tend to sprinkle punctuation like pepper over their pages. Do not use punctuation to spice up your writing. Punctuation marks are functional: they indicate to the reader how the various parts of a sentence relate to one another. By changing the punctuation, you can change the meaning of a sentence. Here are two examples to prove the point.

1. An instructor wrote the following sentence on the board and asked the class to punctuate it: "Woman without her man is nothing."

   The men wrote, "Woman, without her man, is nothing."
   The women wrote, "Woman! Without her, man is nothing."

2. Now it's your turn. Punctuate this sentence: "I think there is only one person to blame myself."

   If you wrote, "I think there is only one person to blame, myself," the reader will understand that you believe only one person—who may or may not be known to you—is to blame.

   If you wrote, "I think there is only one person to blame: myself," the reader will understand that you are personally accepting responsibility for the blame.

The comma is the most frequently used—and misused—punctuation mark in English. One sure sign of a competent writer is the correct use of commas, so it is very important that you master them. This chapter presents five comma rules that cover most instances in which you need to use commas. If you apply these five rules faithfully, your reader will never be confused by missing or misplaced commas in your writing. And if, as occasionally happens, the sentence you are writing is not covered by one of our five rules, remember the first commandment of comma usage: WHEN IN DOUBT, LEAVE IT OUT.

Five Comma Rules

1. Use commas to separate three or more items in a series. The items may be expressed as words, phrases, or clauses.

Words   The required subjects in this program are *math, physics,* and *English.*

Phrases   Punctuation marks are the traffic signals of prose. They tell us *to slow down, notice this, take a detour,* and *stop.* (Lynne Truss)

Clauses   *Karin went to the movies, Jan and Yasmin went to play pool,* and *I went to bed.*

The comma before the *and* at the end of the list is optional, but we advise you to use it. Occasionally, misunderstandings can occur if it is left out.

Exercise 31.1*

Insert commas where necessary in the following sentences. Answers for exercises in this chapter begin on page 536.

1. Holly held two aces a King a Queen and a Jack in her hand.

2. The food at the Thai Palace is colourful spicy delicious and inexpensive.

3. Life would be complete if I had a Blackberry a Porsche a Sea-Doo and a job.

4. The gear list for the Winter Wilderness course includes woollen underwear snowshoes Arctic boots and a toque.

5. In the summer, a cup of coffee a croissant and a glass of juice are all I want for breakfast.

6. Don't forget to bring the videos maps and souvenirs of your trip to Australia.

7. In Ontario, the four seasons are summer winter winter and winter.

Punctuation

8. My doctor and my nutritionist agree that I should eat better exercise more and take vitamins.

9. Sleeping through my alarm dozing during sociology class napping in the library after lunch and snoozing in front of the TV after supper are symptoms of my overactive nightlife.

10. Welcome home! Once you have finished your homework taken out the garbage and done the dishes, you can feed the cat clean your room and do your laundry.

---

2. Put a comma between independent clauses when they are joined by these connecting words:

for	but	so
and	or	
nor	yet	

(You can remember these words easily if you notice that their first letters spell FANBOYS.)

I hope I do well in the interview, for I really want this job.

I like Norah Jones, but I prefer Diana Krall.

We shape our tools, and our tools shape us. (Marshall McLuhan)

I knew I was going to be late, so I went back to sleep.

Be sure that the sentence you are punctuating contains two independent clauses rather than one clause with a single subject and a multiple verb.

We loved the book but hated the movie.
(We is the subject, and there are two verbs, loved and hated. Do not put a comma between two or more verbs that share a single subject.)

We both loved the book, but Kim hated the movie.
(This sentence contains two independent clauses—We loved and Kim hated—joined by *but*. The comma is required here.)

Exercise 31.2*

Insert commas where they are needed in the following sentences, then check your answers.

1. Either it is very foggy this morning or I am going blind.

2. We have an approved business plan and budget but we're still looking for qualified and experienced staff.

3. Talk shows haven't said anything new in years nor have they solved a single one of the problems they endlessly discuss.

4. We discovered that we both had an interest in fine art so we made a date to go to an exhibition at the art gallery next week.

5. Canadians are proud of their country but they don't approve of too much flag-waving.

6. Take good notes for I'll need them in order to study for the exam.

7. I'll rent a tux but I will not get a haircut or my shoes shined.

8. I chose a quiet seat on the train and two women with bawling babies boarded at the next station.

9. I have travelled all over the world yet my luggage has visited at least twice the number of countries that I have.

10. Jet lag makes me look haggard and ill but at least I resemble my passport photo.

3. Put a comma after an introductory word, phrase, or dependent clause that comes before an independent clause.

Lucas, you aren't paying attention. (word)

After staying up all night, I staggered into class 15 minutes late. (phrase)

If that's their idea of a large pizza, we'd better order two. (clause)

Until she got her promotion, she was quite friendly. (clause)

> 4. Use commas to set off any word, phrase, or dependent clause that is NOT ESSENTIAL to the main idea of the sentence.

Following this rule can make the difference between your reader's understanding and misunderstanding what you write. For example, the following two sentences are identical, except for a pair of commas. But notice what a difference those two tiny marks make to meaning:

The children who were dressed in clown costumes had ice cream. (Only the children wearing clown costumes ate ice cream.)

The children, who were dressed in clown costumes, had ice cream. (All the children wore costumes and had ice cream.)

To test whether a word, phrase, or clause is essential to the meaning of your sentence, mentally put parentheses around it. If the sentence still makes complete sense (i.e., the main idea is unchanged; the sentence just delivers less information), the material in parentheses is *not essential* and should be set off from the rest of the sentence by a comma or commas.

Nonessential information can appear at the beginning of a sentence,[1] in the middle, or at the end of a sentence. Study the following examples.

Alice Munro ⸨ one of Canada's best-known novelists ⸩ spends summer in Clinton and winter in Comox.

Most readers would be puzzled the first time they read this sentence because all the information is presented without punctuation, so the reader assumes it is all equally important. In fact, the material in broken parentheses is extra information, a supplementary detail. It can be deleted without changing the sentence's meaning, and so it should be separated from the rest of the sentence by commas:

Alice Munro, one of Canada's best-known novelists, spends summer in Clinton and winter in Comox.

Here's another example to consider:

The Queen ⸨ who has twice as many birthdays as anyone else ⸩ officially celebrates her birthday on May 24.

---

[1] Comma Rule 3 covers nonessential information at the beginning of a sentence.

Again, the sentence is hard to read. You can't count on your readers to go back and reread every sentence they don't understand at first glance. As a writer, your responsibility is to give readers the clues they need as to what is crucial information and what isn't. In the example above, the information in broken parentheses is not essential to the meaning of the sentence, so it should be set off by commas:

> The Queen, who has twice as many birthdays as anyone else, officially celebrates her birthday on May 24.

In this next sentence, the nonessential information comes at the end.

> Writing a good letter of application isn't difficult ⁅ if you're careful ⁆ .

The phrase "if you're careful" is not essential to the main idea, so it should be separated from the rest of the sentence by a comma:

> Writing a good letter of application isn't difficult, if you're careful.

And finally, consider this sentence:

> Writing a letter of application ⁅ that is clear, complete, and concise ⁆ is a challenge.

If you take out "that is clear, complete, and concise," you change the meaning of the sentence. Not all letters of application are a challenge to write. Writing vague and wordy letters is easy; anyone can do it. The words "that is clear, complete, and concise" are essential to the meaning of the sentence, and so they are not set off by commas.

> Writing a letter of application that is clear, complete, and concise is a challenge.

Exercise 31.3*

Insert commas where they are missing in the following sentences, then check your answers.

1. A good day in my opinion always starts with a few cuts of high-volume heavy metal.
2. This photograph which was taken when I was four embarrasses me whenever my parents display it.
3. Mira's boyfriend who looks like an ape is living proof that love is blind.

4. Isn't it strange that the poor who often are bitterly critical of the rich keep buying lottery tickets?
5. A nagging headache the result of last night's great party made me miserable all morning.
6. Our ancient car made it all the way to Saskatoon without anything falling off or breaking down a piece of good luck that astonished everyone.
7. Professor Repke a popular mathematics teacher won the Distinguished Teaching Award this year.
8. We're going to spend the afternoon at the mall a weekly event that has become a ritual.
9. No one who ever saw Patrick Roy play doubts that he was a superstar.
10. Classical music which I call Prozac for the ears can be very soothing in times of stress.

Exercise 31.4*

Insert commas where they are needed in the following sentences. Check your answers on page 538 before continuing.

1. Unfortunately we'll have to begin all over again.
2. Mr. Dillinger the bank would like a word with you.
3. In college the quality of your work is more important than the effort you put into it.
4. Hopelessly lost my father still refused to stop and ask for directions.
5. Finally understanding what she was trying to say I apologized for being so slow.
6. After an evening of watching television I have accomplished as much as if I had been unconscious.
7. Since the doctor ordered me to walk to work every morning I have seen three accidents involving people walking to work.
8. Having munched our way through a large bag of peanuts while watching the game we weren't interested in supper.
9. Whenever an optimist is pulled over by a police officer the optimist assumes it's to ask for directions.
10. That same year Stephen Leacock bought his summer home in Orillia, Ontario.

---

5. Use commas between coordinate adjectives but not between cumulative adjectives.

Coordinate adjectives are those whose order can be changed, and the word *and* can be inserted between them without changing the meaning of the sentence.

Our company is looking for energetic, courteous salespeople.

The adjectives *energetic* and *courteous* could appear in reverse order, and you could put *and* between them: "Our company is looking for courteous and energetic salespeople."

In a series of **cumulative adjectives**, however, each adjective modifies the word that follows it. You cannot change their order, nor can you insert *and* between them.

The bride wore a pale pink silk dress, and the groom wore a navy wool suit.

You cannot say "The bride wore a silk pink pale dress" or "The groom wore a navy and wool suit," so no commas are used with these adjectives.

One final note about commas before you try the review exercises: never place a SINGLE comma between a subject and its verb.

Wrong: <u>Those</u> who intend to register for hockey, <u>must be</u> at the arena
          by 8:00 a.m.

Right: <u>Those</u> who intend to register for hockey <u>must be</u> at the arena
          by 8:00 a.m.

Two commas, however, between a subject and its verb are correct if the commas set off nonessential material.

<u>Saied and Mohamed</u>, who intend to register for hockey, <u>have</u> never <u>played</u> before.

Punctuation

Exercise 31.5*

Insert commas where they are needed in the following sentences. Check your answers before continuing.

1. The desk was made of dark brown carved oak.
2. Do you want your portrait in a glossy finish or a matte finish?
3. Bright yellow fabric that repels stains is ideal for rain gear.
4. Toronto in the summer is hot smoggy and humid.

5. Today's paper has an article about a new car made of lightweight durable aluminum.
6. Dietitians recommend that we eat at least two servings daily of green leafy vegetables.
7. This ergonomic efficient full-function keyboard comes in a variety of pastel shades.
8. We ordered a large nutritious salad for lunch, then indulged ourselves with a redcurrant cheesecake for dessert.
9. Danny bought a cute cuddly purebred puppy.
10. Ten months later that cute puppy turned into a vicious man-eating monster.

The rest of the exercises in this chapter require you to apply all five comma rules. Before you start, write out the five rules and keep them in front of you as you work through the exercises. Refer to the rules frequently as you punctuate the sentences. After you've finished each exercise, check your answers and make sure you understand any mistakes you've made.

Exercise 31.6*

1. Pinot noir which is a type of grape grown in California Oregon British Columbia and Ontario produces a delicious red wine.
2. There are I am told people who don't like garlic but you won't find any of them eating at Freddy's.
3. I use e-mail to communicate with my colleagues a fax machine to keep in touch with clients and Canada Post to send greetings to my relatives.
4. Your dogs Mr. Pavlov seem hungry for some reason.
5. According to G. K. Chesterton "If a thing is worth doing it is worth doing badly."
6. Looking for a competent computer technologist we interviewed tested investigated and rejected 30 applicants.
7. How you choose to phrase your resignation is up to you but I expect to have it on my desk by morning.
8. Your superstitious dread of March 13 Senator Caesar is irrational and silly.
9. The lenses of my new high-fashion sunglasses are impact-resistant yellow UV-reflective optical plastic.
10. Canada a country known internationally for beautiful scenery peaceful intentions and violent hockey always places near the top of the United Nations' list of desirable places to live.

Exercise 31.7*

1. Whereas the Super Bowl tradition goes back about four decades the Grey Cup has a history that stretches back to the 19th century.
2. Otherwise Mrs. Lincoln said she had very much enjoyed the play.
3. Our guard dog a Rottweiler caught an intruder and maimed him for life.
4. Unfortunately my Uncle Ladislaw was the intruder and he intends to sue us for every penny we have.
5. The year 1945 marked the end of World War II and the beginning of assistance to war-torn nations.
6. We bought a lovely old mahogany dining table at auction for $300.
7. If there were more people like Gladys global warming would be the least of our worries.
8. We are pleased with your résumé and are offering you an interview this week.
9. Deciding on the midnight blue velvet pants was easy but paying for them was not.
10. Igor asked "May I show you to your quarters or would you prefer to spend the night in the dungeon?"

GO TO WEB

EXERCISES 31.1, 31.2, 31.3

Exercise 31.8

To test your mastery of commas, provide the necessary punctuation for the following paragraph. There are 15 errors.

When my brother and I were growing up my mother used to summon us home from playing by ringing a solid brass bell that could be heard for miles. All of the other kids to our great embarrassment, knew when our mother was calling us and they would tease us by making ringing noises. We begged her to yell like all the other moms but she knew she had a foolproof system and wouldn't change. One day while we were playing with our friends in the fields behind our homes the bell rang in the middle of an important game. The other kids began their usual taunts that our mother was calling but this time we bravely ignored the bell. When it rang the second time we ignored it again. By the third ring, however we knew that we were in big trouble so we dashed for home. We agreed on the way that we would tell our mother that we just didn't hear the bell. We arrived hot sweaty and panting from our run. Before Mom could say a word my brother blurted out, "We didn't hear the bell until the third ring!" Fortunately for us our mother couldn't stop laughing and we escaped the punishment we deserved.

Summary

The Five Comma Rules

1. Use commas to separate items in a series of three or more. The items may be expressed as words, phrases, or clauses.
2. Put a comma between independent clauses when they are joined by *for, and, nor, but, or, yet,* or *so.*
3. Put a comma after an introductory word, phrase, or dependent clause that comes before an independent clause.
4. Use commas to set off a word, phrase, or dependent clause that is NOT ESSENTIAL to the main idea of the sentence.
5. Use commas between coordinate adjectives but not between cumulative adjectives.

32

The Semicolon

The semicolon and the colon are often confused and used as if they were interchangeable. They have distinct purposes, however, and their correct use can dramatically improve a reader's understanding of your writing. The semicolon has three functions.

1. A semicolon can replace a period; in other words, it can appear between two independent clauses.

You should use a semicolon when the two clauses (sentences) you are joining are closely connected in meaning, or when there is a cause-and-effect relationship between them.

I'm too tired; I can't stay awake any longer.

Montreal is not the city's original name; it was once called Ville Marie.

A period could have been used instead of a semicolon in either of these sentences, but the close connection between the clauses makes a semicolon more effective in communicating the writer's meaning.

2. Certain transitional words or phrases can be put between independent clauses to show a cause-and-effect relationship or the continuation of an idea.

Words or phrases used in this way are usually preceded by a semicolon and followed by a comma:

; also,	; furthermore,	; nevertheless,
; as a result,	; however,	; on the other hand,
; besides,	; in addition,	; otherwise,
; consequently,	; in fact,	; then,
; finally,	; instead,	; therefore,
; for example,	; moreover,	; thus,

The forecast called for sun; instead, we got snow.

My monitor went blank; nevertheless, I kept on typing.

"I'm not offended by dumb blonde jokes because I know I'm not dumb; besides, I also know I'm not blonde." (Dolly Parton)

In other words, *a semicolon + a transitional word/phrase + a comma* = a link strong enough to come between two related independent clauses.

Note, however, that, when these transitional words and phrases are used as nonessential expressions rather than as connecting words, they are separated from the rest of the sentence by commas (Chapter 31, Rule 4, page 420).

I just can't seem to master particle physics, however hard I try.

The emissions test, moreover, will ensure that your car is running well.

3. To make a COMPLEX LIST easier to read and understand, put semi-colons between the items instead of commas.

A complex list is one in which at least one component part already contains commas. Here are two examples:

I grew up in a series of small towns: Cumberland, B.C.; Red Deer, Alberta; and Timmins, Ontario.

When we opened the refrigerator, we found a limp, brown head of let-
tuce; two small containers of yogurt, whose "best before" dates had long
since passed; and a hard, dried-up piece of cheddar cheese.

Exercise 32.1*

Put a check mark next to the sentences that are correctly punctuated. Check
your answers before continuing. Answers for this chapter begin on page 539.

1. _____We've eaten all the food, it's time to go home.
2. _____Many doctors claim weather affects our health; in fact, baro-
metric pressure has a direct effect on arthritis.
3. _____ Your instructor would like to see you pass, however, there may be
a small fee involved.
4. _____ Molly is going to Chicago, she wants to appear on *Oprah*.
5. _____ Many people dislike hockey; because some of the players act like
goons rather than athletes.
6. _____ Orville tried and tried; but he couldn't get the teacher's attention.
7. _____ She presented her report using coloured charts and diagrams;
these visual aids woke up even the accountants.
8. _____ Tomorrow is another day, unfortunately it will probably be just
like today.
9. _____ Rumours of a merger had begun to circulate by five o'clock; so
it's no wonder many employees looked nervous on their way
home.
10. _____We knew the party had been a success when Uncle Morty, drunk
as usual, tap-danced across the top of the piano, Aunt Madeline,
who must weigh at least 80 kg, did her Cirque du Soleil routine,
and Stan punched out two of his cousins.

Exercise 32.2*

Correct the faulty punctuation in Exercise 32.1.

GO TO WEB

EXERCISES 32.1, 32.2

Punctuation

Exercise 32.3*

Insert semicolons where necessary in these sentences. Then check your answers.

1. The rain has to stop soon otherwise, we'll have to start building an ark.
2. Our finances are a mess the only way we can repay our debts would be to stop paying for rent and food.
3. We need you at the meeting, however, since you have another engagement, we will have to reschedule.
4. A day without puns is like a day without sunshine, it leaves gloom for improvement.
5. I work on an assembly line, all of us workers believe that if a job is worth doing; it's worth doing 11,000 times a day.
6. It is not impossible to become wealthy, if you're under 20, all you need to do is put the price of a pack of cigarettes into an RRSP every day, and you'll be a millionaire by the age of 50.
7. If, on the other hand, you continue to spend your money on smokes, the government will make the millions that could have been yours, you'll die early and broke.
8. As a dog lover and the owner of an Afghan, I suffer a great deal of abuse, for example, for my birthday, my wife gave me a book rating the intelligence of Afghans as 79th out of 79 breeds tested.
9. A plateau, according to the *Dictionary of Puns*, is a high form of flattery, this may be low humour, but it's a clever remark.
10. According to a *Gourmet Magazine* poll, four of the top ten restaurants in the world are in Paris, three—those ranking eighth, ninth, and tenth—are in the United States, two are in Tokyo and the other is in Thailand.

GO TO WEB

EXERCISE 32.3

Exercise 32.4

Test your mastery of semicolons and commas by correcting the punctuation in these sentences.

1. Growing old has never really bothered me in fact I consider aging a huge improvement over the alternative.
2. I visit a chiropractor twice a month, if I miss a treatment I have to crawl into work.

3. Our marketing campaign is based on sound principles, for example if we are sufficiently annoying people will buy our product just to make us go away.

4. The construction was so far behind schedule that we couldn't make up the time, consequently we lost our performance bonus our chance to bid on the next contract and an important client.

5. Among the many products being standardized by the European Community is the condom however a number of nations have officially complained that the standard size is too small.

6. Failing to stop at the light turned out to be the least of his offences the police were much more interested in his expired driving licence.

7. In her fridge we found a pound of butter dating from last August a mouldy piece of cake three containers of unidentifiable fur-bearing substances and an open can of beer.

8. A practice that works well in one country may not work in another for example every man in Switzerland is required to own a rifle. Such a policy might find acceptance in the United States however anyone who proposed it in Canada would be thought insane.

9. While some people find bird watching an exciting hobby and others are drawn to rock climbing or heli-skiing my own preference is for less strenuous pastimes such as those involving food.

10. To use or not to use the semicolon is sometimes a matter of the writer's choice, on the other hand, a few syntactical constructions require a semicolon, no other punctuation mark will do.

Punctuation

33

The Colon

The **colon** functions as an introducer. When a statement is followed by a list, one or more examples, or a quotation, the colon alerts the reader that some sort of explanatory detail is coming up.

When I travel, I am never without three things: sturdy shoes, a money belt, and my journal.

There is only one enemy we cannot defeat: time.

We have two choices: to study or to fail.

Early in his career, Robert Fulford did not think very highly of intellectual life in Canada: "My generation of Canadians grew up believing that, if we were very good or very smart, or both, we would someday *graduate* from Canada."

The statement that precedes the colon must be a complete sentence (independent clause).

A colon should never come immediately after *is* or *are*. Here's an example of what *not* to write.

The only things I am violently allergic to are: cats, ragweed, and country music.

This is incorrect because the statement before the colon is not a complete sentence.

1. Use a colon between an independent clause and a LIST or one or more EXAMPLES that define, explain, or illustrate the independent clause.

The information after the colon often answers the question "what?" or "who?"

I am violently allergic to three things: (what?) cats, ragweed, and country music.

Business and industry face a new challenge: (what?) offshore out-sourcing.

The president has found the ideal candidate for the position: (who?) her brother.

2. Use a colon after a complete sentence introducing a quotation.

Lucille Ball observed that there were three secrets to staying young: "Live honestly, eat slowly, and lie about your age."

3. Finally, use a colon to separate the title of a book, film, or TV show from a subtitle.

Word Play: What Happens When People Talk

Ace Ventura: Pet Detective

Trading Spouses: Meet Your New Mommy

If you remember this summary, you'll have no more trouble with colons: the colon follows an independent clause and introduces an example, a list, or a quotation that amplifies the meaning of that clause.

Exercise 33.1*

Put a check mark next to the sentences that are correctly punctuated. Check your answers before going on. Answers for this chapter begin on page 540.

1. _____ Believe it or not, the country that produces the most films every year is: India.

Punctuation

2. _____ Jordan wants to go home to be comforted by the only person in the world who truly understands him: his mother.

3. _____ In this region, the three grapes most commonly grown for wine are Chardonnay, Merlot, and Riesling.

4. _____ The most annoying sound in the world has to be that produced by: bagpipes.

5. _____ The company's bankruptcy resulted from the CEO's management style. He relied on: crisis management, seat-of-the-pants planning, and excessive profit-taking.

6. _____ One topic has dominated the health concerns of the world since the late 1980s: AIDS.

7. _____ Two of Canada's highest awards in professional sports are the Stanley Cup and the Grey Cup.

8. _____ All most students ask is that their teachers treat them with: courtesy, fairness, and respect.

9. _____ Of course, there are always a few students who demand what no true professional will provide special treatment.

10. _____ Our department's proposal is unique it has the CEO's approval.

Exercise 33.2*

Insert colons in the following sentences where necessary and then check your answers. If you find you've made any mistakes, review the explanations on pages 432–33, study the examples, and be sure you understand why your answers were wrong before going on.

1. I have set myself three goals this year to achieve an 80 percent average, to get a good summer job, and to buy a car.

2. Right after we moved in, we discovered we had a problem termites.

3. After our bankruptcy, our credit card consultant asked us an interesting question "Why don't you cut up your credit cards?"

4. Several Canadian writers are even better known abroad than they are at home Carol Shields, Neil Bissoondath, and Michael Ondaatje are three examples.

5. There are a number of inexpensive activities that will improve physical fitness; swimming, tennis, jogging, even brisk walking.

6. Jocelyn is trying to accomplish two mutually contradictory tasks a significant weight loss and success as a restaurant critic.

7. Several of the animals on the international list of endangered species are native to Canada; the wood bison, the northern kit fox, and the whooping crane.

8. We'll finish the assignment by tomorrow only if we stay up all night and consume vast quantities of pizza and black coffee.

9. The majority of Canada's population is worn out and exhausted at the end of a long, hard winter, but most people are able to console themselves with one comforting thought, spring will arrive sometime in May or June.

10. There are several troublesome implications of biological engineering, but one in particular is frightening to most people the cloning of human beings.

Exercise 33.3*

Correct the incorrectly punctuated sentences in Exercise 33.1.

GO TO WEB

EXERCISES 33.1, 33.2, 33.3, 33.4

Exercise 33.4

To test your mastery of colons and semicolons, correct the errors in the following sentences.

1. The person who comes to mind when I am asked to name a female role model is: Adrienne Clarkson.

2. The TV is always asking me challenging questions "It's 11:05. Do you know where your children are?"

3. You have all the qualities of a pit bull: except one, loyalty.

4. Hippocrates, the father of modern medicine, is responsible for the first rule of medical practice "First, do no harm."

5. One of the symptoms of an approaching nervous breakdown is: the belief that one's work is terribly important. (Bertrand Russell)

6. You should use a colon in this sentence: and there's one place to put it here.

7. Contrary to the words of the popular song from the 1950s: breaking up is easy to do.

8. There are many countries on my "must visit" list, including: Brazil, Ukraine, Sweden, and Slovenia.

Punctuation

9. Studies have shown that in most offices the Internet is used primarily for nonwork-related activities: such as personal e-mail, random surfing, and game playing.

10. Having failed to impress Cara with his charm, Sean decided to try gifts; roses, chocolates, and perfume.

34

Quotation Marks

Quotation marks are used to set off direct speech (dialogue), quoted material, and some titles. For information how to punctuate and insert quoted material into your papers, see pages 280–86. To review when to use quotation marks for titles, see page 292.

Direct Quotations

A **direct quotation** is someone's exact words, spoken or written. It is usually introduced by a reporting expression such as *she said, he replied,* or *they shouted.* Put quotation marks before and after the person's exact words.

Tim asked angrily, "Did you delete my entire address book?"

"No, a virus attacked the computer and ate your files," I replied.

Do not use quotation marks with **indirect quotations** (reported speech):

Tim asked angrily if I had deleted his entire address book. (These are not Tim's exact words, so no quotation marks are necessary.)

I replied that a virus attacked his computer and ate his files. (Note that indirect quotations are often introduced by *that.*)

Use single quotation marks to enclose a quotation within a quotation:

"I don't understand what you mean by the term 'creative memory,'" said Lauren.

Punctuation

The final thing you need to know about direct quotations is how to punctuate them. Here are the rules to follow.

1. Separate a reporting expression and a quotation with a comma.

Professor Lam announced, "You will write the mid-term test on Tuesday."

"You will write the mid-term test on Tuesday," announced Professor Lam.

2. If there is no reporting verb, use a colon after an independent clause to introduce a quotation.

Too late, I remembered Professor Lam's advice at the beginning of term: "Keep up with your work each week, and the tests will cause you no trouble."

3. Begin each quoted sentence with a capital letter. If a quoted sentence is divided into two parts, begin the second part with a small letter.

"**O**ur national anthem," John informed us, "**w**as written by Calixa Lavillée. First composed in French, it was later translated into English."

4. If the end punctuation is part of the direct quotation, put commas, periods, question marks, and exclamation marks *inside* the second quotation mark of a pair.

"Could you help me?" the woman asked. "I'm trying to find Melrose Avenue." Almost in tears, she went on, "I'm already late for my job interview!"

5. If the end punctuation is *not* part of the direct quotation, put it *outside* the second quotation mark. (It's part of your sentence, not the speaker's.)

Did the woman say, "I'm late for my job interview"?

6. Put colons and semicolons *outside* the second quotation mark (unless they are part of the direct quotation).

Near tears, the woman cried, "Please help me": we could hardly leave her standing there alone.

The woman cried, "Please help me"; she was near tears.

"Please help me; I'm late for my job interview," cried the woman.

Exercise 34.1

Punctuate the following sentences correctly, using quotation marks and other punctuation marks where they are needed. Answers are provided on page 541.

1. Did you see the look on her face asked Roderick.
2. Frank asked Jenna if she would like to play bridge.
3. I'd love to, she replied, if only I knew how.
4. Pardon me, boys, is this the Transylvania Station asked the man in the black cape.
5. When I pointed out to Wayne that he was wearing one green sock and one brown sock, he replied what's wrong with that? My brother has a pair just like it.
6. When I asked the guide if people jumped from the CN Tower very often, he replied no, just the once.
7. Pierre Trudeau once told Canadians that the state had no business in the nation's bedrooms.
8. Just as well, muttered Terry, because I wouldn't want the state to see what's growing on my bedroom windowsill.
9. I knew that Microsoft had lost its corporate mind when my computer flashed the following blue-screen error message No keyboard detected. Press any key to continue.
10. The psychiatrist said to the woman whose husband thought he was a horse I can cure your husband, but it will take a long time and be very costly. Money is no object, replied the woman. He just won the Queen's Plate.

Punctuation

35

Question and Exclamation Marks

The Question Mark

Everyone knows that a question mark follows an interrogative, or asking, sentence, but we all sometimes forget to include it. Let this chapter serve as a reminder not to forget!

> The **question mark** is the end punctuation for all interrogative sentences.

The question mark gives your readers an important clue to the meaning of your sentence. "There's more?" is vastly different in meaning from "There's more!" and that difference is communicated to readers by the punctuation alone.

The only time you don't end a question with a question mark is when the question is part of a statement.

Is anyone there? (question)
I asked if anyone was there. (statement)
Do you understand? (question)
I wonder whether you understand. (statement)

Exercise 35.1*

Supply the correct end punctuation for the following sentences. Then check your answers. Answers for this chapter are on page 542.

1. Do you ever wonder why we park in a driveway and drive on a parkway

2. I cannot understand how you can listen to that music

3. I cannot believe that you would question my integrity

4. I wonder if my apartment will ever be the same after their visit

5. What's another word for thesaurus

6. If we can't finish the project on time, will we lose the contract

7. I question the results you got on your survey

8. Did you know there are only 18,000 elephants in all of India

9. Human Resources wants to know why we hired an unqualified, inexperienced person for such a sensitive position

10. If corn oil comes from corn, where does baby oil come from

---

GO TO WEB

EXERCISES 35.1, 35.2

The Exclamation Mark

In informal or personal writings, the exclamation mark is a useful piece of punctuation for conveying your tone of voice to your readers. There is a distinct difference in tone between these two sentences:

There's a man behind you.

There's a man behind you!

In the first sentence, information is being supplied, perhaps about the line-up at a grocery-store checkout counter. The second sentence might be a shouted warning about a mugger.

Punctuation

> Use an **exclamation mark** as end punctuation in sentences requiring extreme emphasis or dramatic effect.

Exclamation marks have "punch" or drama only if you use them sparingly. If you use an exclamation mark after every third sentence, how will your readers know when you really mean to indicate excitement? Note also that exclamation marks are seldom used in academic or professional writing.

Practically any sentence could end with an exclamation mark, but remember that the punctuation changes the meaning of the sentence. Read each of the following sentences with and without an exclamation mark and picture the situation that would call for each reading.

He's gone   Don't touch that button

The room was empty   There she goes again

Exercise 35.2*

Supply the correct end punctuation for each of the following sentences. In many cases, the punctuation you use will depend on how you want the sentence to be read.

1. You must be kidding

2. Turn left Now

3. I can't believe I actually passed

4. Oh, great We're moving to Backwater, Alberta

5. Run It's right behind you

6. I'm freezing Turn the heat up

7. "Workers of the world, unite" (Karl Marx)

8. Finally Someone is coming to take our order

9. For the last time, leave me alone

10. What a great game I've never seen a better one.

GO TO WEB

EXERCISES 35.3, 35.4, 35.5

Exercise 35.3

1. We asked whether there is intelligent life in Arkansas

2. Don't shoot I'm on your side

3. What in the world were you thinking when you had "file not found" tattooed on your arm

4. Whenever the power goes out, we wonder if the outage affects everyone or just us

5. Would you believe that the heaviest world-champion boxer, Primo Carnera, weighed 123 kg for a 1933 fight

6. That's one king-size heavyweight

7. Do you really believe that Al found a lamp that held a genie who gave him three wishes

8. That's outrageous

9. I often think about my future. Will I become an architect A fashion designer Or a movie director

10. Hooray This chapter is finished

36

Dashes and Parentheses

When you are talking with someone, you use your voice to punctuate: you pause for a short time (commas) or for a longer time (semicolons and periods); you shout (exclamation marks); or you query (question marks). In writing, punctuation substitutes for these vocal markers: it helps you ensure that your writing will make sense to your readers.

One way you can add variety and flexibility to your sentences is by inserting words or phrases that add to but are not essential to the sentence's meaning. That is, the word or phrase could be omitted, and the sentence would still be complete and would still make sense. It might, however, lack grace or interest.

You can use three punctuation marks to add nonessential material to your sentences: commas, dashes, and parentheses. You are already familiar with the first one. Here is your opportunity to master the last two: the **dash**—which looks like this—and **parentheses** (round brackets). (If you are typing, the dash is two hyphens with no space on either side.)

Dashes

Dashes are used to mark a break in thought or an abrupt shift in emphasis.

1. Use a dash to introduce a word, phrase, or clause that summarizes or restates what has just been said.

I still love dried apricots and pickled beets—foods my mother gave me as treats when I was a child.

Perseverance, spirit, and skill—these three qualities ensure a good game.

Atwood, Ondaatje, Laurence, Davies, Clarke, and Richler—for a country with a relatively small population, Canada has produced an extraordinary number of internationally acclaimed novelists.

2. Use a pair of dashes to enclose a series of items separated by commas.

Four of the managers—Olive, Muhsin, Luis, and Neville—are new to the McDonald's franchise at the zoo.

Because they were afraid of the police, my so-called friends—Roman, Shane, and Mark—all betrayed me.

The apartment he showed me would have been fine, had it not been for the tenants—moths, cockroaches, and silverfish—already making it their home.

3. Use a dash or a pair of dashes to set off from the rest of the sentence a climactic or emphatic moment.

I expect—and so does the college—that students at this level should be self-motivated.

Our neighbour—an animal-rights activist—keeps rabbits in his backyard.

If you really want to go—even though you haven't been invited—I'll take you.

Note that dashes set off material that is not grammatically part of the sentence. If you were to omit the words between the dashes, the sentence would still make sense.

Dashes can be misused if you use them too frequently. Unless you are writing very informally—in a personal letter, for instance—save dashes for the very occasional phrase to which you want to draw emphatic attention.

Punctuation

Exercise 36.1*

Add dashes where they are appropriate. Answers for this chapter begin on page 542.

1. One Aboriginal tribe in England painted themselves blue with dye made from a plant woad.
2. My purpose in moving from Vancouver to Hope like that of hundreds of people before me was to find affordable housing.
3. We shall have to start without her again!
4. Skiing and skating if you like these sports, you'll love Quebec.
5. Tending to his garden, writing his memoirs, and dining with friends these were the pleasures Arnold looked forward to in retirement.
6. What is missing in his life is obvious rest and relaxation!
7. Zoe should do well in fact, I'm sure she will in the engineering program.
8. Alexei was amazed positively thunderstruck when he learned Uncle Vladimir had won a million dollars.
9. Historians, diarists, and chroniclers these are the recorders of our past.
10. Dashes a kind of silent shout allow you to insert an occasional exclamation into your sentences.

Parentheses

Like dashes, parentheses are used to enclose an interruption in a sentence. The difference between them is a matter of tone: dashes SHOUT—they serve to draw the reader's attention to the material they enclose—but parentheses (which should be used sparingly) "whisper." Parentheses are similar to theatrical asides; they are subordinate to the main action but are not to be missed.

1. Use parentheses around additional information that you wish to include but not emphasize.

Giselle's teaching schedule (she is in class seven hours a day) gives her little time to meet with students individually.

They brought me to their village and presented me to their chief (a woman) and to the tribal councillors.

Note the difference in tone your choice of punctuation makes. Compare the examples above with the following versions.

Giselle's teaching schedule—she is in class seven hours a day—gives her little time to meet with students individually.

They brought me to their village and presented me to their chief—a woman—and to the tribal councillors.

2. Use parentheses to enclose explanatory material that is not part of the main sentence.

"Lightweight Lit." (an essay in Part 4) was written by an English teacher who would have preferred to remain anonymous.

The Malagasy (people of Madagascar) like to eat a kapoaka of rice (enough to fill a condensed-milk can) three times a day.

3. Use parentheses to enclose reference data in a research paper. (See Chapter 20.)

Exercise 36.2*

Add parentheses where they are appropriate.

1. Five of the students I was asked not to name them have volunteered to be peer tutors.
2. The apostrophe is explained in the unit on spelling pages 463–70.
3. Jason complained that being a manager he became one in March was like being a cop.
4. I have enclosed a cheque for one hundred and fifty dollars $150.
5. More members of the Canadian Armed Forces died in World War I 1914–18 than in any war before or since.
6. Although Mozart lived a relatively short time he died when he was 36, he composed hundreds of musical masterpieces.
7. As news of her miracle cures spread patients began to come to her from all over the province, the doctor had to move her clinic to a more central location.
8. The new contract provided improved working conditions, a raise in salary 3 percent, and a new dental plan.

Punctuation

9. Ontario and British Columbia now produce world-class wines from their small estate wineries Inniskillin, Hillebrand, Quails' Gate that compete and win internationally.

10. "One of the most important tools for making paper speak in your own voice is punctuation; it plays the role of body language; it helps readers hear you the way you want to be heard" Baker, 48–49.

GO TO WEB

EXERCISE 36.1

Exercise 36.3

Insert dashes and parentheses where appropriate in the following sentences.

1. The function of parentheses see the explanation on page 446 is to set apart material that interrupts the main idea of the sentence and that the writer does not want to emphasize.

2. Dashes, on the other hand bold, dramatic dashes are used to set off an emphatic interruption.

3. We should we must find a way to cut expenses by at least 10 percent.

4. On their first and last date, Rupert took Freda bowling.

5. Proof of the need for investment in infrastructure see the appendix to the Building Committee Report is that the building has twice failed fire code inspections.

6. We wanted it to be warm for our week at the ocean, but it was so hot 40 degrees hot that we didn't even want to leave the hotel to go to the beach.

7. This comic book comics may not be great literature, but they are important cultural documents cost me 10 cents and is now worth more than $4,000.

8. There are a few people obnoxious people like Dwight and Daisy who light up the room when they leave.

9. For my birthday, my sister gave me a pair of hand-knit socks I'm allergic to wool, a box of chocolates I'm on a diet, and a coffee mug with the Nortel logo on it.

10. Canadian sports broadcaster, Foster Hewitt, created a sports catch phrase "He shoots! He scores!" during an overtime game between the Rangers and the Leafs on April 4, 1933. The Rangers won.

Correct the following paragraph, which contains 20 errors (each set of dashes and parentheses counts as two errors).

As a final review of punctuation here's a paragraph that should contain all the punctuation marks we have discussed in this section of the book however 20 pieces of punctuation are missing. Your job is to provide the missing punctuation. Let's quickly deal with punctuation marks one by one. The comma probably the hardest-working of them all is used to separate items in a series to set off nonessential material to join with a conjunction to separate independent clauses and to set off material that comes before a main clause. Whew. The semicolon can replace a period it often separates two independent clauses that are closely connected in meaning. The colon has a different function it follows an independent clause and introduces a list a clarification or a quotation. Did you remember that a colon should never follow "is" or "are". A question mark must be used at the end of all interrogative sentences. We all know this but sometimes we forget. Exclamation marks are used at the end of sentences for one purpose only to supply dramatic effect. But remember that they are seldom used in academic writing. Finally dashes and parentheses allow a writer to interrupt a train of thought and insert an "aside" into a sentence. That's it. If you have correctly inserted all the punctuation in this paragraph then you are ready to tackle Hazardous Homonyms.

Punctuation

37

Hazardous Homonyms

This chapter focuses on homonyms—words that sound alike or look alike and are easily confused: *accept* and *except*; *weather* and *whether*; *whose* and *who's*; *affect* and *effect*. A spell checker will not help you find spelling mistakes in these words because the "correct" spelling depends on the sentence in which you use the word. For example, if you write, "Meat me hear inn halve an our," no spell checker will find fault with your sentence—and no reader will understand what you're talking about.

Careful pronunciation can sometimes help you tell the difference between words that are often confused. For example, if you pronounce the words *accept* and *except* differently, you'll be less likely to use the wrong one when you write. You can also make up memory aids to help you remember the difference in meaning between words that sound or look alike.

Below is a list of the most common homonym hazards. Only some of the words on this list will cause you trouble. Make your own list of problem pairs and tape it on the inside cover of your dictionary or post it close to your computer. Get into the habit of checking your document against your list every time you write.

accept except	*Accept* means "take" or "receive." It is always a verb. *Except* means "excluding." I **accepted** the spelling award, and no one **except** my mother knew I cheated.
advice advise	The difference in pronunciation makes the difference in meaning clear. *Advise* (rhymes with *wise*) is a verb. *Advice* (rhymes with *nice*) is a noun. I *advise* you not to listen to free *advice*.

affect effect	*Affect* as a verb means "change." Try substituting *change* for the word you've chosen in your sentence. If it makes sense, then *affect* is the word you want. As a noun, *áffect* means "a strong feeling." *Effect* is a noun meaning "result." If you can substitute *result,* then *effect* is the word you need. Occasionally, *effect* is used as a verb meaning "to bring about."

> Learning about the *effects* (results) of caffeine *affected* (changed) my coffee-drinking habits.
> Depressed people often display inappropriate *affect* (feelings).
> Antidepressant medications can *effect* (bring about) profound changes in mood.

a lot allot	*A lot* (often misspelled *alot*) should be avoided in formal writing. Use *many* or *much* instead. *Allot* means "distribute" or "assign."

>   *many*   *much*
> He still has ~~a lot of~~ problems, but he is coping ~~a lot~~ better.
> The teacher will *allot* the marks according to the difficulty of the questions.

aloud allowed	*Aloud* means out loud, not a whisper. *Allowed* means permitted.

> We were not *allowed* to speak *aloud* during the performance.

amount number	*Amount* is used with uncountable things; *number* is used with countable things.

> You may have a large *number* of jelly beans in a jar but a small *amount* of candy.
> (Jelly beans are countable; candy is not.)

are our	*Are* is a verb. *Our* shows ownership.

> Marie-Claire Blais and Margaret Atwood *are* two of Canada's best-known writers.

> Canada is *our* home and native land.

assure ensure insure	*Assure* means "state with confidence; pledge or promise."

> She *assured* him she would keep his letters always.

> The prime minister *assured* the Inuit their concerns would be addressed in the near future.

Ensure means "make certain of something."

> The extra $20 will *ensure* that you get a good seat.
>
> No number of promises can *ensure* that love will last.

Insure means "guarantee against financial loss." We *insure* lives and property.

> Kevin *insured* the book before he sent it airmail.
>
> We have *insured* both our home and our car against fire and theft.

choose
chose

Pronunciation gives the clue here. *Choose* rhymes with *booze* and means "select." *Chose* rhymes with *rose* and means "selected."

> Please *choose* a topic.
>
> I *chose* filmmaking.

cite
sight
site

To *cite* is to quote or mention. A lawyer *cites* precedents. Writers *cite* their sources in research papers. You might *cite* a comedian for her wit or a politician for his honesty. A *site* is a place.

> You have included only Internet sources in your Works *Cited* list.
>
> The Plains of Abraham is the *site* of a famous battle.
>
> Tiananmen Square is the *site* of the massacre.
>
> Pape and Mortimer is the *site* of our new industrial design centre.

A *sight* is something you see.

> With his tattooed forehead and three nose rings, he was a *sight* to behold.

coarse
course

Coarse means "rough, unrefined." (Remember: the word *arse* is co*arse*.) For all other meanings, use *course*.

> That sandpaper is too *coarse*.
> You'll enjoy the photography *course*.
> Of *course* you'll do well.

| complement compliment | A *complement* completes something. A *compliment* is a **gift** of praise. |

> A glass of wine would be the perfect *complement* to the meal.
>
> Some people are embarrassed by *compliments*.

| conscience conscious | Your *conscience* is your sense of right and wrong. *Conscious* means "aware" or "awake"—able to feel and think. |

> After Katy cheated on the test, her *conscience* bothered her.
>
> Katy was *conscious* of having done wrong.
>
> The injured man was *unconscious* for an hour.

| consul council counsel | A *consul* is a government official stationed in another country. A *council* is an assembly or official group. (Members of a council are *councillors*.) *Counsel* can be used to mean both "advice" and "to advise." (Those who give advice are *counsellors*.) |

> The Canadian *consul* in Mexico was very helpful.
>
> The Women's Advisory *Council* meets next month.
>
> Maria gave me good *counsel*.
>
> She *counselled* me to hire a lawyer.

| continual continuous | *Continual* refers to an action that goes on regularly but with interruptions. *Continuous* refers to an action that goes on without interruption. |

> The student *continually* tried to interrupt the lecturer, who droned on *continuously*.
>
> There is a *continuous* flow of traffic during rush hour.

| credible credulous creditable | *Credible* means "believable"; *credulous* describes the person who believes an incredible story. |

> Nell was fortunate that the police officer found her story *credible*.
>
> My brother is so *credulous* that we call him Gullible Gus.

Creditable means "worthy of reward or praise."

Spelling

After two semesters, Eva has finally begun to produce *creditable* work.

desert
dessert

A *désert* is a dry, barren place. As a verb, *desért* means "leave behind." *Dessért* is the part of the meal you'd probably like a double serving of, so give it a double *s*.

The tundra is Canada's only *desert* region.
My neighbour *deserted* her husband and children.
Dessert is my favourite part of the meal.

dining
dinning

You'll spell *dining* correctly if you remember the phrase "wining and dining." You'll probably never use *dinning*. It means "making a loud noise."

The children are in the *dining* room.
We are *dining* out tonight.
The noise from the bar was *dinning* in our ears.

disburse
disperse

Disburse means "to pay out money," which is what **bur**sars do. *Disperse* means "to break up"; crowds are sometimes *dispersed* by the **p**olice.

The college's financial-aid officer will *disburse* the students' loans at the end of this week.
The protesters were *dispersed* by the police.

does
dose

Pronunciation provides the clue. *Does* rhymes with *buzz* and is a verb. *Dose* rhymes with *gross* and refers to a quantity of medicine.

John *does* drive quickly, doesn't he?
My grandmother gave me a *dose* of cod liver oil.

farther
further

You'll have no trouble distinguishing between these two if you associate *farther* with *distance* and *further* with *time*.

Dana wanted me to walk a little *farther* so we could discuss our relationship *further*.

faze
phase

Fazed usually has a *not* before it; to be *not fazed* means to be not disturbed, or concerned, or taken aback. *Phase* means "stage of development or process."

Unfortunately, Theo was not the least bit *fazed* by his disastrous grade report.

Since Mei Ling works full-time, she has decided to complete her degree in *phases*.

fewer less	*Fewer* is used with countable things, *less* with uncountable things.

In May, there are *fewer* students in the college, so there is *less* work for the faculty to do.

The *fewer* attempts you make, the *less* your chance of success.

With units of money or measurement, however, use *less*:

I have *less* than $20 in my wallet.

Our house is on a lot that is *less* than four metres wide.

forth fourth	*Forth* means "forward" or "onward." *Fourth* contains the number *four*, which gives it its meaning.

Please stop pacing back and *forth*.

The B.C. Lions lost their *fourth* game in a row.

hear here	*Hear* is what you do with your **ears**. *Here* is used for all other meanings.

Now *hear* this!

Ray isn't *here*.

Here is your assignment.

imply infer	A speaker or writer *implies*; a listener or reader *infers*. To *imply* is to hint or say something indirectly. To *infer* is to draw a conclusion from what is stated or hinted at.

I *inferred* from his sarcastic remarks that he was not very fond of Sheila.

In her introduction of the speaker, Sheila *implied* that she greatly admired him.

it's its	*It's* is a shortened form of *it is*. The apostrophe takes the place of the *i* in *is*. If you can substitute *it is*, then *it's* is the form you need. If you can't substitute *it is*, then *its* is the correct word.

Spelling

It's really not difficult. (*It is* really not difficult.)

The book has lost *its* cover. ("The book has lost *it is* cover" makes no sense, so you need *its*.)

It's is also commonly used as the shortened form of *it has*. In this case, the apostrophe replaces the *ha* in *has*.

It's been a good year for us.

later latter	*Later* refers to time and has the word **late** in it. *Latter* means "the second of two" and has two *t*s. It is the opposite of *former*. It is *later* than you think. You take the former, and I'll take the *latter*.
loose lose	Pronunciation is the key to these words. *Loose* rhymes with *goose* and means "not tight." *Lose* rhymes with *ooze* and means "misplace" or "be defeated." A *loose* electrical connection is dangerous. Some are born to win, some to *lose*.
martial marshal	*Martial* refers to warfare or military affairs. *Marshal* has two meanings. As a noun, it refers to a person who has high office, either in the army or (especially in the United States) the police. As a verb, it means to arrange or assemble in order. She is a *martial* arts enthusiast. When the troops were *marshalled* on the parade grounds, they were reviewed by the army *marshal*.
miner minor	A **miner** works in a **mine**. *Minor* means "lesser" or "not important." For example, a *minor* is a person of less than legal age. Liquor can be served to *miners*, but not if they are *minors*. For me, spelling is a *minor* problem.

moral morale	Again, pronunciation provides the clue you need. *Móral* refers to the understanding of what is right and wrong. *Morále* refers to the spirit or mental condition of a person or group.

> People often have to make *moral* decisions.
> The low *morale* of the workers prompted the strike.

peace piece	*Peace* is what we want on **Earth**. *Piece* means "a part or portion of something," as in "a **piece** of **pie**."

> Everyone hopes for *peace* in the Middle East.
> A *piece* of the puzzle is missing.

personal personnel	*Personal* means "private." *Personnel* refers to the group of people working for a particular employer or to the office responsible for maintaining employees' records.

> The letter was marked *"Personal* and Confidential."
> We are fortunate in having qualified *personnel.*
> Fatima works in the *Personnel* Office.

principal principle	*Principal* means "main." A *principle* is a rule.

> A *principal* is the main administrator of a school.
> Oil is Alberta's *principal* industry.
> I make it a *principle* to submit my essays on time.

quiet quite	If you pronounce these words carefully, you won't confuse them. *Quiet* has two syllables; *quite* has only one.

> The librarian asked us to be *quiet.*
> We had not *quite* finished our homework.

roll role	Turning over and over like a wheel is to *roll*; a bun is also a *roll*. An actor playing a part is said to have a *role*.

> His *role* called for him to fall to the ground and *roll* into
> a ditch, all the while munching on a bread *roll*.

Spelling

simple simplistic	*Simple* means uncomplicated, easily understood. Something described as *simplistic* is too simple to be acceptable; essential details or complexities have been overlooked.

> This problem is far from *simple*. Your solution to it is *simplistic*.

stationary stationery	*Stationary* means "fixed in place." *Stationery* is writing paper.

> Sarah Ferguson works out on a *stationary* bicycle.
>
> Please order a new supply of *stationery*.

than then	*Than* is used in comparisons. Pronounce it to rhyme with *can*. *Then* refers to time and rhymes with *when*.

> Rudi is a better speller *than* I.
>
> He made his decision *then*.
>
> Eva withdrew from the competition; *then* she realized the consequences.

their there they're	*Their* indicates ownership. **There** points out something or indicates place. It includes the word *here*, which also indicates place. *They're* is a shortened form of *they are*. (The apostrophe replaces the *a* in *are*.)

> It was *their* fault.
>
> *There* are two weeks left in the term.
>
> You should look over *there*.
>
> *They're* late, as usual.

too two to	The *too* with an extra *o* in it means "more than enough" or "also." *Two* is the number after one. For all other meanings, use *to*.

> He thinks he's been working *too* hard. She thinks so *too*.
>
> There are *two* sides *to* every argument.
>
> The *two* women knew *too* much about each other *to* be friends.

weather whether wether	*Whether* means "which of the two" and is used in all cases when you aren't referring to the climatic conditions outside (*weather*). A *wether* is a castrated ram, so that word's uses are limited.

Whether you're ready or not, it's time to go.

No one immigrates to Canada for its *weather*.

were where we're	If you pronounce these three carefully, you won't confuse them. *Were* rhymes with *fur* and is a verb. **Where** is pronounced "hwear," includes the word **here**, and indicates place. *We're* is a shortened form of *we are* and is pronounced "weer."

You were joking, *weren't* you?

Where did you want to meet?

We're on our way.

who's whose	*Who's* is a shortened form of *who is* or *who has*. If you can substitute *who is* or *who has* for the *who's* in your sentence, then you are using the right spelling. Otherwise, use *whose*.

Who's coming to dinner? (*Who is* coming to dinner?)

Who's been sleeping in my bed? (*Who has* been sleeping in my bed?)

Whose calculator is this? ("*Who is* calculator" makes no sense, so you need *whose*.)

woman women	Confusing these two is guaranteed to irritate your female readers. *Woman* is the singular form; compare **man**. *Women* is the plural form; compare **men**.

A *woman's* place is wherever she chooses to be.

The *women's* movement promotes equality between women and men.

you're your	*You're* is a shortened form of *you are*. If you can substitute *you are* for the *you're* in your sentence, then you're using the correct form. If you can't substitute *you are*, use *your*.

You're welcome. (*You are* welcome.)

Unfortunately, *your* hamburger got burned. ("*You are* hamburger" makes no sense, so *your* is the word you want.)

In Exercises 37.1 and 37.2, choose the correct word from those in parentheses. If you don't know an answer, go back and reread the explanation. Check your answers after each set. Answers for this chapter begin on page 543.

Exercise 37.1*

1. The limited (coarse course) selection will (affect effect) our academic development and subsequent job opportunities.
2. (Are Our) you going to (accept except) the offer?
3. Eat your vegetables; (than then) you can have your (desert dessert).
4. If (your you're) overweight by 20 kg, (loosing losing) the excess will be a long-term proposition.
5. It's (quiet quite) true that they did not get (hear here) until 2:00 a.m.
6. It is usually the saint, not the sinner, (who's whose) (conscience conscious) is troubled.
7. He (assured ensured insured) me he would keep the (amount number) of changes to a minimum.
8. (Its It's) hard to tell the dog from (its it's) owner.
9. To (choose chose) a (coarse course) of action against your lawyer's (advice advise) would be foolish.
10. (Continual Continuous) (dining dinning) out becomes boring after a while.

Exercise 37.2*

1. It is (simple simplistic) to claim that our society's (morals morales) have declined drastically over the last 20 years; to do so (infers implies) that morality is an absolute value.
2. After the accident, the (moral morale) of the (miners minors) did not recover for many months, but the owners appeared not to be (fazed phased) by the disaster.
3. The chief librarian did not mean to (imply infer) that (farther further) cuts to services are being considered by the board, which, in the circumstances, has done a very (credible credulous creditable) job.
4. The (affect effect) of trying to (disperse disburse) the mob of (less fewer) than 20 people was to cause a riot involving hundreds.
5. (Who's Whose) (principals principles) are so firm that they wouldn't pay (fewer less) tax if they could get away with it?
6. By reading between the lines, we can (infer imply) (wether weather whether) the author intends his (forth fourth) chapter to be taken seriously.

7. It's (your you're) fault that we are (continually continuously) harassed by salespeople because your welcoming smile (assures insures ensures) that they will return again and again.

8. Are you (conscious conscience) of the fact that (choosing chosing) this (site cite sight) for your business will take you (farther further) away from your client base?

9. Gloria could not (accept except) the fact that the (councillors counsellors) rejected her plan to (phase faze) out parking in the downtown core.

10. The (amount number) of people (aloud allowed) to participate depends on (fewer less) (then than) a dozen (woman women) who are entrusted with making the decision.

_____(Exercise 37.3*)

Each of the items below is followed by two statements. Identify the one that makes sense as a follow-up to the introductory sentence.

1. All former students will be welcomed back to class.
   a. We will except all former students.
   b. We will accept all former students.

2. The lawn mower next door has been running nonstop for over an hour.
   a. The continual noise is driving me crazy.
   b. The continuous noise is driving me crazy.

3. This author only hints at how the story ends.
   a. She implies that they live happily ever after.
   b. She infers that they live happily ever after.

4. Your proposal is not worth our consideration
   a. It's simple.
   b. It's simplistic.

5. We're looking for a female role model.
   a. The women must lead by example.
   b. The woman must lead by example.

6. How many assistants will be required?
   a. The amount of help we will need is hard to estimate.
   b. The number of helpers we will need is hard to estimate.

7. While their skill sets are very different, together, the two make a good team.
   a. She compliments his weaknesses.
   b. She complements his weaknesses.

8. Are you permitted to talk during the lectures?
   a. It is not allowed.
   b. It is not aloud.

Spelling

9. When did she wake up?
   a. She regained her conscience during the prayers.
   b. She regained her consciousness during the prayers.
10. How many kilometres are left in your journey?
    a. We have only a little farther to go.
    b. We have only a little further to go.

GO TO WEB

EXERCISES 37.1, 37.2, 37.3, 37.4

Exercise 37.4

Now test your mastery of homonyms by correcting the 10 errors in the following paragraph.

I would advice anyone who's schedule seems to be full to try the solution I came up with less then three months ago. I pulled the plug on my TV. Overwhelmed with assignments and unable to chose among priorities, I realized I was making the problem worse by sitting for three or four hours a night in front of the tube. I decided I should spend more time on my coarses and less on watching television. To avoid temptation, I put the TV set in the closet. The results have been more dramatic then I thought possible. My apartment is now a haven of piece and quiet, and some of my assignments are actually handed in before their due. Occasionally there is a twinge of regret that I no longer know whose doing what to whom in the latest reality contest, but overall, I'm much happier for choosing to loose the tube.

38

The Apostrophe

Most punctuation marks indicate the relationship among parts of a sentence. Apostrophes and hyphens, on the other hand, indicate the relationship between the elements of a word. That's why we've chosen to discuss them in this section, along with other spelling issues.

Misused apostrophes display a writer's ignorance or carelessness. They can also confuse, amuse, and sometimes annoy readers.

- Sometimes you need an apostrophe so that your reader can understand what you mean. For example, there's a world of difference between these two sentences:

  The instructor began class by calling the students' names.

  The instructor began class by calling the students names.

- In most cases, however, misused apostrophes just amuse or irritate an alert reader:

  The movie had it's moments.

  He does a days work for every weeks salary.

  The Lion's thank you for your contribution.

It isn't difficult to avoid such mistakes. Correctly used, the apostrophe indicates either **contraction** or **possession**. It never makes a singular word plural. Learn the simple rules that govern these uses and you'll have no further trouble with apostrophes.

Spelling

Contraction

Contraction is the combining of two words into one, as in *they're* or *can't*. Contractions are common in conversation and in informal written English. Unless you are quoting someone else's words, however, you should avoid them in the writing you do for college or work.

The rule about where to put an apostrophe in a contraction is one of those rare rules that has no exception. It *always* holds.

> When two words are combined into one, and one or more letters are left out, the apostrophe goes in the place of the missing letter(s).

Here are some examples.

I am	→ I'm	they are	→ they're
we will	→ we'll	it is	→ it's
she is	→ she's	it has	→ it's
do not	→ don't	who has	→ who's

Exercise 38.1*

Correct these sentences by placing apostrophes where needed. Answers for this chapter begin on page 544.

1. Yes, its a long way from Halifax to Vancouver, but weve been in training for three months.
2. Were taking the train to Antigonish, and were biking to Halifax; then well begin the big trip west.
3. There wasnt a dry eye in the theatre when Spielbergs film reached its climax.
4. Whos discovered whats wrong with this sentence?
5. Wasnt it Mark Twain who said, "Its easy to stop smoking; Ive done it dozens of times"?

GO TO WEB

EXERCISES 38.1, 38.2

In some formal kinds of writing—academic, legal, and technical, for example—contractions are not acceptable. A good writer is able not only to contract two words into one, but also to expand any contraction into its original form: a two-word phrase. In the following paragraph, find and expand the contractions into their original form.

I'm writing to apply for the position of webmaster for BrilloVision.com that you've advertised in the *Daily News*. I've got the talent and background you're looking for. Currently, I work as a Web designer for an online publication, Vexed.com, where they're very pleased with my work. If you click on their website, I think you'll like what you see. There's little in the way of Web design and application that I haven't been involved in during the past two years. But it's time for me to move on to a new challenge, and BrilloVision.com promises the kind of opportunity I'm looking for. I guarantee you won't be disappointed if I join your team!

Possession

The apostrophe is also used to show ownership or possession. Here's the rule that applies in most cases.

> Add 's to the word that indicates the *owner*.
> If the resulting word ends in a double or triple *s*, delete the last *s*, leaving the apostrophe in place.[1]

---

[1]Many writers today prefer to keep the final *s* when it represents a sound that is pronounced, as it is in one-syllable words such as *boss* and *class*, and in some names such as *Harris* and *Brutus*.

Spelling

Here are some examples that illustrate the rule.

singer + 's = singer's voice
band + 's = band's instruments
players + 's = players'$ uniforms

women + 's = women's voices
student + 's = student's transcript
students + 's = students'$ transcripts

To form a possessive correctly, you must first identify the word in the sentence that indicates possession and determine whether it is singular or plural. For example, "the managers duties" can have two meanings, depending on where you put the apostrophe:

the manager's duties (the duties belong to one *manager*)
the managers' duties (the duties belong to two or more *managers*)

To solve an apostrophe problem, follow this two-step process:
1. Find the owner word.
2. Apply the possession rule.

Problem: Carmens hair is a mess.
Solution: 1. The word that indicates possession is *Carmen* (singular).
         2. Add 's to *Carmen*.

Carmen's hair is a mess.

Problem: The technicians strike halted the production.
Solution: 1. The word that indicates possession is *technicians* (plural).
         2. Add 's to *technicians*, then delete the second *s*, leaving the apostrophe.

The *technicians'* strike halted the production.

Sometimes the meaning of your sentence is determined by where you put the apostrophe.

Problem: I was delighted by the critics response to my book.

Now you have two possibilities to choose from, depending on your meaning.

Solution A: 1. The owner word is *critic* (singular).
          2. Add 's to *critic*.

I was delighted by the *critic's* response to my book.

Solution B: 1. The owner word is *critics* (plural).
2. Add *'s* to *critics*, then drop the second *s*, leaving the apostrophe.

I was delighted by the *critics'* response to my book.

Both solutions are correct, depending on whether the book was reviewed by one critic (A) or by more than one critic (B).

Possession does not have to be literal. It can be used to express the notion of "belonging to" or "associated with." That is, the owner word need not refer to a person or group of people. Ideas or concepts (abstract nouns) can be "owners" too.

a month's vacation = a vacation of one month
a year's salary = the salary of one year
"A Hard Day's Night" = the night that follows a hard day

Note that a few words, called **possessive pronouns**, are already possessive in form, so they don't have apostrophes.[2]

yours   ours   whose
hers, his, its   theirs

His music is not like *yours.*

Whose lyrics do you prefer, *theirs* or *ours*?

The dog lost *its* bone.

Four of these possessive pronouns are often confused with the contractions that sound like them. It's worth taking a moment to learn how to avoid this confusion. When you are trying to decide which spelling to use,

1. Expand the contraction into its original two words.
2. Then substitute those words for the contraction in your sentence.
3. If the sentence still makes sense, use the contraction. If it doesn't, use the possessive spelling.

---

[2]If you add an apostrophe to any of these words, you create an error. There are no such words as *your's, her's, their's,* or *our's.*

Spelling

Possessive		Contraction	
its	= *It* owns something	it's	= it is/it has
their	= *They* own something	they're	= they are
whose	= *Who* owns something	who's	= who is/who has
your	= *You* own something	you're	= you are

Error: They're (they are) going to sing they're (~~they are~~) latest song.
Revision: They're going to sing *their* latest song.

Exercises 38.3 and 38.4 will test and reinforce your understanding of both contraction and possession.

Exercise 38.3*

Correct the following sentences by adding apostrophes where necessary.

1. The cars brakes are worn and its tires are nearly bald.
2. Diplomatic ambassadors wives or husbands are often as important to a missions success as the ambassadors themselves.
3. Near Chicoutimi is one of the countrys most beautiful parks, where the skills of canoeists, fishermen, and wildlife photographers can be put to the test on a summers day.
4. Janis career got its start when she sang seafarers songs in the yacht clubs dining lounge.
5. A countrys history is the main determinant of its national character.

Exercise 38.4*

In each of the sentences below, choose the correct word from those in parentheses. Check your answers before going on.

1. Where (your you're) going, (your you're) biggest problem will be maintaining (your you're) health.
2. (Someones Someone's) got to take responsibility for the large numbers of domestic animals (whose who's) owners have abandoned them.
3. The (ships ship's ships') captain agreed to donate a (weeks week's weeks') salary to the Scott Mission.
4. Contrary to some (people's peoples) opinions, postal (workers worker's workers') contracts are most often settled by both (sides side's sides') willingness to bend long before a strike is necessary.
5. My (turtles turtle's) legs are shorter than your (turtles turtle's), but I bet (its it's) going to run (its it's) laps faster than (yours your's).

EXERCISES 38.3, 38.4

Plurals

The third apostrophe rule is very simple. Memorize it, apply it, and you will instantly correct many of your apostrophe errors.

Never use an apostrophe to make a word plural.

The plural of most English words is formed by adding *s* to the root word (not *'s*). The *s* alone tells the reader that the word is plural: e.g., *memos, letters, files, broadcasts, newspapers, journalists.* If you add an apostrophe + *s*, you are telling your reader that the word is either a contraction or a possessive.

Incorrect: Never use apostrophe's to make word's plural.
Correct: Never use apostrophes to make words plural.

Exercise 38.5*

Correct the misused and missing apostrophes in the following sentences. There are 10 errors in this exercise.

1. When you feel like a snack, you can choose between apples and Timbit's.

2. Annas career took off when she discovered its easy to sell childrens toys.

3. Golfing requires the use of different club's: woods for long shots, irons for short ones.

4. Poker's an easy game to play if you are dealt ace's more often than your opponent's are.

5. Good writing skill's dont guarantee success in you're career, but they help.

Spelling

Exercise 38.6

Before you try the final exercise in this chapter, carefully review the information in the Summary box below. Then test your mastery of apostrophes by correcting the 15 errors in the passage below.

The following advisory for American's heading to Canada was compiled from information provided by the U.S. State Department and the CIA. It is intended as a guide for American traveller's:

Canada is a large foreign country, even bigger than Texas. It has 10 states (called provinces) and it's only neighbour is America. Canadas contributions to Western civilization include bacon, hockey players, geese, doughnut's, and the Mountie's red uniform's.

Canadians stand in line without complaining, seldom raise they're voices, and cheer politely when the home or visiting teams players do something worthwhile. Canada has two language's: French and American. Other linguistic oddities include "eh," which can turn any statement into a question, and the pronunciation of *ou* as *uoo*, as in *huoose* or *abuoot*.

The bright color's and funny picture's of Canadian currency may make the unwary tourist think of it as play money, but each blue Canadian five-dollar bill is worth about two real dollars. The one- and two-dollar coins, called loonies and toonies, make good souvenir's.

The Canadian government is somewhat left-leaning, providing health care for all and refusing to execute criminal's. Tourists are advised to avoid all political discussion and to remember that politician's in Canada are like politician's anywhere: popular with some people, unpopular with others.

Summary

- When contracting two words into one, put an apostrophe in the place of the missing letters.
- Watch for owner words: they need apostrophes.
- To indicate possession, add *'s* to the owner word. (If the owner word already ends in *s*, just add the apostrophe.)
- Possessive pronouns (e.g., *yours, its, ours*) do not take apostrophes.
- Never use an apostrophe to form the plural of a word.

39

The Hyphen

The **hyphen** (-) has three different functions:

- as part of the correct spelling of a word (e.g., mother-in-law, self-esteem)
- to divide a word at the end of a line
- to separate or join two or more words or parts of words. There are five rules to follow.

1. Use a hyphen to divide a word at the end of a written or typed line.

Your dictionary tells you where words can be divided. Most dictionaries mark the syllables of a word with a dot: syl·lables = syl-lables.

Never divide a word of only one or two syllables. Use a hyphen at the end of a line for words of three or more syllables (e.g., commu-nity). If the word is already hyphenated (e.g., self-reliance, ex-president), break it after the hyphen.

2. Use a hyphen to separate a prefix from the main word when two of the same vowels occur together.

Examples: re-elected, co-operate, anti-imperalism

When the two vowels are different, however, no hyphen is required: semiautomatic, realign, preamble

3. Use a hyphen with compound numbers from twenty-one to ninety-nine, with fractions, and with dimensions.

Examples: forty-six, one-eighth, ninety-eight, six-by-eight

4. Use a hyphen to join two or more words that serve as an adjective *before* a noun.

Examples: The (first-born) child is often the best loved.

The (best-loved) child is often the first born.

(Word-of-mouth) advertising is very effective.

A good writer has a (well-thumbed, up-to-date) dictionary.

5. Use a hyphen to avoid ambiguity.

Examples: The contractor re-covered the roof with asphalt shingles. (He repaired the roof.)

The contractor recovered his money. (He got his money back.)

The government's plan provided for nursing-home care. (care in a nursing home)

The government's plan provided for nursing home-care. (care at home by nurses)

The prime minister will address small business owners. (Do you really want to say he will talk only to short people?)

The prime minister will address small-business owners. (These people are owners of small businesses.)

Exercise 39.1*

Most of the following sentences require one or more hyphens. Review the rules in the boxes above, then try your hand at correcting these sentences. Answers for this chapter are on page 545.

1. Jill decided to sublet her fifth floor apartment.

2. Fraser claims he is allergic to classical music but addicted to hip hop music.
3. Just before the critical play, the hard fought game was preempted by the movie *Heidi*!
4. Hand knit sweaters are usually more expensive than factory produced ones.
5. In 1950, at the age of forty seven, George Orwell died of tuberculosis.

GO TO WEB

EXERCISE 39.1

Exercise 39.2*

In the following sentences, some hyphens are missing, and some are included where they don't belong. Correct the errors in these sentences.

1. For months after Saddam Hussein was over-thrown, the world was shocked by revelations of the repression suffered by the Iraqi people.
2. Would you re-lay this message to Mr. Chan: the masons would like to relay the bricks this evening?
3. Our next door neighbour teaches in a high-school, but she does not like to be introduced as a high school teacher.
4. A face to face meeting with an antiintellectual always gets my adrenalin going.
5. Because Angela was an attorney at law and had once been an all Canadian athlete, her former coach was not surprised when she became Minister-of-Recreation.

Exercise 39.3

This last exercise is a mastery test. Insert hyphens where they are needed and delete them where they are not.

1. At 20 years-of-age, Trudy began to reorganize her life.
2. Because she is the instructor who is the most up to date with trends in the industry, Alysha is the coordinator of our program.
3. Only one third of the team seemed to be reenergized by the 20 minute break.
4. Vernon wore his hand tailored three piece suit to his former-girlfriend's wedding.
5. In spite of its country garden atmosphere, the hotel's up to the minute décor and facilities could not be faulted.

Spelling

6. The space shuttle will reenter the atmosphere in exactly eighty five seconds.
7. Tim began to recover from his career threatening injury after taking an antiinflammatory.
8. Some very successful businesses are coowned by the employees; these cooperative ventures ensure that workers' hard earned dollars are put to work on their-own behalf.
9. Computer generated graphics are ninety nine percent of our over the counter business.
10. Trevor was treated for post traumatic stress after his no hope last minute attempt to pass chemistry.

40

Capital Letters

Capital letters belong in a few specific places and nowhere else. Some writers suffer from "capitalitis." They put capital letters on words without thinking about their position or function in a sentence.

Capitalize the first letter of a word that fits into one of the six categories listed below:

1. The first word of a sentence, a direct quotation, or a sentence from a quoted source.

Are you illiterate? Write to us today for free help.
The supermodel cooed, "I just love the confidence makeup gives me."
Lister Sinclair claims that the only thing Canadians have in common is that "We all hate Toronto."

Exercise 40.1*

Add the seven missing capital letters to the following sentences. Answers for exercises in this chapter begin on page 545.

1. time is nature's way of keeping everything from happening at once.

2. Brad sang, "there's a light in the Frankenstein house."

3. Learning Standard english is, for many people, like learning another Language.

4. Richard Harkness, writing in *The New York Times*, said "a committee is a group of the unwilling, picked from the unfit, to do the unnecessary."

Spelling

5. in conclusion, I want you to consider the words of Wendell Johnson: "*always* and *never* are two words you should always remember never to use."

---

2. The names of specific people, places, and things.

Names of people (and their titles):

Shania Twain, Governor General Michaëlle Jean, the Rev. Henry Jones, the Hon. Eugene Forsey, Senator Anne Cools

Names of places, regions, and astronomical bodies (but not general geographic directions):

Stanley Park, Lake Superior, Cape Breton Island; Nunavut, the Prairie Provinces, the Badlands; Saturn, Earth, the Moon, the Asteroid Belt; south, north

Names of buildings, institutions, organizations, companies, departments, products, etc.:

the Empress Hotel; McGill University, Red Deer College; the Liberal Party, the Kiwanis Club; Petro-Canada, Radio Shack; the Department of English, the Human Resources Department; Kleenex, Volvo, Labatt's

Exercise 40.2*

Add capital letters where necessary in the following sentences. There are 30 errors in this exercise.

1. After a brief stay in the maritimes, captain tallman and his crew sailed west up the st. lawrence.

2. The broadcast department of niagara college has ordered six sony cameras for their studios in welland, ontario.

3. Do you find that visa is more popular than American express when you travel to faraway places such as mexico, france, or jupiter?

4. Our stay at the seaview hotel, overlooking the pacific ocean, certainly beat our last vacation at the bates motel, where we faced west, overlooking the city dump.

5. As the fundraiser for our alumni association, I am targeting companies like disney, canadian tire, the bank of montreal, and the cbc, all of which employ our graduates.

3. Names of major historical events, historical periods, religions, holy texts, and holy days.

World War II, the Depression; the Renaissance; Islam, Judaism, Christianity, Buddhism, Hinduism; the Torah, the Koran, the Bible, the Upanishads; Ramadan, Yom Kippur, Easter

Exercise 40.3

Add the 20 capital letters that are missing from the following sentences.

1. The crusades, which were religious wars between muslims and christians, raged through the middle ages.

2. The hindu religion recognizes and honours many gods; islam recognizes one god, allah; buddhism recognizes none.

3. The koran, the bible, and the torah agree on many principles.

4. The jewish festival of hanukkah often occurs near the same time that christians are celebrating christmas.

5. After world war I, many jews began to emigrate to Palestine, where they and the muslim population soon came into conflict.

Spelling

GO TO WEB

EXERCISE 40.1

4. The days of the week, months of the year, and specific holidays, but not the seasons.

Wednesday; January; Remembrance Day, Canada Day; spring, autumn

Exercise 40.4*

The following sentences contain both missing and unnecessary capitals. Find and correct the 15 errors.

1. My favourite months are january and february because I love all Winter sports.

2. This monday is valentine's day, when messages of love are exchanged.

3. In the summer, big meals seem too much trouble; however, after thanksgiving, we need lots of food to survive the winter cold.

4. A National Holiday named flag day was once proposed, but it was never officially approved.

5. By thursday, I'll have finished my st. patrick's day costume.

5. The main words in titles of published works (books, magazines, films; essays, poems, songs; works of art; etc.). Do not capitalize minor words (articles, prepositions, conjunctions) in titles unless the word is the first word in the title.

The Colony of Unrequited Dreams   *The Thinker*
Of Mice and Men   "An Immigrant's Split Personality"
Maclean's   "In Flanders Fields"
A Room with a View   "If I Had a Million Dollars"

Add the 30 capital letters that are missing from the following sentences.

1. The review of my book, *the life and times of a chocoholic*, published in *the globe and mail*, was not favourable.

2. Clint eastwood fans will be delighted that the two early movies that made him internationally famous, *a fistful of dollars* and *for a few dollars more,* are now available on DVD.

3. Joseph Conrad's short novel *heart of darkness* became the blockbuster movie *apocalypse now*.

4. My poem, "a bright and silent place," was published in the april issue of *landscapes* magazine.

5. Botticelli's famous painting, "birth of venus," inspired my poem "woman on the half shell."

Pay special attention to this next category. It is one that often causes trouble.

6. The names of specific school courses.

Marketing 101, Psychology 100, Mathematics 220, English 110,

but

a) not the names of general school subjects

    e.g., marketing, sociology, mathematics

b) *unless* the subjects are languages or pertain to specific geographical areas whose names are capitalized

    e.g., English, Greek, the study of Chinese history, modern Caribbean literature, Latin American poetry

(Names of languages, countries, and geographical regions are always capitalized.)

Exercise 40.6*

Add capital letters where necessary in the following sentences. There are ten errors in this exercise.

1. After studying geography for two years, I began taking courses in ancient greek and modern history.

2. We began our study of sociology with the concept of relationships.

3. By taking Professor Subden's noncredit course, introduction to wine, I qualified to register for oenology 120 the next semester.

4. While math is her strong subject, Laurie has trouble with accounting, english, and conversational french.

5. The prerequisite for theology 210 is introduction to world religions, taught by Professor Singh.

GO TO WEB

EXERCISE 40.2

Exercise 40.7

The following exercise is the mastery test and contains 30 errors. Before you begin, it would be a good idea to review the six capitalization rules presented in this chapter.

1. On the first official friday of Spring, we always celebrate by going fishing on lake winnipeg.

2. Failing Sociology is like eating soup with a fork: it's difficult, but you can do it if you really try.

3. July First is Canada day, when we celebrate the anniversary of confederation, which occurred in 1867.

4. Although Ms. Lau is a member of the new democratic party, she is quite Conservative in her thinking on Economic and social issues.

5. She may look like a sheep, but I'll have you know she's a purebred afghan hound.

6. Trying to learn english as quickly as possible, Wong Bao Lin took two Night School classes a week and listened to audiotapes several hours every day.

7. When travelling abroad, canadians can readily identify each other by their mountain equipment co-op backpacks, tilley hats, and roots clothing.

8. If I drop Math and Accounting, I will be able to concentrate on english and Marketing, but it will mean adding a semester to my program.

9. Citroen, Renault, and Peugeot are french cars that sell well in Europe, but have never caught on in north America.

10. Sally and Kendra are packing away the essentials like cigarettes, doritos, and Beer in preparation for the end of the World, which, they are convinced, will occur on December 31, 2010.

Spelling

41

Numbers

Numbers may be expressed as words (*one, four, nine*) or as figures (*1, 4, 9*), depending on the kind of assignment you are writing and what the numbers refer to. In a few circumstances, a combination of words and figures is required. In scientific and technical papers, numbers are normally given in figures; in humanities papers, numbers that can be expressed in one or two words are spelled out. For college papers, ask your instructor which style he or she prefers. For general purposes, including most business writing, follow the guidelines given below.

When to Use Words

1. Use words to express whole numbers one through nine and simple fractions. Use figures for numbers 10 and above.

The novel's three parts chronicle the nine-week journey of the five Acadian teenagers.

China and India together account for more than one-third of the Earth's population.

Approximately 30 years ago, Paul Henderson scored the most famous goal in the history of Canadian hockey.

There are two exceptions to this general rule.

A. Spell out any number that begins a sentence, or rewrite the sentence so that the number does not come first.

Incorrect: 157 students submitted essays to the awards committee.

Correct: One hundred and fifty-seven students submitted essays to the awards committee.

Also correct: The awards committee received essays from 157 students.

B. Use either figures *or* words to express numbers that modify the same or similar items in one sentence. (That is, be consistent within a sentence.)

We are looking for 3 accountants, 15 salespeople, and 2 customer service representatives. (*not* "three, 15, and two")

Only 9 of the 55 applicants had both the qualifications and the experience we required. (*not* "nine of the 55 applicants")

2. Treat ordinal numbers (first, second, etc.) as you would cardinal numbers (one, two, etc.).

Up to its sixth or seventh month, an infant can breathe and swallow at the same time.

In a 1904 speech, Sir Wilfrid Laurier declared that the 20th century would belong to Canada.

Exercise 41.1*

Applying the two highlighted rules in this chapter, correct any errors in the following sentences. Answers begin on page 547.

1. This applicant claims to speak more than 7 languages, but from her résumé, I'd say that English is not 1 of them.

2. This is the 3rd time the Accounting Department has filed its report 2 days late.

Spelling

3. 54 eager people have signed up for the 2nd annual Pool Tournament.

4. Of the 12 cuts on her new DVD release, the 1st two are my favourites.

5. Gavin, who works for the garage where I take my car, was unable to answer twelve of the twenty-three questions on the Mechanic Certification Exam.

6. In the Great Fire of 1666, 1/2 of London burned down, but only 6 people lost their lives.

7. If the diesel mixture contains 3/4 of a litre of regular gasoline, it will make your truck easier to start in those 4 or 5 really cold weeks of winter.

8. When I was twenty-seven and had been unemployed for nearly 3 years, I decided to return to college for 2 years of practical training.

9. In the United States, 1 of the reasons that hemp is illegal is that about eighty years ago, cotton growers lobbied against its cultivation because they saw it as competition.

10. Only eight out of forty-seven trivia players were able to name Jay Silverheels of Brantford, Ontario, as the original Tonto in *The Lone Ranger.*

GO TO WEB

EXERCISE 41.1

When to Use Figures

As a general rule, you should use figures when you are presenting technical or precise numerical information or when your sentence or paragraph contains several numbers.

3. Use figures to express dates, specific times, addresses, and percentages; with abbreviations or symbols; and with units of currency.

Dates	April 1, 2006, *or* 1 April 2006
Times	8:45 a.m. *or* 08:45, 7:10 p.m. *or* 19:10 (Use words with *o'clock*: e.g., *nine o'clock*)
Addresses	24 Sussex Drive, 2175 West 8th Street
Percentages	19 percent, a 6.5-percent interest rate (Use the % sign only with figures in tables or in series: e.g., "From 2003 to 2005, our sales increased by 8%, 13%, and 19%.")
With abbreviations or symbols	7 mm, 293 km, 60 km/h, 40 g, 54 kg, 18°C, 0.005 cm, 1.5 L, 8½", p. 3
Amounts of money	79 cents *or* $0.79, $2, $100, $30,000, $20 million, $65 billion (Use words if the unit of currency follows whole numbers one through nine: e.g., *two dollars*, *seven euro*s, unless the number includes a decimal: e.g., *1.5 trillion dollars*.)

Exercise 41.2*

With rule 3 in mind, correct the errors in the following sentences.

1. Researchers at Cornell University conducted a study that showed that sixty-six percent of all businessmen wear their ties too tight.

2. More than ten percent of those studied wore their ties so tight that blood flow to the brain was diminished.

3. 99 percent of the people who read the report wondered why Cornell had conducted such a study.

4. 1 plan is to retire on December seventeenth, 2055.

5. At precisely eight-ten p.m. on June third, your flight will leave for Whitehorse.

6. You will arrive at approximately 10 o'clock on June fourth if you make all your connections.

7. I won 5 dollars from Ted by proving that February Eighteen Sixty-five was the only month in recorded history not to have a full moon.

Spelling

8. You must be present at one thirty-three West Eighteenth Street by exactly 7:00 o'clock to claim your prize.

9. So far this year, I have spent thirty-eight thousand dollars, or twenty percent more than my anticipated income for the entire year, and it's only May fifteenth!

10. At the Indianapolis Speedway, the race cars burn approximately four L of fuel for each lap, while the ship *Queen Elizabeth II* moves just fifteen cm for every 4 L of fuel it burns.

GO TO WEB

EXERCISE 41.2

When to Use Both Words and Figures

4. When one number immediately follows another, spell out the one that makes the shorter word.
5. For numbers over a million, express introductory whole numbers 10 and above in figures, and the quantity in words. (If the numbers involve decimals, use figures.)

The Grey Cup is contested by *two 12-man* teams of heavily padded and helmeted warriors.

Our local car dealers sold more than *200 four-wheel* drive vehicles the day after our first big storm.

The human stomach contains more than *35 million* digestive glands.

The Earth's population in 2005 was *6.54 billion*.

The following exercises will test your ability to apply all of the rules and exceptions presented in this chapter.

_____ Exercise 41.3*

Correct any errors in the expression of numbers in the following sentences.

1. The speedboat is powered by 2 80-horsepower outboard motors.

2. 1 8-cylinder SUV emits more pollution than two four-cylinder Volkswagens or 3 Toyota gas-electric hybrids.

3. Because she sold seven $2,000,000 homes last year, she topped the agency's earnings list.

4. Eighty-two percent of people whose net worth is over two million dollars say they got rich by hard work.

5. 200 people were invited to celebrate my parents' twenty-fifth wedding anniversary on August Thirty-first, 2005.

6. A total of 10 fifteen-year-old girls and 4 fifteen-year-old boys applied for the commercial acting position we advertised.

7. Our lawyer told us that thirty-eight % of people who die between the ages of 45 and 54 have not prepared a will.

8. Canada's population of about 30,000,000 puts us in twenty-ninth place on the list of most populous countries.

9. 10 years ago, the average speed on urban freeways was fifty kph, but it has been steadily declining and is expected to be thirty kph within the next 5 years.

10. 7,000 ecstatic fans celebrated their team's unexpected two–one win in the Memorial Cup final, partying in the streets until four-thirty a.m.

GO TO WEB

EXERCISE 41.3

Spelling

Exercise 41.4

Before you tackle this final exercise, review the five highlighted rules given in this chapter. It's a good idea to write them out on a single sheet of paper and keep them before you as you go through this exercise. There are 15 errors in this paragraph.

Here's a news flash: Canadians trust neither politicians nor the media! A poll conducted for the CBC revealed that just under 2/3 of Canadians have little or no confidence in their political leaders. Furthermore, 1/3 of the respondents said they have little or no confidence in the media who report on the politicians; only eleven percent had a great deal of confidence in the media. But Canadians aren't just unhappy with the usual targets; they also have lost confidence in religious leaders (forty % have little or no confidence in them). Business leaders are slightly more trusted than religious leaders, with four % more people showing faith in them. In the poll, which surveyed just one thousand five hundred of Canada's 33,000,000 citizens, there was a little good news: seventy-two % of those polled said they didn't really expect politicians to keep their promises. That's down 2 percentage points from 2004. The CBC is careful to point out that the poll is accurate to within two point six percentage points nineteen times out of twenty, but even within that small margin of error, there is little here to surprise anyone. In their report on the poll, the CBC seemed most perturbed by the finding that so few had faith in the media. If Canadians are anything, it's news-savvy, and they are perfectly aware of the media's tendency to sensationalism, simplistic reporting of complex stories, and editorial bias. This distrust is most evident among young people: ask ten nineteen-year-old Canadians where they get their information about the world, and 8 will tell you, "The Internet."

List of Terms: A Vocabulary of Writing

The following list contains definitions of some common terms referring to syntax and style. For some of the terms, you will find further information in the book or on the *Essay Essentials* website (www.essayessentials4e. nelson.com). If a term you are looking for is not listed, check the index or consult your dictionary. For punctuation marks, see Chapters 31 to 36 and Chapters 38 and 39.

abstract, concrete	See **noun**.
active voice	See **voice**.
adjective	A word that modifies (describes) a noun or a pronoun. Adjectives usually answer the questions What kind? How many? Which? E.g., The *best* example; *three* strikes; *my morning* class. Nouns, phrases, and clauses can also function as adjectives: *ground* control; *up-to-the-minute* news. See also Parts of Speech on the *Essay Essentials* website.
adverb	A word that modifies a verb, adjective, or other adverb. Adverbs usually answer the questions When? How? Where? Why? How much? E.g., Nino talks fast (*fast* modifies the verb *talks*); he is a very fast talker (*very* modifies the adjective *fast*); he talks really fast (*really* modifies the adverb *fast*). Adverbs often—but not always—end in *-ly*. A phrase or a clause can also function as an adverb. See also Parts of Speech on the *Essay Essentials* website.
agreement	Grammatical correspondence in person and number between a verb and its subject, or in person, number, and gender between a pronoun and its antecedent. See Chapters 28 and 30.
analogy	A comparison between two dissimilar things that share at least one element or characteristic in common; e.g., Time is like a river. Just as the river flows from higher to lower ground, so time

flows from the past into the future. Analogies are often used for stylistic or dramatic effect as well as to explain or illustrate a point.

anecdote A short account of an event or incident, used to illustrate a point and sometimes intended to entertain. See paragraph 10 of Carol Geddes' "Growing Up Native" (page 165).

antecedent From Latin for "coming before; preceding." An antecedent is the word or words that a pronoun refers (usually back) to or stands for: My sister thinks *she* is always right (*sister* is the antecedent of the pronoun *she*).

article Often classed as adjectives, the definite article *the* and the indefinite articles *a* and *an* are "determiners" that precede nouns: *the* umpire; *a* baseball bat; *an* orange.

auxiliary A "helping" verb used with a main verb to form different tenses. The auxiliary verbs are *be, have, do, may, can, ought, must, shall, will* and their various forms.

clause A group of words containing a subject and a verb. If the group of words can stand by itself as a simple sentence, it is an **independent** (or **main**) **clause**: Great minds think alike. A **dependent** (or **subordinate**) **clause** cannot stand alone as a sentence; it must be linked to a main clause: *Because great minds think alike,* I am sure you will agree with me. See Chapter 23.

cliché A phrase that has become meaningless through overuse. See Chapter 2.

coherence The logical consistency and stylistic connections between ideas, sentences, and paragraphs in a piece of writing. See Chapter 8.

collective noun A noun that names a group; for example, class, faculty, jury, choir. Collective nouns are singular when the group is considered as a unit, plural when the focus is on individual members: The <u>class</u> <u>wants</u> a mid-term break. The <u>class</u> <u>have</u> not yet <u>handed</u> in *their* papers. See **agreement**.

colloquialism A word or group of words that is appropriate in casual conversation and informal—but not formal—writing. Some common examples are guy, kid, flunk.

comma splice Two independent clauses joined with a comma: The comma splice is a type of run-on sentence, it is a serious error. See Chapter 24.

complement A word or phrase that completes the meaning of a verb. Also called a **subjective completion**, a complement is a noun, pronoun, or adjective that follows a linking verb: Jamie is the *manager* (noun complement); The winner was *she* (pronoun complement); Her paper will be *excellent* (adjective complement).

complex sentence A sentence consisting of one independent clause and one or more subordinate clauses. See also Sentences: Kinds and Parts on the *Essay Essentials* website.

compound	Two or more grammatical elements (words, phrases, clauses) joined so that they function as a unit: *Hans, Peter, and Walter* are brothers (compound subject); Hans *works and studies* (compound verb); Peter expects an *A or a B+* (compound object). Also called **multiple** subjects, verbs, objects, or complements.
compound sentence	A sentence consisting of two or more independent clauses. See also Sentences: Kinds and Parts on the *Essay Essentials* website.
compound-complex sentence	A sentence consisting of two or more independent clauses and one or more subordinate clauses. See also Sentences: Kinds and Parts on the *Essay Essentials* website.
concrete, abstract	See **noun**.
conjunction	A part of speech. **Coordinating** conjunctions (*for, and, nor, but, or, yet, so*) join equal grammatical elements such as nouns, verbs, phrases, or clauses. **Subordinating** conjunctions are words or phrases that join dependent clauses to main clauses. Some examples are although, because, after, in order that, as soon as. See **dependent clause cues** in Chapter 23. For **correlative** conjunctions, see Parts of Speech on the *Essay Essentials* website.
conjunctive adverb	An adverb such as however, therefore, thus, and nevertheless used to indicate a logical relationship between two independent clauses. Conjunctive adverbs are preceded by a semicolon and followed by a comma: Jordan hates math; *therefore*, he is not going to be an engineer.
connotation	The positive or negative meaning associated with a word; for example, *slender* and *skinny* both mean *thin*, but to describe someone as *slender* is a compliment, while to describe someone as *skinny* suggests disapproval.
contraction	The combining of two words into one, spelled with an apostrophe to mark the missing letter or letters: isn't (is not), here's (here is), should've (should have). Contractions are not appropriate in formal writing unless they are part of quoted speech.
dangling modifier	See **modifier**.
declarative sentence	See Sentences: Kinds and Parts on the *Essay Essentials* website.
demonstrative	See **pronoun**.
denotation	The specific meaning of a word; the dictionary definition. Compare **connotation**.
dependent clause	See **clause**.
dependent clause cue	A word or phrase that introduces a dependent clause. See Chapter 23.

diction   A writer's choice and use of words. Diction is a feature of style and can be colloquial, informal, or formal. Within the context of a sentence, paragraph, or paper, diction can be appropriate (consistent and suitable to the target audience) or inappropriate (inconsistent and unsuited to the target audience).

direct object   See **object**.

ellipsis   The three spaced periods (. . .) used to indicate that a word or words have been omitted from a quoted passage. See Chapter 19.

exclamatory sentence   See Sentences: Kinds and Parts on the *Essay Essentials* website.

fragment   A group of words, punctuated like a sentence, that cannot stand alone as a sentence. The word group may be missing a subject, verb, or both subject and verb, or it may be a dependent clause. See Chapter 23.

fused sentence   Two independent clauses with no punctuation between them: The fused sentence is a type of run-on it is a serious error. See Chapter 24.

gender   Nouns and pronouns may be masculine (father, boy, stallion; he, his, him), feminine (mother, girl, mare; she, hers, her); or neuter (laughter, book; it).

gender-biased language   See **sexist language**.

grammar   The description and study of how the elements of language function, by themselves and in relation to one another. See also Grammar Basics on the *Essay Essentials* website.

helping verb   See **auxiliary**.

homonyms   Two or more words that are identical in sound (e.g., meet, meat, mete) or spelling (e.g., bank—a place to deposit money; bank—a slope) but different in meaning. See Chapter 37.

imperative sentence   Also called a **command**. See Sentences: Kinds and Parts on the *Essay Essentials* website.

indefinite pronoun   See **pronoun**.

independent clause   See **clause**.

indirect object   See **object**.

infinitive   A verb form usually consisting of *to* + the base form of the verb: to be, to walk, to read, to procrastinate. An infinitive or infinitive phrase can function as a noun, adjective, or adverb, but never as the main verb in a clause. E.g., I offered to help (*to help* functions as a noun, direct object of the verb *offered*).

interrogative sentence	See Sentences: Kinds and Parts on the *Essay Essentials* website.
irony	A way of saying one thing while implying something else, often the opposite of what the words themselves signify. For an extended example of irony, see "A Tree-Planting Primer" (pages 180–84). Situations can also be ironic: in "Pucker Up" (pages 195–96), for example, we learn that a beauty product is made from disgusting materials; in "The Telephone" (pages 226–32), the instrument that was supposed to enhance the life of a village in fact destroys it.
irregular verb	A verb that does not form its past tense and past participle by adding *-ed* or *-d*; for example, write, wrote, written; sing, sang, sung. See Chapter 29.
jargon	Strictly, the specialized technical vocabulary of a particular profession. More broadly, **pretentious language**: wordy, confusing language that is intended to impress the reader. See Chapter 2.
linking verb	See **verb**.
misplaced modifier	See **modifier**.
modifier	A word or group of words that describes, qualifies, or restricts another word, phrase, or clause in a sentence. A modifier can act as an adjective or as an adverb. If there is no word in the sentence to which the modifier can logically refer, or if the modifier refers grammatically to a word it doesn't actually modify, it is a **dangling modifier**: Standing on the dock, many fish could be seen. A **misplaced modifier** is not placed close enough to the word it is intended to modify: Our team has *nearly* lost half its regular players. See Chapter 25.
noun	A word that names a person, place, thing, idea, quality, action, or event, and that can be made possessive. **Concrete** nouns name things we know through our five senses and can be **proper** (naming a particular person, place, thing, etc.: John, Alberta, July, the *Bluenose*, World War II), or **common** (naming one or more members of a class of things or qualities: boy(s), province(s), month(s), ship(s), war(s)). **Abstract** nouns name ideas or qualities that we know with our minds: truth, excellence, anger. See also Parts of Speech on the *Essay Essentials* website.
number	The form of a verb, a noun, or a pronoun may be singular or plural.
object	A noun or noun substitute (pronoun, phrase, or clause) that receives the action expressed by a transitive verb, or that completes a prepositional phrase. Objects of transitive verbs can be **direct** (David wanted a *raise*; Mira promised *to give David a raise*) or **indirect** (Mira gave *David* a raise). The object of a preposition usually follows the preposition (in the *book*, before the *class*),

except in direct questions (*What* are you writing *about*?) and indirect questions (I'm not sure *what* to write *about*).

parallelism Use of the same form for words, phrases, or clauses that have equal grammatical value and similar function in a sentence or paragraph. Parallel elements match each other in structure as well as meaning: Hot weather makes people *tired, cranky,* and *quarrelsome; What I said* and *what I meant* are two different things. See Chapter 26.

paraphrase To paraphrase is to rephrase another writer's idea in your own words. A good paraphrase reflects both the meaning and the tone of the original passage. It is usually approximately the same length or shorter than the original. Be sure to acknowledge the source of any material you paraphrase.

participle A verb form regularly ending in *-ing* or *-ed* that can be used as an adjective (the *weeping* willows, a *completed* work) or with an auxiliary as part of a verb phrase (am *succeeding*, have been *rented*). For past participles of irregular verbs, see Chapter 29 or a dictionary.

parts of speech The nine categories into which traditional grammar classifies words according to their function in a sentence: noun, pronoun, verb, adjective, adverb, conjunction, preposition, article, expletive. See also Parts of Speech on the *Essay Essentials* website.

passive voice See **voice**.

person A quality of pronouns and verbs that shows whether they refer to someone speaking (**first person:** I, we); to someone being spoken to (**second person:** you), or to someone or something being spoken about (**third person:** he, she, it, they, everyone).

personal pronoun See **pronoun**.

phrase A group of meaning-related words lacking a subject and/or a verb; compare **clause**. The different kinds of phrases function as grammatical units (parts of speech) and syntactical elements (subject, verb, object, etc.). For example,

Please order more legal-size file folders. (noun phrase acting as object of verb *order*)

I must have been sleeping when you called. (verb phrase acting as main verb in independent clause)

prefix One or more letters that can be added to the beginning of a word (1) to make a new word or (2) to change its part of speech.

1. a + sexual = asexual
   contra + diction = contradiction
   mis + spell = misspell
   un + thinkable = unthinkable

2. de + nude (adjective) = denude (verb)
   in + put (verb) = input (noun)
   con + temporary (adjective) = contemporary (noun, adjective)

Some prefixes require a hyphen: e.g., *anti*-reform, *all*-Canadian, *mid*-season, *self*-control. See Chapter 39.

preposition	A word that links a noun, pronoun, or phrase (object of the preposition) to some other word(s) in the sentence. Prepositions may be a single word (from, upon, within, to, for) or a phrase (apart from, on account of, in spite of).
prepositional phrase	A group of words consisting of a preposition and its object(s), along with any modifiers. Prepositional phrases usually function as adjectives or adverbs:

Mine is the second office *on the right.* (adjective modifying noun *office*)

Please go *into my office.* (adverb modifying verb *go*)
See the list of prepositional phrases on page 334.

pretentious language	Wordy, roundabout, or unintelligible language. Also called gobbledygook. Pretentious writing is a kind of jargon characterized by wordiness, long words, vague abstract nouns, and frequent use of the passive voice. See Chapter 2.
principal parts	The forms of a verb from which all its tenses are derived: the **infinitive** (or **base**) **form** (walk, write, drink), the **present participle** (walking, writing, drinking), the **past tense** (walked, wrote, drank), and the **past participle** (walked, written, drunk). The principal parts of irregular verbs are listed in the dictionary. See Chapter 29.
pronoun	A word that stands for or refers to a noun or another pronoun (its antecedent). There are several kinds of pronouns:

personal:	I, we, you, he, she, it, they (subject forms) me, us, him, her, it, them (object forms)
possessive:	my, our, your, his, her, its, their
demonstrative:	this, these, that, those
relative:	who, which, that, whom, whose
interrogative:	who, whose, whom, which, what
indefinite:	any, some, all, one, everybody, anything, each, either, few, none, several, etc.

See **antecedent**, **number**, **person**, and Chapter 30.

run-on	Two or more independent clauses lacking appropriate punctuation between them. See Chapter 24.
sentence	The basic unit of connected speech and writing. A sentence can assert, question, request, command, or exclaim. See Sentences: Kinds and Parts on the *Essay Essentials* website.

sexist language	Writing that calls attention unnecessarily to the sex of the being person written about: actress, waitress, female author. Also, the use of masculine nouns and pronouns to refer to persons of both sexes: A good *salesman* listens to *his* customers. See Chapter 2.
slang	A highly colloquial word or phrase, used by speakers belonging to a particular group; e.g., high-school students, music lovers, or sports fans. Slang is not appropriate in academic or professional writing. See Chapter 2.
style	A characteristic of written language; good style, whether formal or informal, is concise, clear, and pleasing.
subject	In a sentence, the person, place, thing, or concept that the sentence is about (see Chapter 22). In a paper, what the essay is about—the topic (see Chapter 3).
subordinate clause	See **clause**.
suffix	One or more letters added to the end of a word (1) to change its meaning, (2) to change its grammatical function, or (3) to change its part of speech.

1. king + dom = kingdom
   tooth + less = toothless
   few + er = fewer

2. love (base form) + s = loves (3rd person singular, present tense)
   student (singular) + s = students (plural)
   eat (base form) + en = eaten (past participle)

3. happy (adjective) + ness = happiness (noun)
   happy (adjective) + ily = happily (adverb)
   hope (noun) + ful = hopeful (adjective)

tense	The quality of a verb that indicates time: past, present, or future. The tense of a verb is indicated by its ending (pla*ys*, pla*ying*, play*ed*) and by any auxiliary verbs associated with it (*will* play, *has* played, *must have* played).

Simple tenses	Perfect tenses
present: ask, asks	has (have) asked
past: asked	has (have) asked
future: will ask	will have asked

The simple and perfect tenses can also be **progressive**: am asking, have been asking, will be asking.

thesis	The idea or point about a subject that an essay sets out to prove or explain. See Chapter 5.
tone	A writer's attitude toward his or her subject and intended audience, conveyed through style and ideas. Tone is an emotional quality, and there are as many different kinds of tone as there are emotions: objective, angry, sarcastic, humorous, solemn, anxious, concerned, etc. See Chapter 8.

transition	Any device used to connect ideas within a sentence, a paragraph, or a paper. See Chapter 8.
unity	The quality of oneness in a sentence, paragraph, or essay. A piece of writing should focus on a single topic or thesis; everything in the piece should relate directly to the topic or thesis; there should be no unrelated ideas or digressions.
usage	The customary or conventional way of using words and combinations of words in a language. The incorrect use of words and expressions (called "abusages" in this book) is a sign of nonstandard English. See Chapter 2.
verb	A part of speech that indicates one of three states:

action: Ravi stopped the ball. (physical action)
               Nina believed the team would win. (mental action)

occurrence: Father's Day falls on the third Sunday in June.

condition: Minnie felt ill.

Transitive verbs require a direct object: I *hate* chemistry; Minnie *lifts* weights.

Intransitive verbs do not require an object: Please *listen* and *learn*.

Linking verbs require a noun or adjective as their complement: Phil is the *manager* of our department (noun); Phil is *ambitious* (adjective).

The most common linking verb is *be* (*am, is, are, was, were*, etc.) Other linking verbs are *appear, become, feel, grow, look, taste, remain, seem, smell,* and *sound*.

See also **auxiliary** verb and Parts of Speech on the *Essay Essentials* website.

voice	A quality of verbs, which may be either **active** or **passive**. With an active voice verb, the subject of the verb is performing the action (I *read* your essay); with a verb in the passive voice, the subject of the sentence is being acted upon (Your essay *was read* by me). See Chapter 29.

APA Format and Documentation[1]

Formatting an APA-Style Research Paper

TITLE PAGE

In APA style, a research paper or essay requires a separate title page. On the title page (and all other pages) include a running header consisting of an abbreviated version of your title and the page number. Leave 1.25 cm of space between the title abbreviation and the numeral. Choose a concise title that identifies the subject of your paper, and then shorten it for the running header. Capitalize main words, but don't underline, italicize, or put quotation marks around your title. Centre the title in the upper half of the page (quadruple-space it from the top of the page). If the title is more than one line, double-space between the lines.

After the title, centre your name, the course you are preparing the paper for, the professor's name, and the date of submission; double-space between each of these elements. A sample APA-style title page follows. The italicized words to the left of the page identify the components of the title page.

---

[1]The information in Appendix B has been adapted from Centennial College's *Revised Style Sheet: A Guide to Format and Documentation*. Permission is gratefully acknowledged.

Running header   Multigenerational Families   1

Title   Conflict in Multigenerational Families

Name   Wendy Garriques

Course number   CS 101

Professor's name   Professor Xiu

Date submitted   April 27, 2005

HEADER, PAGE NUMBERS, AND SPACING

Number your pages consecutively throughout the paper, beginning with the title page and ending with the last page of the References list. Use the right header function of your word processor and key in the abbreviated title and the page number. Include only your abbreviated title + 1.25 cm space + the numeral—no punctuation or *p*.

Double-space between all lines of your paper, including the title page, abstract, headings (if any), pages of the text itself, quotations, and References list. Indent all paragraphs 1.25 cm.

ABSTRACT

Some assignments require you to provide an abstract—a short summary of the contents of your whole paper. It should give the purpose of your paper and the key ideas; that is, it should give your reader a preview of your paper. An abstract is usually one paragraph long. It must be well organized and carefully written.

Type the abstract on a separate page that includes the running header and the page number (2). Centre the word "Abstract" at the top of the page. Type the abstract paragraph itself in block format (without indentation).

FIRST PAGE OF TEXT

On page 3 (following the title page and abstract), centre the full title of your research paper. Double-space, and begin the text of your essay.

Parenthetical Reference Citations

Parenthetical reference citations serve two functions: (1) they tell your reader that this material comes from somewhere else, and (2) they point the reader to full information about sources in the References list at the end of your paper.

To cite an author's work, name the author of the source in your own sentence and include the date of publication in parentheses immediately after the author's name. If you do not name the author in your sentence, put author's surname + comma + date in parentheses right after your quotation, summary, or paraphrase. (See the examples below.)

If you are quoting from a source, you must include in your parenthetical citation the page number(s) on which the quotation appears, using the abbreviation *p.* (page) or *pp.* (pages). Do not give page numbers if you are summarizing or paraphrasing, however. (See the examples below.)

Electronic sources (discussed below) do not follow the author/date-based citation method because they often do not have an identifiable author and rarely include page numbers.

EXAMPLES OF PARENTHETICAL CITATIONS: TRADITIONAL PRINT SOURCES

- **Author's name given in your paragraph**

  Kevin Patterson (2000) writes about his sailing journey from British Columbia to the South Pacific and back: "Suffused with optimism and rum, I told Peter I wanted to sail to Tahiti" (p. 6).

For the entry for this source, see item 7 in the sample References list on page 511.

APA FORMAT AND DOCUMENTATION · 501

- **Author's name not given in your paragraph**

  Long voyages by sea, especially in small boats, present clear dangers depending on the ocean and the season of crossing: "The North Pacific is cold and volatile in the autumn and anyone who knew enough about the sea to consider sailing to Canada knew that much" (Patterson, 2000, p. 249).

- **No author named in source**

  Legislation to reduce the amount of pollution generated by large-scale vehicles has been on the federal agenda for some time: "Canada has said it will toughen pollution-emission rules for all new vehicles, ending a loophole that allowed less stringent standards for popular sport-utility vehicles and minivans" (Canada to toughen, 2002, p. A6).

When no author is named, as in the example above, give the first words of the title. For the entry for this source, see item 2 in the sample References list.

- **Source with two authors**

Name both in the order in which their names appear on the work.

  Norton and Green (2005) observe that inexperienced writers achieved superior results when they spent half the allotted time on planning and drafting, and the other half on revising.

If you do not name the authors in your own sentence, use an ampersand (&) instead of *and* in the parenthetical reference.

  One approach to writing recommends that students divide the process of revising into three steps or stages (Norton & Green, 2005).

- **Classical works**

The first time you quote or paraphrase from a classical work of literature (such as Shakespeare) or the Bible, identify in parentheses the version or edition you are using, and give the book, chapter, canto, act, scene, verse, and/or line numbers. Do not include this kind of source in your References list. The lines of such works are numbered systematically in all editions.

  In the Bible, it is clear that people who have suffered exile from their land are not allowed to subjugate others because they themselves have suffered and understand the suffering of the oppressed: "Also thou shalt not oppress a stranger, seeing ye were strangers in the land of Egypt" Exodus 23:8 (King James Version).

Further information on APA parenthetical citations (e.g., two or more books by the same author, a work in an edited anthology, a work cited in a secondary source) can be found on the APA website (http://www.apa.org).

EXAMPLES OF PARENTHETICAL CITATIONS: ELECTRONIC SOURCES

If the electronic source lists an author, give the surname and the publication date in your reference citation. This is all the information your reader needs in order to find the full bibliographical data in your References list. Example:

> Planespotting is a popular hobby, even an obsession, for growing numbers of people who are fascinated with aviation: "Some spotters take photographs. Others make videotapes. But the majority flock to airports around the world, equipped with scanners and notepads with one goal in mind—recording the registration numbers painted on airplane tails" (Bourette, 2002).

The quotation in the example above comes from *Shift*, an online magazine. (See item 1 in the sample References list.)

If the electronic source does not list an author, use the document title (or a shortened version of the title) instead of the author's name.

> Statistics Canada calculates that the nation's infant mortality rate in 1997 was 5.5 for every 1,000 live births (Statistics Canada, 2002).

The information in the example above comes from the Statistics Canada website. (See item 9 in the sample References list.)

Electronic sources don't usually include page numbers or other navigation devices. If there are page, paragraph, or section numbers that could guide your reader to the specific material being quoted, include them. Your parenthetical reference should include the author's name (unless you've mentioned it in your own paragraph), followed by a comma, the date, and the sections or paragraph numbers, abbreviated as *par.* or *pars.* For example:

> In the short story "The Necklace," Mme. Loisel undergoes a dramatic change after she loses her friend's jewels:

> The frightful debt must be paid. She would pay it. They dismissed the servant; they changed their rooms; they took an attic under the roof.
>
> She learned the rough work of the household, the odious labors of the kitchen. She washed the dishes, wearing out her pink nails on the greasy pots and the bottoms of the pans. (Maupassant, 1907, pars. 98–99)

The quotation in the example above comes from an online edition of Guy de Maupassant's story "The Necklace."

If a source does not give page, paragraph, or section numbers that you can use to identify a quotation, give the author's name or the title in parentheses. If no publication date is given, use the date that you accessed the material in day-month-year format. If a reader needs to locate the source, Web browser search engines can help find it using keywords or phrases.

More information on the treatment of electronic sources can be found on the APA website (http://www.apa.org).

APA List of References

A page headed *References* is included at the end of your paper (see the sample References list). It gives detailed bibliographical information for all sources that you have quoted, summarized, or paraphrased in your essay.

The References list enables your reader to assess the extent of your research and to locate every source. In other documentation styles, this list is called Bibliography or Works Cited, but APA format prescribes *References* as the list heading.

Begin the References list on a new page. Two spaces below your header (abbreviated title + 1.25 cm space + page number), centre the word "References" on the page. Leave a double space between the title and the first entry, and double-space the entire document.

Begin each entry at the left margin. If the entry runs more than a single line—and most do—indent the second and subsequent lines 1.25 cm. (Use the five-space tab that you use for paragraph indentation.) This format is called a "hanging indent" and can be found in most word-processing packages.

Arrange the entries in your References list alphabetically, beginning with the first word in the entry (usually the surname of the author). If no author is listed, alphabetize by the first main word in the title, ignoring *A, An*, or *The*. For example, *The Canadian Encyclopedia* would be alphabetized under C, for Canadian. Do *not* number the entries.

BOOKS AND OTHER NONPERIODICAL WORKS

Below is the basic model for a book entry. (Note the capitalization, punctuation, and order of the information.) Leave one space between initials in author' names as well as after commas, colons, semicolons, and periods that separate parts of the reference citation. Give the author's surname, a comma, and initials only. Then, in parentheses, give the year the book was copyrighted. Only proper names and the first word of the title (and subtitle, if any) are capitalized, and the title/subtitle is italicized (or underlined). Use the first city if several cities are listed. Shorten the publisher's name (e.g., Alfred A. Knopf, Inc. to Knopf).

> Last name of author, Initials. (Year of Publication). *Title of book: Subtitle.* City: Publisher.

If you are citing an essay or chapter within a larger book, capitalize only the first word of the title (as above), but do not italicize the title or place in quotation marks.

> Turner, L. J. (2001). Truth or consequences. In S. Norton & B. Green, *The bare essentials, form A* (pp. 303–304). Toronto: Harcourt.

- **Book by one author**

> Patterson, K. (2000). *The water in between: A journey at sea.* Toronto: Vintage Canada.

> Turner, C. (2004). *Planet Simpson: How a cartoon masterpiece defined a generation.* Cambridge, MA: Da Capo.

- **Book by two authors**

> Leakey, R., & Lewin, R. (1992). *Origins reconsidered: In search of what makes us human.* New York: Doubleday.

- **Selection from an anthology or collection (with an editor)**

> Mistry, R. (2001). Journey to Dharmsala. In C. Meyer & B. Meyer (Eds.), *The reader: Contemporary essays and writing strategies* (pp. 38–51). Toronto: Prentice.

- **Unidentified author**

  Roget's Thesaurus. (3rd ed.). (1998). New York: Random House.

PERIODICALS

Periodicals are publications that appear regularly at fixed intervals such as newspapers, magazines, and academic journals.

Begin your entry with the author's name (if available)—surname first followed by a comma—and initials. Then add the date in parentheses. For magazines and newspapers, give the year, followed by a comma and then the month and day. (For a magazine published once a month, give the month.) Do not abbreviate names of months. Reference entries for a newspaper include its name as it appears on the masthead (e.g., *The Globe and Mail*). Titles of periodicals are capitalized in the normal way.

Give page numbers for each article in your list. Cite all of the page numbers. For example, if the article begins on page 27 and concludes on page 29, follow the title with a comma and the span of pages (e.g., *Saturday Night*, 27–29). If the article is not printed on consecutive pages (if it begins, let's say, on pages 27 to 29 and concludes on page 40), provide all page numbers separated with commas: 27–29, 40.

In newspapers, the sections are usually paginated separately, so include the section number as well as the page number (e.g., *The Vancouver Sun*, pp. B1–2).

Note the order, punctuation, and capitalization in the model below.

> Author's last name, Initials. (Year, quarter, month, or month + day). Title of article. *Title of Periodical,* page numbers.

- **Article in a scholarly journal**

  Forrester, S., & Beggs, B. (2005, Winter). Gender and self-esteem in intramural sports. *Physical and Health Education Journal, 70*(4), 12–19.

  Lemire, J. A. (2001). Preparing nurse leaders: A leadership model. *Nursing Leadership Forum, 6*(2), 39–44.

In the examples above, note that the volume number is italicized as if it were part of the title, while the issue number (enclosed in parentheses) is not.

- **Article in a monthly magazine**

    Reece, E. (2005, April). Death of a mountain: Radical strip mining and the leveling of Appalachia. *Harper's,* 41–60.

- **Article in a weekly magazine**

    Hawaleshka, D. (2005, February 28). Power hungry. *Maclean's,* 22–23.

- **Article in a newspaper**

    Canada to toughen auto-emissions rules. (2002, April 5). *The Wall Street Journal,* p. A6.

Note that APA style requires you to include *p.* or *pp.* for page number(s) in newspaper entries, but not in entries for magazines or journals.

- **Review**

    Houpt, S. (2005, March 19). Spamalot a spoof to end all spoofs [Review of the play *Monty Python's Spamalot.*] *The Globe and Mail,* p. R7.

AUDIOVISUAL SOURCES

- **Movie or video recording**

    Moore, M. (Writer, Producer, Director). (2002). *Bowling for Columbine* [Motion picture]. Canada. Alliance Atlantis.

- **Television show**

    Neilson, L. (Performer). (2002, March 5). *Rock stars: The world of curling.* [Television Broadcast]. Toronto: Canadian Broadcasting Company. CBLT.

- **Radio show**

    Hallway Confidential. (2005, March 23). *Outfront* [Radio broadcast]. Toronto: CBC Radio One. Toronto.

ELECTRONIC SOURCES

Entries for electronic sources should identify the source and provide enough information to enable a reader to locate the material (e.g., author, title, publication information, and date). Be sure to include the URL (Uniform Resource Locator)—the sequence of words, abbreviations, numbers, and characters that identifies the source's location in cyberspace. You should also download and print the material you're using for your paper so that you can verify it if it is revised, unavailable, or inaccessible at a later date.

Do not use a hyphen to divide a URL over two lines, even if it is very long, because it introduces a symbol that will invalidate the URL. Put the URL on a single line, or break it only after a slash or before a period, even if doing so results in uneven lines. You can prevent your typed URLs from turning into hyperlinks (which don't print). In *Word 2000* and *Word 2003*, go into "Tools," choose "AutoCorrect," click on "AutoFormat As You Type," and delete the check mark in front of "Internet and network paths with hyperlinks."

Along with the URL, you must provide two dates: (1) the date of the publication of the material (if available) and (2) the date that you, as the researcher, located the information. The date of publication goes at the end of the entry and is placed in parentheses. Your access date follows the title and is introduced by the word "Retrieved."

Below is a basic model for online source entries in a References list:

> Author's Last Name, and Initials [if known]. (Date of publication if known). Title of document. *Title of complete work or site.* Retrieved month day, year, from Protocol and URL address

"Protocol" refers to a particular set of rules for performing tasks on the Internet such as Hypertext Transfer Protocol (HTTP), File Transfer Protocol (FTP), and telnet.

- **Online information database or scholarly project**

> Goofs browser. (1997–2002). *The Internet movie database.* Retrieved March 7, 2002, from http://us.imdb.com/Sections/Goofs

> Vassanji, M. G. (1997, August 8). *Canadian literature research service.* Retrieved April 28, 2005, from http://collection.nlc-bnc.ca/ 100/201/301/lecture/vassanji.htm

- **Personal or professional website**

  Shark byte. (1997–2002). *Jump the shark: The turning point of television programming.* Retrieved March 30, 2002, from http://www.jumptheshark.com/page.htm

  Shakespeare: Chill with Will. Retrieved May 22, 2005, from http://library.thinkquest.org/19539/front.htm

- **Online book or literary work**

  Maupassant, G. (1907). The necklace. *Bartleby.com: Great books online.* Retrieved March 7, 2005, from http://www.bartleby.com/195/20/html

  Service, R. (February 23, 2002). The cremation of Sam McGee. *The Robert W. Service home page.* Retrieved June 5, 2005, from http://www.ude.net/verse/cremation.html

- **Article in an online periodical**

  Bourette, S. (2002, March). Planespotting. *Shift.* Retrieved March 14, 2005, from http://www.shift.com/content/10.1/53/1.html

  Wahl, A. (2005, February 28). Emission impossible. *Canadian Business,* 24. Retrieved March 21, 2005, from eLibrary Canada database.

- **Online encyclopedia**

  Art Deco. *Encyclopaedia Britannica.* Retrieved April 22, 2005, from Encyclopaedia Britannica Online.

  Charter comes into effect. *The Canadian Encyclopedia 2001.* Retrieved March 14, 2005, from http://tceplus.com/Timeline/charter_frame.htm

- **Online government publication**

  Canada. Health Canada. Health Products and Food Branch. (2003, June). *Natural health products in Canada: A history.* Retrieved April 4, 2005, from http://www.hc-sc.gc.ca/hpfb-dgpsa/nhpd-dpsn/history_e.html#top

- **Newspaper article from an online (library subscription) database**

    Deutsch, C. H. (2005, February 27). Are women responsible for their
    own low pay? *New York Times*. Retrieved March 22, 2005,
    from National Newspaper Abstracts, ProQuest database.

- **CD-ROM**

    Canadian encyclopedia world edition. (1999). (Version 5). Toronto:
    McClelland & Stewart.

- **Online news service**

    MSNBC News Services. (2005, February 10). Images show wide rifts
    in tsunami seabed. Retrieved March 1, 2005, from the
    MSN.Com website: http://www.msnbc.msn.com/id/6946276/

- **Online posting, discussion group, or listserv**

    Fox, F. (2004, March 12). Nanotech—The next controversy alike
    GM? Message posted to http://www.euroscience.net/
    article6.html

- **Personal communications (electronic)**

E-mail, electronic bulletin board messages, and the like (along with non-
electronic personal communications such as letters, memos, and telephone
conversations) do not provide recoverable data and therefore are not
included in the References list. Cite personal communications, including
electronic communications, in your paper only. Give the surname and initials of the communicator along with the date. E.g.,

    (J. K. Smith, personal communication, June 13, 2005)

Never provide your source's e-mail address or telephone number.

SAMPLE REFERENCES LIST

Note that entries in a References list are arranged alphabetically according to the first word in the entry. Entries in a References list are *not* numbered. (The numbers listed to the right of the sample page are included only to help you find the entry format for some of the reference citations given earlier in Appendix B.)

The sample References list below includes the following sources:

1. Article in an online periodical
2. Article in a newspaper
3. Book by three authors
4. Article in a scholarly journal
5. Selection from an anthology
6. Movie
7. Book by one author
8. Article in a monthly magazine
9. Online government publication
10. Online database
11. Magazine article from an online (library subscription) database

Title of Paper 29

References

Bourette, S. (2002, March). Planespotting. *Shift*. Retrieved March 14, 2005, from http://www.shift.com/content/10.1/53/1.html

Canada to toughen auto-emissions rules. (2002, April 5). *The Wall Street Journal*, p. A6.

France, H., Rodriguez, M., & Hett, G. (2004). *Diversity, culture and counselling: A Canadian perspective.* Calgary: Detselig.

Helson, R., & Pals, J. (2000). Creative potential, creative achievement, and personal growth. *Journal of Personality*, *68*(2), 39–44.

Mistry, R. (2001). Journey to Dharmsala. In C. Meyer & B. Meyer (Eds.), *The reader: Contemporary essays and writing strategies.* (pp. 38–51). Toronto: Prentice.

Moore, M. (Writer, Producer, Director). (2002). *Bowling for Columbine* [Motion picture]. Canada: Alliance Atlantis.

Patterson, K. (2000). *The water in between: A journey at sea.* Toronto: Vintage Canada.

Sreenivasan, A. (2002, February). Keeping up with the cones. *Natural History*, 40–46.

Statistics Canada. (2002, October 11). Infant mortality rates. Retrieved October 12, 2005, from http://www.statcan.ca/english/Pgdb/ health21.htm

Vassanji, M. G. (1997, August 8). *Canadian literature research service.* Retrieved April 28, 2005, from http://collection.nlc-bnc.ca/100/201/ 301/lecture/vassanji.htm

Wahl, A. (2005, February 28). Emission impossible. *Canadian Business*, 24. Retrieved March 21, 2005, from eLibrary Canada database.

1.

2.

3.

4.

5.

6.

7.

8.

9.

10.

11.

APPENDIX C

Answers for
Selected Exercises

Answers for Chapter 1: Your Audience and You (pages 9–23)

Exercise 1.1

1. Audience: Literate readers who are interested in exploring a serious analysis of what is usually treated as a trivial topic.

    Writer's role: To provide information.

    Language: Formal. Sentences vary in length; one is quite long and complex. While there are no technical terms, the writer assumes the reader has a broad general vocabulary and good reading ability. Use of third-person point of view contributes to the impersonal tone.

2. Audience: Experts in woodworking.

    Writer's role: To provide information in an accessible way. The writer is not instructing the reader, but outlining the function of the tool and some of its possible applications.

    Language: General level, combining technical vocabulary with an informal tone. Sentences vary in length. Writer addresses reader as "you."

3. Audience: Educated business owners or high-level managers who are interested in doing business in China.

    Writer's role: To inform Canadian entrepreneurs who have little experience with Chinese business culture that it is very different from the Canadian culture, and that considerable preparation is needed if one is to be successful in that market.

    Language: Formal. Sentences are long and complex; vocabulary is highly sophisticated and includes a few examples of business jargon: e.g., "principals," "power brokers." Tone is serious.

4. Audience: General readers, probably not just parents of young children as might be suggested by the content.

    Writer's role: To make a point in an amusing, friendly way.

    Language: Informal. Includes contractions and colloquialisms ("kids," "slick operator") and slang ("junkies"), but also a couple of challenging phrases and words (e.g., "disdainfully"). Writer addresses readers as "you," as if speaking directly to them.

5. Audience: English professor.

   Writer's role: To demonstrate that she can write a good research paper.

   Language: Formal. Student assumes reader is familiar with Brontë's novel and presents her findings in sentences of varying lengths. Each conclusion is supported with an appropriate quotation from the text. Paragraph is fairly long (11 sentences), and tone is impersonal.

Answers for Chapter 2: Choosing the Right Words (pages 24–38)

Exercise 2.1 (suggested answers)

1. I do not think there is any basis for believing in UFOs.
2. I prefer contemporary furniture to antiques.
3. I think Alison is pretending to be sick so she won't have to go to work.
4. Our competitor's products, although inferior to ours, are selling better than ours.
5. My essay is as good as Jill's and deserves an equivalent mark, but the professor hates me.
6. I doubt that this innovation will succeed.
7. A course in English basics is a prerequisite to success in college, business, and the community.
8. "As a new teacher," we told our English instructor, "you should understand that you can't gain our respect if you insist on grammar rules that inhibit our creativity."
9. This trend can probably be reversed if we go back to our design fundamentals and introduce a few manufacturing innovations.
10. We have deleted any unlawful descriptors, such as race, age, gender, religion, and marital status, and now all our personnel documents are practically identical.

Exercise 2.4 (suggested answers)

1. When the rain began, we turned on the windshield wipers.
2. Young people often have difficulty communicating with parents and others in authority.
3. The witness lied when she claimed that the accused had confessed in a meeting with her.
4. The results of our study demonstrate that our survey instrument is as valid as any other.
5. Cancelling IMF loans to Pacific Rim countries could affect the relationship between developed and developing nations.

Exercise 2.6 (suggested answers)

1. The well-known producer Elaine May often regrets that she cannot go out in public without attracting the attention of fans and photographers.
2. Amy King first joined the company as a salesperson; only 10 years later, she was promoted to president.

3. An executive sitting in the first-class cabin rang for the flight attendant, a friendly woman who quickly arrived to assist him.
4. The list of ingredients on food packages contains information that may be important to consumers, especially if they are the parents of young children.
5. The typical family is often hard-pressed to find time for family recreation.

Exercise 2.7 (suggested answers)

1. Regardless of what you think, the problem between her and me has nothing to do with you.
2. If you want to be in the office pool, I need $5.00 from you today because there will be no spots left by tomorrow.
3. Because they didn't finish the job themselves the way they should have, we have to work late to get it done.
4. I didn't feel like seeing anybody, so I went home, turned on the TV, and did nothing for the rest of the night.
5. This used to be a good place to work, but now we're supposed to work a full shift every day, or a penalty is deducted from our pay.
6. Many young people today are trying to fight prejudice not only in society but also within themselves.
7. I'm supposed to ask you if the reason for the delay is that it's raining. (*Better:* . . . ask you if the rain is the reason for the delay.)
8. It's irresponsible of us to blame television or any other medium for causing violence.
9. Television is responsible, however, for the fact that many ungrammatical expressions sound all right to us.
10. Between you and me, the reason I didn't speak to anyone about Elmo's cheating on the test is that he would have broken my arm.

Answers for Chapter 3: Selecting a Subject (pages 39–43)

Exercise 3.1

1. significant
2. significant
3. revise
4. significant
5. revise
6. significant
7. revise

Exercise 3.2

1. revise
2. revise
3. revise
4. single (the subject is *the accuracy of reporting*, not the two media)
5. single
6. revise
7. revise

Exercise 3.3
1. specific
2. revise
3. specific
4. revise
5. revise
6. revise
7. specific

Exercise 3.4
1. supportable
2. supportable
3. supportable
4. revise
5. revise
6. revise
7. supportable

Exercise 3.5
1. not specific
2. not single
3. not supportable
4. satisfactory
5. not specific

Answers for Chapter 4: Managing the Main Points (pages 44–60)

Exercise 4.6
1. cell (not distinct, overlaps with *telephone*)
2. distance from suppliers and markets (not related)
3. repetitive (not related: repetition is a programming problem, not a characteristic of commercials)
4. procrastination (not distinct, overlaps with *poor study habits*)
5. *find a reliable real-estate agent* overlaps with *seek expert advice*; also not necessarily relevant—not all people need an agent
6. *competitors offer better pay* overlaps with *salary lower than industry standard*

Exercise 4.7
1. chronological (5, 1, 4, 3, 2)
2. climactic (2, 1, 3, 4)
3. random
4. climactic (3, 1, 2. This order reflects the amount of time it takes for a smoker to quit using each method and also the amount of agony the smoker will suffer in the process.)
5. random

Answers for Chapter 5: Writing the Thesis Statement (pages 61–70)

Exercise 5.1
1. <u>Students who try to combine a full-time job with a full-time program face problems</u> <u>at school</u>, <u>at work</u>, and <u>at home</u>.
2. <u>To be successful in a broadcasting career</u>, you must be <u>talented</u>, <u>motivated</u>, and <u>hardworking</u>.
3. <u>The ideal notebook computer for business applications</u> is <u>reliable</u>, <u>lightweight</u>, <u>powerful</u>, and <u>flexible</u>.
4. <u>Establishing a local area network</u> would increase <u>efficiency</u> and <u>flexibility</u> in the office.
5. <u>The chairperson's job calls for a responsible and sensitive person</u>, someone who is <u>knowledgeable about company policy</u>, <u>sensitive to personnel issues</u>, and <u>a creative problem solver</u>. It wouldn't hurt if he or she could also walk on water.
6. <u>The business traveller can learn much from the turtle</u>. <u>Carry everything you need with you</u>. <u>Move slowly but with purpose and consistency</u>. <u>Keep your head down until you are sure you know exactly what is going on</u>.
7. Large energy producers and some provincial governments say we cannot afford to live up to the terms of the Kyoto Accord, which seeks to reduce the production of greenhouse gases. <u>But can we afford not to comply with this international agreement</u>? <u>Can we afford to compromise the health of Canadians</u> by continuing to pollute? <u>Can we afford to risk the effects of global warming</u> on our environment? <u>Can we afford to fall behind the rest of the world in research and development leading</u> to a solution to the problem of greenhouse gases?

Exercise 5.6 (suggested answers)
1. When choosing between two fast-food restaurants, consider food, atmosphere, service, and price.
2. Urban overcrowding results in traffic jams, air pollution, homelessness, and violence.
3. Successful small businesses are usually those with adequate capital, a marketable product, dedicated personnel, and a workable business plan.

Answers for Chapter 7: Understanding Paragraph Form and Function (pages 81–97)

Exercise 7.3
1. Canada makes no economic sense.
2. All sports can be made ridiculous because the essence of sport is rules.
3. In reality, taste buds are exceedingly small.
4. Scholarly explanations of humor fall into three major categories.
5. With the huge variety of computers now on the market, the determining factor in a purchase should be the job the machine will be expected to do.

*Answers for Chapter 8: Keeping Your Readers with You
(pages 98–109)*

Exercise 8.1

1. sentence 6
2. sentence 4
3. sentence 5
4. sentence 5
5. sentence 6

Exercise 8.2

1. Therefore, ...
2. Finally, . . . but . . . .
3. Unfortunately, however, ...
4. On the other hand, ...
5. For example, ... In addition, ...

Exercise 8.4

The transitions in this exercise are identified by category. See the numbered list of coherence strategies on page 102.

1.   Finally (5), developing the proper attitude is the key to winning tennis. I define winning tennis (1) as playing the game to the best of your ability, hitting the ball as well as you can, and enjoying the feeling of practised expertise (4). Winning tennis (1) has little to do with defeating an opponent. Naturally (5), if you learn the basics, practise sufficiently, and concentrate (4), you will win many matches, but that is the reward of playing well, not the reason for playing well (4). People who swear and throw their racquets when they lose are very useful: they (3) are the most satisfying players to trounce. But I do not understand why they (3) play a game (2) that causes them such pain. Tennis players who enjoy the feel of a well hit ball and the satisfaction of a long, skillfully played rally are winners, regardless of the score.

2.   Travel abroad offers you the best education you can get. For one thing (5), travel (1) is a course in communication skills. In order to function in a foreign language, you must practise every aspect of the communication process (1, 2) from body language to pronunciation. In fact (5), just making yourself understood is a lesson in creativity, a seminar in sign language, and a lab in communication theory (2, 4). Another educational aspect of travel (5) is the history, geography, and culture (4) that you learn about almost unconsciously. Everywhere you go, you encounter memorable evidence of historic events (2) you may dimly recall from school, and you are continually confronted by the practical realities of geography (1) as you try to find your way around. As for culture (1, 5), no book or course of study could provide you with the understanding and appreciation of another society that living in it (3) can. A third way (5) in which travel (1) educates is through teaching you about yourself. Your ability—

or inability—to cope with unfamiliar customs, with language difficulties, and with the inevitable problems of finding transportation and accommodation (4) will tell you more than you might want to know about yourself (2). Without the safety net of family and friends, perhaps without even the security of knowing where you'll spend the night, you develop self-reliance or you go home. Either way (5), you learn valuable lessons. While you may not get a diploma from Travel U., you'll learn more about the world, about people, and about yourself (1, 4) than you will in any classroom.

Exercise 8.6
(We've italicized the words and phrases that require revision to change the tone of this paragraph from tactless to tactful. We've given some revision suggestions in square brackets following the offensive phrases.)

I'm from the city, so I may not know much about the subject, but it seems to me that we urban-dwellers have lost touch with the food we eat. By this I mean, *obviously,* [delete] that we no longer appreciate the farmers and farm workers who supply the food that we enjoy every day. *Anyone with half a brain should realize that* [delete] Most of the food we buy is prepackaged in Styrofoam, wrapped in plastic, or precooked and frozen by huge corporations *whose goal is to make humongous profits by selling us the packaging, not the contents.* [that put at least as much effort into designing attractive packaging as they do into preparing food.] *Do any urban consumers understand that* [How many urban consumers think about the fact that] their ketchup is made from farm-grown tomatoes? Do *any advertising-driven* [delete] supermarket shoppers *really think about the fact* [stop to consider] that those *over-* [delete] packaged frozen pork chops, so irresistible with their sprig of parsley, were once a pig, raised by a farmer? *Not only are we ignorant, but also we could care less* [Let's face the facts: Do many of us know or even care] about the journey our food makes from farm to fridge[?] My guess is that if you asked most *city kids* [urban children] where their food comes from, they'd say, "the food factory."

Here is how a final draft of this revision might read. (Note that we've added a conclusion to the paragraph.)

It seems to me that we urbanites have lost touch with the food we eat. By this I mean that we no longer appreciate the farmers and farm workers who supply the food that we enjoy every day. Most of the food we buy is prepackaged in Styrofoam, wrapped in plastic, or precooked and frozen by huge corporations that put at least as much effort into designing attractive packaging as they do into preparing food. How many urban consumers think about the fact that ketchup is made from farm-grown tomatoes? Do supermarket shoppers stop to consider that those packaged frozen pork chops, so irresistible with their sprig of parsley, were once a pig, raised by a farmer? Let's face facts: how many of us know or even care about the journey our food makes from farm to fridge? My guess is that if you asked most urban children where their food comes from, they'd say, "the food factory." But the correct answer is, "Canadian farmers." They deserve our attention and support.

Answers for Chapter 10: The Three Steps to Revision (pages 125–39)
Exercise 10.1

Attention-getter: As the recipient of approximately 1,000 business-related e-mail messages every month, I am something of an expert on what is effective and what is not in e-mail correspondence.

Thesis statement: The three areas that need attention in most e-mail messages are the subject line, the content and format of the message, and the use of attachments.

Main points:

I. Subject line
   A. Never leave the subject line blank (*or* Always include a subject line)
   B. Make sure the subject line states clearly what the message is about

II. Message
   A. Content
      1. Be concise and to the point
      2. Tell the reader what action is needed, by whom, and when
      3. Use plain English, not "cyberspeak"
      4. Use an appropriate level of language in your message as well as in your salutation and signature
   B. Format
      1. Use bullets to identify points you want to emphasize
      2. Leave white space between points
      3. Avoid sending your message in uppercase letters (shouting)
      4. Avoid smilies and other "cute" computer shorthand symbols

III. Attachments
   A. Use only if necessary
      1. may carry viruses
      2. take time to transfer and to open
   B. Attach text-only files, unless a graphic is absolutely necessary

Summary: If you follow my recommendations on these three points whenever you write an e-mail, you will make the recipient of your message very happy.

Memorable statement: Especially if you're writing to me.

Exercise 10.2 (suggested answer)

In the following answer, we have corrected only the errors in paragraph structure, sentence structure, and grammar. The passage still contains errors in spelling, punctuation, and usage. We will correct those errors at Step 3.

1   As the recipient of almost 1,000 business-related e-mail messages every month, I am something of an expert on what is effective and what is not in e-mail correspondence. The three areas that need attention in most e-mail messages are the subject line, the **content and format** of the message, and the use of attachments.

2   Some people leave the subject line blank**.** **T**his is a mistake. I want to know what the message is about before I open it, so I can decide if it needs my immediate attention **or** can wait until later. A message with no subject line**,** or with a line that **doesn't** tell me **anything** about the content of the e-mail**,** **gets** sent to the bottom of my "to-do" list. There are lots of readers like me: busy people who receive tons of e-mail, much of it unsolicited advertising that **clutters** up **our** in-boxes. For this reason the subject line should always clearly state the subject of the message and should never be vague or cute**,** like "hello**,**" or "message**,**" or "are you there?"

3   As for the message itself, it's function should be to tell the reader what action **you want. Y**ou need to be clear about this and be as brief as possible. What is it that you want the recipient to do. Who else needs to be involved. By when does the action need to take place. Communicate your message in plain English, not in "cyberspeak**.**" Not everyone knows Net lingo, and even some who are famliar with it find it irritating**,** not charming. Use an appropriate level of language (general level Standard English **is** always appropriate) to convey you're message. Use the same level of language in you're salutation and closing or "signature." **Never** sign off a message to you're client or you're boss with "love and kisses."

4   Format you're message so that the recipient **can read it quickly and understand** it easily. Use bullets to identify points you want to emphasize **and** separate the bullets with white space so **that your points** can be read at a glance and reviewed individually if neccessary.

5   There are some important points of e-mail etiquette that you should observe. Don't type you're message in upper case letters**.** **This is** considered "shouting." Do avoid "smilies" and other "cute" computer shorthand symbols. Some of you're readers won't understand them**.** **O**thers will have seen them so often they will be turned off.

6   Attachments should be included only if they are really necessary**.** **One reason is that** they may carry virruses and some people won't open them. Another disadvantage is that **attachments** take time to send download and open. Unless I am sure that an attachment is both urgent and vitally important—the agenda of tomorrow's meeting, for example—I don't bother to open it**.** **F**or all I know, it might contain not only a virus but also footage of the sender's toddler doing her latest photogenic trick. As a general rule **you should** attach only what you must and attach text-only files. Try to include everything you need to say in the message itself**;** use attachments only as a last resort. Think of them as equivalent to footnotes**:** supplementary to the message**,** not an essential part of it.

7   If you follow my recommendations on these three points whenever you write an e-mail, you will make the recipient of your message very happy, especially if you're writing to me.

Exercise 10.3 (suggested answers)
1. I **expect** a salary **commensurate** with my qualifications and experience.
2. I have **learned** the Microsoft Word and **Excel spreadsheet programs**.
3. I received a **plaque** for being salesperson of the year.
4. Reason for leaving last job: **maternity** leave.
5. You will want me to be a **manager** in no time.
6. I am a perfectionist and rarely **if ever** forget details.

7. Marital status: **single**.

8. In my previous job, I **learned to trust no one**.

9. As **indicated**, I have **more than** five years **experience in** analyzing investments.

10. I was responsible for **running** a Western chain store. (*Better:* I was responsible for managing a Western chain store.)

Exercise 10.4 (suggested answer)

(Words that have been omitted are indicated by ***.)

1   As the recipient of approximately 1,000 business-related e-mail messages every month, I am something of an expert on what is effective and what is not in e-mail correspondence. The three areas that need attention in most e-mail messages are the subject line, the content *** and format of the message, and the use of attachments.

2   Some people leave the subject line blank. This is a mistake. I want to know what the message is about before I open it, so I can decide if it needs my immediate attention or can wait until later. A message with no subject line, or with a line that doesn't tell me anything about the content of the e-mail, gets sent to the bottom of my "to-do" list. There are lots of readers like me: busy people who receive tons of e-mail, much of which is unsolicited advertising that clutters up our in-boxes. For this reason, the subject line should always clearly state the subject of the message and should never be vague or cute. **Some examples of inappropriate subject lines include** "Hello," *** "Message," **and** "Are you there?"

3   As for the message itself, **its** function should be to tell the reader what action you want **taken**. *** Be clear about this, and be as brief as possible. What is it that you want the recipient to do? Who else needs to be involved? By when does the action need to **be completed?** Communicate your message in plain English, not in "cyberspeak." Not everyone knows Net lingo, and even some who are **familiar** with it find it irritating, not charming. Use an appropriate level of language (general level Standard English is always appropriate) to convey **your** message. Use the same level of language in **your** salutation and closing or "signature." Never sign off a message to **your** client or **your** boss with "love and kisses."

4   Format **your** message so that the recipient can read it quickly and understand it easily. Use bullets to identify points you want to emphasize, and separate the bullets with white space so that your points can be read at a glance and reviewed individually, if **necessary**.

5   There are some important points of e-mail etiquette that you should observe. Don't type **your** message in uppercase letters. This is considered "shouting." Do avoid "smilies" and other "cute" computer shorthand symbols. Some of **your** readers won't understand them. Others will have seen them so often **that** they will be turned off.

6   Attachments should be included only if they are really necessary. One reason is that they may carry **viruses,** and some people won't open them. Another disadvantage is that attachments take time to send, download, and open. Unless I am sure that an attachment is both urgent and vitally important—the agenda of tomorrow's meeting, for example—I don't bother to open it. For all I know, it might contain not only a virus but also footage of the sender's toddler doing her latest photogenic trick. As a general rule, you should attach only what you must, and

attach text-only files. Try to include everything you need to say in the message itself; use attachments only as a last resort. Think of them as equivalent to footnotes: supplementary to the message, not an essential part of it.

7   If you follow my recommendations on these three points whenever you write an e-mail, you will make the recipient of your message very happy, especially if you're writing to me.

Exercise 10.5

According to a recent survey in *Maclean's* magazine, only 43 percent of Canadians are satisfied with their jobs. What can you do to ensure that you will not be one of the 57 percent who are unhappy with the work they do**?** There are three questions to consider when seeing employment that will provide satisfaction as well as a paycheque.

First**,** are you suited to the kind of work you are applying for**?** If you enjoy the outdoors, for example, and like to be active, **you are** not going to be happy with a nine-to-five office job, no matter how much it pays.

Second**,** is the job based in a location compatible with your **preferred** lifestyle**?** No matter how much you like your work, if you go home every night to an **environment** you are miserable in, it will not be long before you start **transferring** your **dissatisfaction** to your job. If you like the amenities and **conveniences** of the city, you probably will not enjoy working in a small town. If, on the other hand, you prefer the quiet and security of small town life, you may find the city a stressful place in which to live.

Finally, is **the company you are applying to** one that you want to work for**?** Do you need the security of generous **benefits**, a good pension plan, and incentives to stay and grow with one company? Or are you an **ambitious** person who is looking for variety, quick advancement, and a high salary**?** If so, you may have to forego security in favour of commissions or cash incentives and be willing to move as quickly and as often as opportunities occur. Some **careful** self-analysis now, before you start out on your career path, will help you **choose** a direction that will put you in the 43 percent minority of satisfied Canadian workers.

Answers for Chapter 20: Documenting Your Sources (pages 290–305)

Exercise 20.2

Works Cited

American Institute of Stress. 2 May 2005 <http://www.stress.org>.

Cleeland, Nancy. "As Jobs Heat Up, Workers' Hearts Take a Beating." *Vancouver Sun*
    Mar. 2005: A2.

Dubrin, Andrew. *Getting It Done: The Transforming Power of Self-Discipline*.
    Princeton, NJ: Pacesetter, 1995.

Ford, Janet. "Time Management." E-mail to Sarah Norton. 5 June 2005.

Selye, Hans. Interview. 1 Jan. 1982.

White, Linda A. "Child Care, Women's Labour Market Participation and Labour
    Market Policy Effectiveness in Canada." *Canadian Public Policy* 27.4 (2001):
    385–405.

Answers for Chapter 22: Cracking the Sentence Code (pages 327–38)

Exercise 22.1

1. I <u>bought</u> a used car.
2. The used <u>car was</u> cheap.
3. <u>It needed</u> some repairs.
4. Unfortunately, the <u>repairs were</u> expensive.
5. <u>Insurance</u> for the car <u>was</u> expensive, too.
6. <u>Buying</u> a car <u>is</u> costly.
7. According to the salesman, the <u>car was</u> not <u>overpriced</u>.
8. <u>[You]</u> Always <u>get</u> a second opinion.
9. After 10 years, <u>cars</u> sometimes <u>develop</u> serious problems.
10. <u>Paying</u> for repairs <u>compensates</u> for the cheap price.

Exercise 22.2

1. Here <u>is</u> an <u>idea</u> to consider.
2. <u>William Lyon Mackenzie led</u> a rebellion against the Government of Canada.
3. <u>He</u> later <u>became</u> the mayor of Toronto.
4. <u>Who wants</u> the last piece?
5. <u>You</u> (understood) <u>Eat</u> slowly.
6. There, beyond the swimming pool, <u>is</u> the <u>gym</u>.
7. A moving <u>chicken is</u> poultry in motion.
8. Far behind the leaders <u>trailed</u> the main <u>group</u> of cyclists.
9. Here <u>are</u> the <u>results</u> of your examination.
10. Irish <u>coffee contains</u> ingredients from all four of the essential food groups: caffeine, fat, sugar, and alcohol.

Exercise 22.3

1. He <u>has talked</u> nonstop for three hours.
2. I <u>am</u> not <u>going</u> to drive.
3. <u>Could they return</u> the goods tomorrow?
4. <u>You cannot eat</u> your birthday cake before dinner.
5. <u>Carla should have been filing</u> the letters and memos.
6. <u>I will be</u> the first member of my family to graduate from college.
7. Paula's <u>lawsuit should</u> never <u>have been allowed</u> to proceed this far.
8. <u>Have you</u> ever <u>been</u> to the Zanzibar tavern?
9. There <u>has</u> never <u>been</u> a better <u>time</u> to travel to Greece.
10. How <u>are</u> the club <u>members identified</u>?

Exercise 22.4

1. ~~Among English teachers,~~ Santa's <u>helpers are known</u> as subordinate clauses.
2. ~~After his death,~~ <u>Terry Fox became</u> a national symbol ~~of heroic courage~~.
3. ~~In the state of Florida,~~ <u>it is</u> illegal ~~for single, divorced, or widowed women~~ to parachute ~~on Sunday afternoons~~.
4. ~~In Kentucky,~~ no <u>woman may appear</u> ~~in a bathing suit on any highway in the state~~ unless escorted ~~by two officers~~ or armed ~~with a club~~.
5. ~~In my wildest imaginings,~~ <u>I cannot understand</u> ~~these laws~~.
6. ~~During a break in the conversation,~~ Darryl's embarrassing <u>comment could be heard</u> ~~in every corner of the room~~.

7. ~~In my lawyer's dictionary~~, a <u>will</u> <u>is defined</u> as a dead giveaway.
8. ~~To the staff and managers of the project~~, I <u>extend</u> my congratulations ~~for an excellent job~~.
9. ~~Against all odds~~, and ~~despite their shortcomings~~, the St. John <u>Miners</u> <u>made</u> it ~~into the playoffs of the Southern New Brunswick Little League~~.
10. [You] <u>Walk</u> a mile ~~in my shoes at high noon with your head held high in order to avoid clichés like the plague~~.

Exercise 22.5

1. <u>Management</u> and <u>union</u> <u>met</u> ~~for a two-hour bargaining session~~.
2. <u>They</u> <u>debated</u> and <u>drafted</u> a tentative agreement ~~for a new contract~~.
3. The <u>anesthetist</u> and the <u>surgeon</u> <u>scrubbed</u> ~~for surgery~~ and <u>hurried</u> ~~to the operating room~~.
4. <u>Frederick Banting</u> and <u>Norman Bethune</u> <u>are known</u> ~~around the world~~ as medical heroes.
5. <u>Kevin</u> and <u>Sandra</u> <u>hiked</u> and <u>cycled</u> ~~across most of Newfoundland~~.
6. My <u>son</u> or my <u>daughter</u> <u>will meet</u> me and <u>drive</u> me home.
7. [You] <u>Knock</u> three times and <u>ask</u> for Stan.
8. ~~In the 17th and 18th centuries~~, the <u>French</u> and the <u>English</u> <u>fought</u> ~~for control of Canada~~.
9. [You] <u>Buy</u> the base model and <u>don't</u> <u>waste</u> your money ~~on luxury options~~.
10. <u>Ragweed</u>, <u>golden rod</u>, and <u>twitch grass</u> <u>formed</u> the essential elements ~~in the bouquet for his English teacher~~.

Answers for Chapter 23: Solving Sentence-Fragment Problems (pages 339–46)

Exercise 23.1 (suggested answers)
We have made the sentence fragments into complete sentences to give you an idea of how the sentences might be formed. Different sentences can be made out of the fragments in this exercise; just be sure each sentence has a subject and a verb.

1. F   My favourite <u>movies</u> <u>are</u> about historical events.
2. F   <u>It</u> <u>is</u> silly to decide on the basis of rumour, not facts.
3. S
4. F   After cooking my famous tuna casserole, my <u>guests</u> politely <u>declined</u> to eat it.
5. F   The party <u>members</u> gathering in the campaign office <u>called</u> for a recount.
6. S
7. F   [You] <u>Put</u> your hands over your head.
8. F   I <u>don't</u> <u>want</u> to go anywhere without my iPod.
9. F   Having worked hard all her life, <u>she</u> <u>was</u> happy to retire.
10. S

Exercise 23.2 (suggested answers)
__F__ Professional athletes <u>make</u> millions of dollars a year. __F__ At the same time, owners of sports franchises <u>grow</u> fantastically rich from the efforts of their employees, the players. __F__ The fans <u>are</u> the forgotten people in the struggle for control over major league sports. __F__ <u>They</u> <u>are</u> the people who pay the money that

makes both owners and players rich. __S__ I have an idea that would protect everyone's interests. __S__ Cap the owners' profits. __S__ Cap the players' salaries. __F__ And, most important, [you] cap the ticket prices. __F__ This <u>plan</u> <u>would ensure</u> a fair deal for everyone. __S__ Fans should be able to see their teams play for the price of a movie ticket, not the price of a television set.

Exercise 23.3
1. F   Although
2. F   Since
3. S
4. F   Whichever
5. F   Before

Exercise 23.4
1. Although
2. As long as
3. Whether
4. Because
5. As

Exercise 23.5

Although many companies are experiencing growth, thanks to a healthy economy, **m**iddle managers are not breathing easily. As long as there is surplus of junior executives, **m**iddle managers will continue to look over their shoulders, never sure when the axe will fall. Whether through early retirement, buyout, or termination, **t**heir positions are being eliminated by cost-conscious firms whose eyes are focused on the bottom line. Because the executive branch of many businesses expanded rapidly during the years of high growth, **n**ow there is a large block of managers who have no prospects of advancement. As one analyst observed, when he examined this block of largely superfluous executives and their chances of rising in the company hierarchy, "You cannot push a rectangle up a triangle."

Exercise 23.6

In spite of what everyone says about the weak economy and the scarcity of jobs, especially for young people, I have financed my college career with a variety of part-time and seasonal jobs. Right now, for instance, while completing my third year at college, I have not one, or two, but three part-time jobs. I am a short-order cook three nights a week for a local bar and diner, **a**nd a telemarketer for a cable company after school **o**r whenever I have free time. I'm also a server at a specialty coffee store on weekends. To maintain any kind of social life **w**hile juggling three jobs and the requirements of my third-year program is not exactly easy, but I find it hard to turn down the opportunity for experience, **n**ot to mention cash. I'm willing to put my social life on hold **f**or a while.

Answers for Chapter 24: Solving Run-On Problems (pages 347–51)

Exercise 24.1
1. This is strong coffee. It has dissolved my spoon!
2. Just let me do the talking. We're sure to get a ticket if you open your mouth.

3. Correct

4. If you have never tried it, hitting a golf ball may look easy, **but** it's not.

5. Correct

6. Montreal used to be known as Ville St. Marie. Before that it was known as Hochelaga.

7. Students today really need summer jobs and part-time employment **because** their tuition and living costs are too high for most families to subsidize.

8. Correct

9. It's very windy, **so** a ball hit deep to centre field will likely go into the stands.

10. "I was married by a judge; I should have asked for a jury." (Groucho Marx)

Exercise 24.2

1. I use a keyboard all the time, **and** my handwriting has become illegible.

2. Despite my parents' objections, I enjoy having long hair **because** it makes me feel attractive.

3. Casual meetings are fine for small groups, **but** more formal settings are appropriate for larger groups.

4. I'd be happy to help you. Just call when you need me; I'll be here all day.

5. In Canada, winter is more than a season. It's a bad joke.

6. Correct

7. For students in most technology programs, the future looks bright; however, a diploma does not guarantee job security.

8. A Canadian who speaks three languages is called multilingual; one who speaks two languages is called bilingual; **and** one who speaks only one language is called an English Canadian.

9. Skilled people are needed in specialized fields; currently, the top three are geriatrics, hospitality, and environmental technology.

10. I believe in a unified Canada. **I** believe that in 1867 the Fathers of Confederation were right: a federation of provinces can make a strong nation.

Answers for Chapter 25: Solving Modifier Problems (pages 352–60)

Exercise 25.1

1. Trevor left out the can of Pet Grrmet he had opened for the dog.

2. On the first day, our supervisor told us no one takes coffee breaks. (*Or:* Our supervisor told us no one takes coffee breaks on the first day.)

3. With no experience whatever, I enthusiastically recommend this candidate.

4. In September, Professor Green told us he thought our class was a hopeless case. (*Or:* Professor Green told us he thought our class was a hopeless case in September.)

5. We enjoyed almost the whole movie; only the ending was a disappointment.

6. In a highrise within walking distance of the campus, Leo and Annie found an apartment with two bedrooms and a sunken living room.

7. There are just enough pieces to go around.

8. It seems there is a game almost every day during baseball season.

9. A charming, intelligent companion who looks good in evening gowns and diamonds is sought by a vertically challenged but wealthy gentleman.

10. Only one of us could go because there was just enough money to buy one ticket.

Exercise 25.2

1. One usually finds the best Chinese food in those restaurants where the Chinese eat.

2. Using his new binoculars, he caught sight of a canary and several finches.

3. Using my camera with automatic functions, I can take professional-quality pictures.

4. The football practices have been organized as a keep-fit measure for players who are not with a team in the summertime.

5. Vancouver is a wonderful city to live in for anyone who likes rain and fog.

6. Some games, such as tiddlywinks, are less demanding in terms of time and equipment.

7. The Human Rights Code prohibits discrimination on the basis of race, religion, sex, or age against anyone who is applying for a job.

8. We looked in a golf store for a birthday present for our boss.

9. Each year, almost 500,000 Canadian men have a vasectomy.

10. Using cash as a motivator, we hope to improve our students' performances.

Exercise 25.3

1. Because she was driving recklessly and without lights, the police stopped Gina at a roadblock.

2. After I had been late twice in one week, my supervisor gave me a lecture about punctuality.

3. After criticizing both my work and my attitude, she fired me.

4. With enough memory to store her favourite movies and more than 10,000 songs, the iBook was the computer Hannah knew she needed.

5. After they spent two weeks quarrelling over money, their relationship was over.

6. As a dedicated fan of Alice Munro, I believe her last book was her best.

7. In less than a minute after applying the ointment, I felt the pain begin to ease.

8. Jake was probably more nervous than Allison, who was making her first formal presentation to her colleagues and her supervisor.

9. When you are handling hazardous waste, the safety manual clearly outlines the procedures to follow.

10. After spending the day in the kitchen preparing a gourmet meal, Kendra felt her efforts weren't appreciated because the guests drank too much wine.

Exercise 25.4

1. She was the baker's only daughter, but she could loaf all day. (*Or:* She was only the baker's daughter, but she could loaf all day.)

2. Being horribly hung over, I came to the realization that the only problem with a free bar is knowing when to quit.

3. Sam finally got the terrified horse, which was rearing and kicking, under control.

4. In a hurry to get to the interview on time, I left my résumé lying on my desk at home.
5. As a college student constantly faced with new assignments, I find the pressure is sometimes intolerable.
6. Listening to the rumours, I'll bet the newlyweds are already on the road to separation.
7. The display of liquor in the duty-free outlet held no interest for me because I am a nondrinker.
8. Quartetto Gelato receives enthusiastic acclaim from Vancouver to St. John's for its original arrangements and witty presentations.
9. Queen Elizabeth couldn't resist the little Corgi puppy, which was rolling on her back, eager to have her tummy scratched.
10. If you wear a small Canadian flag on your backpack or lapel, your reception abroad will be warm and enthusiastic.

Answers for Chapter 26: The Parallelism Principle (pages 361–66)

Exercise 26.1

1. This program is easy to understand and to use.
2. We were told that we would have to leave and that we could take nothing with us.
3. We organized our findings, wrote the report, and finally prepared our PowerPoint presentation.
4. Both applicants were unskilled, unprepared, and unmotivated.
5. Elmer's doctor advised him not to strain his back or his mind.
6. The company is looking for an employee who has a car and who knows the city.
7. If consumers really cared, they could influence the fast-food industry to produce healthy, delicious, inexpensive food.
8. When I want to get away from it all, there are three solitary pleasures that I enjoy: walking quietly in the country, reading a good book, and listening to fine music. (*Or:* . . . a walk in the country, a good book, and fine music.)
9. A recent survey of female executives claims that responsibility for their families, exclusion from informal networks, and lack of management experience are the major factors keeping them from advancement.
10. If it is to be useful, your report must be clearly organized, well written, and thoroughly researched.

Exercise 26.2

1. For my birthday, I requested either a Roots jacket or a Dior scarf.
2. In my community, two related crimes are rapidly increasing: drug abuse and theft.
3. Bodybuilding has made me what I am today: physically perfect, financially prosperous, and practically friendless.
4. After reading all the explanations and completing all the exercises, you'll be a better writer.
5. Bruce claimed that, through repetition and reward, he had trained his centipede to be loyal and obedient.
6. During their vacation in New Brunswick, Tracy and Jane visited many beautiful locations and ate wonderful seafood.

7. I'm an average tennis player; I have a good forehand, an average backhand, but a weak serve.
8. The problem with being immortalized as a statue is that you will be a target for pigeon droppings and graffiti artists.
9. Never disturb a sleeping dog, a happy baby, or a silent politician.
10. I'd like to help, but I'm too tired and too busy.

Exercise 26.3

1. wine	women	song
2. do your best	don't give up	
3. lying about all morning	doing whatever I please	
4. information	education	entertainment
5. as individuals	as a group	
6. privately	publicly	
7. happy	healthy	wise
8. employers	full-time employees	contract workers
9. lack of time	[lack of] money	[lack of] staff
10. French is the language of love	English is the language of business	German is the language of profanity

Exercise 26.4

1. Not being able to speak the language is confusing, frustrating, and embarrassing.
2. Trying your best and succeeding are not always the same thing.
3. The first candidate we interviewed seemed frightened and shy, but the second was composed and confident.
4. Licking one's fingers and picking one's teeth in a restaurant are one way to get attention.
5. Our CEO claims his most valuable business assets are a good backhand and membership at an exclusive golf club.
6. In order to succeed in this economy, small businesses must be creative, innovative, and flexible.
7. Lowering our profit margin, raising our prices, and laying off two managers will enable us to meet our budget.
8. After an enjoyable dinner, I like to drink a cappuccino, eat a dark chocolate mint, and, occasionally, smoke a good cigar.
9. Lying in the sun, consuming high-fat foods, and smoking cigarettes are three dangerous activities that were once thought to be healthy.
10. Business travellers complain of long delays at airports, higher costs for services, and tighter restrictions on their freedom of movement.

Answers for Chapter 27: Refining by Combining (pages 367–71)

Exercise 27.1

1. We cannot sell our cottage, **so** we will live there instead.
2. There are three solutions given for this problem, **and** all of them are correct.
3. The people in our firm work very hard, **but** they wouldn't want it any other way.
4. We could spend our day off shopping at the mall, **or** we could spend the day fishing.

5. Great leaders do not bully their people, **nor** do they deceive them.
6. I will not be able to finish my report, **for** there are only two hours before the deadline.
7. Jennifer knows that she likely will not get the vice-president's job, **yet** (*or* **but**) she wants the experience of applying for it.
8. Finish the estimate, **but** do not begin work until it has been approved.
9. Today has been the worst day of my life, **so** my horoscope was right.
10. The government did not offer me a job, **nor** did it even reply to my letter.

Exercise 27.2 (suggested answers)

1. Leonardo da Vinci was a great artist and inventor **who** invented scissors, among other things.
2. Cats can produce over 100 vocal sounds, **whereas** dogs can make only 10.
3. **Although** it is said that men don't cry, they do while assembling furniture.
4. The name Wendy was made up for a book **that** was called *Peter Pan*.
5. **Although** 10 percent of Canadians are heavy drinkers, 35 percent abstain from alcohol.
6. Travel broadens the mind **even though** it flattens the bank account.
7. We are seeking an experienced and innovative director **who** is fluent in French.
8. One hundred thousand Vietnam veterans have taken their own lives, **which** is twice the number who were killed in action.
9. **After** my cooking class went on a field trip to gather greens for a salad, we discovered that what we thought was watercress was, in fact, poison ivy.
10. Eight of the ten classmates who ate the salad were hospitalized, **although** no one was seriously affected.

Answers for Chapter 28: Mastering Subject–Verb Agreement (pages 372–81)

Exercise 28.1

1. They sell used essays to other students.
2. Those new guidelines affect all the office procedures.
3. All those who shop at Pimrock's receive free cans of tuna.
4. The women maintain that their boss has been harassing them.
5. Those girls' fathers are looking for rich husbands for them.

Exercise 28.2

1. is
2. is
3. is
4. are
5. tempt

Exercise 28.3

1. are
2. registers
3. is

4. wonders
5. puts

Exercise 28.4

1. is
2. involves
3. is
4. wants
5. believes

Exercise 28.5

1. plans
2. has
3. have
4. was
5. are

Exercise 28.6

1. was
2. seems
3. is
4. is
5. seems

Exercise 28.7

1. Neither of the following two sentences **is** correct.
2. The teachers, with the full support of the college administration, **treat** plagiarism as a serious offence.
3. Either good looks or intelligence **runs** in our family, but never at the same time.
4. None of these computer programs **is** able to streamline our billing procedures.
5. The enjoyment of puns and jokes involving plays on words **is** the result of having too little else on your mind.
6. Anyone who jumps from one of Paris's many bridges **is** in Seine.
7. It is amazing how much better the orchestra **plays** now that the conductor is sober.
8. The number of layoffs reported in the headlines **seems** to be rising again.
9. Her supervisors all agree that Emily **needs** further training to be effective.
10. Canada's First Nations population **is** thought to have come to this continent from Asia thousands of years before the Europeans arrived in North America.

Exercise 28.8

Quebec City, along with Montreal, Toronto, and Vancouver, **is** among Canada's great gourmet centres. Whereas Toronto is a relative latecomer to this list, neither Quebec City nor Montreal **is a stranger** to those who **seek** fine dining. Indeed, travel and food magazines have long affirmed that the inclusion of these two cities in a Quebec vacation **is** a "must." Montreal is perhaps more international in its offerings, but Quebec City provides exquisite proof that French-Canadian cuisine and hospitality **are** second to none in the world. Amid the Old World charm of the lower city

are to be found some of the quaintest and most enjoyable traditional restaurants; the newer sections of town **boast** equally fine dining in more contemporary surroundings. The combination of the wonderful food and the city's fascinating charms **is** sure to make any visitor return frequently. Either the summer, when the city blooms and outdoor cafés abound, or the winter, when Carnaval turns the streets into hundreds of connecting parties, **is a** wonderful **time** to visit one of Canada's oldest and most interesting cities.

Answers for Chapter 29: Using Verbs Effectively (pages 382–95)

Exercise 29.1

1. lay
2. eaten
3. ridden
4. sat
5. lie
6. chosen
7. printed
8. lent
9. worn
10. known

Exercise 29.3

1. After he accused me, I **called** him a liar.
2. Hank Aaron broke Babe Ruth's record of 714 home runs in a lifetime when he **hit** number 715 in 1974.
3. Children are quite perceptive and **know** when you are lying to them.
4. She went up to the counter and **asked** for a refund.
5. When Brad Pitt walked into the room, the girls **went** crazy.
6. correct
7. Tim walked into the room, took one look at Leroy, and **smashed** him right through the wall.
8. First you will greet the guests; then you **will show** them to their rooms.
9. The largest cheese ever produced took 43 hours to make and **weighed** a whopping 15,723 kg.
10. He watches television until he finally **goes** to sleep.

Exercise 29.4

For some reason, when mistakes or accidents happen in radio or television, they **are** often hilariously funny. If, in the course of a conversation, someone said, "Here come the Duck and Doochess of Kent," listeners would probably be mildly amused. But many years ago, when an announcer **made** that slip on a live radio broadcast, it **became** one of the most famous blunders in radio history. Tapes of the slip **were** filed in "bloopers" libraries all over the world. This heightened sense of hilarity is the reason that so many people who work in radio **dedicate** their creativity to making the on-air announcer laugh while reading the news. To take one example, Lorne Greene's **was** the deeply serious voice that **was** heard on the CBC news during World War II. He **was** the victim of all kinds of pranks aimed at getting him to break up while reading the dark, often tragic, news of the combat overseas. The pages of his news script **were** set on fire while he **read**. He **was** even stripped naked as he **read**, calmly, and apparently without strain. Lorne Greene **was** a true professional. Many other newscasters, however, **have been** highly susceptible to falling apart on air at the slightest provocation. And there **are** always people around a radio station who cannot resist giving them that little push.

Exercise 29.6

1. The department head called a meeting.
2. The server will make expresso in a few minutes.
3. When it gets cold, we plug in the block heater overnight.
4. For many years, professional athletes have used steroids to improve speed and endurance.
5. You must not knead the dough, or your pastry will be tough.
6. My parents wrote this postcard while they were hiking through Nepal.
7. A crew of students made this movie for less than $900,000.
8. Thieves broke into our neighbours' house while they were vacationing in the Caribbean.
9. You made an error in the code you wrote for this program.
10. The Mighty Ducks have replaced the Red Sox and the White Sox as the team with the stupidest name in sports.

Exercise 29.7

1. Another Juno was won by Sarah McLachlan. (Active is more effective.)
2. The ball was spiked by Carl, after scoring the winning points. (Active is more effective.)
3. A bylaw forbidding smoking in bars and restaurants has been passed by city council. (Passive is more effective, because it focuses the readers' attention on the law rather than on who brought the law into being.)
4. Forty-eight hours later, the technician added 2 mL of sterile water to the culture in the petri dish. (Passive is more effective; it puts the focus on the procedure rather than on the person.)
5. Four tickets for the concert were got by Courtenay after standing in line all night. (Active is more effective.)
6. The truth behind the famous Doobie Brothers scandal was revealed on the 10 p.m. news. (Passive is more effective; what was revealed is of more interest than who revealed it.)
7. The judge finally announced her judgment today, almost a year after the environmental hearings were concluded. (Passive is more effective, for the same reason as in sentence 6.)
8. After a long debate, Yasmin's fundraising proposal was finally endorsed by the committee. (Passive is more effective, because it focuses attention on the individual proposal rather than on the anonymous committee.)
9. Dr. Hans Steiner, a psychologist at Stanford University, has developed a computer program that analyzes speech patterns. (Passive is more effective, for the same reason as in sentence 6.)
10. After years of research among college students, Dr. Steiner has concluded that people who frequently use passive-voice constructions tend to be maladjusted. (Active is more effective.)

Answers for Chapter 30: Solving Pronoun Problems (pages 396–415)

Exercise 30.1

1. No one except you and **me** . . .
2. **He** and I can't figure out this problem set any better than you and **she** could.
3. George and **he** fell asleep . . .
4. Do you want to work with Emma and **her**?
5. We can use the film passes all week, and you and **she** can use them on the weekend when Biff and **I** are going skiing.
6. Thanks to the recommendations provided by your math instructor and **me**, you and **she** got the tutorial jobs.
7. As we were going to class, Karl and **I** heard . . .
8. If it hadn't been for Hassan and **him** . . .
9. Quentin and **he** agreed to split the price of a case with Stan and **me**.
10. Only two students passed the midterm: Nadia and **I**.

Exercise 30.2

1. At 14, my younger brother is already taller than **I** [am].
2. No one likes partying more than **he** and Anne.
3. Would you like to join Daniel and **me** . . . ?
4. Only one person in this firm could manage the department as well as **he** [could].
5. At last I have met someone who enjoys grilled liver as much as **I** [do].
6. We can skate as well as **they**, but they are much better at shooting and defending than **we** [are].
7. More than **I** [do], Serge uses the computer . . . .

Exercise 30.3

1. My boyfriend and **I** . . . .
2. I like fast food better than **he** [does].
3. He likes vegetables better than **I** [do].
4. In fact, between you and **me** . . . .
5. . . . it is difficult for **them** to know where to take him and **me** . . . .
6. The only type of restaurant where **we** and **they** can all have what we like is Italian.
7. There, **he** and his friends . . . .
8. We are probably not as healthy as they, but they don't seem to enjoy their food as much as **we** [do].

Exercise 30.4

1. his
2. her
3. his
4. her
5. himself, he

Exercise 30.5

1. Everyone who enjoys a thrilling match will reserve a seat . . . .
2. . . . everyone climbed to the fourth floor to hand in the course evaluation.

3. Each of her sons successfully completed his diploma.

4. Someone with lots of money left a purse in the women's washroom.

5. All reporters must decide for themselves how far they will go . . . .

Exercise 30.6

1. Virginia claims that every one of her male friends has a room of his own.

2. Almost everyone I know is concerned about finding a suitable job.

3. Anybody who applies for a job with this institution can expect to spend a lot of time in selection committee interviews.

4. Taking pictures of people when they are not looking can produce interesting results.

5. Nearly every man who can cook will tell you that he enjoys preparing food.

Exercise 30.7

1. I know that smoking is bad for me and everyone else, but I can't give up cigarettes.

2. If your pet rat won't eat its food, feed the pellets to the kitty.

3. Our cat is a picky eater; her food preferences are inconvenient and expensive.

4. Whenever Stefan and Matt played poker, Stefan stacked the deck.

5. The gorilla was mean and hungry because he had finished all his food in the morning.

6. Madonna has transformed herself at least four times in her career, an accomplishment that makes her unique.

7. Dani backed her car into a garbage truck and dented her fender.

8. Rocco was suspicious of handgun control because he thought everyone should have a gun for late-night subway rides.

9. Get your ears pierced during this week's special and take home an extra pair of earrings free.

10. Our car is in the shop, but we're still going to the party.

Exercise 30.9

1. The actress **who** saw her first grey hair thought she'd dye.

2. I am a longtime fan of David Cronenberg, a director **who** began his career in Canada.

3. I wonder why we are so often attracted to people **who** are completely opposite to us.

4. I'm one of those people **who** should stay out of the sun.

5. People **who** take afternoon naps often suffer from insomnia as a result.

6. The vacuum-cleaner salesperson **who** came to our door was the sort of person **who** won't take no for an answer.

7. This is the brilliant teacher **who** helped me achieve the grades **that** I had thought were beyond me.

8. Marathon runners **who** wear cheap shoes often suffer the agony of defeat.

9. The math problems **that** we worked on last night would have baffled anyone **who** hadn't done all the problem sets.

10. We took the ancient Jeep, **which** we had bought from a friend **who** had lost his licence, to a scrapyard **that** paid us $200 for it.

Exercise 30.10

1. you
2. you, your
3. a
4. she
5. we

Exercise 30.11

1. People who live in glass houses shouldn't throw stones.
2. Experience is something **you acquire** just after you need it.
3. Anyone who enjoys snowboarding can have **her** (*or* **his** *or* **the**) best holiday ever in western Alberta.
4. When she asked if Peter Tchaikovsky played for the Canucks, **I** knew she wasn't the woman for me.
5. From time to time, most of us think about the opportunities we've missed even if **we're** happy with what **we** have.
6. Managers who are concerned about employee morale should think about ending **their** policy of threats and intimidation and consider other means to improve efficiency.
7. If you are afraid of vampires, **you** should wear garlic around **your** neck and carry a silver bullet.
8. Any woman who wears a garlic necklace probably won't have to worry about men harassing **her**, either.
9. Can you really know another person if you have never been to **his** (*or* **her**) home?
10. A sure way to lose **your** friends is to eat all the ice cream yourself.

Exercise 30.12

When people see a dreadful occurrence on television, such as a bombing, an earthquake, or a mass slaughter, it does not always affect **them.** It is one thing for people to see the ravages of war **themselves** and another thing to see a three-minute newscast of the same battle, neatly edited by the CBC. Even the horrible effects of natural catastrophes that wipe out whole populations are somehow minimized or trivialized when **people** see them on TV. And though viewers may be horrified by the gaunt faces of starving children on the screen, **they** can easily escape into **their** familiar world of Egg McMuffins, Shake'n Bake, and Labatt Blue that is portrayed in commercial messages.

Thus, the impact of television on us is a mixed one. It is true that **we are** shown terrible, sometimes shocking events that **we** could not possibly have seen before television. In this way, **our** world is drawn together more closely. However, the risk in creating this immediacy is that **we** may become desensitized and cease to feel or care about **our** fellow human beings.

Answers for Chapter 31: The Comma (pages 416–26)

Exercise 31.1

1. Holly held two aces**,** a King**,** a Queen**,** and a Jack in her hand.
2. The food at the Thai Palace is colourful**,** spicy**,** delicious**,** and inexpensive.
3. Life would be complete if I had a Blackberry**,** a Porsche**,** a Sea-Doo**,** and a job.

4. The gear list for the Winter Wilderness course includes woollen underwear, snowshoes, Arctic boots, and a toque.
5. In the summer, a cup of coffee, a croissant, and a glass of juice are all I want for breakfast.
6. Don't forget to bring the videos, maps, and souvenirs of your trip to Australia.
7. In Ontario, the four seasons are summer, winter, winter, and winter.
8. My doctor and my nutritionist agree that I should eat better, exercise more, and take vitamins.
9. Sleeping through my alarm, dozing during sociology class, napping in the library after lunch, and snoozing in front of the TV after supper are symptoms of my overactive nightlife.
10. Welcome home! Once you have finished your homework, taken out the garbage, and done the dishes, you can feed the cat, clean your room, and do your laundry.

Exercise 31.2

1. Either it is very foggy this morning, or I am going blind.
2. We have an approved business plan and budget, but we're still looking for qualified and experienced staff.
3. Talk shows haven't said anything new in years, nor have they solved a single one of the problems they endlessly discuss.
4. We discovered that we both had an interest in fine art, so we made a date to go to an exhibition at the art gallery next week.
5. Canadians are proud of their country, but they don't approve of too much flag-waving.
6. Take good notes, for I'll need them in order to study for the exam.
7. I'll rent a tux, but I will not get a haircut or my shoes shined.
8. I chose a quiet seat on the train, and two women with bawling babies boarded at the next station.
9. I have travelled all over the world, yet my luggage has visited at least twice the number of countries that I have.
10. Jet lag makes me look haggard and ill, but at least I resemble my passport photo.

Exercise 31.3

1. A good day, in my opinion, always starts with a few cuts of high-volume heavy metal.
2. This photograph, which was taken when I was four, embarrasses me whenever my parents display it.
3. Mira's boyfriend, who looks like an ape, is living proof that love is blind.
4. Isn't it strange that the poor, who often are bitterly critical of the rich, keep buying lottery tickets?
5. A nagging headache, the result of last night's great party, made me miserable all morning.
6. Our ancient car made it all the way to Saskatoon without anything falling off or breaking down, a piece of good luck that astonished everyone.
7. Professor Repke, a popular mathematics teacher, won the Distinguished Teaching Award this year.

8. We're going to spend the afternoon at the mall, a weekly event that has become a ritual.
9. correct
10. Classical music, which I call Prozac for the ears, can be very soothing in times of stress.

Exercise 31.4

1. Unfortunately, we'll have to begin all over again.
2. Mr. Dillinger, the bank would like a word with you.
3. In college, the quality of your work is more important than the effort you put into it.
4. Hopelessly lost, my father still refused to stop and ask for directions.
5. Finally understanding what she was trying to say, I apologized for being so slow.
6. After an evening of watching television, I have accomplished as much as if I had been unconscious.
7. Since the doctor ordered me to walk to work every morning, I have seen three accidents involving people walking to work.
8. Having munched our way through a large bag of peanuts while watching the game, we weren't interested in supper.
9. Whenever an optimist is pulled over by a police officer, the optimist assumes it's to ask for directions.
10. That same year, Stephen Leacock bought his summer home in Orillia, Ontario.

Exercise 31.5

1. correct
2. correct
3. correct
4. Toronto in the summer is hot, smoggy, and humid.
5. Today's paper has an article about a new car made of lightweight, durable aluminum.
6. Dietitians recommend that we eat at least two servings daily of green, leafy vegetables.
7. This ergonomic, efficient, full-function keyboard comes in a variety of pastel shades.
8. We ordered a large, nutritious salad for lunch, then indulged ourselves with a redcurrant cheesecake for dessert.
9. Danny bought a cute, cuddly, pure-bred puppy.
10. Ten months later that cute puppy turned into a vicious, man-eating monster.

Exercise 31.6

1. Pinot noir, which is a type of grape grown in California, Oregon, British Columbia(,) and Ontario, produces a delicious red wine.
2. There are, I am told, people who don't like garlic, but you won't find any of them eating at Freddy's.
3. I use e-mail to communicate with my colleagues, a fax machine to keep in touch with clients(,) and Canada Post to send greetings to my relatives.
4. Your dogs, Mr. Pavlov, seem hungry for some reason.

5. According to G. K. Chesterton, "If a thing is worth doing, it is worth doing badly."

6. Looking for a competent computer technologist, we interviewed, tested, investigated(,) and rejected 30 applicants.

7. How you choose to phrase your resignation is up to you, but I expect to have it on my desk by morning.

8. Your superstitious dread of March 13, Senator Caesar, is irrational and silly.

9. The lenses of my new high-function sunglasses are impact-resistant, yellow, UV-reflective optical plastic.

10. Canada, a country known internationally for beautiful scenery, peaceful intentions(,) and violent hockey, always places near the top of the United Nations' list of desirable places to live.

Exercise 31.7

1. Whereas the Super Bowl tradition goes back about four decades, the Grey Cup has a history that stretches back to the 19th century.

2. Otherwise, Mrs. Lincoln said, she had very much enjoyed the play.

3. Our guard dog, a Rottweiler, caught an intruder and maimed him for life.

4. Unfortunately, my Uncle Ladislaw was the intruder, and he intends to sue us for every penny we have.

5. correct

6. We bought a lovely, old, mahogany dining table at auction for $300.

7. If there were more people like Gladys, global warming would be the least of our worries.

8. correct

9. Deciding on the midnight blue velvet pants was easy, but paying for them was not.

10. Igor asked, "May I show you to your quarters, or would you prefer to spend the night in the dungeon?"

Answers for Chapter 32: The Semicolon (pages 427–31)

Exercise 32.1

1. incorrect	6. incorrect
2. correct	7. correct
3. incorrect	8. incorrect
4. incorrect	9. incorrect
5. incorrect	10. incorrect

Exercise 32.2

1. We've eaten all the food; it's time to go home.

2. correct

3. Your instructor would like to see you pass; however, there may be a small fee involved.

4. Molly is going to Chicago; she wants to appear on *Oprah*.

5. Many people dislike hockey because some of the players act like goons rather than athletes.

6. Orville tried and tried; but he couldn't get the teacher's attention.

7. correct

8. Tomorrow is another day; unfortunately, it will probably be just like today.

9. Rumours of a merger had begun to circulate by five o'clock, so it's no wonder many employees looked nervous on their way home.

10. We knew the party had been a success when Uncle Morty, drunk as usual, tap-danced across the top of the piano; Aunt Madeline, who must weigh at least 80 kg, did her Cirque du Soleil routine; and Stan punched out two of his cousins.

Exercise 32.3

1. The rain has to stop soon; otherwise, we'll have to start building an ark.

2. Our finances are a mess; the only way we can repay our debts would be to stop paying for rent and food.

3. We need you at the meeting; however, since you have another engagement, we will have to reschedule.

4. A day without puns is like a day without sunshine; it leaves gloom for improvement.

5. I work on an assembly line; all of us workers believe that if a job is worth doing, it's worth doing 11,000 times a day.

6. It is not impossible to become wealthy; if you're under 20, all you need to do is put the price of a pack of cigarettes into an RRSP every day, and you'll be a millionaire by the age of 50.

7. If, on the other hand, you continue to spend your money on smokes, the government will make the millions that could have been yours; you'll die early and broke.

8. As a dog lover and the owner of an Afghan, I suffer a great deal of abuse; for example, for my birthday, my wife gave me a book rating the intelligence of Afghans as 79th out of 79 breeds tested.

9. A plateau, according to the *Dictionary of Puns*, is a high form of flattery; this may be low humour, but it's a clever remark.

10. According to a *Gourmet Magazine* poll, four of the top ten restaurants in the world are in Paris; three—those ranking eighth, ninth, and tenth—are in the United States; two are in Tokyo; and the other is in Thailand.

Answers for Chapter 33: The Colon (pages 432–36)

Exercise 33.1

1. incorrect	6. correct
2. correct	7. correct
3. correct	8. incorrect
4. incorrect	9. incorrect
5. incorrect	10. incorrect

Exercise 33.2

1. I have set myself three goals this year: to achieve an 80 percent average, to get a good summer job, and to buy a car.

2. Right after we moved in, we discovered we had a problem: termites.

3. After our bankruptcy, our credit card consultant asked us an interesting question: "Why don't you cut up your credit cards?"

4. Several Canadian writers are even better known abroad than they are at home: Carol Shields, Neil Bissoondath, and Michael Ondaatje are three examples.

5. There are a number of inexpensive activities that will improve physical fitness: swimming, tennis, jogging, even brisk walking.

6. Jocelyn is trying to accomplish two mutually contradictory tasks: a significant weight loss and success as a restaurant critic.

7. Several of the animals on the international list of endangered species are native to Canada: the wood bison, the northern kit fox, and the whooping crane.

8. correct

9. The majority of Canada's population is worn out and exhausted at the end of a long, hard winter, but most people are able to console themselves with one comforting thought: spring will arrive sometime in May or June.

10. There are several troublesome implications of biological engineering, but one in particular is frightening to most people: the cloning of human beings.

Exercise 33.3

1. Believe it or not, the country that produces the most films every year is India.

2. correct

3. correct

4. The most annoying sound in the world has to be that produced by bagpipes.

5. The company's bankruptcy resulted from the CEO's management style. He relied on crisis management, seat-of-the-pants planning, and excessive profit-taking.

6. correct

7. correct

8. All most students ask is that their teachers treat them with courtesy, fairness, and respect.

9. Of course, there are always a few students who demand what no true professional will provide: special treatment.

10. Our department's proposal is unique: it has the CEO's approval.

Answers for Chapter 34: Quotation Marks (pages 437–39)

Exercise 34.1

1. "Did you see the look on her face?" asked Roderick.

2. correct

3. "I'd love to," she replied. "If only I knew how."

4. "Pardon me, boys, is this the Transylvania Station?" asked the man in the black cape.

5. When I pointed out to Wayne that he was wearing one green sock and one brown sock, he replied, "What's wrong with that? My brother has a pair just like it."

6. When I asked the guide if people jumped from the CN Tower very often, he replied, "No, just the once."

7. correct

8. "Just as well," muttered Terry, "because I wouldn't want the state to see what's growing on my bedroom windowsill."

9. I knew that Microsoft had lost its corporate mind when my computer flashed the following blue-screen error message: "No keyboard detected. Press any key to continue."

10. The psychiatrist said to the woman whose husband thought he was a horse, "I can cure your husband, but it will take a long time and be very costly." "Money is no object," replied the woman. "He just won the Queen's Plate."

Answers for Chapter 35: Question and Exclamation Marks (pages 440–43)

Exercise 35.1

1. question mark
2. period
3. period
4. period
5. question mark
6. question mark
7. period
8. question mark
9. period
10. question mark

Exercise 35.2

1. exclamation mark
2. exclamation mark, exclamation mark
3. exclamation mark
4. exclamation mark, exclamation mark (or period)
5. exclamation mark and period
6. two exclamation marks (or exclamation mark and period)
7. exclamation mark (inside final quotation mark)
8. exclamation mark, exclamation mark (or exclamation mark and period)
9. exclamation mark
10. exclamation mark, exclamation mark (or exclamation mark and period)

Answers for Chapter 36: Dashes and Parentheses (pages 444–49)

Exercise 36.1

1. One Aboriginal tribe in England painted themselves blue with dye from a plant—woad.

2. My purpose in moving from Vancouver to Hope—like that of hundreds of people before me—was to find affordable housing.

3. We shall have to start without her—again!

4. Skiing and skating—if you like these sports, you'll love Quebec.

5. Tending to his garden, writing his memoirs, and dining with friends—these were the pleasures Arnold looked forward to in retirement.

6. What is missing in his life is obvious—rest and relaxation!

7. Zoe should do well—in fact, I'm sure she will—in the engineering program.

8. Alexei was amazed—positively thunderstruck—when he learned Uncle Vladimir had won a million dollars.

9. Historians, diarists, and chroniclers—these are the recorders of our past.

10. Dashes—a kind of silent shout—allow you to insert an occasional exclamation into your sentences.

Exercise 36.2

1. Five of the students (I was asked not to name them) have volunteered to be peer tutors.
2. The apostrophe is explained in the unit on spelling (pages 463–70).
3. Jason complained that being a manager (he became one in March) was like being a cop.
4. I have enclosed a cheque for one hundred and fifty dollars ($150).
5. More members of the Canadian Armed Forces died in World War I (1914–18) than in any war before or since.
6. Although Mozart lived a relatively short time (he died when he was 36), he composed hundreds of musical masterpieces.
7. As news of her "miracle cures" spread (patients began to come to her from all over the province), the country doctor had to move her clinic to a more central location.
8. The new contract provided improved working conditions, a raise in salary (3 percent), and a new dental plan.
9. Ontario and British Columbia now produce world-class wines from three small estate wineries (Inniskillin, Hillebrand, Quail's Gate) that compete and win internationally.
10. "One of the most important tools for making paper speak in your own voice is punctuation; it plays the role of body language; it helps readers hear you the way you want to be heard" (Baker 48–49).

Answers for Chapter 37: Hazardous Homonyms (pages 450–62)

Exercise 37.1

1. course, affect
2. Are, accept
3. then, dessert
4. you're, losing
5. quite, here
6. whose, conscience
7. assured, number
8. It's, its
9. choose, course, advice
10. continual, dining

Exercise 37.2

1. simplistic, morals, implies
2. morale, miners, fazed
3. imply, further, creditable
4. effect, disperse, fewer
5. whose, principles, less
6. infer, whether, fourth
7. your, continually, ensures
8. conscious, choosing, site, farther
9. accept, counsellors, phase
10. number, allowed, fewer, than, women

Exercise 37.3

1. b
2. b

3. a
4. b
5. b
6. b
7. b
8. a
9. b
10. a

Answers for Chapter 38: The Apostrophe (pages 463–70)

Exercise 38.1
1. Yes, **it's** a long way from Halifax to Vancouver, but **we've** been in training for three months.
2. **We're** taking the train to Antigonish, and **we're** biking to Halifax; then **we'll** begin the big trip west.
3. There **wasn't** a dry eye in the theatre when **Spielberg's** film reached its climax.
4. **Who's** discovered **what's** wrong with this sentence?
5. Wasn't it Mark Twain who said, "**It's** easy to stop smoking; **I've** done it dozens of times"?

Exercise 38.2
   I am writing to apply for the position of webmaster for BrilloVision.com that **you have** advertised in the *Daily News*. **I have** the talent and background **you are** looking for. Currently, I work as a Web designer for an online publication, Vexed.com, where **they are** very pleased with my work. If you click on their website, I think **you will** like what you see. **There is** little in the way of Web design and application that I **have not** been involved in during the past two years. But **it is** time for me to move on to a new challenge, and BrilloVision.com promises the kind of opportunity **I am** looking for. I guarantee you **will not** be disappointed if I join your team!

Exercise 38.3
1. The **car's** brakes are worn and its tires are nearly bald.
2. Diplomatic **ambassadors'** wives or husbands are often as important to a **mission's** success as the ambassadors themselves.
3. Near Chicoutimi is one of the **country's** most beautiful parks, where the skills of canoeists, fishermen, and wildlife photographers can be put to the test on a **summer's** day.
4. **Janis'(s)** career got its start when she sang **seafarers'** songs in the yacht **club's** dining lounge.
5. A **country's** history is the main determinant of its national character.

Exercise 38.4
1. you're, your, your
2. Someone's, whose
3. ship's, weeks'

4. people's, workers', sides'
5. turtle's, turtle's, it's, its, yours

Exercise 38.5

1. When you feel like a snack, you can choose between apples and **Timbits**.
2. **Anna's** career took off when she discovered **it's** easy to sell **children's** toys.
3. Golfing requires the use of different **clubs**: woods for long shots, irons for short ones.
4. **Poker's** an easy game to play if you are dealt **aces** more often than your **opponents** are.
5. Good writing **skills don't** guarantee success in **your** career, but they help.

Answers for Chapter 39: The Hyphen (pages 471–74)

Exercise 39.1

1. Jill decided to sublet her **fifth-floor** apartment.
2. Fraser claims he is allergic to classical music but addicted to **hip-hop** music.
3. Just before the critical play, the **hard-fought** game was **pre-empted** by the movie *Heidi*!
4. **Hand-knit** sweaters are usually more expensive than **factory-produced** ones.
5. In 1950, at the age of **forty-seven**, George Orwell died of tuberculosis.

Exercise 39.2

1. For months after Saddam Hussein was **overthrown**, the world was shocked by revelations of the repression suffered by the Iraqi people.
2. Would you **relay** this message to Mr. Chan: the masons would like to **re-lay** the bricks this evening.
3. Our **next-door** neighbour teaches in a **high school**, but she does not like to be introduced as a **high-school** teacher.
4. A **face-to-face** meeting with an **anti-intellectual** always gets my adrenalin going.
5. Because Angela was an **attorney-at-law** and had once been an **all-Canadian** athlete, her former coach was not surprised when she became **Minister of Recreation**.

Answers for Chapter 40: Capital Letters (pages 475–81)

Exercise 40.1

1. **T**ime is nature's way of keeping everything from happening at once.
2. Brad whispered, "**T**here's a light in the Frankenstein house."
3. Learning Standard **E**nglish is, for many people, like learning another **l**anguage.
4. Richard Harkness, writing in *The New York Times*, said "**A** committee is a group of the unwilling, picked from the unfit, to do the unnecessary."
5. **I**n conclusion, I want you to consider the words of Wendell Johnson: "*Always* and *never* are two words you should always remember never to use."

Exercise 40.2

1. After a brief stay in the **M**aritimes, **C**aptain **T**allman and his crew sailed west up the **S**t. **L**awrence.
2. The **B**roadcast **D**epartment of **N**iagara College has ordered six **S**ony cameras for their studios in **W**elland, **O**ntario.
3. Do you find that **V**isa is more popular than American **E**xpress when you travel to faraway places such as **M**exico, **F**rance, or **J**upiter?
4. Our stay at the **S**eaview **H**otel overlooking the **P**acific **O**cean certainly beat our last vacation at the **B**ates **M**otel, where we faced west, overlooking the city dump.
5. As the fundraiser for our alumni association, I am targeting companies like **D**isney, **C**anadian **T**ire, the **B**ank of **M**ontreal, and the **CBC**, all of which employ our graduates.

Exercise 40.3

1. The **C**rusades, which were religious wars between **M**uslims and **C**hristians, raged through the **M**iddle **A**ges.
2. The **H**indu religion recognizes and honours many gods; **I**slam recognizes one god, **A**llah; **B**uddhism recognizes none.
3. The **K**oran, the **B**ible, and the **T**orah agree on many principles.
4. The **J**ewish festival of **H**anukkah often occurs near the same time that **C**hristians are celebrating **C**hristmas.
5. After **W**orld **W**ar I, many **J**ews began to emigrate to Palestine, where they and the **M**uslim population soon came into conflict.

Exercise 40.4

1. My favourite months are **J**anuary and **F**ebruary because I love all **w**inter sports.
2. This **M**onday is **V**alentine's **D**ay, when messages of love are exchanged.
3. In the summer, big meals seem too much trouble; however, after **T**hanksgiving, we need lots of food to survive the winter cold.
4. A **n**ational **h**oliday named **F**lag **D**ay was once proposed, but it was never officially approved.
5. By **T**hursday, I'll have finished my **S**t. **P**atrick's **D**ay costume.

Exercise 40.5

1. The review of my book, ***The Life and Times of a Chocoholic***, published in ***The Globe and Mail***, was not favourable.
2. Clint **E**astwood fans will be delighted that the two early movies that made him internationally famous, ***A Fistful of Dollars*** and ***For a Few Dollars More***, are now available on DVD.
3. Joseph Conrad's short novel ***Heart of Darkness*** became the blockbuster movie ***Apocalypse Now***.
4. Her poem, "**A B**right and **S**ilent **P**lace," was published in the **A**pril issue of ***Landscapes*** magazine.
5. Botticelli's famous painting, ***Birth of Venus***, inspired my poem "**W**oman on the **H**alf **S**hell."

Exercise 40.6

1. After studying geography for two years, I began taking courses in ancient **G**reek and modern history.

2. correct
3. By taking Professor Subden's noncredit course, **I**ntroduction to **W**ine, I qualified to register for **O**enology 120 the next semester.
4. While math is her strong subject, Laurie has trouble with accounting, **E**nglish, and conversational **F**rench.
5. The prerequisite for **T**heology 210 is **I**ntroduction to **W**orld **R**eligions, taught by Professor Singh.

Answers for Chapter 41: Numbers (pages 482–88)

Exercise 41.1

1. This applicant claims to speak more than **seven** languages, but from her résumé, I'd say that English is not **one** of them.
2. This is the **third** time the Accounting Department has filed its report **two** days late.
3. **Fifty-four** eager people have signed up for the **second** annual Pool Tournament.
4. Of the **12** cuts on her new DVD release, the **first** two are my favourites.
5. Gavin, who works for the garage where I take my car, was unable to answer **12** of the **23** questions on the Mechanic Certification Exam.
6. In the Great Fire of 1666, **half** of London burned down, but only **six** people lost their lives.
7. If the diesel mixture contains **three-quarters** of a litre of regular gasoline, it will make your truck easier to start in those **four** or **five** really cold weeks of winter.
8. When I was **27** and had been unemployed for nearly **three** years, I decided to return to college for **two** years of practical training.
9. In the United States, **one** of the reasons that hemp is illegal is that about **80** years ago, cotton growers lobbied against its cultivation because they saw it as competition.
10. Only **8** out of **47** trivia players were able to name Jay Silverheels of Brantford, Ontario, as the original Tonto in *The Lone Ranger*.

Exercise 41.2

1. Researchers at Cornell University conducted a study that showed that **66** percent of all businessmen wear their ties too tight.
2. More than **10** percent of those studied wore their ties so tight that blood flow to the brain was diminished.
3. **Ninety-nine** percent of the people who read the report wondered why Cornell had conducted such a study.
4. One plan is to retire on **December 17, 2055**.
5. At precisely **8:10 p.m.** on **June 3rd**, your flight will leave for Whitehorse.
6. You will arrive at approximately **ten o'clock** on **June 4th** if you make all your connections.
7. I won **five dollars** from Ted by proving that February **1865** was the only month in recorded history not to have a full moon.
8. You must be present at **133 West 18th** Street by exactly **seven o'clock** to claim your prize.

9. So far this year, I have spent **$38,000**, or **20** percent more than my anticipated income for the entire year, and it's only **May 15th**!

10. At the Indianapolis Speedway, the race cars burn approximately **4L** of fuel for each lap, while the ship *Queen Elizabeth II* moves just **15** cm for every 4L of fuel it burns.

Exercise 41.3

1. The speedboat is powered by **two** 80-horsepower outboard motors.

2. **One** 8-cylinder SUV emits more pollution than two 4-cylinder diesel Volkswagens or **three** Toyota gas-electric hybrids.

3. Because she sold seven **$2-million** homes last year, she topped the agency's earnings list.

4. correct

5. **Two hundred** people were invited to celebrate my parents' **25th** wedding anniversary on **August 31**, 2005.

6. A total of **ten 15-year-old** girls and **four 15-year-old** boys applied for the commercial acting position we advertised.

7. Our lawyer told us that **38 percent** of people who die between the ages of 45 and 54 have not prepared a will.

8. Canada's population of about **30 million** puts us in **29th** place on the list of most populous countries.

9. **Ten** years ago, the average speed on urban freeways was **50 kph**, but it has been steadily declining and is expected to be **30 kph** within the next **five** years.

10. **Seven thousand** ecstatic fans celebrated their team's unexpected 2–1 win in the Memorial Cup final, partying in the streets until **4:30 a.m.**

Index